MW01629513

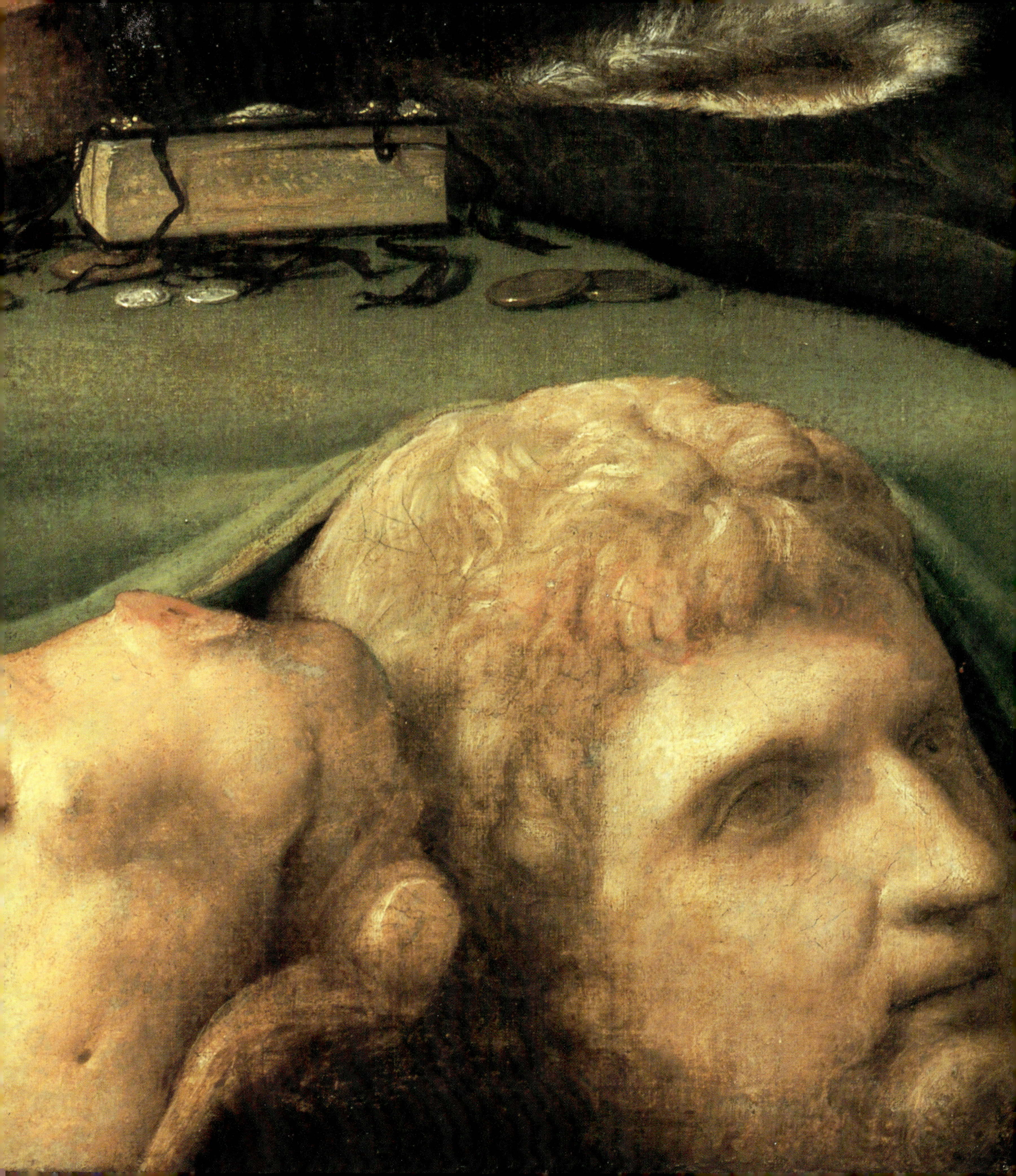

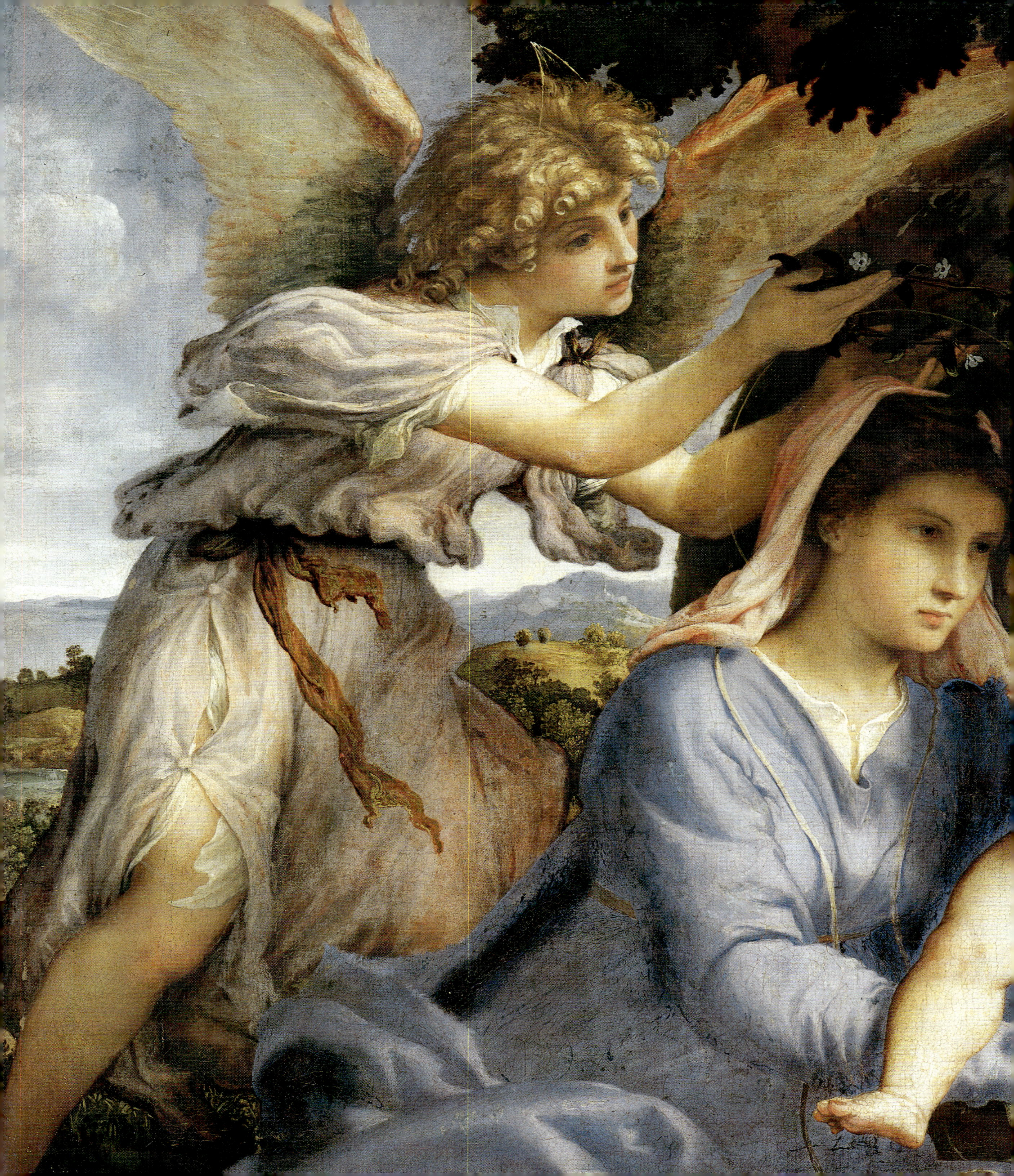

Peter Humfrey

LORENZO LOTTO

Yale University Press
New Haven & London

Copyright © 1997 by Yale University

All rights reserved.
This book may not be reproduced, in whole or in part, in any form (beyond that copying permitted by Sections 107 and 108 of the U.S. Copyright Law and except by reviewers for the public press), without written permission from the publishers.

Designed by Gillian Malpass
Printed in Singapore

Library of Congress Cataloging-in-Publication Data

Humfrey, Peter, 1947–
Lorenzo Lotto / Peter Humfrey.
p. cm.
Includes bibliographical references and index.
ISBN 0-300-06905-7 (cloth: alk. paper)
1. Lotto, Lorenzo, 1480?–1556? 2. Painters–Italy–Biography.
I. Lotto, Lorenzo, 1480?–1556? II. Title.
ND623.L8H86 1997
759.5–dc20 96-27624
CIP

A catalogue record for this book is available from The British Library

Page i: Lotto, detail of pl. 115.

Frontispiece: Lotto, detail of pl. 110.

In memory of my godson
Richard Edlin
1978–1995

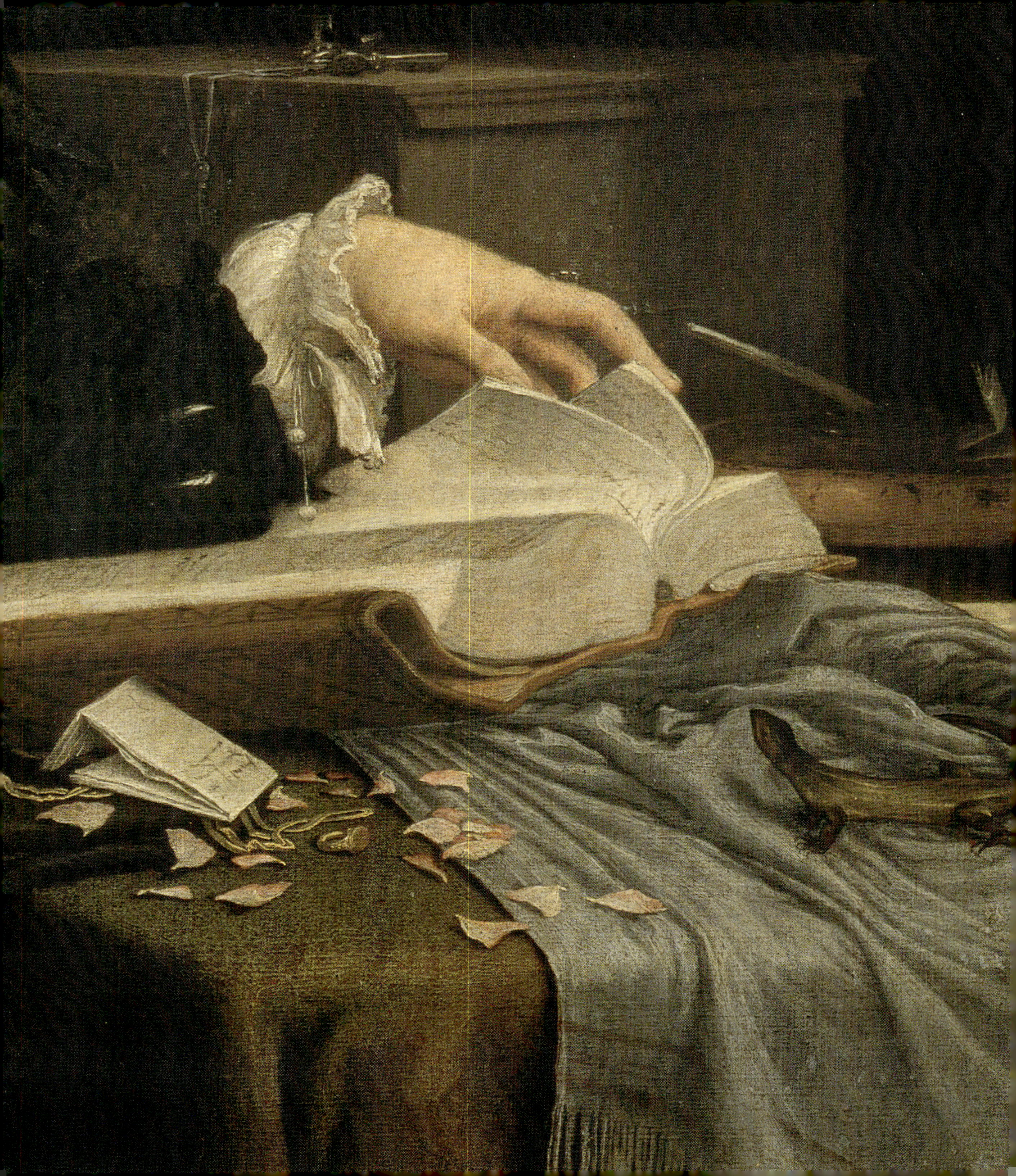

CONTENTS

facing page Detail of pl. 117.

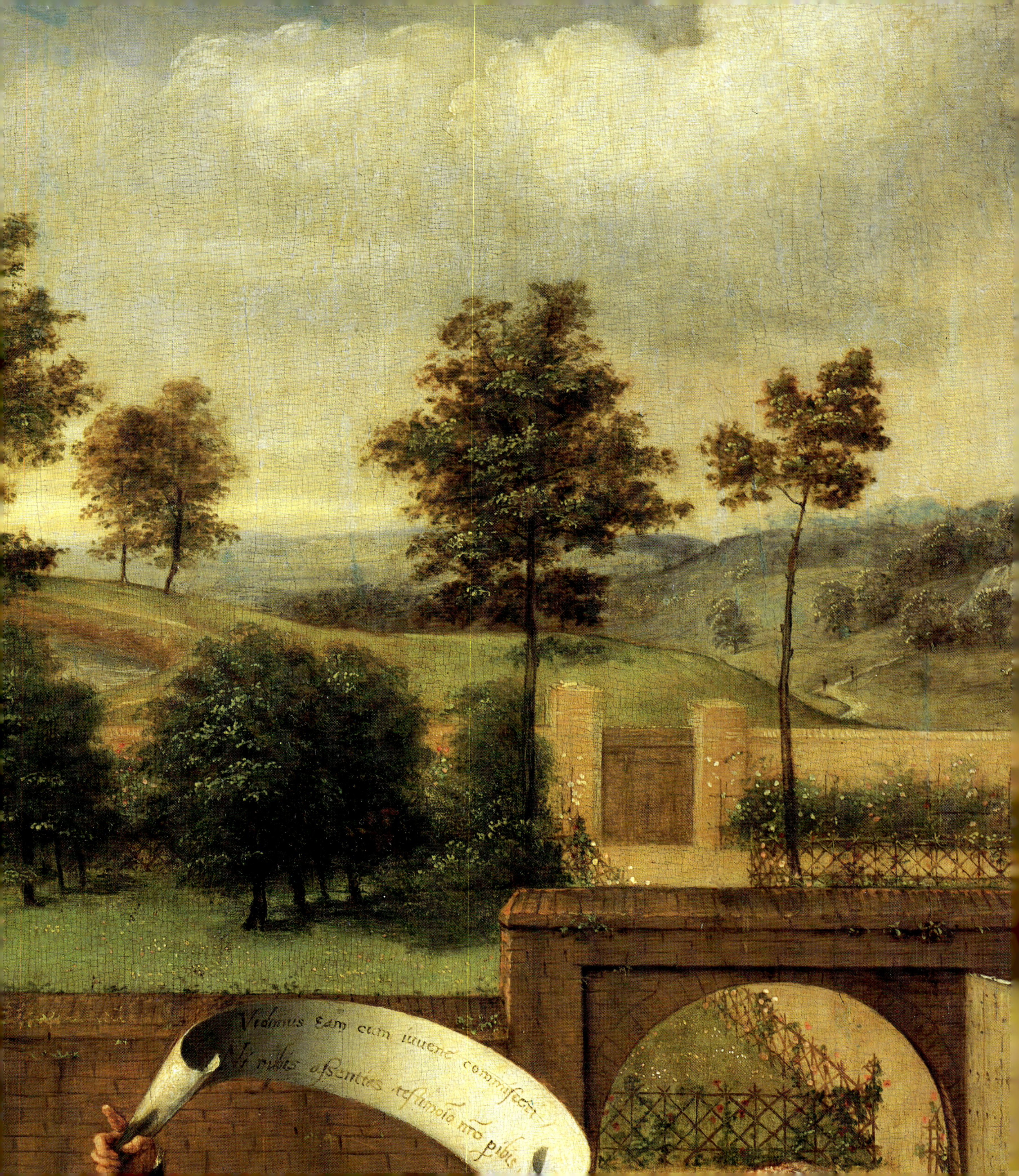
Vidimus eam cum iuuene commisceri
Ut nobis absentes testimonio nro pibis

FOREWORD

THE CELEBRATIONS HELD IN 1980/81 to commemorate the fifth centenary of Lorenzo Lotto's birth were unusually successful in stimulating new research on the painter. All three of the regions of Italy in which he worked – the Veneto, Bergamo and the Marches – held exhibitions and conferences in his honour; and the various publications associated with these events have, in turn, given rise to a further crop of specialised books and articles. Much of this research has been genuinely enlightening, and has uncovered a quantity of new information and ideas about Lotto, his art and his social world. At the same time, however, the Lotto literature has become rather inaccessible to the general reader, partly because of its sheer volume, and partly because much of it has appeared in local publications that are not widely diffused, even in Italy.

The purpose of the present book is, accordingly, to provide an introduction to one of the most attractive and distinctive personalities of Italian Renaissance art, taking particular account of research undertaken during the past fifteen years. The book is intentionally selective, and concentrates on Lotto's finest and most characteristic achievements. It makes no attempt to discuss, or even to mention all of the many pictures by or attributed to him; and as his later works – despite some striking exceptions – undeniably show a gradual decline in quality, his late career is treated more sketchily than its earlier phases. Included in the Appendix is a small, but it is hoped telling and representative, sample from the exceptionally large surviving corpus of Lotto documents.

The opportunity for taking time off teaching to write this book was provided by a generous award from the British Academy under its Research Leave Scheme. An equally welcome opportunity to study in Italy was provided by a European Visiting Research Fellowship, awarded by the Royal Society of Edinburgh in association with the Caledonian Research Foundation. I had the additional good fortune of being able to look at most of Lotto's works in Italy, on a roundabout trip from Bergamo to Rome, in the company of Ulrich Birkmaier, David Alan Brown and Mauro Lucco. My thanks to them for their many stimulating observations made on that memorable occasion. I have also benefited from the learned advice and practical assistance provided by many other friends and colleagues, but in particular by Claudie Balavoine, Jane Bridgeman, Dawson Carr, Anna Coliva, Aldo Corcella, Jill Dunkerton, Augusto Gentili, Marco Lattanzi, John Martin, Louisa Chevalier Matthew, Nicholas Penny and Graham Smith. The draft manuscript was much improved by the suggestions and corrections offered by David Ekserdjian, Deborah Howard, Paul Joannides and Mauro Lucco, as well as by an anonymous reader and by my editor, Gillian Malpass. To all these I am most grateful, as I am to the members of my ever-supportive family: Margaret, Nicholas and Joseph.

St Andrews, December 1995

facing page Detail of pl. 70.

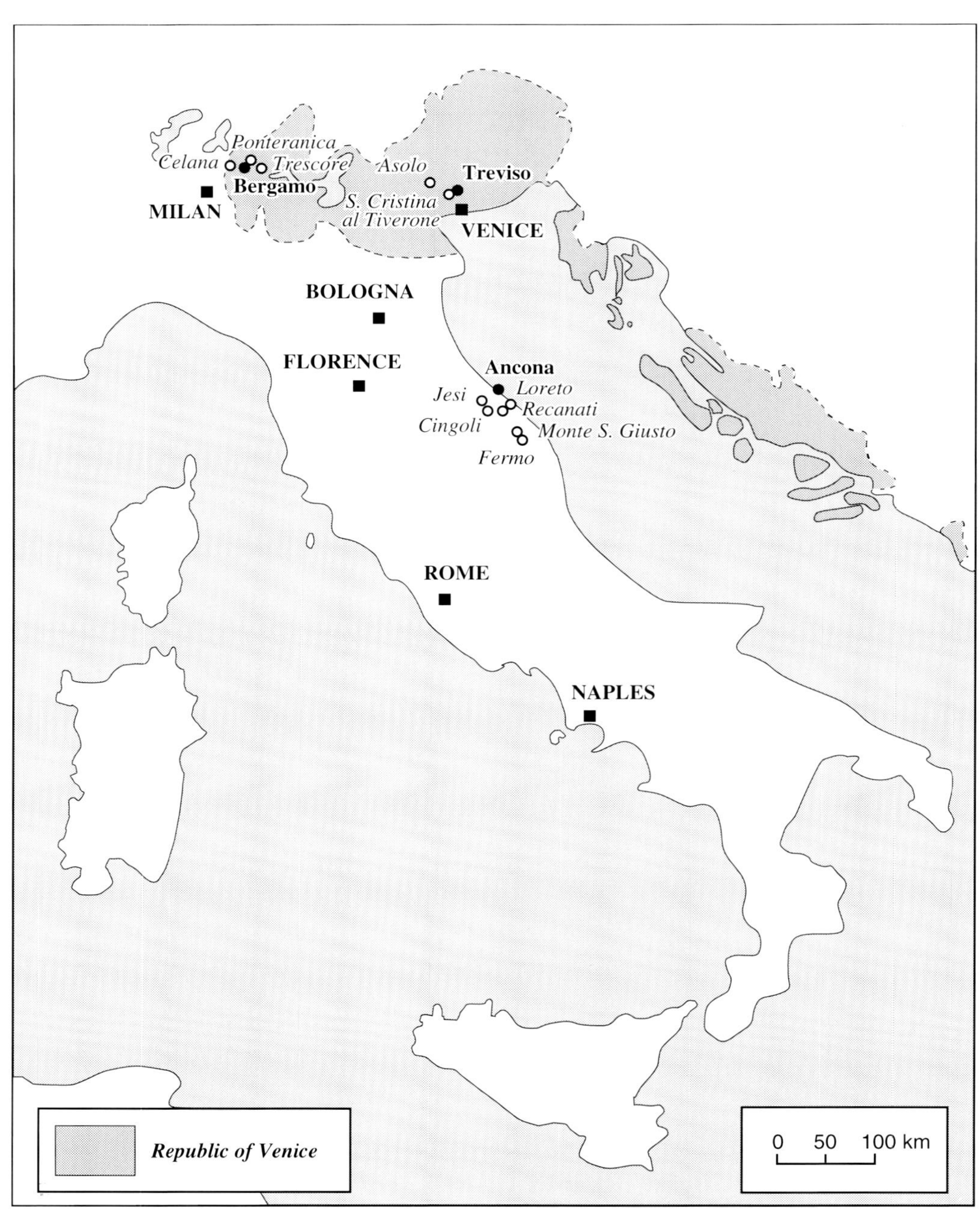

1 Map of Italy, showing principal sites associated with Lotto.

BIOGRAPHICAL OUTLINE

c. 1483?	Born in Venice
1503	June, August, September and December: recorded as a painter in legal documents in Treviso.
	20 September: date inscribed on reverse of *Virgin and Child with St Peter Martyr* (pl. 7).
	27 November: witnessed a will in Venice.
1504	Recorded in further documents in Treviso, including as a member of the Scuola del Santissimo Sacramento (Confraternity of the Holy Sacrament) at the Cathedral.
1505	Recorded in further documents in Treviso. 1 July: date formerly inscribed on reverse of Rossi *Allegory* (pl. 16).
1506	Inscribed date on Louvre *St Jerome* (pl. 22) and Asolo *Assumption* (pl. 25).
	4 May: settlement of dispute over fee for *St Christina* altarpiece (pl. 24).
	17 June: in Recanati to sign contract for San Domenico polyptych (pl. 31).
	18 October: renews lease on house in Treviso before leaving for Recanati.
1508	Inscribed date on San Domenico polyptych and Borghese *Virgin and Child with Saints* (pl. 35).
1509	8 March and 18 September: payments from papal exchequer for work in Vatican Palace.
1511	27 October: undertakes *Entombment* for San Floriano, Jesi (pl. 38).
1512	Inscribed date on Jesi *Entombment* and *Judith* (pl. 44).
1513	13 May: undertakes to paint frescoes of life of St Catherine in Sant' Alessandro in Colonna, Bergamo.
	15 May: undertakes Colleoni Martinengo altarpiece (pls 47, 52).
1515	Inscribed date on *Giovanni Agostino and Niccolò della Torre* (pl. 75).
1516	Inscribed date on Colleoni Martinengo altarpiece.
1517	Inscribed date on *Susannah and the Elders* (pl. 70).
1521	Inscribed date on Santo Spirito and San Bernardino altarpieces (pls 54, 55) and *Christ taking Leave of his Mother* (pl. 63).
1523	Inscribed date on *Mystic Marriage with Niccolò Bonghi* (pl. 74), Washington *Nativity* (pl. 67) and *Messer Marsilio and his Bride* (pl. 80).
	11 December: in Jesi to sign contract for *St Lucy* altarpiece (pl. 123).
1524	Inscribed date on frescoes in Oratorio Suardi, Trescore (pls 85–90).
	12 March and 16 June: undertakes to design cycle of *intarsie* for choir of Santa Maria Maggiore in Bergamo.
	2 September: first of series of letters to Consorzio della Misericordia.

1525 Inscribed date on frescoes in San Michele del Pozzo Bianco, Bergamo, and in San Giorgio at Credaro.

20 December: arrives in Venice, and takes up lodgings at Santi Giovanni e Paolo.

1526 Inscribed date on *Virgin and Child with Sts Joseph and Jerome* for San Francesco al Monte, Jesi (pl. 101), and the Louvre *Christ carrying the Cross* (pl. 106).

1527 Inscribed date on Celana *Assumption* (pl. 99) and *Andrea Odoni* (pl. 115).

1528 1 April: witness to will of Sebastiano Serlio.

1529 Inscription formerly legible on *St Nicholas in Glory* for Santa Maria dei Carmini, Venice (pl. 103).

1531 Inscribed date on *St Christopher* panel (Berlin, Gemäldegalerie) of triptych for San Sebastiano in Castelplanio, near Jesi.

1531 29 September: serves on committee appointed by the Arte dei Depentori (guild of painters) in Venice to administer a legacy left by Vincenzo Catena.

1532 16 March: last of series of letters to Consorzio della Misericordia in Bergamo.

29 August: recorded on a visit to Treviso.

Inscribed date on *St Lucy* altarpiece (pl. 123).

1533 28 January: makes will in Venice (document lost).

1535 Inscribed date on Fermo altarpiece (pl. 129).

August: undertakes to decorate chapel of Palazzo dei Priori, Jesi.

1538 1 August: undertakes *Virgin and Child with Saints* for Sant' Agostino, Ancona (pl. 130).

16 November: earliest entry in the *Libro di Spese Diverse*.

1539 Inscribed date on the Cingoli altarpiece (pl. 131).

14 October: writes to Cingoli from Macerata.

1540 31 January: back in Venice; living in house of Mario d'Armano from 3 July.

1542 Inscribed date on *St Antoninus* altarpiece (pl. 141).

17/18 October: moves from Venice to house of Giovanni dal Saon in Treviso.

1543/4 Executed portraits of Febo da Brescia and Laura da Pola (pls 147–8).

1545 February to July: execution of *Lamentation* for San Paolo, Treviso (pl. 146).

12 December: returns to Venice, to house of Giovanni della Volta.

1546 25 March: makes will (Appendix C).

Inscribed date on San Giacomo dell'Orio altarpiece (pl. 152).

November: stays in house of Bartolomeo Carpan during period of illness.

1546/7 Executed portrait of Fra Gregorio Belo (pl. 155).

1547 20 November: moves to house of Bernardo da Verona.

1548 June: in Ancona, in connection with installation of Mogliano altarpiece.

7 July: moves to house of Arsenio Contarini in Venice.

1549 1 July: arrives in Ancona to paint *Assumption* for San Francesco alle Scale (pl. 156), and stays in adjoining convent.

1550 August: auction of paintings and drawings at Loggia dei Mercanti, Ancona.

13 November: rents house in Ancona.

1552 19 August: undertakes altarpiece for Amici family in Duomo, Jesi.

30 August: takes up residence in Loreto.

1553 17 May and 30 October: visits Jesi in connection with Amici commission.

1554 8 September: enters religious community at Santa Casa, Loreto.
1555 Various payments for work at Santa Casa.
1556 1 September: final entry in *Libro*.
1557 9 July: Lotto recorded as deceased.

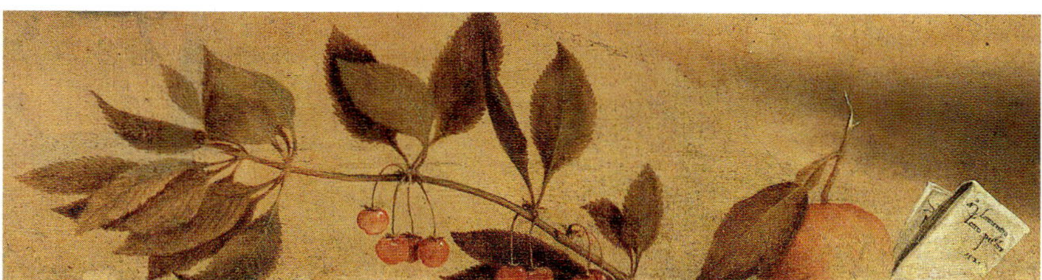

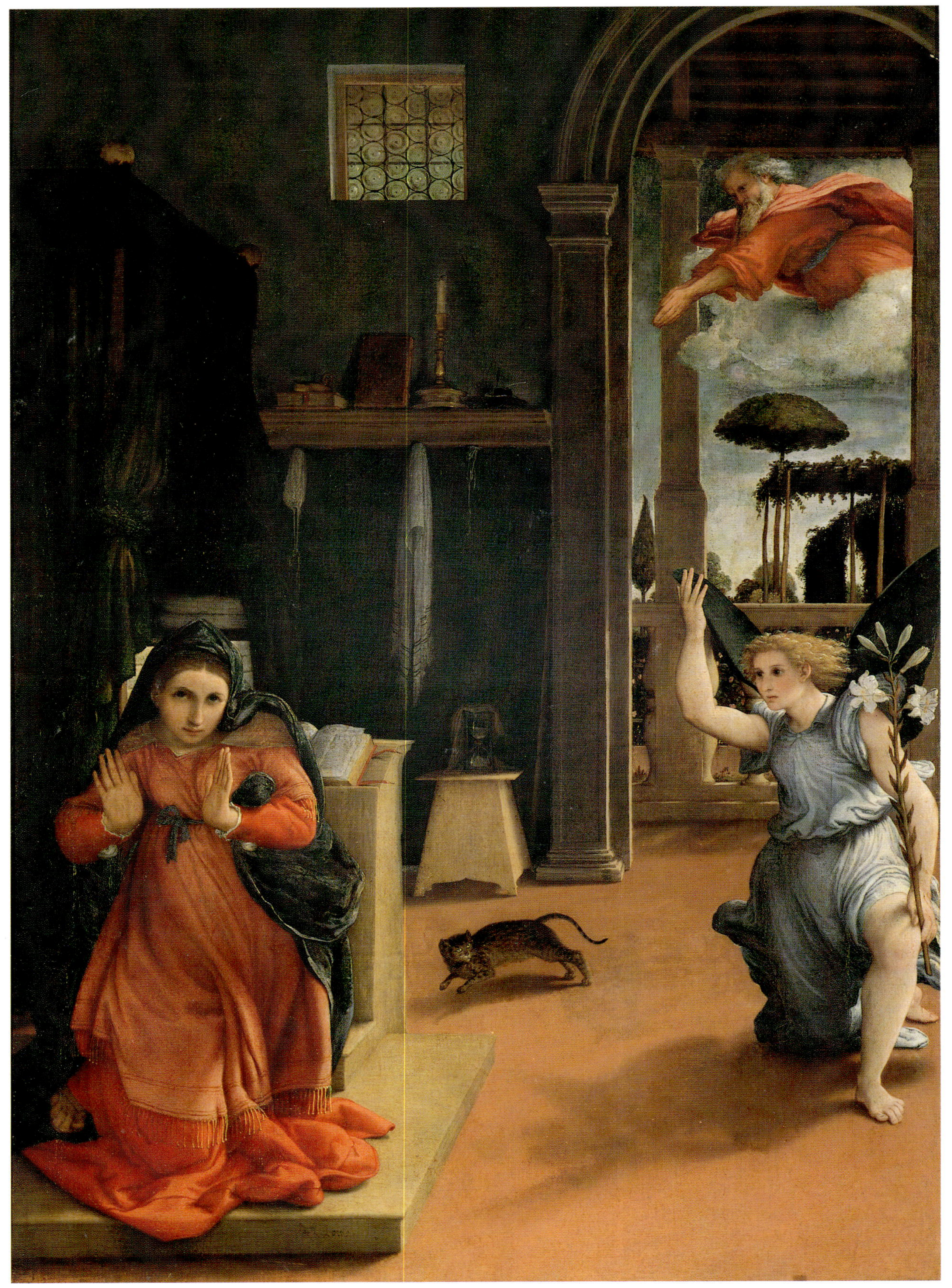

INTRODUCTION

Lorenzo Lotto belonged to the same highly gifted generation of Venetian painters that included, among several others, Giorgione and Titian. In at least one respect Lotto may be regarded as more truly Venetian than either of his two great contemporaries: whereas they were born and brought up on the *terraferma*, he was a native of the city of Venice; and throughout his life he continued proudly to describe himself as such. Yet in most other respects Lotto was always to be an outsider in the artistic world of Renaissance Venice. Immediately after completing his apprenticeship in about 1503 he began his independent career in the mainland city of Treviso; and it was not for another twenty-two years, after phases spent variously in the Marchigian towns of Recanati and Jesi, in Rome and in Bergamo, that he returned to practice as a painter in Venice (pl. 1). Even then he continued to work as much for patrons in his former areas of activity as for Venetians; and it also appears that he spent several more years in the Marches during the 1530s. A second period of residence in Treviso on the mid-1540s was followed in 1549 by another return to the Marches and, finally, in 1554 he decided to spend the remaining few years of his life as a lay brother in the holy city of Loreto.[1]

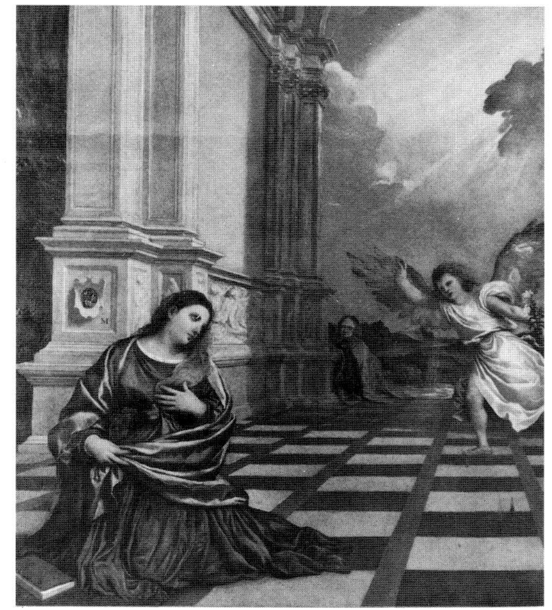

3 Titian. *Annunciation* (*c.*1520–23). Treviso, Duomo.

2 (*facing page*) Lotto. *Annunciation* (*c.*1534–5). Canvas, 166 × 114 cm. Recanati, Pinacoteca Comunale.

In part because of his long periods of absence from his native city, Lotto's art never conformed to what one might describe as the central tradition of Venetian Cinquecento painting. This independence of a norm, represented above all by the art of Titian, is vividly illustrated by the contrast between Lotto's *Annunciation* (pl. 2), probably painted in the early 1530s, for the oratory of a devotional confraternity in Recanati (p. 126), and Titian's rendering of the same subject, painted about a decade earlier for the cathedral of Treviso (pl. 3). Lotto would certainly have known Titian's picture, which may well have served as an inspiration for the unusual compositional device of posing the Virgin frontally, and of showing the angel entering the room from behind her. The grandiose rhetoric of Titian's version, however, made no impression on Lotto. The majestically buxom figure of Titian's Virgin is portrayed as the future Queen of Heaven, as if she were already aware that her response to the angelic salutation will set in train the redemption of mankind. She is accordingly placed within a nobly classicising but indeterminate architectural setting, which opens at the back to reveal a generalised mountain landscape and a flood of supernatural radiance. The contours of the forms are characteristically soft and blurred, and the colours are warm, rich and harmoniously fused. Lotto, by contrast, portrays his Virgin as a shy and startled girl, as if recalling the words of Luke's Gospel (1:29): 'And when she saw him, she was troubled at his saying, and cast in her mind what manner of salutation this should be.' The chamber is full of carefully described, humble domestic objects–bed, books, candle, towel, hour-glass–and the open doorway leads to a tidily cultivated garden. The light is cool and crystalline, and the colour-range is similarly cool, tending to dissonance in the pinks and reds. The gestures of all three figures are slightly stilted but also highly expressive; and the earnestness with which the pale-faced angel fixes his attention on the Virgin is typical of the mixture of sincere directness and touching naïveté with which the event as a whole is portrayed. The central episode of the frightened cat, perhaps symbolic of evil put to flight,[2] adds a paradoxical touch of humour to the scene.

Lotto's extensive travels in the Italian peninsula meant that he had a wider experience of different pictorial cultures than did the majority of his Venetian colleagues. In the Recanati *Annunciation*, a particular interest in Netherlandish painting is evident in the circumstantially described domestic interior; but other pictures variously reflect the painter's contacts with the art of Dürer, Raphael and Leonardo. Sometimes, and especially when working for Venetian patrons, he made more serious effort than in the *Annunciation* to make his handling of form and colour closer to that of Titian; but Lotto's essential independence of Venetian, and indeed of any other local pictorial tradition, was the consequence not simply of his peripatetic way of life, but even more of a personality that was unwilling or simply unable to conform to established aesthetic convention. As illustrated by the *Annunciation*, Lotto was concerned above all to give direct, personal expression to his subject-matter, even to the point of appearing eccentric. Similarly, in a contemporary portrait such as that of the anonymous man in the Galleria Borghese (pl. 5), the rather awkward, demonstrative pose has nothing of the relaxed elegance favoured by Titian (pl. 4); rather, it combines with the intense, brooding melancholy of the face to convey a sense of deep empathy with the sitter's inner thoughts and feelings.

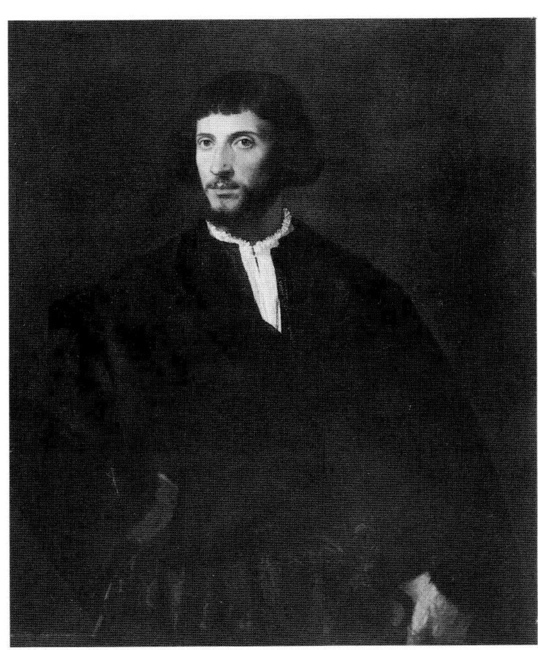

4 Titian. *Portrait of a Man* (*c.*1520). Paris, Musée du Louvre.

The distinctiveness of Lotto's personality is everywhere apparent in his art, but to an extent unusual among Italian, and especially Venetian painters of the Renaissance period, it also emerges from a large corpus of written material. His works are exceptionally well documented by inscribed dates and signatures, and also by official records such as contracts and payments. But beyond these, there survive three documents of major importance, which shed light not just on the external circumstances of his career, but also on his emotional reaction to them. The first of these documents is a series of thirty-nine letters, written by Lotto after his return to Venice in 1525 to the Confraternity of the Misericordia in Bergamo concerning the progress of a commission to design a cycle of *intarsie* for the church of Santa Maria Maggiore in that city.[3] This was a commission close to the painter's heart, but also one that over the years turned out to be frustrating and burdensome. The second document is a very detailed, almost autobiographical will, which he drew up in Venice in 1546, but subsequently revoked (see Appendix C, p. 179). The third, and most important document is the *Libro di Spese Diverse*: that is to say, Lotto's account-book regularly kept during the last sixteen years of his life spent in Venice, Treviso and the Marches, from 1540 to 1556.[4] The *Libro*, like the recently published *Libro Secondo* of Jacopo Bassano and his workshop,[5] naturally provides a mine of information about the works executed during the period it covers, and about the circumstances surrounding their commission; and beyond that, it represents a major source of information on the business practices and day-to-day operations of an Italian Renaissance workshop in general.[6] But whereas the Bassano *Libro Secondo* has the impersonality that would be expected of an account-book, Lotto's *Libro*, like his will, is full of personal observations that offer an extraordinary insight into the painter's inner concerns and preoccupations.[7] Although the precise significance of many of the events and comments recorded in the three documents remains ambiguous and subject to differing interpretations, together the documents provide a fairly clear picture of Lotto the person: introspective, hypersensitive, often prickly and quick to take offence; but also generous in his affections, tender in his humanity and possessing a quirky sense of humour. He never married and, especially in his later life, he clearly suffered from loneliness and from the lack of a family. He was obviously also of a

5 (*facing page*) Lotto. *Portrait of a Man* (*c.*1535). Canvas, 118 × 105 cm. Rome, Galleria Borghese.

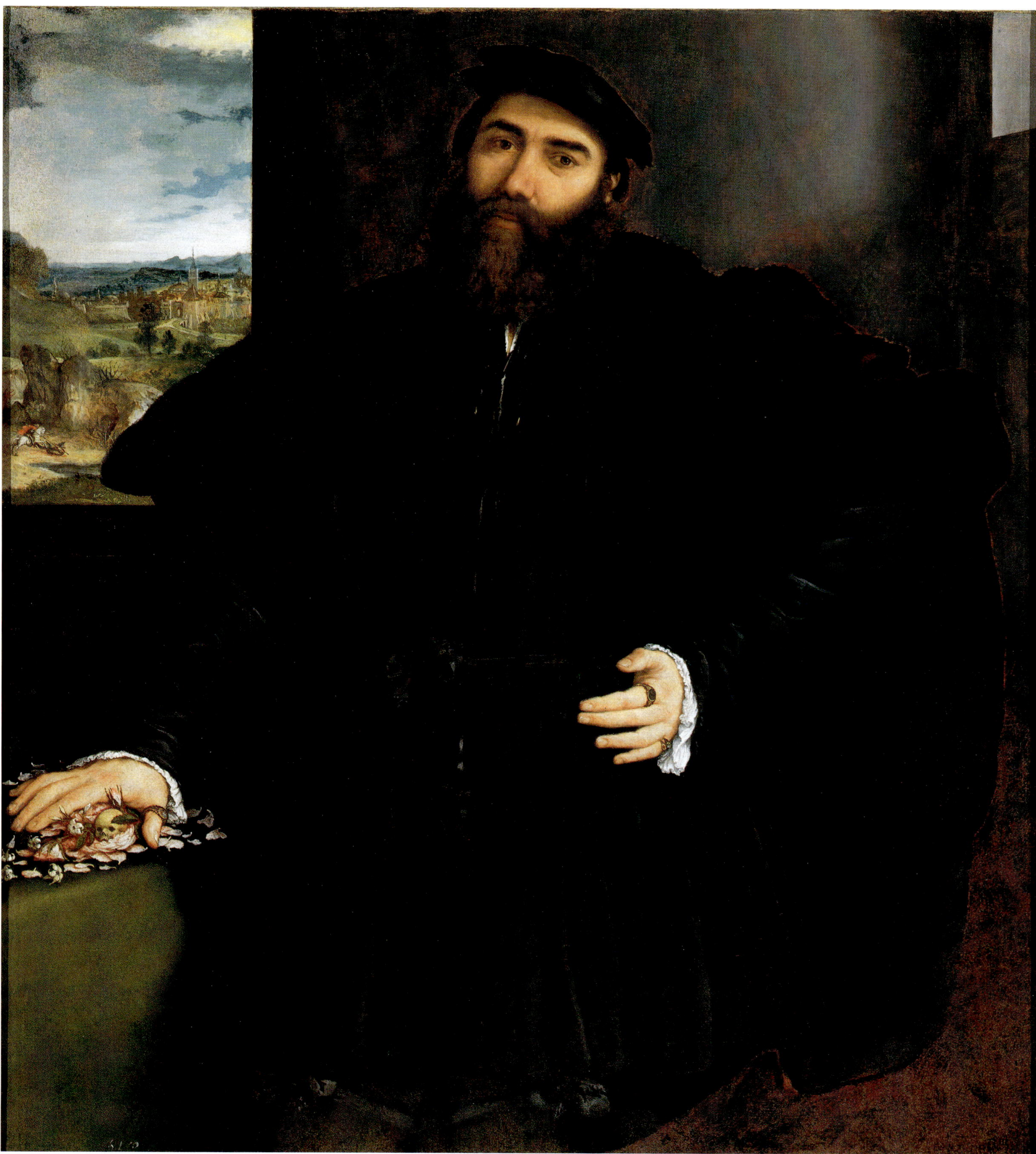

deeply religious sensibility, and felt much troubled by the crisis in the Church provoked by the Reformation.

In contrast to this abundant documentary information about Lotto's life and works, the information provided by the early critics and historians is decidedly thin. Probably the most interesting evaluation of Lotto's art written in his lifetime was provided by the influential critic Pietro Aretino, in the form of an open letter to the painter dated April 1548 (pp. 156–8). Aretino had praise for the 'miracles' performed by Lotto's brush, which he said surpassed the efforts of most other painters; and he also spoke highly both of Lotto's critical judgement and of his personal goodness and religious piety. But for Aretino, no painter could compete with his hero Titian and, without giving any particular reason, he made clear his opinion that Lotto was the lesser of the two. More forthcoming on the nature of Lotto's supposed deficiencies was Lodovico Dolce, who in a brief dismissive comment in his *Dialogue on Painting, entitled Aretino* of 1559, spoke of the *cattive tinte* (bad colours) of Lotto's *St Nicholas* altarpiece of 1527–9 (pl. 103; see p. 96). But like Aretino, after whom the *Dialogue on Painting* is named, Dolce was not seeking to be objective in his criticism, but to boost the reputation of Titian; and the strikingly effective, but quite un-Titianesque use of colour in the *St Nicholas* altarpiece is chosen as a foil for the author's eulogistic analysis of Titian's own practice as a colourist. Compared with the two Venetian critics, Giorgio Vasari was benevolently bland in his comments. In a single short paragraph devoted to Lotto in the first edition of the *Lives* (1550), Vasari listed a handful of works (including the *St Nicholas* altarpiece), and concluded – in contrast to Dolce – that Lotto was a very fine colourist, and that his early works in particular were admirably finished.[8] As a Tuscan, Vasari may well have been instinctively attracted by Lotto's relatively cool, un-Venetian palette and refined attention to detail; and in the second edition of the *Lives* (1568), where the list of works was considerably expanded, the author's assessment was again exclusively positive. Thus he found the portrait of Andrea Odoni (pl. 115) 'molto bello', the landscape of the *St Nicholas* altarpiece similarly 'bellissimo', and the now lost predella of the San Domenico polyptych (pl. 31) 'cosa rara'. Like Aretino, he also admired Lotto for his personal unworldliness and for being a 'good Christian'.[9] Vasari's biography, which is combined with that of Palma Vecchio, is disappointing chiefly for its brevity – especially considering that author and painter were both in Venice at the same time in 1541–2, and they almost certainly, therefore, knew one another. Yet the brevity is itself indicative that Vasari, despite his positive epithets, did not consider Lotto to be a major figure in the great artistic revival of his age. Indeed, for a critic who held in the highest admiration the classicising, normative aesthetic ideals of High Renaissance Florence and Rome, a work such as the Recanati *Annunciation* would certainly have appeared too particularised and too idiosyncratic to merit serious attention.

Principally because of the prevalence of an academic artistic taste that shared the prejudices of Vasari, but also because so little of Lotto's work was to be seen in the major artistic centres, his name was largely forgotten for three centuries after his death. It is true that several of his portraits and domestic religious pictures painted for Venetian patrons subsequently entered the princely collections of seventeenth-century Europe, including those of Charles I in England (where the *Goldsmith in Three Views* (pl. 119) clearly impressed Van Dyck) and of the Archduke Leopold Wilhelm in Brussels; by this time, however, such works had often acquired attributions to more familar Old Masters, such as Titian or Correggio.[10] Then, towards the end of the nineteenth century, two complementary developments began to stimulate a new interest in Lotto, and to promote a radical reassessment of his art-historical position. In the first place, local historians in Venice, Treviso, Bergamo and the various towns of the Marches began to rediscover and publish original documents relating to him, including the will of 1546 and the account-book.[11] At the same time, a new approach to art criticism, one that was both analytically rigorous and liberated from traditional academic tastes, led to a new scrutiny of the works themselves, and to a new realisation of their qualities. One of the principal founders of the modern study of Italian Renaissance painting, Bernard Berenson, experienced a powerful early attraction towards the art of Lotto; and in his monograph of 1895 he combined close visual analysis with the evidence of the newly discovered documents, to create the first coherent account of the painter's character and stylistic development.[12] Berenson's monograph has provided an essential basis for the considerable amount of further scholarly research on all aspects of Lotto that has taken place during the course of the twentieth century, and in particular in its second half.[13] It has also provided the basis for the widespread appreciation of him today as one of the most engaging artistic personalities of the sixteenth century.

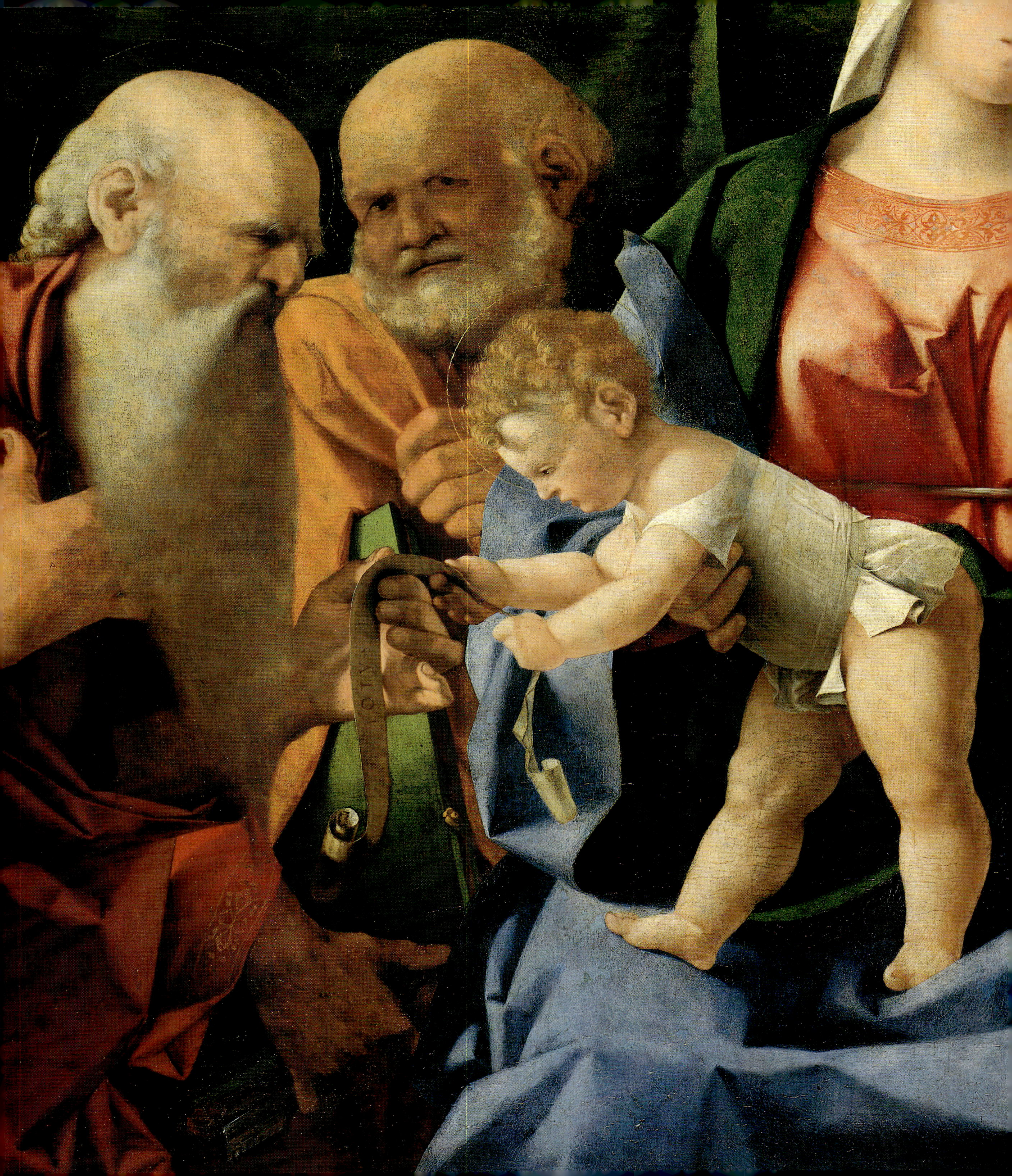

Chapter 1

TREVISO *c.* 1503–1506

THE EARLIEST CERTAIN RECORDS of Lorenzo Lotto date from the summer of 1503, when he was living and already active as a painter in the Venetian mainland city of Treviso.[1] It is not known exactly what age he had reached in that year: on the basis of a statement made in his will of 1546, to the effect that he was then aged 'about sixty-six', historians have generally assumed that he was born in Venice very close to 1480; but, given the imprecise wording of this statement made in old age, it remains possible that he was born a few years later, aboout 1483.[2] Certainly the unusual self-description as 'LAURENT LOTUS IUNIOR' in the Asolo *Assumption* of 1506 (pl. 25) implies that in that year he had not yet reached the majority age of twenty-five; while the visual evidence of his earliest known work (pl. 7), which is inscribed with the date of 1503 on its back,[3] indicates that he had only very recently graduated as a master, presumably at the customary age of about eighteen to twenty. Numerous documents then record his continuing presence in Treviso for the next three years, until the autumn of 1506, when he moved south to Recanati in the Marches.

It is not clear why Lotto chose to set up shop in Treviso, where such leading local painters as Vincenzo dai Destri and Pier Maria Pennacchi were decidedly provincial compared with their Venetian metropolitan counterparts.[4] But Treviso, situated on the principal trade route from Venice to southern Germany, was a relatively large and prosperous city of some 10,000 inhabitants, and it could offer a young painter of ambition considerable opportunities for commissions. There had long existed a lively literary culture in Treviso, represented in the last decade of the fifteenth century above all by the fantastic antiquarianism of Fra Francesco Colonna's *Hypnerotomachia Poliphili*, composed in the city between about 1485 and 1495, but also by the works of the neo-Petrarchan poet Giovanni Aurelio Augurelli and the Latinist Giovanni Bologni.[5] Then in 1499, a fresh impetus to the cultural life of Treviso had been given by the appointment of Bernardo de' Rossi as bishop.[6] This energetic but controversial personality, a member of a noble family of Parma in Emilia, almost immediately attracted the hostility of the Venetian secular authorities by appointing several of his Parmese compatriots to key posts in the cathedral chapter. But his humanist-inspired programme of ecclesiastical reform was combined with a discerning interest in painting, and during the three years of Lotto's residence in Treviso, Rossi did much to promote his career, both by prompting the commission of altarpieces within his diocese, and by commissioning a number of smaller pictures for his own private use. The earliest of these was the previously mentioned work of 1503, the *Virgin and Child with St Peter Martyr*, now in Naples (pl. 7).

There is physical evidence that this picture has been tampered with, probably in the later sixteenth century, and that originally the figure presented by Peter Martyr to the Virgin and Child was not the feebly painted child Baptist, but a portrait of a cleric kneeling in profile, almost certainly identifiable with Rossi himself.[7] This type of image, introduced into Venetian painting by Giovanni Bellini, was well established by

6 Detail of pl. 27.

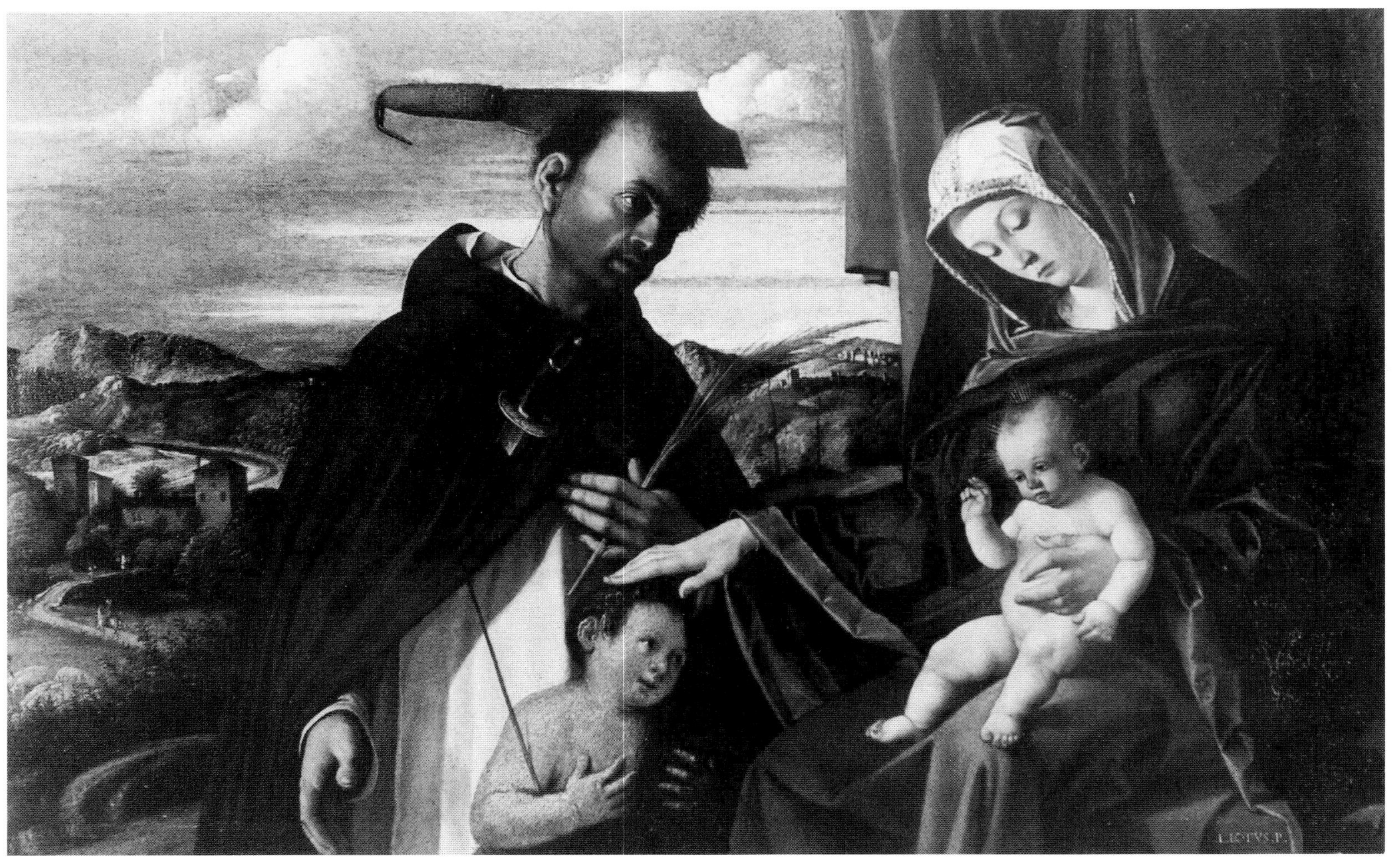

7 Lotto. *Virgin and Child with St Peter Martyr* (1503). Panel, 55 × 88 cm. Naples, Galleria Nazionale di Capodimonte.

the first decade of the sixteenth century, but the choice of the Dominican saint Peter Martyr as intercessor raises questions, because Rossi was not a Dominican and is not otherwise known to have had a special devotion to this saint. One possible explanation for the choice may lie in the date inscribed on the reverse, which implicitly relates the commission to a dramatic event that took place on 29 September 1503, when an attempt was made by the Venetian *podestà* and a group of Trevigian noblemen on the bishop's life.[8] The picture, in which the instruments of Peter Martyr's assassination are given special prominence, would thus constitute a commemoration by Rossi of his deliverance through heavenly assistance from violent death.

One of the reasons for supposing that in 1503 Lotto's career as an independent master had only just begun is that, of all his works, the *Virgin and Child with St Peter Martyr* is the most derivative in terms of style and motif. Deeply indebted to the example of Giovanni Bellini, for example, is not just the general compositional formula, with its three-quarter-length figures set against a distant landscape, but also the specific motif of the Virgin and Child, which is borrowed very literally from a design known in numerous versions by Bellini and his followers (pl. 8).[9] The figure of Peter Martyr, on the other hand, with his half-open mouth and expression of yearning pathos, recalls similar friar-saints in the work of Cima, as in the St Francis in his *Lamentation over the Dead Christ* of about 1495–7 now in Modena (pl. 10). Yet Lotto's pictorial handling, with its use of hard surfaces, bright enamelled colours, angular draperies and sharp contours, does not particularly resemble that of either the late

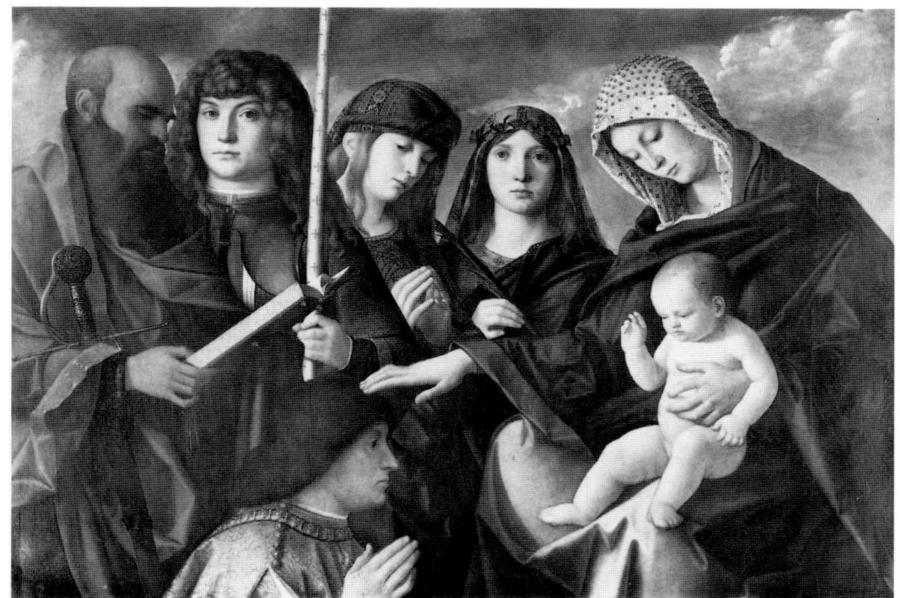

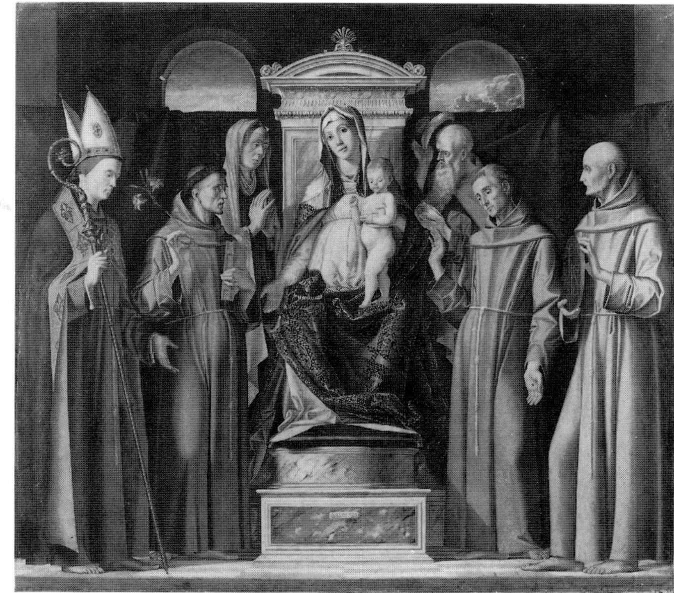

8 (*above left*) Workshop of Giovanni Bellini. *Virgin and Child with Saints and a Donor* (*c.*1500). New York, Pierpont Morgan Library.

9 (*above right*) Alvise Vivarini. *Virgin and Child with Saints* (1480). Venice, Gallerie dell'Accademia.

Bellini or of Cima, it is much closer to that of a third leading master in late fifteenth-century Venice, Alvise Vivarini. One of Alvise's most important altar paintings had, in fact, been painted in 1480 for a church in Treviso (pl. 9), where Lotto would certainly have had recent opportunity to study it. But the fact that the similarities between the altarpiece and Lotto's *Virgin and Child with St Peter Martyr* are not superficial ones of motif but more fundamental ones of style, suggests that they are due to a close personal contact between Lotto and Alvise, perhaps over a number of years. In other words, it is likely that Lotto's training as a painter took place in the Venetian workshop of Alvise Vivarini.[10]

Despite the somewhat old-fashioned hardness of his handling, Lotto's modernity in relation to the members of the elder generation of Venetian painters is evident in his use of more dramatic contrasts of light and shade, and in his creation of a landscape background that is not serenely unruffled, as in Cima's *Lamentation*, but charged with atmospheric tension. In the portrait of Bernardo de' Rossi (pl. 12), painted a year or two later in 1504–5,[11] Lotto's own personal voice is already to be heard more distinctly, even though, as in virtually all his works of the early Treviso period, the basic compositional formula remains rooted in the art of late Quattrocento Venice. The portrait shares with Bellini's *Doge Leonardo Loredan* of about 1501–2, for example (pl. 11), the firmly pyramidal structure and the relationship of the head to the frame; and, as in Bellini's portrait, a strong illumination from the left plays over the features, providing a crisp definition of every protruberance of bone and cartilage, and every crease of flesh. Unlike the doge, however, Rossi fixes his gaze directly on the viewer, and his lips seem about to move; and in this respect, Lotto owes more to the example of portraits by Alvise Vivarini such as the *Portrait of a Man* of 1497 (pl. 13), and to the Venetian portaits of Antonello da Messina. Lotto also follows Alvise in the extension of the format to include the sitter's hand and part of his forearms; and, more effectively than in Alvise, this inclusion combines with the half-open mouth and the sharply-focused gaze to create a striking effect of mental and physical alertness. Although the *Bernardo de' Rossi*, like the *Doge Loredan*, presents a dignified and credible image of a holder of high office, Rossi does not appear as an ideal embodiment of that office, but rather as its particular holder in a particular historical situation. Surrounded by controversy and the recent survivor of an assassination attempt, Rossi grips his scroll in his

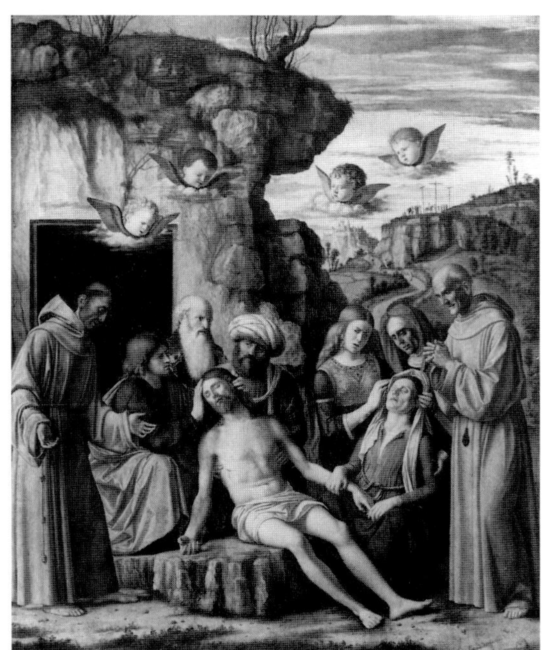

10 Cima da Conegliano. *Lamentation over the Dead Christ* (*c.*1495–7). Modena, Galleria Estense.

12 (*right*) Lotto. *Bishop Bernardo de' Rossi* (*c.*1504–5). Panel, 54.5 × 42 cm. Naples, Galleria Nazionale di Capodimonte.

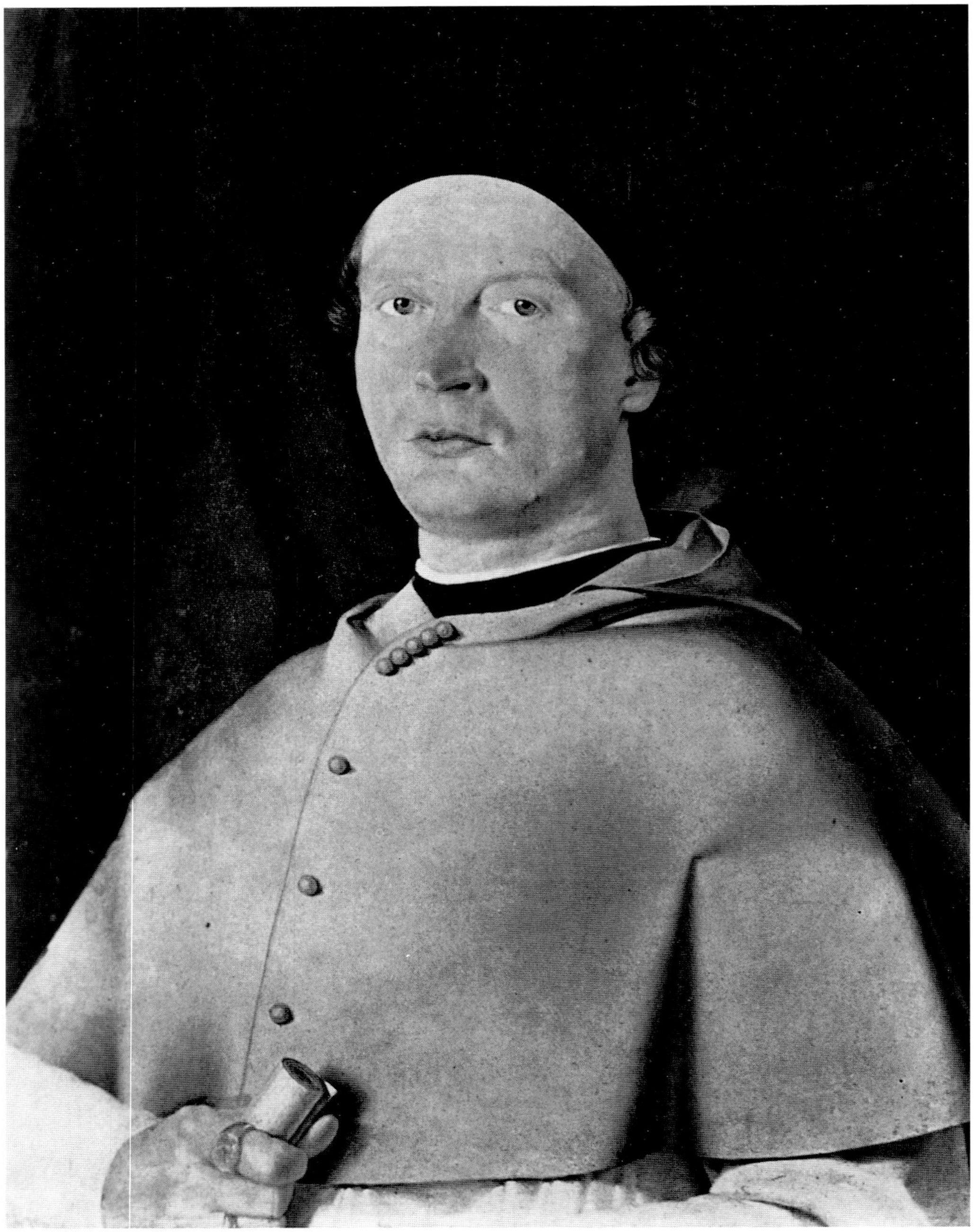

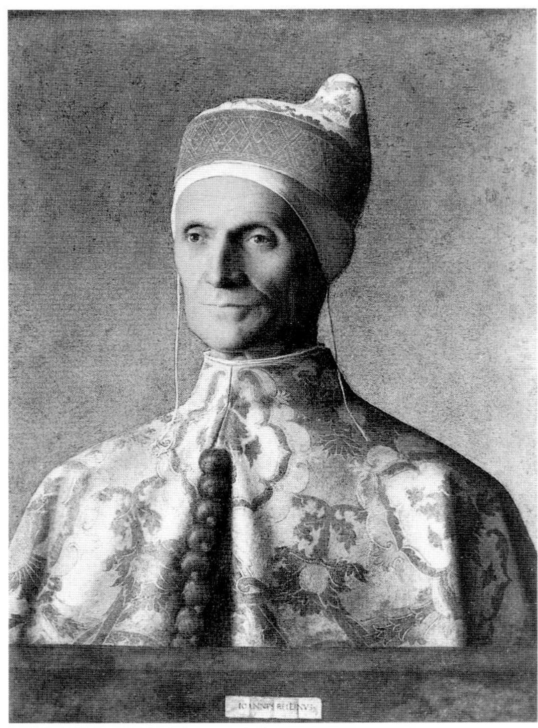

11 Giovanni Bellini. *Doge Leonardo Loredan* (*c.*1501–2). London, National Gallery.

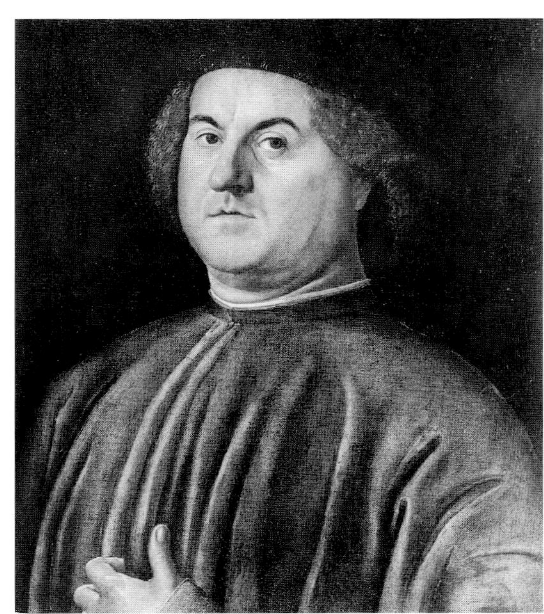

13 Alvise Vivarini. *Portrait of a Man* (1497). London, National Gallery.

clenched fist, and confronts the viewer with a stare that is at once defensive and somewhat aggressive.

The expressive intensity and meticulous realism of the *Bernardo de' Rossi* has reminded some critics of only slightly earlier portraits by Albrecht Dürer, such as the *Self-portrait* of 1498 (Madrid, Prado) and the *Oswald Krel* of 1499 (Munich, Alte Pinakothek). Any resemblance must be fortuitous, however, since Lotto cannot have seen these pictures, and Dürer's engraved portraits all date from much later in his career. On the other hand, Lotto does indeed seem to have known and responded to Dürer's subject-engravings from an early stage in his career, as is already evident in the *Allegory* completed for Bishop Rossi on 1 July 1505 as a cover for his portrait (pl. 16).[12] From the descriptions by Marcantonio Michiel of pictures in Venetian and Paduan private collections it emerges that was not unusual for portraits of the period to be equipped with wooden or canvas covers, the original function of which was to protect them from dust or damage, but which could also be decorated with appropriate symbolic or heraldic devices or inscriptions or both. Sometimes, as in a surviving example mentioned by Michiel, the portraits of Alvise Contarini and *A Nun of San Secondo* by Jacometto Veneziano of about 1480–90 (New York, Metropolitan Museum of Art, Lehman Collection), a pair of portraits was hinged to form a folding diptych, which was then also painted on its two reverses. In the case of the Rossi portrait, however—and probably also of Lotto's closely contemporary *Portrait of a Woman* now in Dijon (p. 12)—the cover consisted of a slightly larger, separate panel, which was probably originally attached to the portrait by a sliding mechanism similar to the one still retained by Dürer's portrait of *Hieronymus Holzschuher* of 1526 (Berlin, Staatliche Museen).[13] But whatever the type of physical arrangement, the pairing of a portrait with a complementary image had an obvious analogy with the traditional placing of a personal *impresa* on the reverse of a portrait medal; and painted covers could similarly, therefore, be used to provide a pithy summary of the sitter's inner personality or philosophy in the language of allegory.[14] Although the iconography of the Rossi cover is more complex than that by Jacometto, and the meaning of some of the details remains obscure, its general tenor seems clear enough.[15] The division of the composition by the central tree-trunk into two vertical halves, each showing a landscape of a sharply contrasting character, obviously invites a comparison between the two halves. On the left—the side towards which Rossi's escutcheon with its rampant lion inclines—the ground is stony and the hedge thorny; yet the kneeling putto amid his mathematical and musical instruments is industrious and attentive. Above him, a branch of the dead tree bursts into leaf, and beyond him the sea is calm and the land sunny. Half way up the background slope the figure of another putto—or perhaps the same one now rewarded with a pair of wings—is to be seen ascending towards a dazzling radiance. On the right side, by contrast, the vegetation is lush and inviting, and the pleasures of wine are freely available. But the lounging satyr has abandoned himself to idleness and luxury, while an urn on its side spills its contents; and in the background, dark storm-clouds gather over a shipwreck. On this side, the tree remains barren, and the crystal escutcheon with the gorgon's head signals petrification and death. Clearly then, while the path of virtue and reason may be hard and stony, it will eventually lead to happiness and fulfilment; whereas the indulgence of man's purely sensual appetites, while bringing pleasure in the short term, will inevitably lead to disaster.

Rossi's desire for his portrait to be complemented by an image setting out his stoical philosophy of life would certainly have been coloured by the crisis of 1503; and against this background, it is probably reasonable to interpret the central tree as a reference to a verse in the Book of Job (14:7): 'For there is hope of a tree, if it be cut down, that it will sprout again, and that the tender branch thereof will not cease.' Rossi is known to have owned a copy of the *Moralia* of Gregory the Great, which included a commentary on the Book of Job; and he may well have seen himself as the just man, afflicted with suffering and surrounded by enemies, but who nevertheless survived and flourished through steadfast virtue.[16]

Stylistically, the *Allegory* is one of the most original of the works of Lotto's early career in Treviso, and its landscape, much more than that of the *Virgin and Child with St Peter Martyr*, is strikingly independent of the example of Bellini, Cima or Alvise. In its bipartite division by a central tree the composition bears a general resemblance rather to that of Dürer's engraving of *Hercules at the Crossroads* of 1498 (pl. 14),[17] a source that might have been inspired by the fact that Hercules, too, was required to choose between harsh virtue and seductive vice. Dürer's prints were readily available in Treviso by this date, as is evident from a very literal borrowing of one of his landscape

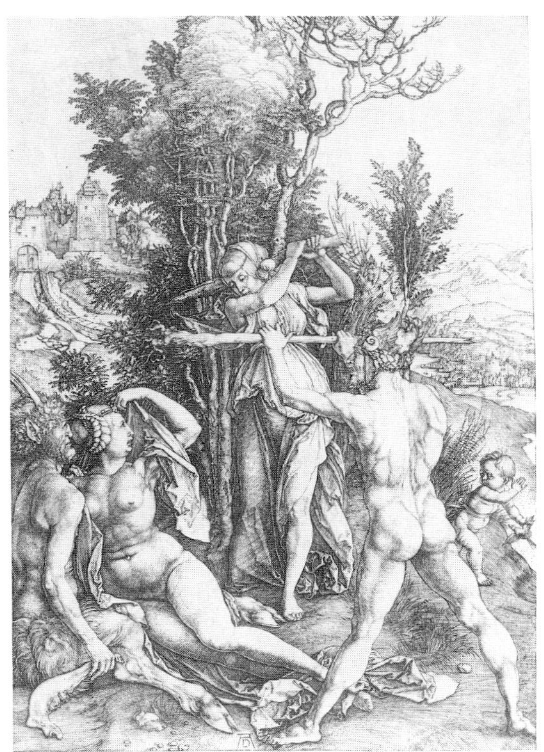

14 Albrecht Dürer. *Hercules at the Crossroads* (1498). Engraving.

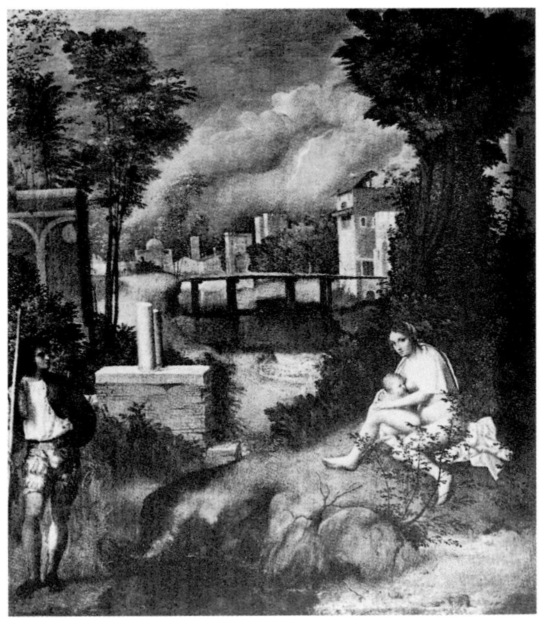

15 Giorgione. *Tempest* (*c.*1505–6). Venice, Gallerie dell'Accademia.

16 (*facing page*) Lotto. *Allegory* (1505). Panel, 56.5 × 42.2 cm. Washington, DC, National Gallery of Art. Samuel H. Kress Collection.

motifs by the local painter Pier Maria Pennacchi in a *Dead Christ with Angels* of about 1497.[18] Lotto's own borrowing from Dürer in the *Allegory* is by no means as literal; indeed, it would be possible to deny any compositional dependence of the painting on the *Hercules* engraving in particular. It is nevertheless a sign of Lotto's growing maturity that he was beginning to absorb a wider range of artistic experiences on a deeper level; and surely indebted to Dürer's prints in general is the taut dynamism of the landscape, with its energetic curvilinear rhythms and its vigorously thrusting vegetation.[19] It may be that Lotto was further encouraged in this direction by an acquaintance with the revolutionary art of his slightly older contemporary Giorgione, and in particular with his *Tempest* (pl. 15), which itself owes much to a knowledge of Dürer's prints. But apart from the fact that the date of the *Tempest* is matter of critical controversy, and the *Allegory* may actually have been painted earlier, the graphic clarity with which Lotto describes his forms, so different from Giorgione's *sfumato*, implies that his lessons from Dürer were derived directly from the prints, and not by way of Giorgione.

The inspiration of Dürer is again apparent in the so-called '*Maiden's Dream*' (pl. 17), another small panel, probably painted not more than a year later, in which mythological figures inhabit a poetically suggestive, northern-looking landscape. But in this case, while the landscape and smaller figures continue to reflect Lotto's interest in Dürer's prints in general, the central figure of the resting woman bears a close resemblance to one work in particular, a drawing of a nude dated 1501, now in Vienna (pl. 18).[20] Lotto is bound to have been aware that in the autumn of 1505 the great German artist arrived in Venice in person, to paint his *Feast of the Rosegarlands* (Prague, National Gallery) for the church of San Bartolomeo at Rialto; and the borrowing from the Vienna drawing (or from another very like it) implies that Lotto must have gone to the capital to meet Dürer, perhaps soon after his arrival there.

Like the Rossi *Allegory*, the '*Maiden's Dream*' was almost certainly painted as the cover of a portrait, the most likely candidate for which is the *Portrait of a Woman* now in Dijon (Musée des Beaux-Arts).[21] Although the picture has sometimes similarly been interpreted in narrative terms, as the story of Danaë, or of the nymph Rhodos, it almost certainly constitutes an allegory, conveying a message similar to that of the Rossi picture.[22] As before, the composition is structured to convey a dialectical contrast, in this case between the female figure in the centre, clothed in shining white, and the satyrs at either side, who more obviously belong to the shadowy world of the forest. Like that in the Rossi *Allegory*, the two satyrs allude to man's lower nature, and to the animal pleasures of the senses: thus the female satyr on the left lustfully ogles her male companion, who pours wine from a vase into his mouth. By contrast, the pure maiden at the centre leans against an olive tree, symbolic of the wisdom of Minerva, and experiences a vision of a heavenly cupid, who blesses her with a shower of luminous blossoms. A number of different texts and images have been suggested as sources for the various motifs in the picture: thus the central figure, seated by a clear stream and showered with petals, may have been intended to evoke Petrarch's Laura, as portrayed in his Sonnet CXXVI; it may also have been inspired by the woodcut representing a similarly reclining figure, *Nymph at the Fountain*, in the celebrated *Hypnerotomachia Poliphili* of 1499 (pl. 19). But any such sources, presumably proposed by the unknown patron whose portrait the picture was designed to accompany, are then varied and combined by Lotto into a new poetic unity.

Another small-scale, Düreresque landscape by Lotto, this time almost certainly commissioned by Rossi, is a *St Jerome*, signed and dated 1506 (pl. 22).[23] As with the *Allegory*, the theme of the scholar heroically struggling to follow the stony path of Christian righteousness and to reject the temptations of the world, would have had a particular personal relevance for the embattled bishop.[24] But small-scale representations of the penitent Jerome in the desert had become a highly popular genre by the later

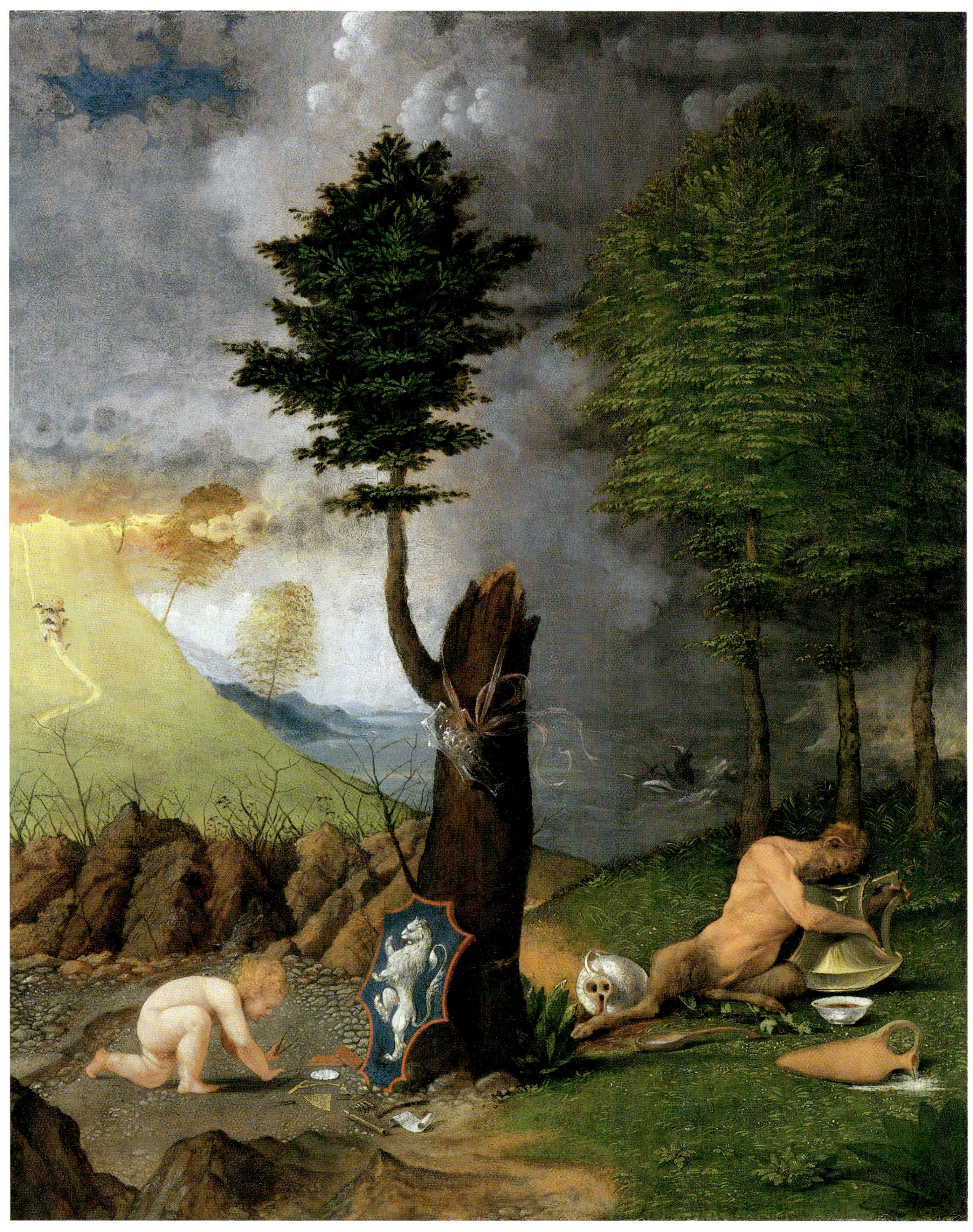

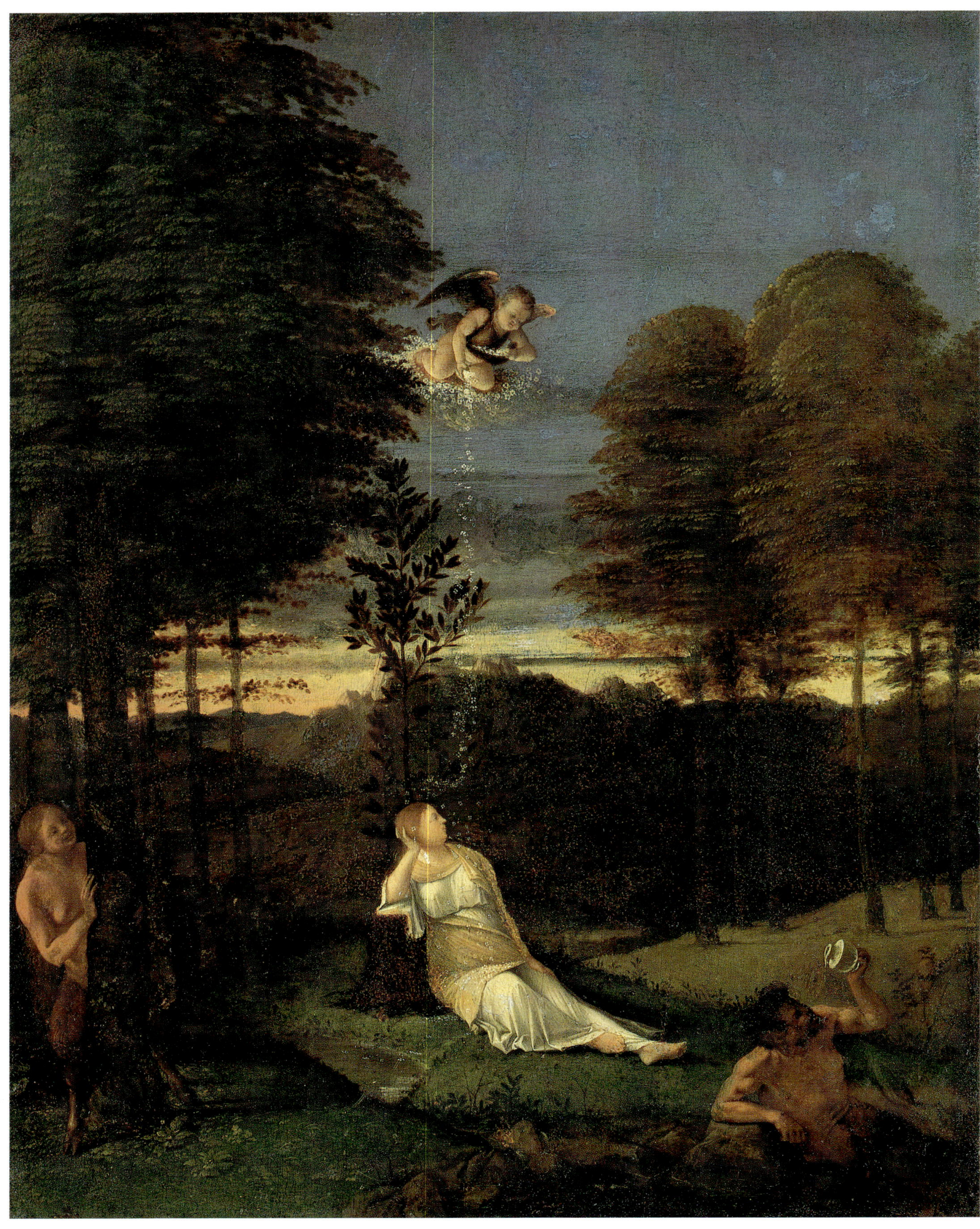

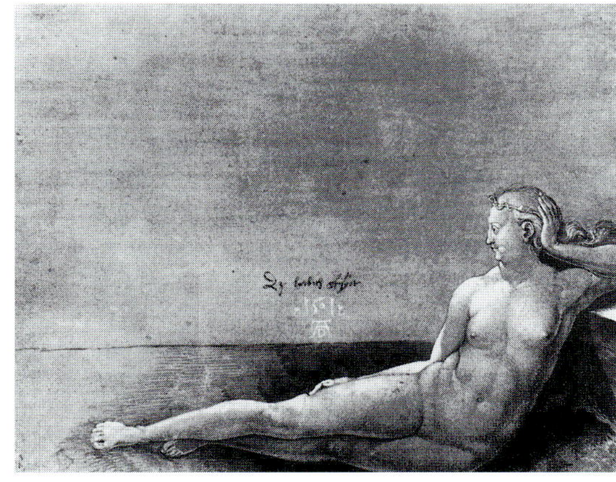

18 Albrecht Dürer. *Nude* Drawing (1501), Vienna, Albertina.

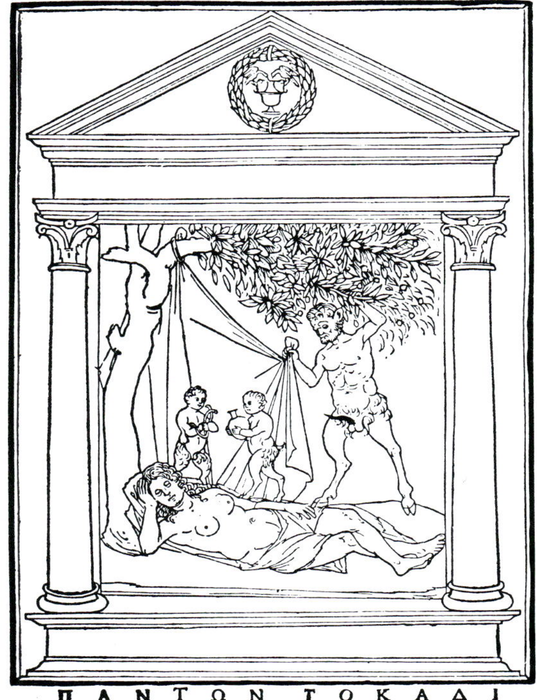

19 *Nymph at the Fountain.* Woodcut from *Hypnerotomachia Poliphili* (1499).

17 (*facing page*) Lotto. '*A Maiden's Dream*' (*c.*1505–6). Panel, 42.9 × 33.7 cm. Washington, DC, National Gallery of Art. Samuel H. Kress Collection.

20 (*right*) Detail of pl. 17.

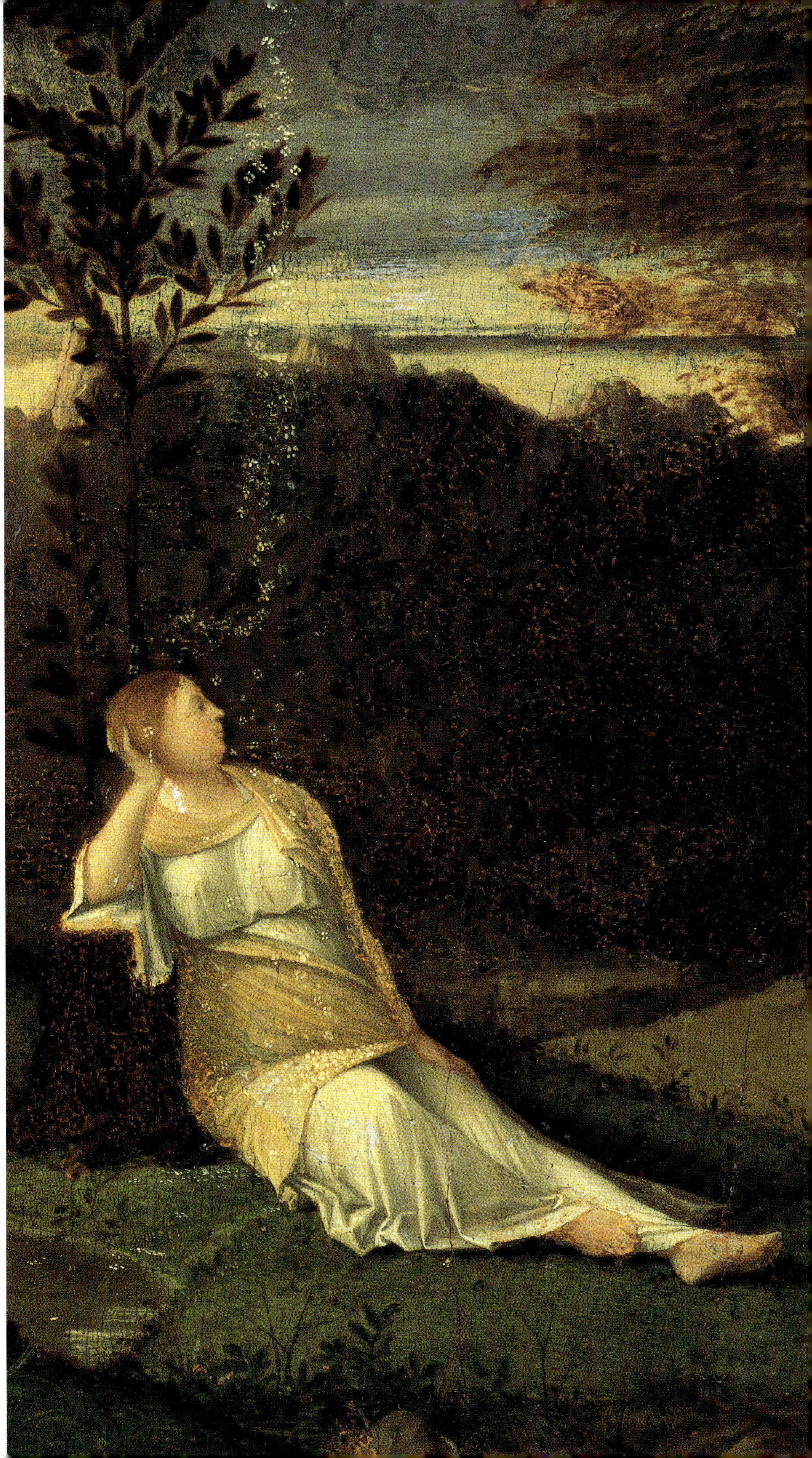

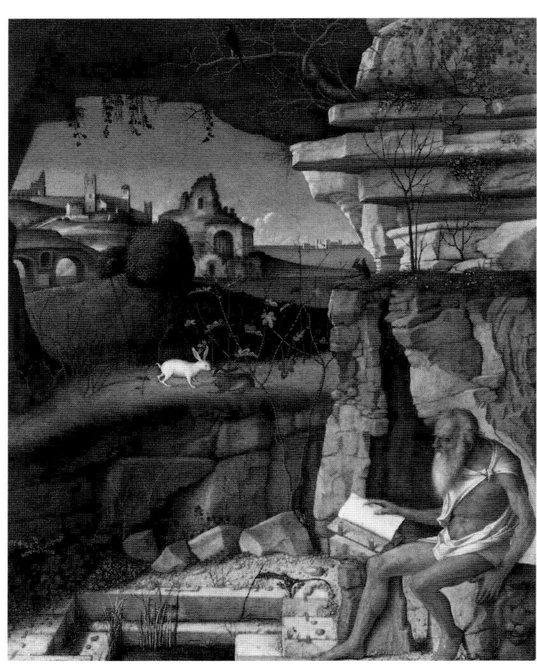

21 Giovanni Bellini. *St Jerome* (*c.*1505). Washington, DC, National Gallery of Art. Samuel H. Kress Collection.

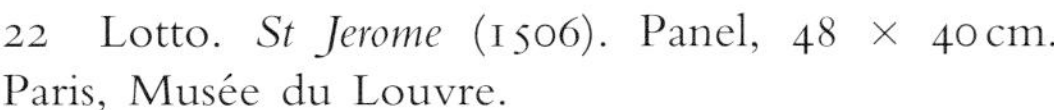

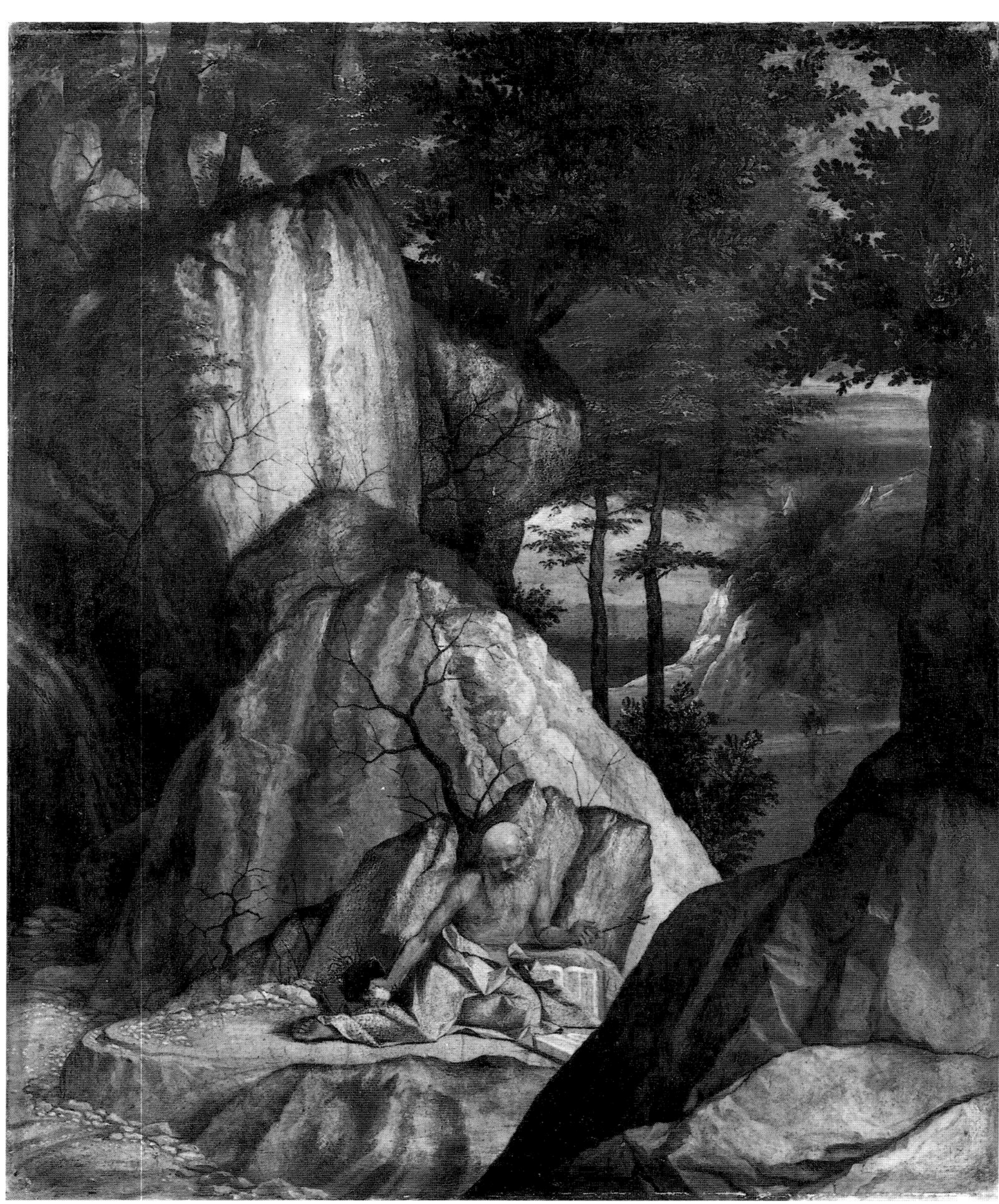

22 Lotto. *St Jerome* (1506). Panel, 48 × 40 cm. Paris, Musée du Louvre.

fifteenth century in Venice, thanks above all to the pioneering contribution made by Giovanni Bellini. In a rather late example by Bellini, dated to the previous year (pl. 21), the saint is characteristically set against a serene and humanised landscape, which recedes in orderly fashion from the foreground rocks across a grassy knoll to the mouth of a river and a bridge, and thence to picturesque ruins and a seascape beyond. By contrast, Lotto's interpretation of the theme – the first of a number of variations he was to paint throughout his career (see pls 36, 59, 153) – is highly dramatic. Smaller in relation to the frame and set back from the foreground plane, his saint is deeply immersed in a wilder and more rugged landscape, dominated by huge rocks and towering trees, which appear to grow infinitely upwards and outwards. Instead of Bellini's carefully constructed grid of verticals and horizontals, Lotto's composition, like that of Dürer's *Hercules*, is dominated by bold, sweeping diagonals, which further contribute to the effect of a natural world in the process of active growth. Similarly indebted to Dürer and uncharacteristic of Bellini are the sudden contrasts of scale and breaks in spatial recession, and the use of jagged silhouettes. Independent of graphic inspiration, however, is the mood of poetic mystery created, as in the '*Maiden's Dream*', by the evening twilight, and by the occasional glimpses between the dark rocks and trees of a sunset sky.

It was probably some time in the previous year, 1505, that Lotto received his first commission to paint a large-scale public work, his altarpiece for the parish church of Santa Cristina al Tiverone, a village just outside Treviso (pl. 24). In 1504 Bishop Rossi had released funds for the rebuilding and refurbishment of the church, and the choice by the parish priest, one Pre Franchino, of Lotto to decorate its main altar was probably made on the recommendation of the bishop. This seems especially likely because, when Lotto was involved in litigation with the priest over the fee for the completed work in May 1506, Rossi again intervened on the painter's behalf. A further document, dated November 1507 and recording payments to a wood-carver and a gilder for their work on the frame, suggests that Lotto's panels had not yet been framed or installed above the altar at the time of his departure for Recanati in the autumn of 1506.[25]

The overall design of the altarpiece for Santa Cristina, consisting of a main field capped by a separate lunette, had become old-fashioned by metropolitan standards by the early sixteenth century, and its choice here may have been determined as much by the parish priest and his chapter as by the painter. But as in an earlier venture into new territory, the *Virgin and Child with St Peter Martyr* of 1503, the pictorial composition is itself unusually conservative and derivative for Lotto, and it follows a standard Venetian formula for Madonna and saints altarpieces going back a quarter of a century. The original, documented frame is lost, but as in the work's Venetian prototypes, the architectural forms of the frame would almost certainly have repeated those of the main panel, and would have united with them to enhance the illusion of a box-like space.[26] The most obvious model is that of Bellini's great San Zaccaria altarpiece, completed very recently in 1505 (pl. 23), from which Lotto has borrowed not just the general symmetrical arrangement and the illusionistic linkage with the architectonic frame, but such specific motifs as the half-dome, with its golden mosaic and curling vegetal ornament, and even the identity of the two male saints at either side. It would have been customary, of course, for the patron to make the principal decisions regarding the choice of saints, and in this case the two inside saints obviously directly reflect local interests. Thus the saint in the place of honour immediately to the right of the Virgin and Child is the titular of the parish, Christina, holding a very prominent mill-wheel as an attribute of her martyrdom; while opposite her is the patron saint of Treviso, the warrior Liberale, holding a model of the city in his left hand. But the more generally popular and less locally specific figures of Peter and Jerome may have been introduced on Lotto's own initiative, in tribute to Bellini's masterpiece. The figure of the Dead Christ with mourning angels in the lunette also takes up a theme closely associated with Bellini, as in the apex of his much earlier *St Vincent Ferrer* polyptych of about 1464–8 (Venice, Santi Giovanni e Paolo), from which Lotto has taken over the touching motif of Christ's limp right hand held up by the angel. But Lotto clearly took the opportunity to study the altarpieces of other painters as well, including Antonello da Messina's San Cassiano altarpiece of 1475–6 (fragment in Vienna, Kunsthistorisches Museum), which provided appropriate models for the figures of both Christina and Liberale.

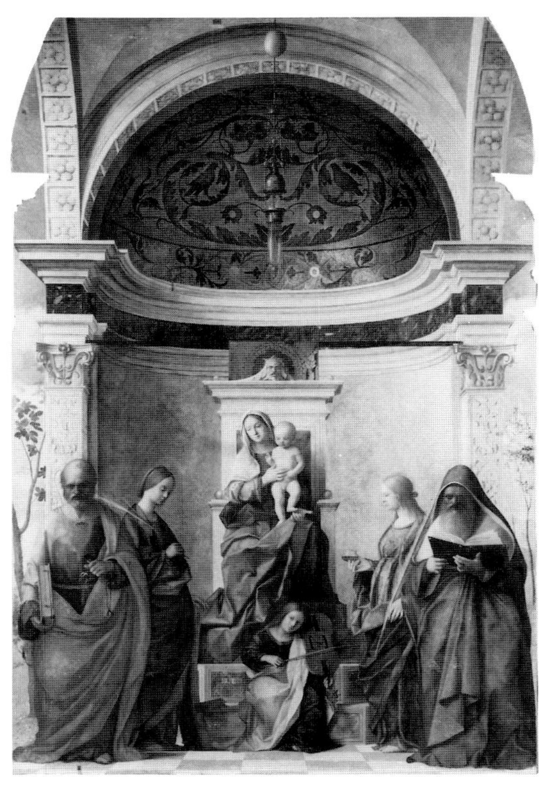

23 Giovanni Bellini. *Virgin and Child with Saints* (1505). Venice, San Zaccaria.

The *St Christina* altarpiece does not, however, constitute a mere pastiche of Venetian prototypes; with a precocious self-confidence, Lotto succeeds in combining his borrowings in a way that already reveals his quite distinctive character as a painter of religious images. The compositional harmony of the San Zaccaria altarpiece is disrupted by a number of minor but telling asymmetries, such as the contrast between the darkness on the extreme left and the view to the open sky on the right, and the

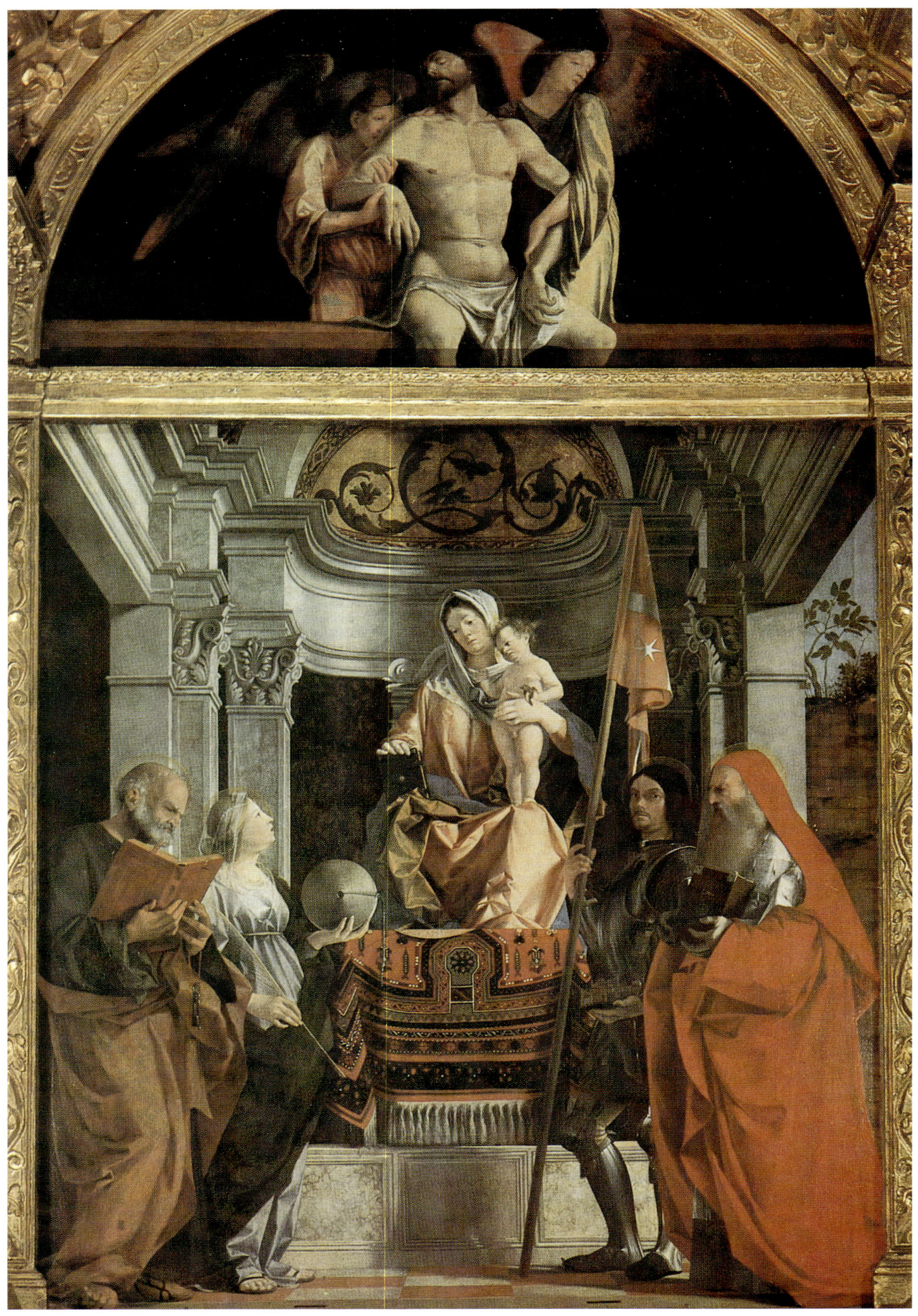

24 Lotto. *St Christina* altarpiece (1504–6). Two panels: 175 × 162 cm (main field); 90 × 180 cm (lunette). Santa Cristina al Tiverone (Treviso) parish church.

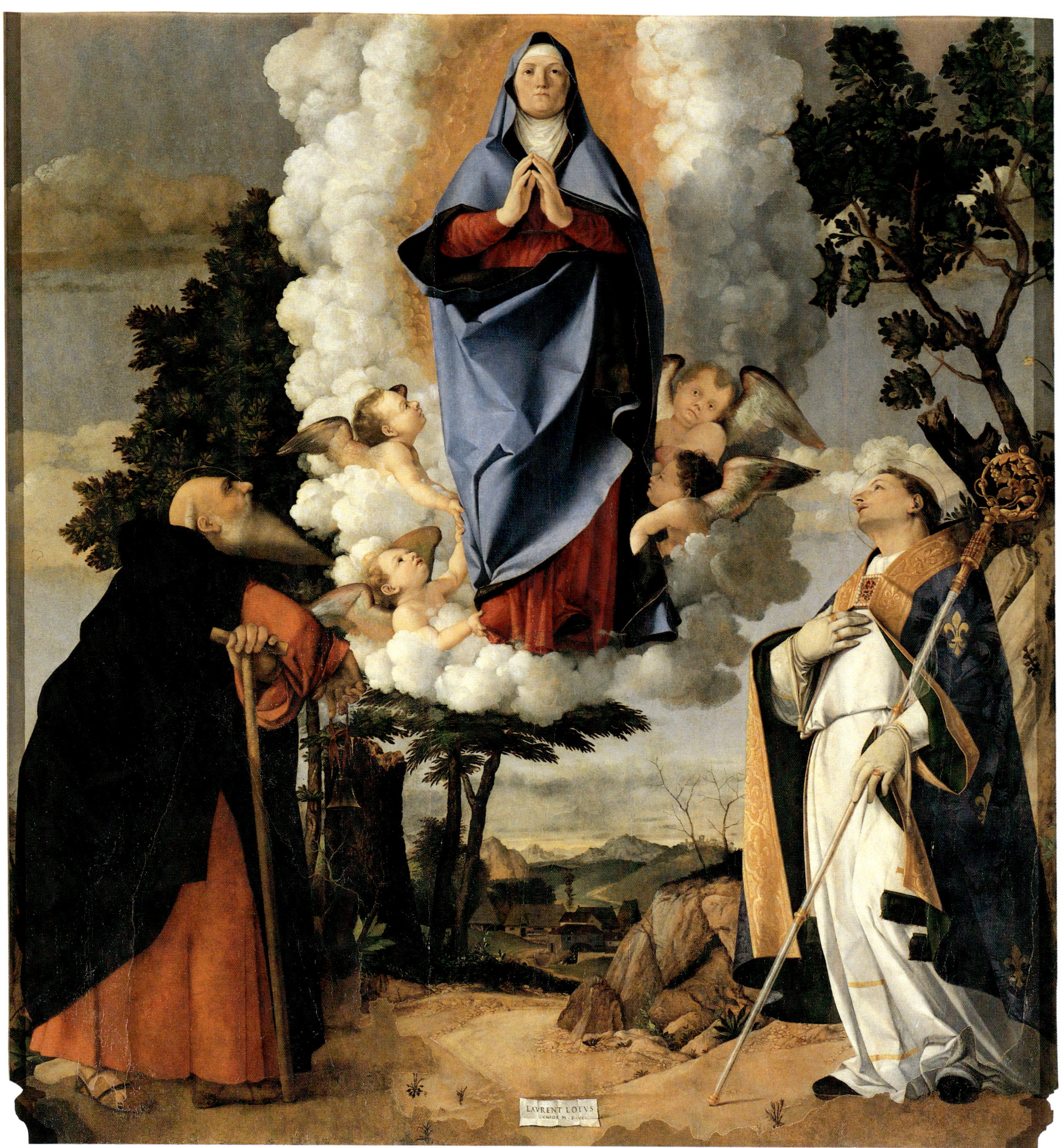

25 Lotto. *Assumption of the Virgin with Sts Anthony Abbot and Louis of Toulouse* (1506). Panel, 175 × 161 cm. Asolo, Duomo.

combined attention of the Virgin and Child on a single figure, Christina. Similarly disruptive of any overall harmony is the almost obsessive attention to subordinate details: the oriental carpet; the ermine-tails on the fur lining of Jerome's robe; the straps of Liberale's armour; the metal brackets fixed to the tiled floor in the foreground. Again, the light is not warm and evenly diffused, but cool and sharply directed, creating complicated angular patterns in the folds of the draperies and a hard glitter on Liberale's armour. The saints are not calmly absorbed in their own thoughts, but nervous and restless, reacting to each other and to the spectator. It is as if the tragic mood of the *Pietà* in the lunette has encroached upon the normally serene theme of the *sacra conversazione*, and filled the saints with melancholy foreboding.[27]

Following hard on the *St Christina* altarpiece came a second commission for an altarpiece within the diocese of Treviso, the *Assumption of the Virgin* of 1506 (pl. 25), now in the Duomo of Asolo, but originally apparently painted for the neighbouring meeting-house of a devotional confraternity, the Scuola di Santa Maria dei Battuti.[28] This confraternity was closely involved in the administration of a local hospital entrusted with the care of the poor and the sick; and this fact may help explain the presence, in addition to that of the Scuola's patron, the Virgin, of Anthony Abbot, a saint traditionally invoked for protection against disease, and of Louis of Toulouse, who renounced a royal birthright to serve the needs of the poor.[29] While portraying both saints in attitudes of fervent adoration of the hovering Virgin, Lotto makes a highly effective contrast between their two characters, the one an old, bearded hermit with a rustic stick, the other a young, aristocratic bishop, dressed in a splendid cope adorned with the lilies of France and holding a precious crozier of silver and gold.

The precise subject represented by Lotto has been the matter of considerable recent critical debate, since the historical witnesses of the Assumption of the Virgin were not, of course, Anthony and Louis, but the twelve apostles, as shown by Lotto himself in two of his later altarpieces (pls 99, 156). The Asolo picture, together with Giovanni Bellini's iconographically similar altarpiece for Santa Maria degli Angeli on Murano (now in nearby San Pietro Martire),[30] which Lotto must certainly have known, has consequently often been interpreted instead as a representation of the mystery of the Immaculate Conception.[31] But there are no unambiguous references in the representations of either Bellini or Lotto to this somewhat contentious doctrine, which in this period was promoted chiefly by the Franciscan order; and it was not, in fact, at all unusual in altarpieces for the principal figure or episode of a sacred event to be accompanied by saints that were entirely anachronistic. The Duomo of Asolo was dedicated to the Virgin of the Assumption, and so presumably was the Scuola di Santa Maria dei Battuti. Lotto's altarpiece may thus be read as an iconic image of the confraternity's principal protectress in this guise – unusually, but perfectly appropriately shown as an old woman – together with two other saints to which its members were particularly devoted.

Of the various other pictures that may be assigned to Lotto's early career in Treviso, none has a secure date or patron. In addition to the *Bernardo de' Rossi*, he painted several portraits of now anonymous sitters, and of these perhaps the finest is the *Young Man with a Lamp* in Vienna (pl. 26).[32] Although still restricted to a bust-length format, this portrait closely resembles the *Rossi* in its use of a curtain-backdrop and its precise, 'warts and all' rendering of the features, and especially also in the enquiring, somewhat hostile glance outwards and the mobile lips. Unlike that in the *Rossi*, the curtain here is slightly drawn to reveal a burning lamp with its snuffer at the top right, hinting at an interior space beyond that of the immediate foreground, and implying that the lamp carries some allegorical meaning relevant to the sitter's personality, destiny or both. It is not entirely clear from his costume whether he is a secular scholar or a cleric, but in

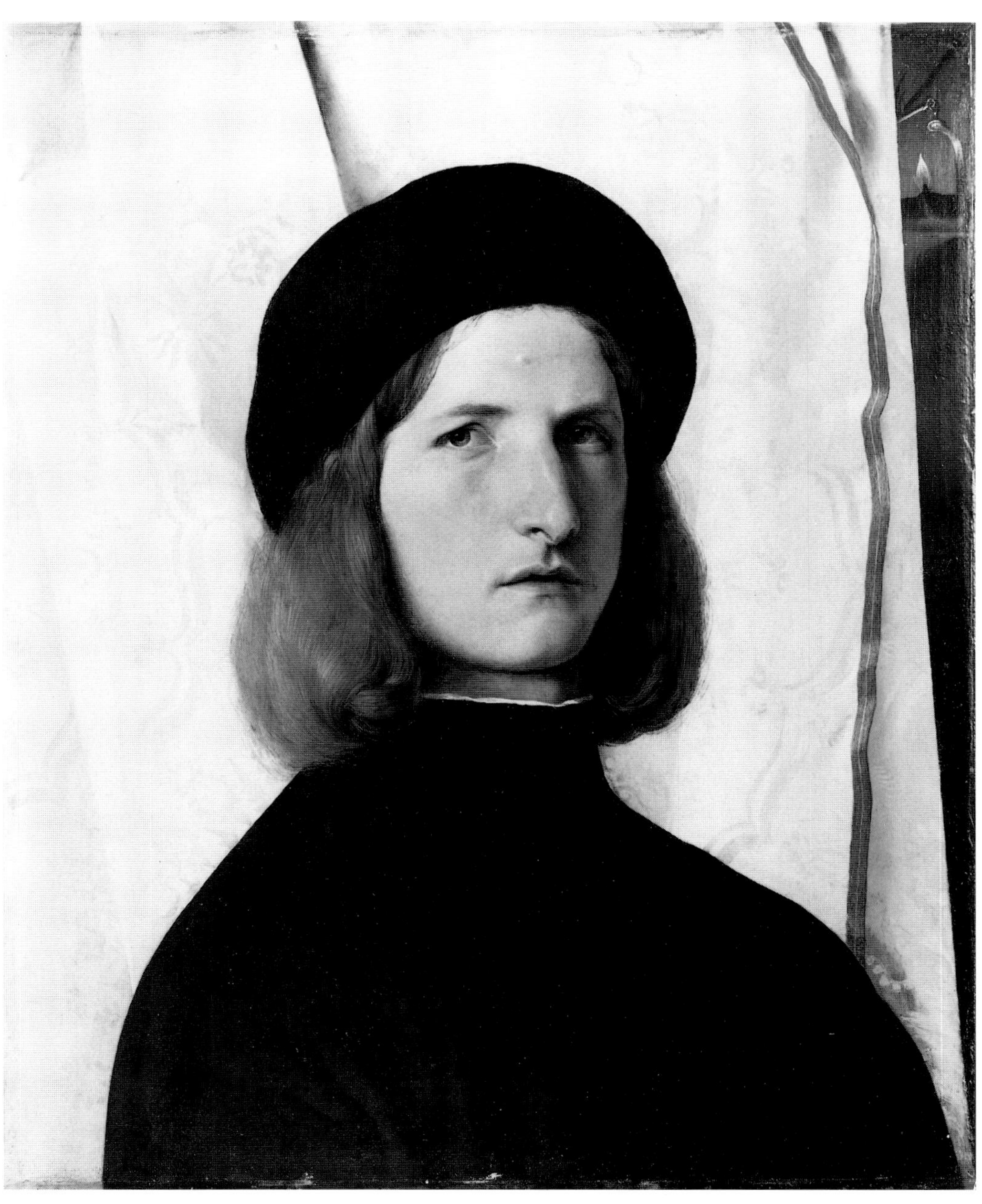

26 Lotto. *Young Man with a Lamp* (*c.*1506). Panel, 42.3 × 35.3 cm. Vienna, Kunsthistorisches Museum.

either case the lamp, by analogy with the lamps prepared by the Wise Virgins in Christ's parable, may refer to true wisdom as the guiding light of a young man of contemplation.[33] Alternatively, and in keeping with an interpretation of lamp symbolism provided by the hieroglyphic scholar Pierio Valeriano, the motif would refer to the uncertainty of human life, constantly in danger of being snuffed out.[34] Although Valeriano did not publish his authoritative compilation *Hieroglifica* until 1557, it is significant that like Lotto, he was a protégé of Bishop de' Rossi in the first decade of the century, at a time when he had already begun work in Venice on his huge opus.[35]

Lotto's other two most important religious pictures of the period both represent variations on the theme already essayed in his first known work, that of the half-length Virgin and Child with saints against a landscape. The composition of the earlier, now in Edinburgh (pl. 27),[36] remains close to fifteenth-century tradition; and the way in

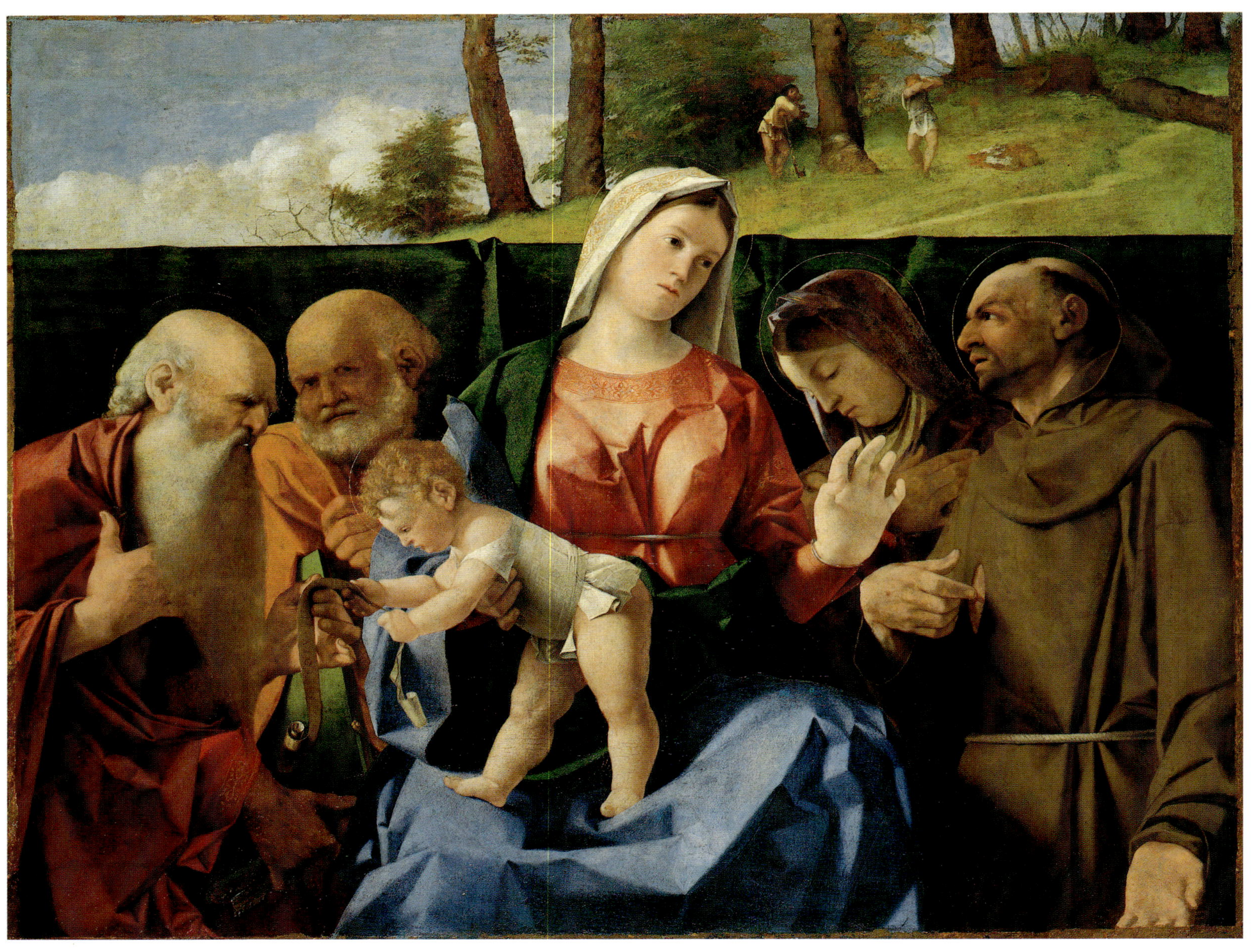

27 Lotto. *Virgin and Child with Saints* (*c.*1504–5). Panel transferred to canvas, 82 × 105 cm. Edinburgh, National Gallery of Scotland.

which the Virgin and the Christ Child lean in different directions, with the Child playing with the attribute of one of the saints, is particularly characteristic of earlier examples of the genre by Cima. Consistent with this are the still markedly Cimesque figures of the Virgin and the aged prophet on the left, perhaps identifiable as Jeremiah.[37] At the same time, the figures are all broader-boned than their counterparts by Cima or Bellini, with larger, less elegant and more expressive hands; and, as in the probably exactly contemporary Santa Cristina altarpiece, Lotto has succeeded, by means both of gesture and motif, in endowing the conventional theme with a new sense of spiritual urgency. Highly expressive is the half-playful motif at the left, with the Child carefully scrutinising the prophet's scroll, since it also carries a poignant implication of his future Passion and death. This idea is also conveyed by the unusually emphatic way in which the prophet's counterpart on the right, Francis, points to the wound in his side, and especially by the figures of the woodcutters in the landscape, whose cutting down of growing trees serves as a potent metaphor for the Crucifixion.[38] The treat-

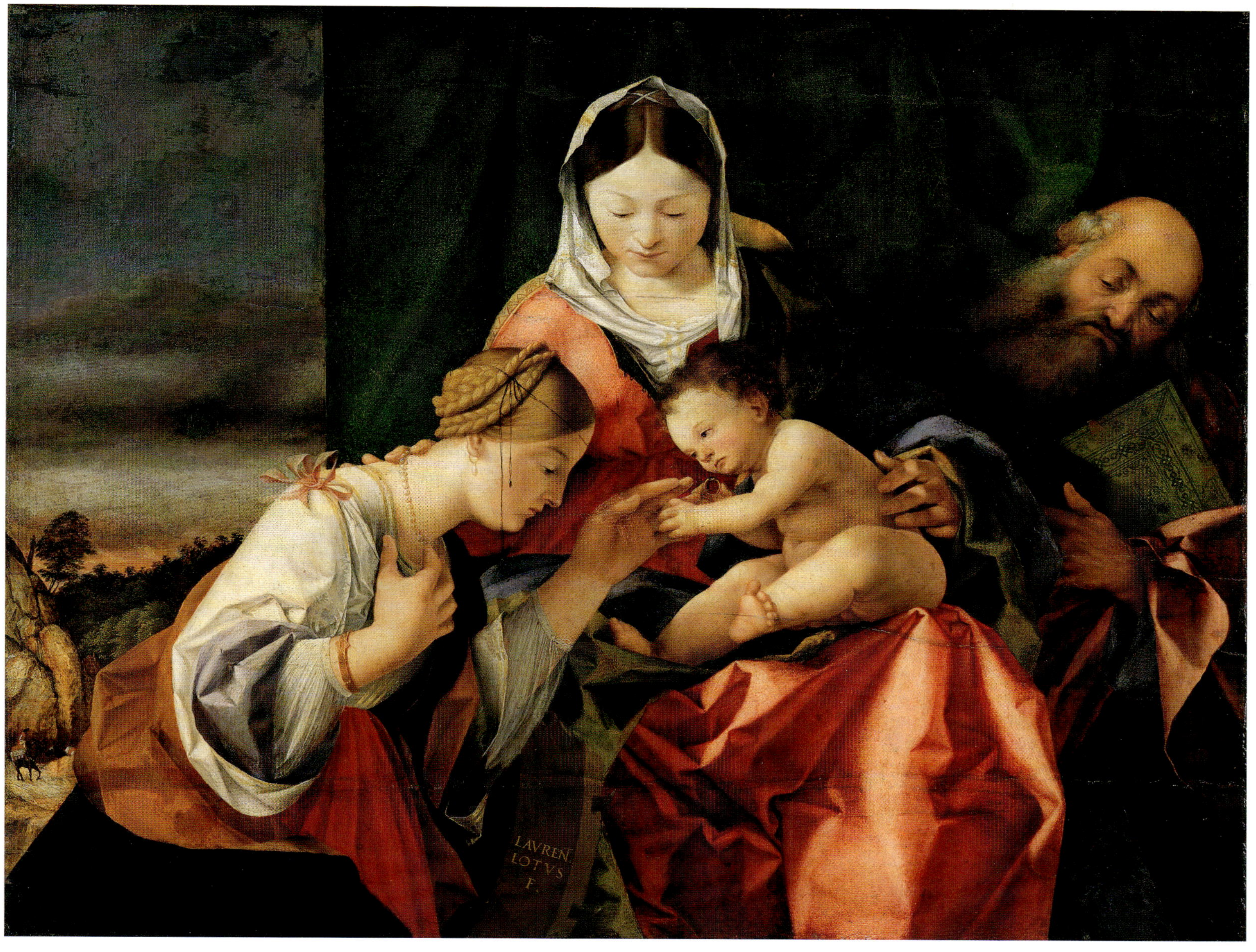

28 Lotto. *Mystic Marriage of St Catherine* (*c.*1505–6). Panel, 71.3 × 91.2 cm. Munich, Alte Pinakothek.

ment of this enticing sylvan scene as a juxtaposed vignette, seeming as much to hover above the saints as to take place in the distance beyond them, serves as a highly effective reinforcement of its underlying symbolic significance.

Probably only slightly later than the Edinburgh picture is the *Mystic Marriage of St Catherine* in Munich (pl. 28),[39] in which the Child's close involvement with one of the two flanking saints has reduced the second – presumably, but not unambiguously identifiable as Joseph[40] – to the role of a passive witness. Stimulated, perhaps, by the narrative element, referring to the mystic betrothal of the saintly princess to Christ, Lotto has loosened the traditional symmetry of design by introducing a strongly directed diagonal that runs from the bottom left to the upper right. As in the Santa Cristina altarpiece, the dark foil at one edge is loosely balanced by a view to the open air at the other, in this case to a mysteriously evocative sunset landscape very similar to that half-glimpsed in Rossi's *St Jerome* of 1506.

Already in the three to four years that he spent in Treviso, Lotto undertook

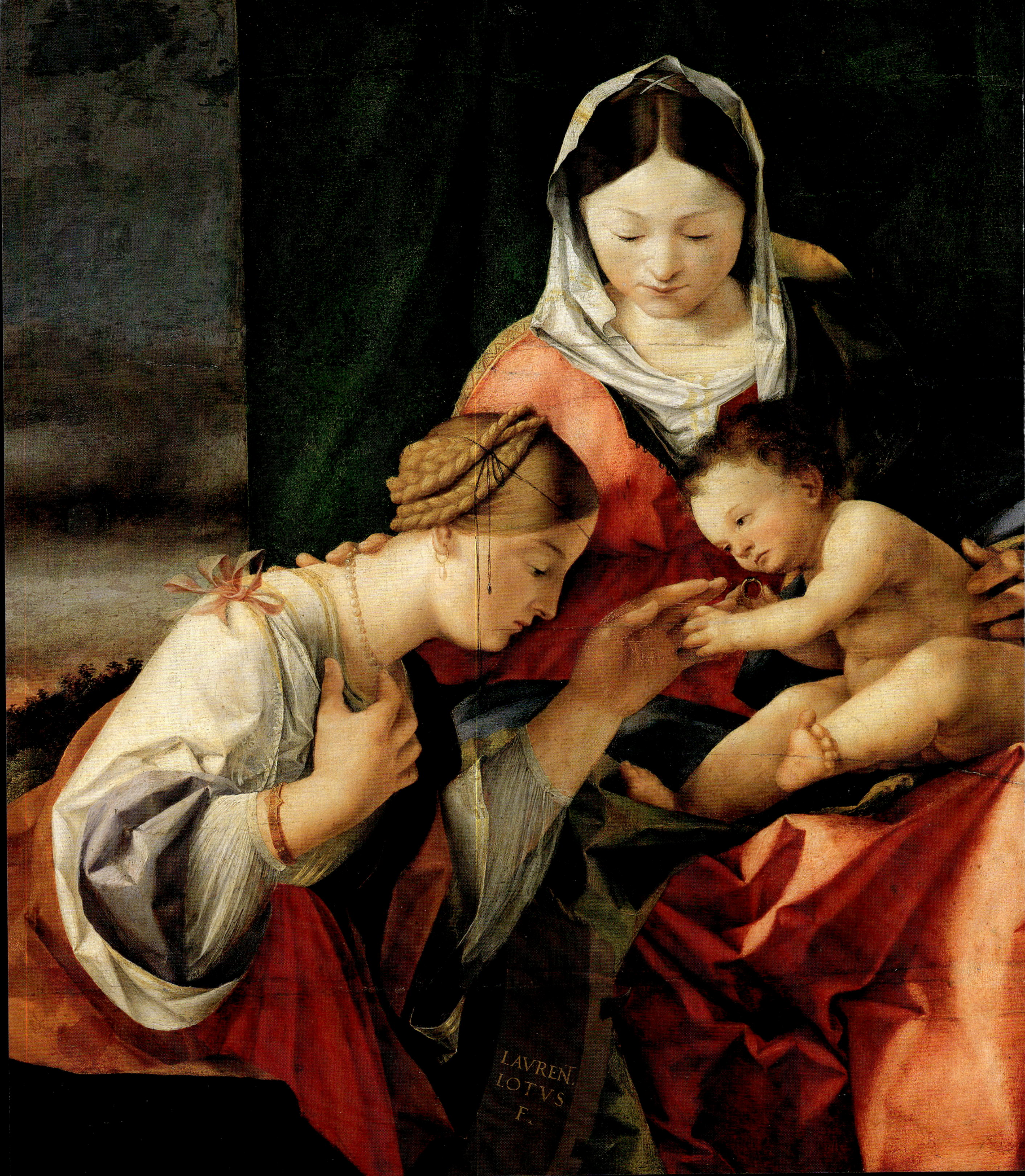
LAVREN.
LOTVS
F.

commissions in all the main genres he was to practise in his subsequent career. Religious subjects, in the form of altarpieces and smaller-scale devotional pictures, already predominate; but his earliest works also include a number of penetrating portraits, as well as secular allegories. And although a fresco representing a pair of standing pages below the Onigo tomb in San Niccolò, Treviso, is surely not by Lotto,[41] the fact that he was called to Rome in 1508/9 to paint frescoes suggests that he did indeed have early experience as a fresco painter in Treviso or the surrounding region. During this period his compositional habits and pictorial style remained rooted in fifteenth-century Venetian tradition, as represented in particular by Giovanni Bellini and Alvise Vivarini; and technically, too, he remained a traditionalist, continuing to use a well-prepared panel support rather than canvas, and to apply his paint in thin, superimposed layers over a careful underdrawing. Almost from the beginning, however, the same temperamental aversion to a normative, generalised classicism, already noted in a mature work such as the Recanati *Annunciation* (pl. 2; pp. 1–2), drew Lotto towards the more accentuated expressiveness and greater intensity of realism of German art; and as early as 1504 his interest in Dürer lent his work a flavour that was both modern and quite distinctive. By contrast, the impact of Lotto's only slightly older contemporary Giorgione was to remain limited. Despite the undeniable resemblance of the landscape background of the Asolo *Assumption* to that of Giorgione's *Adoration of the Shepherds* (Washington, National Gallery of Art),[42] there is no echo of the latter's Castelfranco altarpiece in Lotto's altarpiece for nearby Santa Cristina al Tiverone; and his early portraits have nothing of the poetic langour of those by Giorgione. More fundamentally, the crispness of Lotto's forms and the cool sharpness of his colours reveal little interest in the tonal revolution that Giorgione was in fact only just beginning to create at the time of Lotto's departure from the Veneto in 1506. Although subsequently, and particularly in the 1520s, he could scarcely avoid responding to certain aspects of Giorgione's art, alone of his generation of Venetian painters Lotto never went through a phase of development that may be categorised as Giorgionesque. Indeed, many of the characteristics of style that he developed during his early career in Treviso were to remain with him, essentially unaltered, for the rest of his long life.

29 Detail of pl. 28.

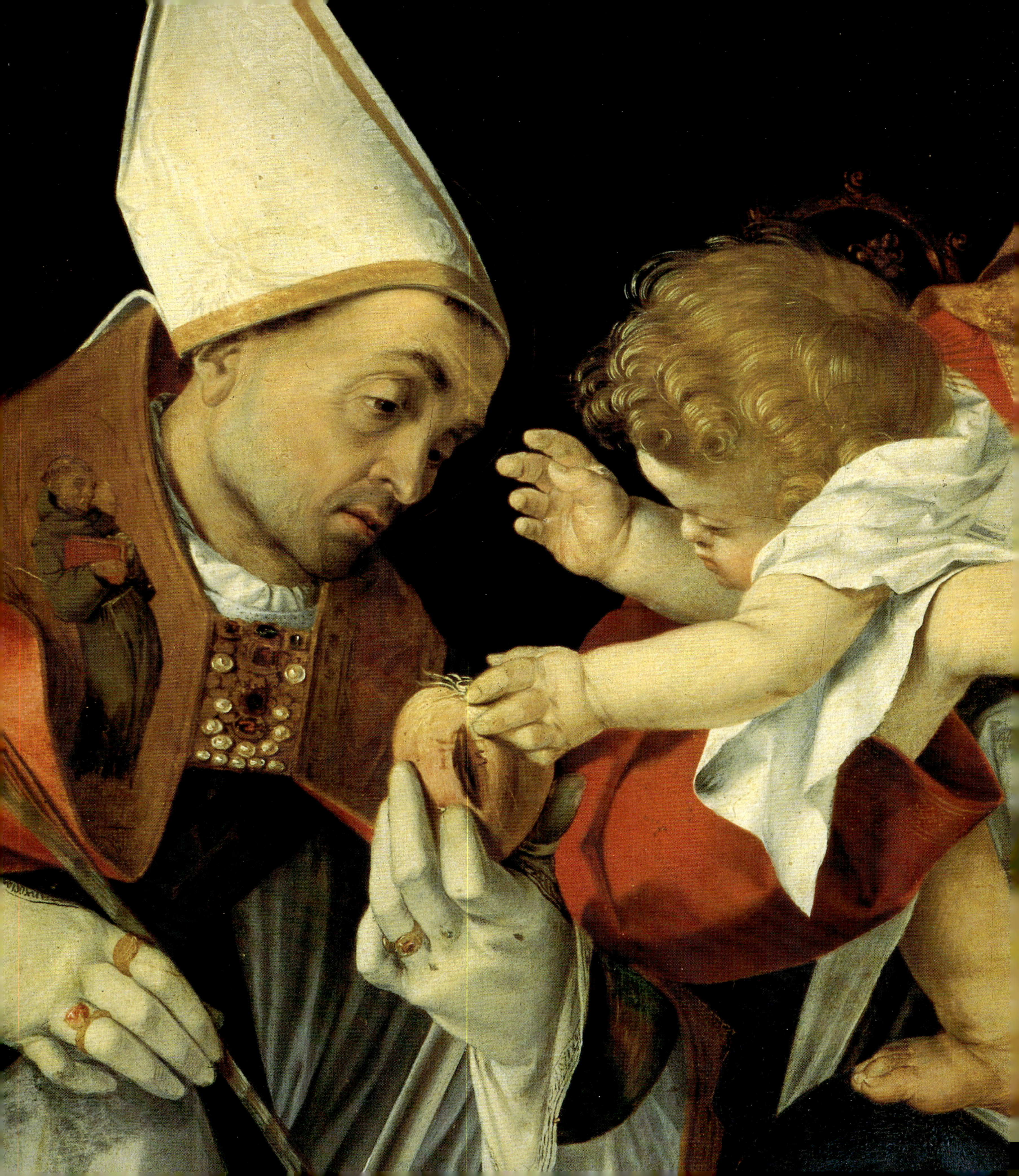

Chapter 2

THE MARCHES AND ROME 1506–1513/14

In June 1506, probably while he was still working on the Asolo *Assumption*, Lotto paid a brief visit to the Marches to sign the contract to paint the high altarpiece of the church of San Domenico in Recanati. In October of the same year, having fulfilled his outstanding obligations in Treviso, he moved to Recanati, where he lived within the convent of San Domenico until the completion of the altarpiece, probably in the late summer of 1508. Then in March and September 1509, he is recorded in Rome, working in one of the state apartments in the Vatican Palace. His movements during the subsequent years are not quite clear, but it is often reasonably supposed that after the Roman sojourn he briefly visited Florence before returning to the Marches. Certainly he was in Jesi, not far from Recanati, in October 1511; and he completed commissions for each of these two towns before again moving on, this time to Bergamo in Venetian Lombardy, in 1513/14.[1]

There had long existed close commercial and cultural ties between Venice and the papal states bordering the Adriatic coast, and since the fourteenth century Venetian painters had been in the habit of sending altarpieces to cities in the Marches.[2] Despite the example of Carlo Crivelli, however, who had settled in Ascoli Piceno in about 1469 as a fugitive from justice in his native Venice, it was usual practice to execute such works at home rather than on the spot; and it is curious, therefore, that Lotto should rather have decided to abandon Treviso and the Veneto and to take up residence in Recanati. His decision is all the more surprising, considering that the early support lent by Bishop Rossi was just beginning to bear fruit in large-scale commissions; furthermore, with Giorgione still working largely in the private sphere, and Sebastiano del Piombo and Titian only just beginning to emerge as independent artists, Lotto would have been well placed to embark upon a successful career in Venice itself. By comparison with Venice and even Treviso, Recanati was small, with a population of no more than 7,000, and it was also provincial, being distant from its capital, Rome, and separated from it by mountainous terrain. Situated in the province of Macerata in the central area of the Marches, Recanati also fell outside the artistic orbit both of Urbino to the north and Ascoli to the south; and there were no local painters of any real consequence. On the other hand, the commission at San Domenico was an important one for Lotto, involving a large and complex public work, and an exceptionally generous honorarium of 700 florins (the equivalent of about 320 Venetian ducats). He may also have calculated—correctly, as it turned out—that the region would offer as many possibilities for future commissions as the Veneto. Further, he would have been well aware of the close proximity of Recanati to Loreto, a Marian shrine much favoured by the reigning pope, Julius II, and where Luca Signorelli and Melozzo da Forlì had executed important works in the 1470s and 1480s; and it would have been natural to expect that this proximity might lead to fruitful contacts with members of the papal curia.[3]

30 Detail of pl. 35.

The Gothic church of San Domenico, one of the largest and most important in

Recanati, is situated in the central piazza, close to the Palazzo Comunale, the seat of civic government. Three days before Lotto signed his contract on 20 June 1506, the *comune* agreed to make a substantial contribution towards the funding of the commission, on the condition that the altarpiece include the images of the local patron saints, Flavian and Vitus.[4] The painter presumably knew of this and other iconographical requirements in advance, since the contract does not itemise them, but merely refers with approval to a compositional drawing that he had provided for the occasion. The contract was made with the Dominicans, who agreed to provide food and lodging for Lotto and his assistant during the course of the execution; but the continuing involvement of the civic authorities is illustrated by a document of November of the same year, which records that they provided twenty-five planks for the construction of the panels. The respective interests of the Dominican clergy on the one hand, and of the *comune* on the other, are almost diagrammatically evident in the choice of the eleven principal saints represented in two lower registers of the altarpiece (pl. 31).[5] Thus the principal panel appropriately celebrates St Dominic as titular of the church, and shows him kneeling before the Virgin and Child, while an angel invests him with the white scapular of the Dominican habit. Each of the other four panels similarly contains a Dominican saint. But St Thomas Aquinas and Peter Martyr in the full-length panels are paired with the bishop Flavian and the soldier Vitus; and at least one of the pope-saints flanking the Virgin's throne was chosen for his close association with the city of Recanati.[6] The same balance of interests was to be found in the three panels of the predella, now missing but recorded *in situ* by Vasari. To the left and right were scenes from the life of St Dominic; but the central scene – the carrying by angels of the Holy House from Dalmatia to its final resting-place in Loreto – celebrates a miraculous event central to the religious and civic dignity of the *comune* of Recanati.[7]

Partly to accommodate this complex iconographical programme, and partly no doubt to conform with provincial Marchigian tastes, Lotto was evidently required by his employers to design the altarpiece in the somewhat old-fashioned form of a polyptych. But whereas earlier Marchigian polyptychs, as represented above all by those of Crivelli, had been characterised by limited effects of spatial depth or unity, Lotto succeeded in introducing into his own polyptych many of the features of an up-to-date Venetian *sacra conversazione*. Unfortunately the present Renaissance-style frame dates only from 1912, and the original is long since lost; but as already at Santa Cristina al Tiverone (pl. 24), its forms are likely to have repeated those of the architecture represented in the three main panels, and to have linked up with them to reinforce the illusion of a chapel-like space at the centre, with chambers leading off to either side. The motifs of the central coffered barrel vault, of the mosaic half-domes at the sides and of the musician angels at the foot of the throne, all have precedents in the *sacra conversazione* altarpieces of Giovanni Bellini (see pl. 23);[8] and to a greater extent than in the self-consciously Bellinesque *St Christina* altarpiece, the main panels of the Recanati polyptych also reflect the compositional habits of Alvise Vivarini. Clearly derived from Alvise in particular is the placing of two attendant figures beside and slightly behind the Virgin's throne (see pl. 9);[9] and almost equally Alvisesque are the slightly fussy crowding of the figures and the effects of twitching movement. At the same time, many of Lotto's own innovations in the *St Christina* altarpiece are here taken further, as in the asymmetry created by the placing of the vested angel and St Dominic, and in the brooding introspection of the Virgin and saints. Entirely characteristic of Lotto is the contrast between the general mood of melancholy, which reflects that of the *Pietà* in the apex, and the amusing detail in the lower foreground of the child angels, who recoil as if startled by the entrance of Dominic. Even more than before, there is a close attention paid to tiny details of jewellery and metalwork, and to the way in which things function: to how, for example, the armour and elaborate ribbons of Vitus are

31 Lotto. San Domenico polyptych (1506–8). Six panels: 227 × 108 cm (centre); 155 × 67 cm (sides, lower); 67 × 67 cm (sides, upper); 80 × 108 cm (apex). Recanati, Pinacoteca Comunale.

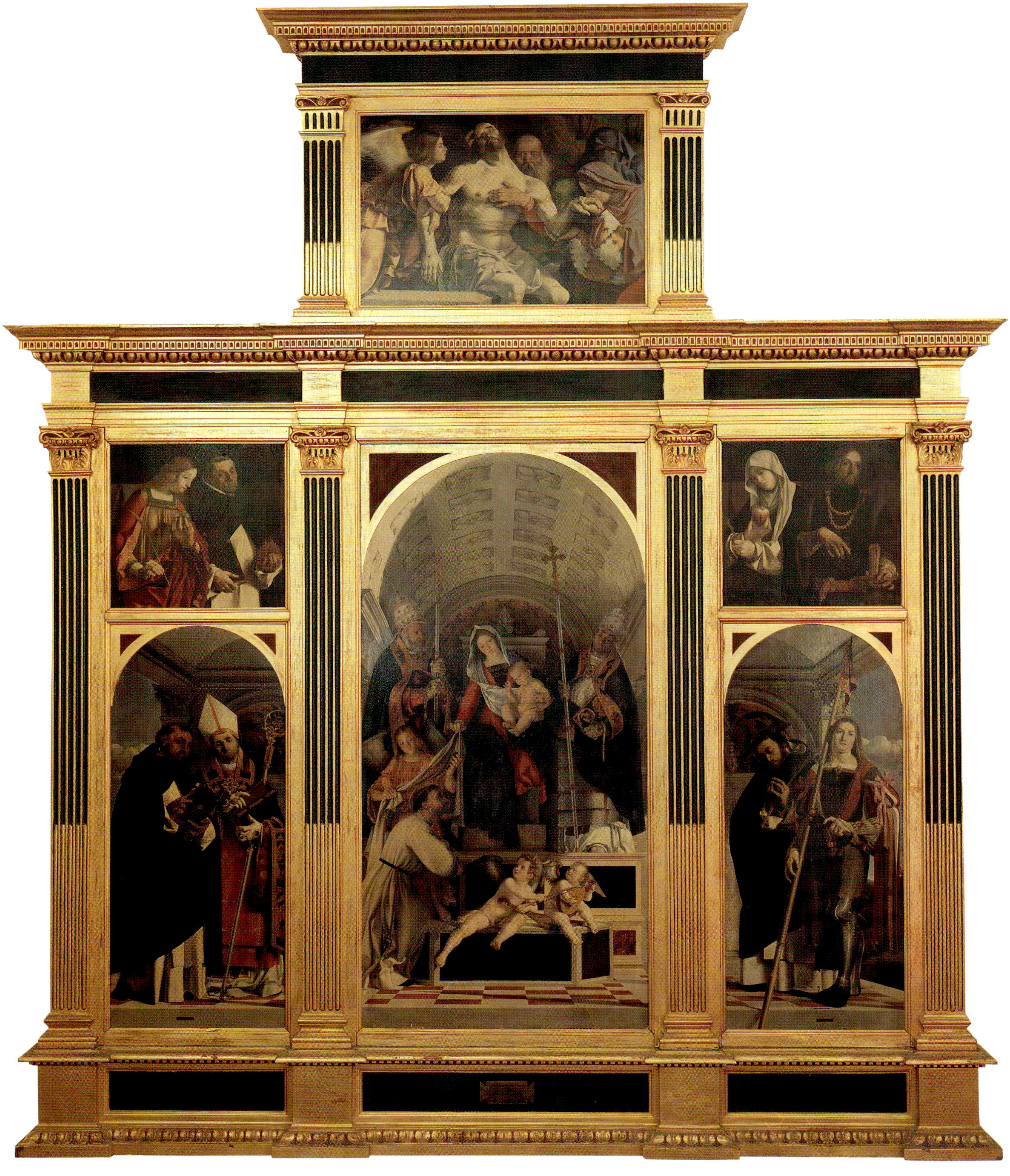

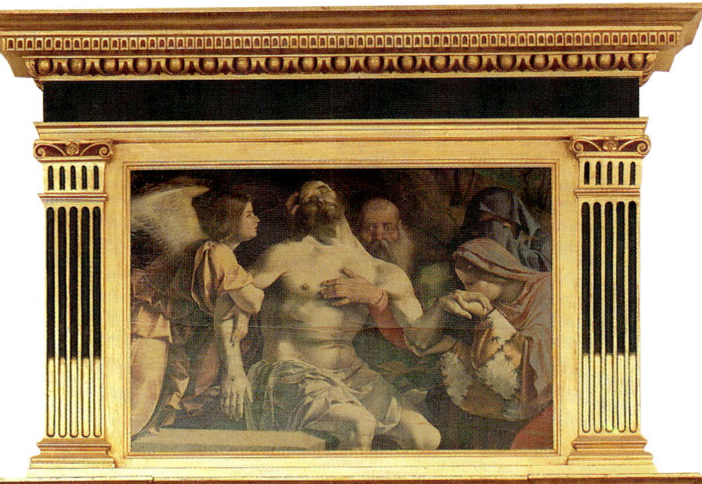

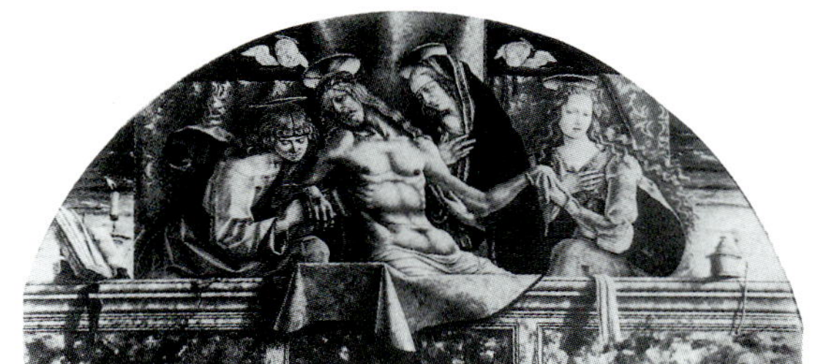

32 Carlo Crivelli. *Pietà* (1493). Milan, Pinacoteca di Brera.

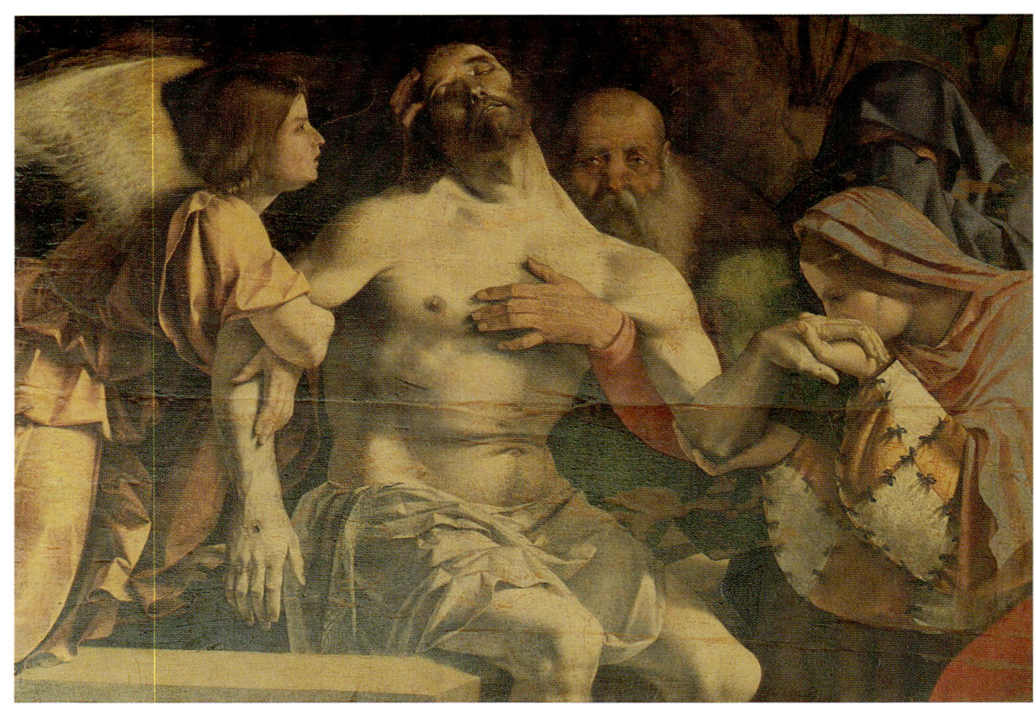

33 (*right*) Detail of pl. 31.

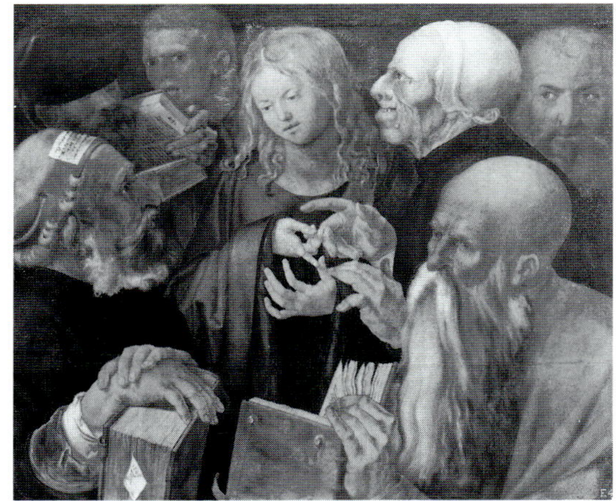

34 Albrecht Dürer. *Christ among the Doctors* (1506). Madrid, Fundacion Colección Thyssen-Bornemisza.

strapped and laced together; or to how the wings of the child angels grow out of their shoulders.

In terms of style and motif, the Recanati polyptych shows little response by Lotto to the local pictorial culture of the Marches, except perhaps in the *Pietà*, which in its dense, relief-like packing of the forms and its expression of desperate grief has analogies with the similarly placed *pietà* groups in the polyptychs of Crivelli (pl. 32).[10] But much more striking are the formal similarities between Lotto's *Pietà* and a recent painting by Dürer, the *Christ among the Doctors* of 1506 (pl. 34). Like that of Dürer, Lotto's composition lays particular stress on large, expressive, somewhat ungainly heads and hands, which stand out clearly against a dark background. Particularly Düreresque is the bald, walrus-moustached head of Joseph of Arimathea, which combines elements of both figures at the right edge of *Christ among the Doctors*. In his earliest works, such as the Rossi *Allegory* and the *St Jerome*, Lotto's response to Dürer had been based on his prints, in which landscape tended to predominate; and even in the *'Maiden's Dream'*, where the central figure implies knowledge of a work by Dürer's own hand (pl. 18), the source had been a graphic one, and Lotto's treatment of it is correspondingly fine and linear. The much more robust Dürerism of the polyptych, by contrast, indicates that before his departure from the Veneto in October 1506, Lotto must have taken the opportunity of studying paintings with large-scale figures executed by Dürer during his year-long sojourn in Venice: the *Feast of the Rosegarlands*, as well as the *Christ among the Doctors*.

There exists some disagreement among Dürer scholars about whether the artist executed the latter work while still in Venice in the late summer or early autumn of 1506, or some months later in Rome.[11] In the latter case, Lotto's knowledge of it when painting the Recanati polyptych would have had to have been based on Dürer's preparatory drawings, which could well have been made in Venice, rather than on the completed painting. By 1508, however, the date inscribed on the even more markedly Düreresque *Virgin and Child with Sts Ignatius of Antioch and Onophrius* now in the Galleria Borghese (pl. 35), Lotto had clearly come to know Dürer's painting; and if

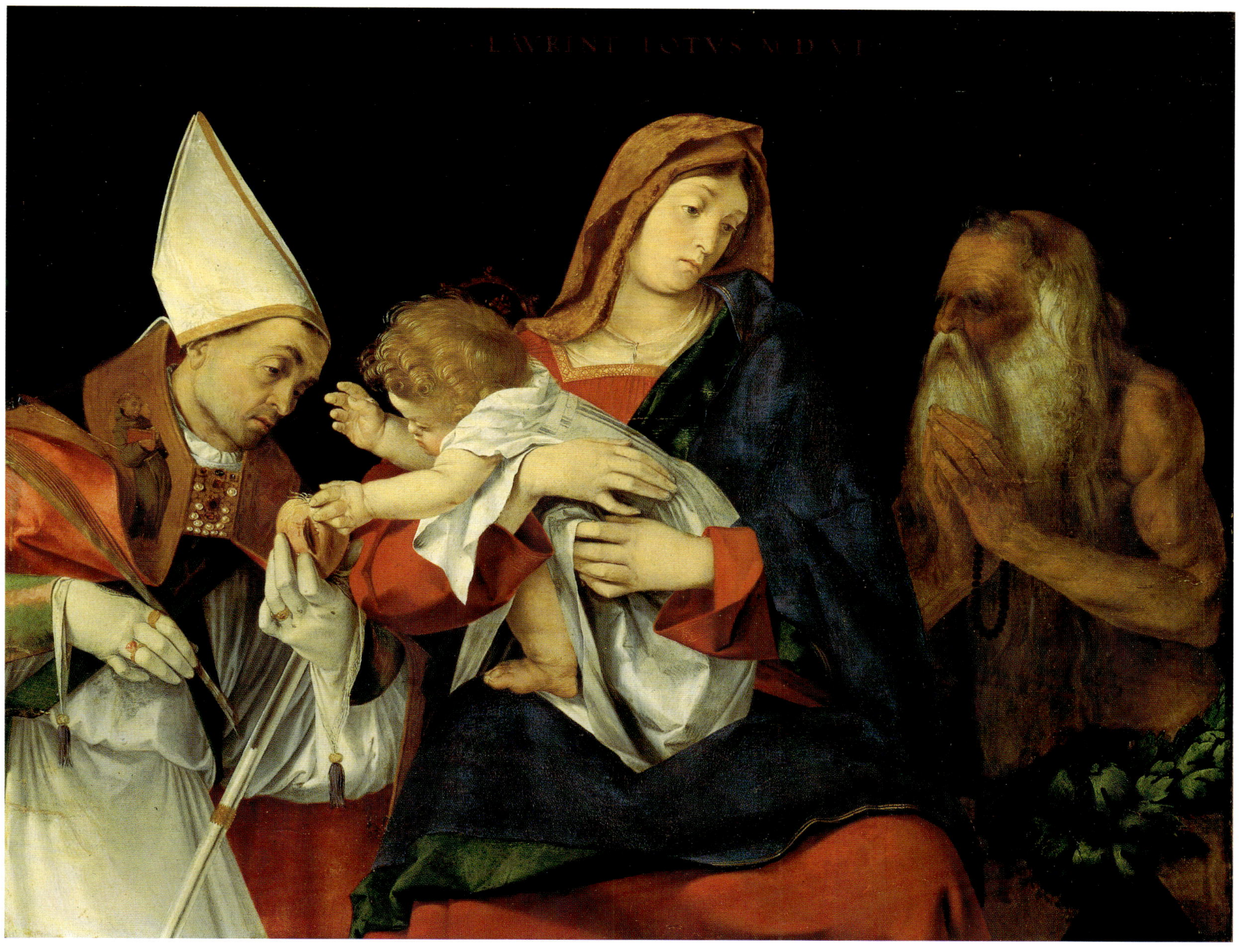

35 Lotto. *Virgin and Child with Sts Ignatius of Antioch and Onophrius* (1508). Panel, 53 × 67 cm. Rome, Galleria Borghese.

Dürer did indeed execute the *Christ among the Doctors* in Rome, it is likely that Lotto likewise painted his own panel in the papal capital, presumably immediately on his own arrival towards the end of 1508, rather than earlier in the year in the Marches, as is usually supposed.[12] In any case, the Borghese picture may be seen as standing in an analogous relation to the earlier, compositionally similar *Virgin and Child with Saints* in Edinburgh (pl. 27) as the Recanati polyptych does with the *St Christina* altarpiece. Thus, while the poses of the Virgin and Child, as in the Edinburgh picture, diverge to communicate with the saints at either side, the movement of the Child is now more dramatic, and the draperies are broader and more fluent. But even more than in the polyptych, the figure types have moved away from those of fifteenth-century Venetian tradition towards the decidedly unbeautiful, physiognomically sharply characterised types of Dürer's strange but compelling virtuoso piece. Similarly Düreresque are the bright enamelled colours of the draperies, arranged in contrasting planes, very different from the papery, Bellinesque folds of the Edinburgh picture; while the atmospheric landscape of the earlier work has been suppressed, as in the *Christ among the Doctors*, in favour of a dark, neutral background, the spacelessness of which is emphasised by the placing of the artist's signature in neat golden majuscules on its surface.

The precise circumstances surrounding Lotto's stay in Rome remain unclear and subject to conjecture.[13] All that is known for certain is that he received two payments totalling one hundred and fifty ducats for work in one of the Vatican Stanze, respectively in March and September 1509. From this it may be deduced that he was one of the team of pan-Italian artists called to the city in 1508 on the instructions of Pope Julius II to undertake a grandiose scheme for the redecoration of the Vatican Palace. In May of that year Michelangelo started planning his frescoes for the ceiling of the Sistine Chapel; in the autumn, Perugino, Sodoma and Bramantino were engaged in the pope's suite of private apartments; and probably some time in the summer Raphael arrived to paint the room subsequently known as the Stanza della Segnatura. According to Vasari, Raphael was summoned on the recommendation of the papal architect, Bramante; and it has been plausibly suggested that Lotto, too, owed his commission to Bramante, who is known to have been in Loreto in the second half of 1508, in connection with work on the Marian sanctuary.[14] Lotto's frescoes were almost certainly painted in the room adjoining the Stanza della Segnatura, now called the Stanza d'Eliodoro, probably for its ceiling;[15] but they would then have been destroyed almost immediately, when Raphael was commissioned to redecorate the room in 1512–14. Clearly—and perhaps hardly surprisingly—the pope was much less impressed by Lotto than by Raphael; and sensing that he had no future in Rome, Lotto may already have left by the end of 1509.

One of the few surviving pictures by Lotto generally agreed to have been painted during the Roman phase is the *St Jerome*, still in Rome at the Castel Sant'Angelo (pl. 36).[16] The contrast with the earlier version, painted in Treviso only three or four years before, is striking. The inspiration of Dürer is still unmistakable in the left background, where twisting roots, jagged branches and steep rocks provide an appropriately harsh environment for the secondary, small-scale representation of the saint in active penitence. But the sunlit foreground, where Jerome the scholar reclines comfortably with his books, and the spacious vista on the right, are quite different in character; and they recall rather the gently rolling Umbrian landscapes of Perugino and the early Raphael, with their feathery trees, and their distant buildings evoking human civilisation. Appropriate to the Roman origins of the picture is the resemblance of the battlemented fortress with its bridge to the Castel and Ponte Sant'Angelo. Similarly, the figure of the saint is proportionately larger in relation to the field than in the earlier *St Jerome*, and with his heroic seated pose he resembles some antique river god.[17]

Despite this classical reference, Lotto, unlike Michelangelo and Raphael, remained comparatively indifferent to the art of pagan antiquity, and he probably never felt at home in the cultural climate of Julian Rome. The principal reason, in fact, for supposing that he made a brief visit to Florence in 1510 is that several of his immediately subsequent works show the influence of Fra Bartolomeo,[18] a painter who managed to create a fully up-to-date classicising language of form without recourse to antique statuary, and in a way that was entirely appropriate to his uncompromisingly Christian message. In any case, by the autumn of 1511, and perhaps as much as a year earlier, Lotto was back in the Marches, where by 1512 he had completed two major altarpieces, both commissioned by local devotional confraternities, and both with narrative subjects. The first of these, the *Transfiguration* (pl. 39), was painted for the high altar of the Benedictine church of Santa Maria di Castelnuovo, just outside Recanati.[19] To judge from a document of February 1507 in which the Confraternity of Santa Maria followed the example of the local Dominicans in requesting a subvention from the *comune* towards the cost of their proposed new altarpiece (p. 28), the *Transfiguration* was originally commissioned while Lotto was still engaged on the polyptych; and by

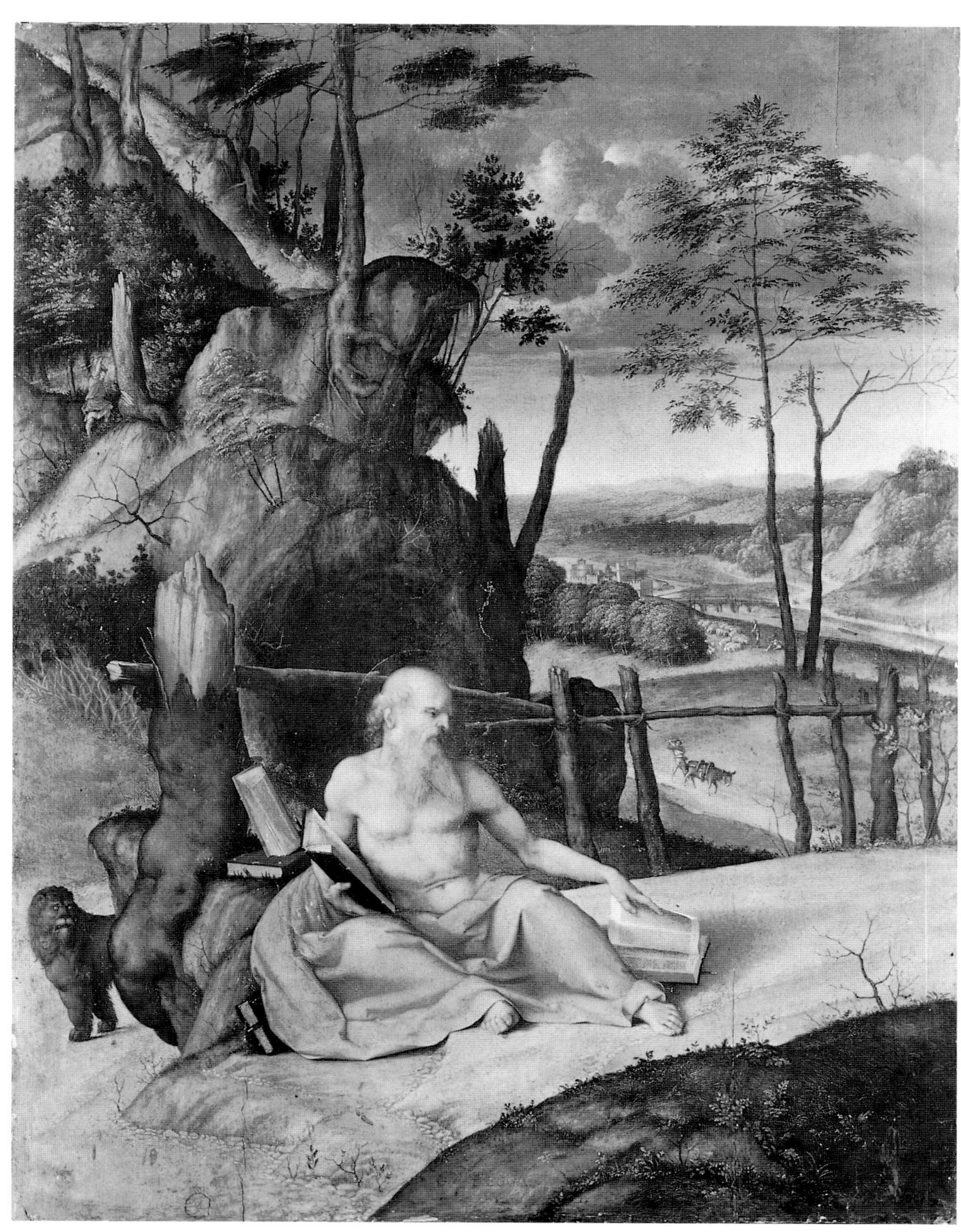

36 Lotto. *St Jerome* (*c.*1509). Panel, 80.5 × 61 cm. Rome, Museo Nazionale di Castel Sant'Angelo.

the time of a renewed request to the *comune* for the promised sum in September 1511, Lotto may already have made considerable headway with the work, if indeed he had not already completed it.[20] Then in the following month, he signed a contract to paint a second new altarpiece, the *Entombment* dated 1512 (pl. 38).[21] This was commissioned by the Confraternity of Buon Gesù for its altar in the Franciscan church of San Floriano in the town of Jesi, about twenty-five miles north-west of Recanati, in the province of Ancona.[22]

Three years earlier this confraternity – officially dedicated to the Holy Name of Jesus – had commissioned Signorelli to paint its altarpiece, but for some reason the painter had failed to fulfil his commitment. The subject given to Lotto was the same as that given to his predecessor; and as it inevitably involved the prominent representation of the naked body of Christ, it was a natural choice for the confraternity. A direct reference to the dedication of the confraternity, and presumably of the altar as well, is provided by the wooden tablet inscribed 'INRI' in the foreground, and by the glory in the apex with the IHS monogram. It has often been suggested that Lotto's composition is loosely based on Raphael's version of the same subject, painted in 1507 for San Francesco in Perugia (pl. 37); but the suggestion has also been vigorously denied.[23] It is true that the relationship is not so close as to be unmistakable, and it is possible to identify a number of other sources of inspiration. In some respects, for example, Lotto's composition is more reminiscent of Mantegna's engraving of about 1470–5, with which it also shares a mood of bitter anguish.[24] Similarly, Lotto's emotionally fraught and pathetically helpless figures retain more in common with those of Crivelli (pl. 32) than with the heroic, Michelangelesque types of Raphael. Again, much of the altarpiece's modernity, and in particular its treatment of landscape, may owe as much to recent works by Fra Bartolomeo, such as the *Assumption of the Virgin* of 1507–8 (destroyed; formerly Berlin, Kaiser-Friedrich Museum), which Lotto could have see in Florence. Yet none of these other sources can adequately account for the general similarity between the compositions of the two *Entombments*: in the placing, for example, of the dead Christ diagonally across the centre, or in the centrifugal movements of the mourners; or in the view of the three crosses on a grassy hill in the background. Furthermore, Lotto's colour-scheme, with its light vermilions, pinks, emerald greens and yellows, while similar to that found in the work of Fra Bartolomeo, even more closely resembles that of Raphael, and is in any case distinctly different from the darker, richer range of his pre-Roman phase.[25] It is probably only to be expected, in fact, that when composing his first altarpieces with narrative subjects, Lotto should have looked to Raphael, already recognised as a supreme master of dramatic composition, and with whom he had worked in close proximity in the Stanze for much of 1509. Other signs of Lotto's continuing interest in Raphael include the motif at the apex, with the golden disc encircled by clouds and flying putti, which recalls a similar motif at the centre of the *Disputa*; and the oblique, decentralised placing of the sarcophagus is very similar to that found in another early work by Raphael in San Francesco, Perugia, the Oddi *Coronation of the Virgin* of about 1503 (Rome, Vatican Museum).[26] All this indicates that Lotto must at some point have visisted Perugia, perhaps on his way back from Florence to the Marches in 1510 or early 1511.

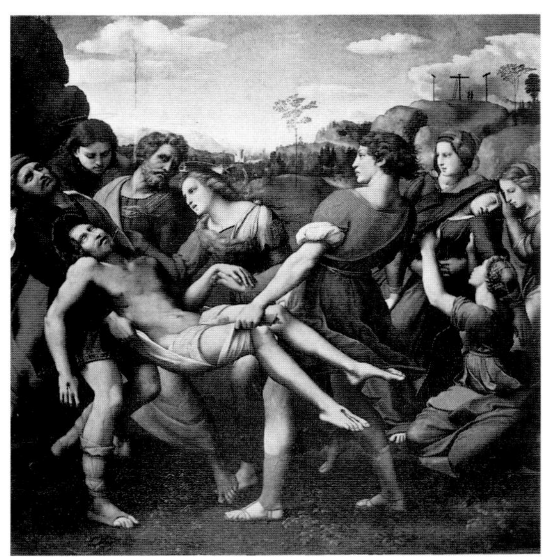

37 Raphael. *Entombment* (1507). Rome, Galleria Borghese.

Lotto's *Entombment* is a highly ambitious and eloquent work, in which characteristically unheroic but expressive elements such as the man holding the shroud with his teeth, or John clenching his fists under his cloak, are subjected to a new sense of drama and a new formal discipline, evident in the reduction of the naturalistic observation to a few telling details. A similar combination of a pronounced Raphaelism of style and motif with a very un-Raphaelesque expressionism and pathos is also to be found in the rather more experimental, and probably slightly earlier *Transfiguration* (pl. 39). The subject is not necessarily one that demands high drama, and six years earlier, at the time of the Asolo *Assumption*, Lotto would certainly have adopted the solemn, meditative approach of Bellini's version of the subject of about 1480 (Naples, Museo di Capodimonte). The contact with Raphael, and perhaps especially again with the elevated rhetoric of the *Disputa*, has resulted instead in a new emphasis on narrative, and on the psychological interaction between moving, gesticulating figures.[27] Particularly Raphaelesque in type is the figure of Peter, with his violet-blue robe decorated with fine golden embroidery, and his sharply foreshortened left arm. As in the Jesi *Entombment*, the colours are lighter in tone, and the draperies are more rhythmically composed than in Lotto's pre-Roman period. But again, and less obviously appropriately than in the tragic subject of the *Entombment*, the curiously stunted figures appear agitated and tormented, and Raphael's complex but harmonious and spatially expansive

38 (*facing page*) Lotto. *Entombment* (1511–12). Panel, 298 × 198 cm. Jesi, Pinacoteca Civica.

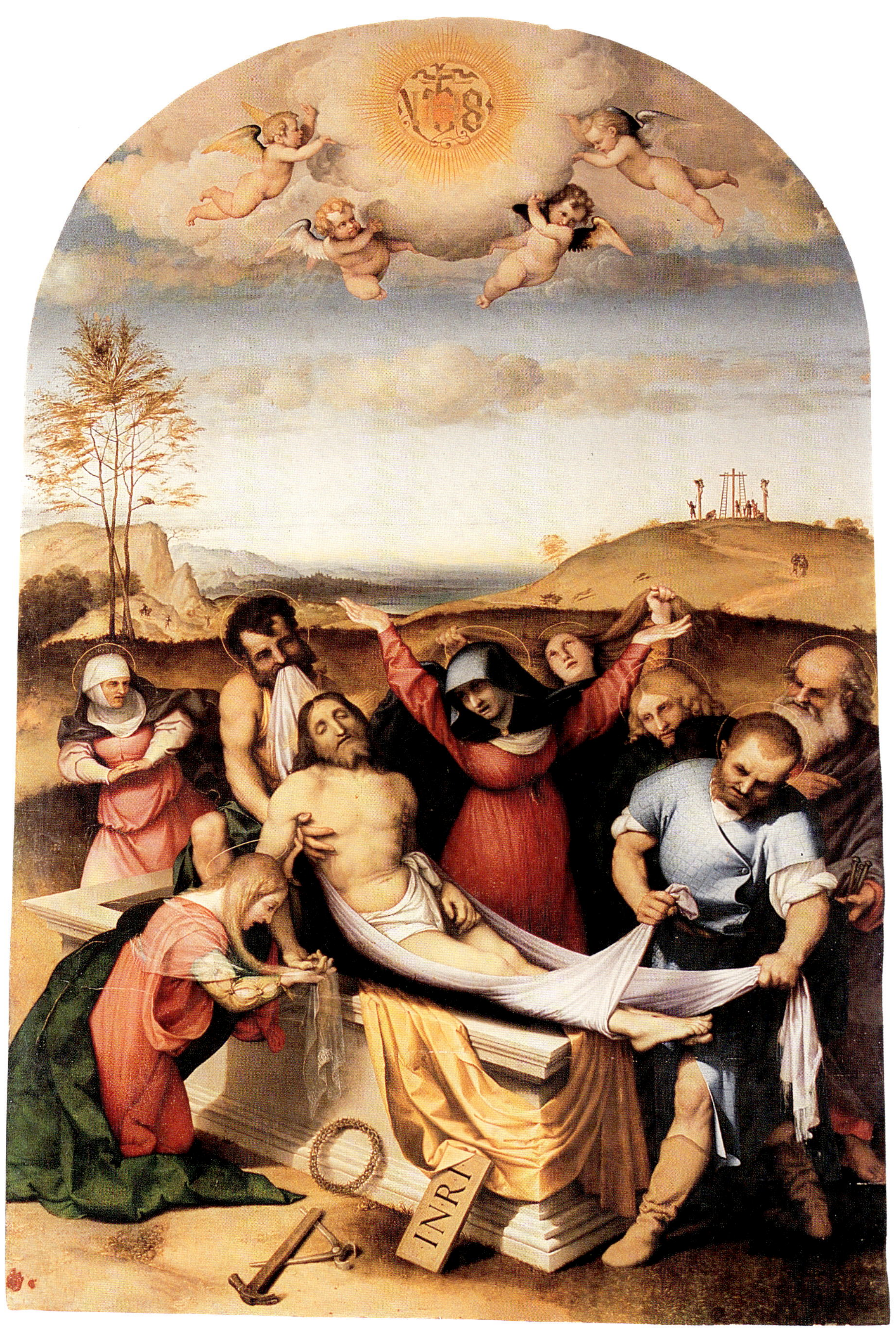
INRI

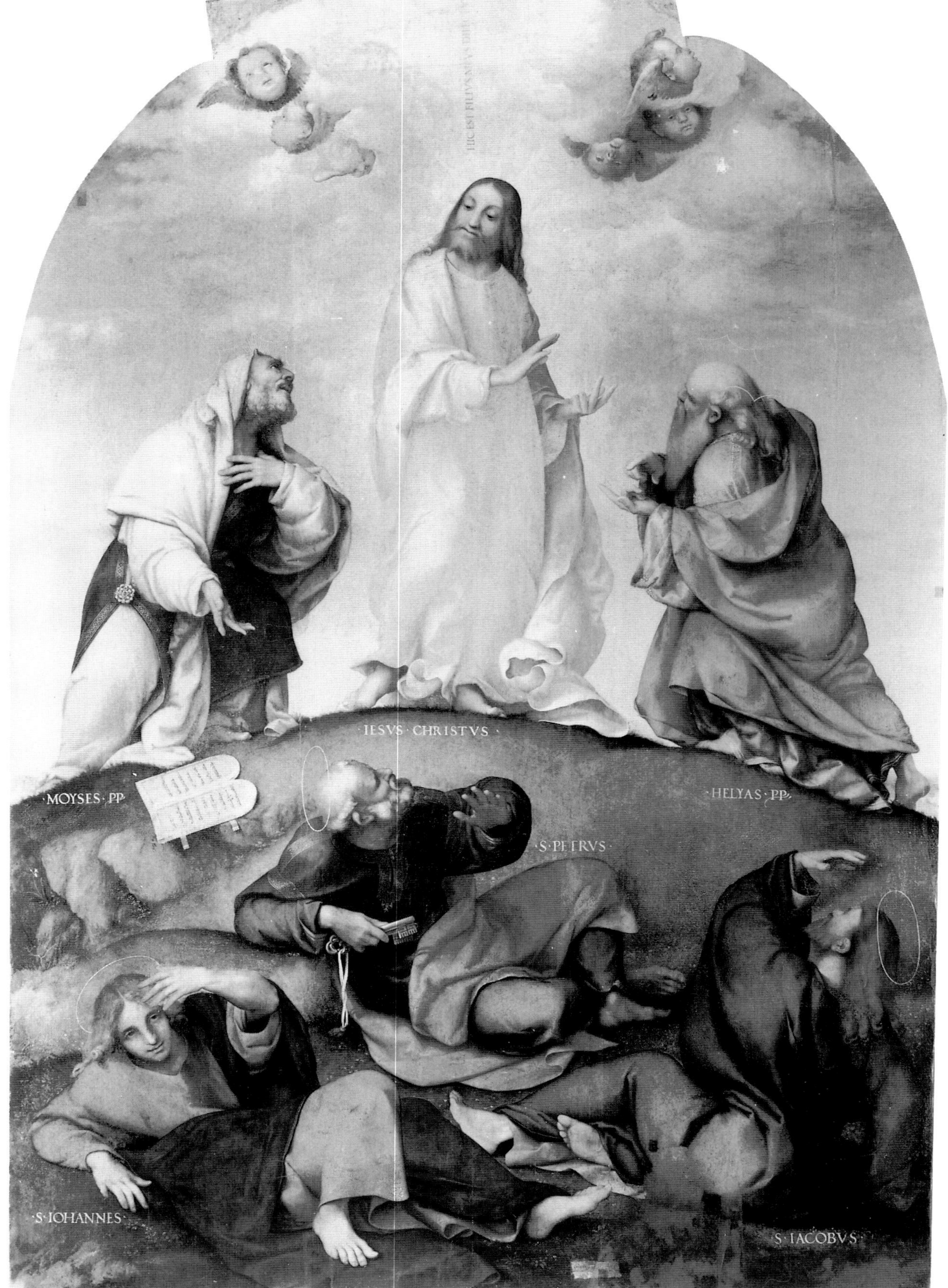
IESVS CHRISTVS
MOYSES PP
HELYAS PP
S PETRVS
S IOHANNES
S IACOBVS

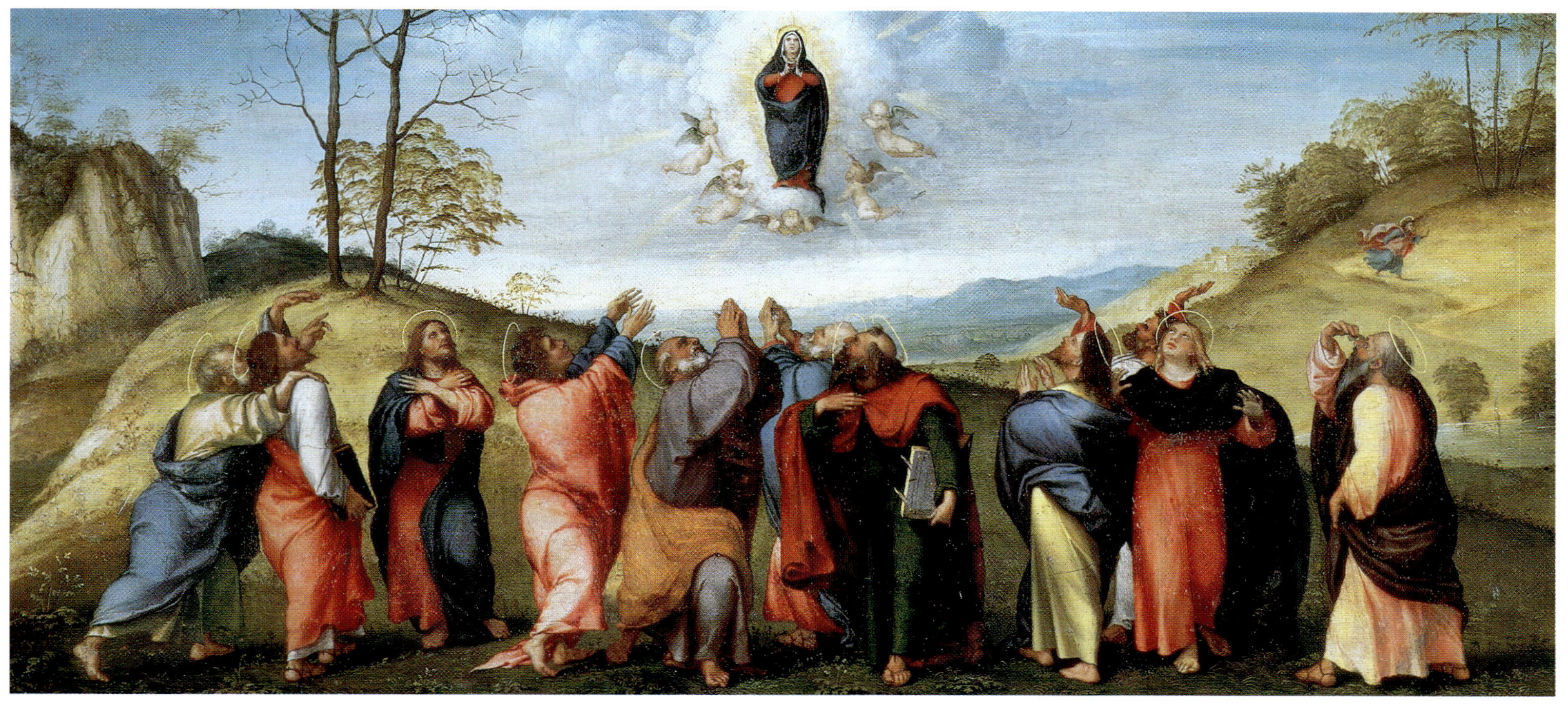

40 Lotto. *Assumption of the Virgin* (*c.*1512). Panel, 27 × 56 cm. Milan, Pinacoteca di Brera.

39 (*facing page*) Lotto. *Transfiguration* (*c.*1510–11). Panel, 300 × 203 cm. Recanati, Pinacoteca Comunale.

use of *contrapposto* has become transformed into an uncomfortable contortion within a single plane. This anti-spatial emphasis on the picture surface is then further heightened by the use, as in the Borghese *Virgin and Saints* (pl. 35; p. 32), of archaising golden inscriptions, labelling the figures and quoting the divine voice from out of the clouds ('Hic est filius meus dilectus').[28] Ultimately, in fact, the comparison with Raphael only serves to underline the remoteness of Lotto's conception from the human and pictorial ideals of the Roman High Renaissance.

Since the church of Santa Maria di Castelnuovo was dedicated to the Assumption of the Virgin, the choice of the Transfiguration of Christ as the subject for its high altarpiece demands some explanation. According to one recent suggestion, the Confraternity of Santa Maria, supported by the *comune* of Recanati, may have wanted to express thereby its loyalty to the papacy, especially at a moment of crisis, when the German emperor and the king of France had jointly taken up arms against the pope, and the Church was threatened with schism.[29] Certainly the figure of St Peter, at the apex of the triangle of crouching apostles, holding out his key and receiving the direct attention of Christ, is unusually prominent in the composition. The didactically assertive use of inscriptions is also consistent with the supposition that the confraternity intended the altarpiece to convey a topical message boldly and clearly. If so, the tension and anxiety conveyed by the picture may owe as much to the external circumstances of the commission as to Lotto's inner state of mind.

As with the Recanati polyptych, Vasari recorded that the *Transfiguration* was accompanied by three predella panels, in this case representing *Christ leading the Apostles to Mount Tabor*, the *Agony in the Garden* and the *Ascension of Christ*.[30] The first of these is clearly identical with a panel now in the Hermitage, St Petersburg; the second is lost; and the third has often been identified with an *Assumption of the Virgin* now in the Brera, Milan (pl. 40), on the supposition that Vasari must have been careless in his description of the subject. Certainly the pictorial style of the *Assumption* is consistent with a date of about 1511–12; and here, too, the expressive idiosyncrasy characteristic of Lotto, as in the detail of the apostle on the far right, peering through his spectacles at the ascending

Virgin, co-exists with a rhythmical figure composition and light colour-range derived from both Fra Bartolomeo and Raphael. Consistent with the theory that the panel once belonged with the *Transfiguration* is the dedication of Santa Maria di Castelnuovo to the Assumption, and also the fact that the height of the *Assumption* is virtually identical with that of *Christ leading the Apostles*.[31] This theory has recently been convincingly challenged, however, by the observation that the three Christological subjects described by Vasari are perfectly coherent, both with each other and with the theme of the Transfiguration; further, that the eucharistic subject of the *Agony* would have been entirely appropriate for the centre of the predella; and finally, that the centralised composition of the *Assumption* implies that it, too, originally occupied the centre rather than the right side of a predella. The conclusion must be, therefore, that the *Ascension* is still missing, and that the *Assumption* must belong to the predella of a different altarpiece.[32] The obvious candidate for this altarpiece is the Jesi *Entombment*, despite the fact that the documents make no mention of any predella and that the theme of the *Assumption* has no direct connection with the cult of the Name of Jesus. But Lotto's two recent altarpieces for Recanati, as well as his later *St Lucy* altarpiece for the same church in Jesi (p. 115), were all equipped with predellas, and the contract for the *Entombment* is very vague in its wording. Moreover, the cult of the Virgin of the Assumption, like that of the Name of Jesus, was one vigorously promoted by the Franciscan order. A final point in favour of an original association between the *Assumption* and the *Entombment* is the visual echo of the circular motif surrounding the IHS monogram in the angelic glory surrounding the figure of the ascending Virgin.[33]

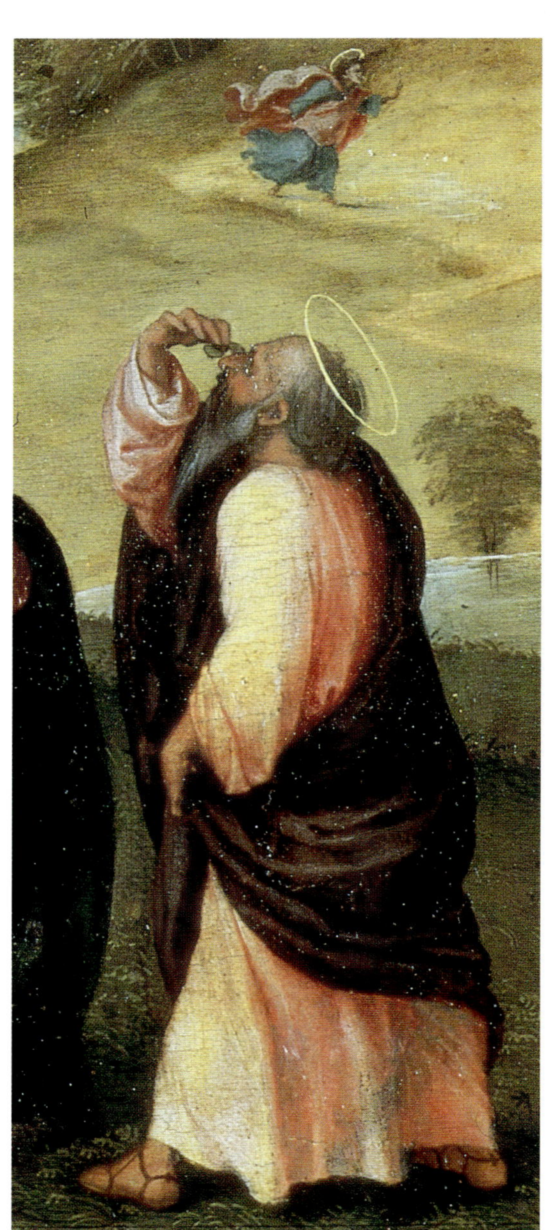

41 Detail of pl. 40.

The atmosphere of impending disaster that hung over the cities of the Marches in the years 1511–12 also affected another work probably painted in this phase, the *St Vincent Ferrer* fresco, painted for the wall at the end of an aisle in San Domenico in Recanati (pl. 43).[34] The fiery Spanish preacher, who had lived at the time of the Great Schism a century earlier, was already included in the upper left panel of Lotto's polyptych for the same church (pl. 31). But whereas there he was passive and introverted, now he is presented highly dramatically, arriving on a cloud borne by angels, gesturing vigorously heavenwards and displaying his favourite text from the Apocalypse: 'Fear God and give glory to him, for the hour of his judgement is come.'[35] The fresco is damaged at both top and bottom, and originally the trumpeting angels at the top would presumably have emanated from a now lost figure of Christ as Judge in the apex. This combination of an upward-pointing St Vincent with a Christ in glory was certainly inspired by a similar image painted by Fra Bartolomeo for the church of San Marco in Florence just before Lotto's visit there;[36] and it is highly significant that in his own version, Lotto has given the saint the features of a more recent Dominican prophet of doom, the late prior of San Marco, Fra Girolamo Savonarola.[37] Originally the saint hovered high above a panoramic landscape, seen in bird's-eye view at the base of the composition.[38] Especially because of the associations of the subject, the source of the compositional idea may be traced to Dürer's woodcut of *St Michael and the Dragon* (pl. 42) from the Apocalypse series of 1496–8. At the same time, the Raphaelism evident in the saint's *contrapposto*, and in particular in the plastic modelling of the angels, is perhaps more pronounced here than in any of Lotto's other works, and suggests a date still close to the Roman experience.

Like the Jesi *Entombment* inscribed with the date 1512, but very different in character from this group of urgently expressive religious works, is a tiny, exquisitely executed panel representing *Judith with the Head of Holofernes* (pl. 44). This category of image, showing the beautiful Old Testament heroine in half-length and in close-up, with or without her maidservant, had become highly popular in Venice under the influence of Giorgione, as is illustrated by a highly sensuous rendering by Cariani (pl. 45), datable to about the same time.[39] The comparison highlights Lotto's stylistic remoteness from

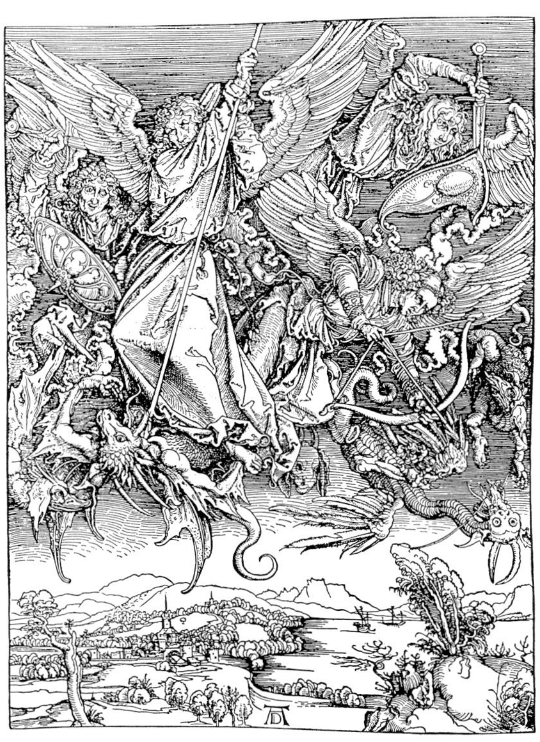

42 Albrecht Dürer. *St Michael and the Dragon* (1496–8). Woodcut.

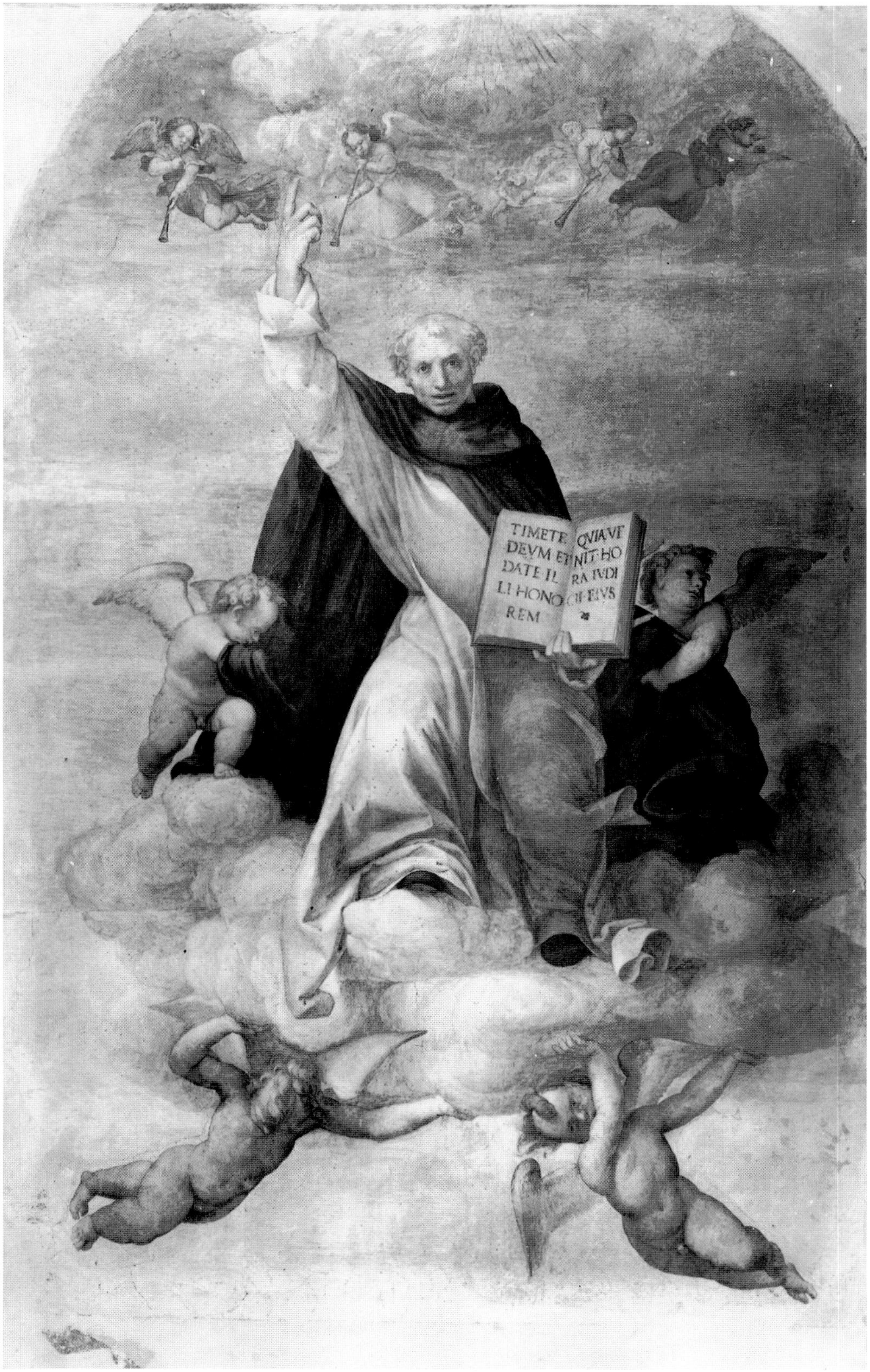

43 Lotto. *St Vincent Ferrer* (*c.*1511). Fresco, 265 × 166 cm. Recanati, San Domenico.

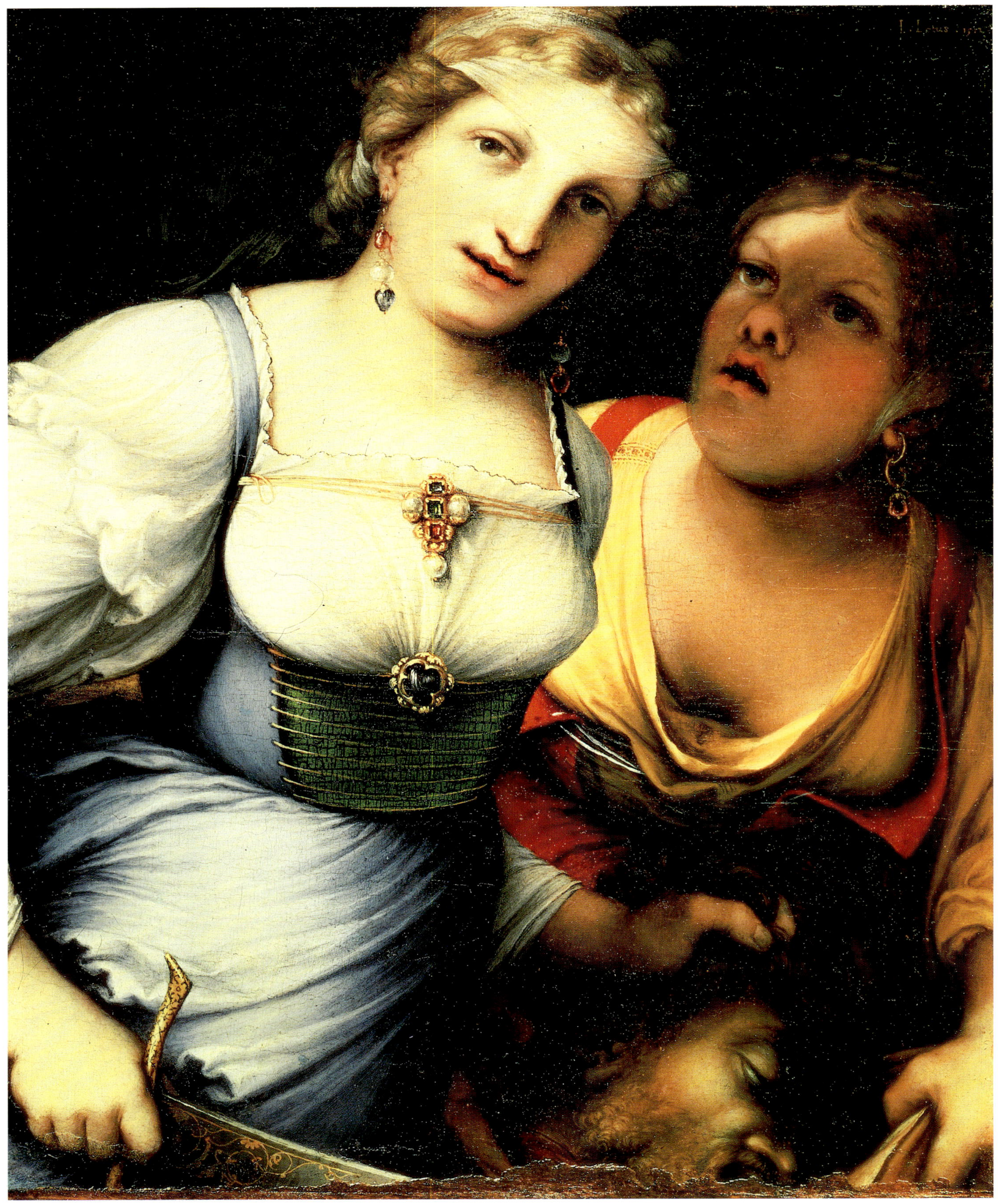

Venice at this time—the crisp-edged, flowing patterns of his draperies are quite unlike the thickly impasted, suggestively evoked folds of Cariani—but the problem remains of how Lotto became acquainted with a compositional type that had only emerged during the period of his absence in central Italy. A possible explanation is that Lotto developed the type not on the basis of any Giorgionesque model, but on one by Giovanni Bellini, now known only in versions by the Romagnuol painter Marco Palmezzano.[40] In the latter's composition the figures are still relatively small in relation to the frame, and they compete for prominence with their circumstantially described surroundings; but already included is the half-length, fashionably dressed Judith, complete with jewellery and a curving scimitar. Or it may be that a Giorgionesque version had already reached Rome, and that Lotto, as a Venetian painter, was asked by a Roman patron to produce a variant that preserved its portrait-like immediacy. In any case, the picture is painted with a self-conscious aestheticism that points to the probability that it was painted for a discerning collector in the papal capital, rather than for some merchant or cleric in the Marches; and it may be significant in this connection that the first recorded mention of the picture occurs in the inventory of a princely collection in seventeenth-century Rome.[41]

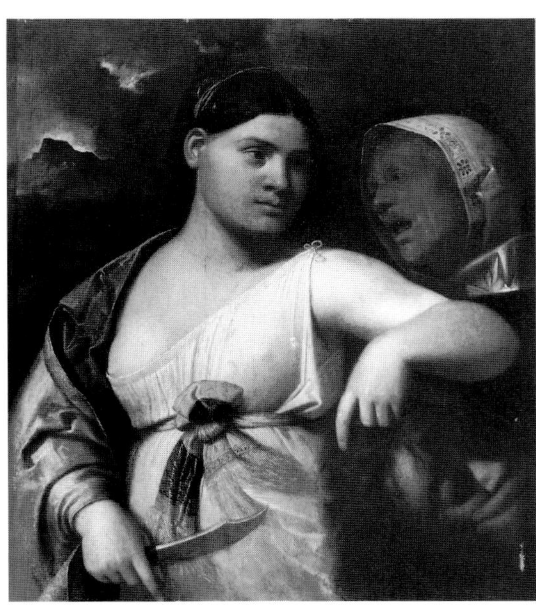

45 Giovanni Cariani. *Judith* (*c.*1510). Private collection.

Lotto's presence in Bergamo is first definitely recorded on 13 May 1513.[42] Two days later he signed the contract to paint a huge altarpiece for the local nobleman, Alessandro Colleoni Martinengo; and since the contract mentions that Lotto was awarded it following a competition with a number of other painters (p. 43), it is likely that he had already been in the city for several weeks. Given the uncertainty of the circumstances surrounding an open competition, however, it is also likely that he had not yet taken up permanent residence in Bergamo, and that during 1513–14 he continued to maintain a base in the Marches.[43] This would repeat the pattern of 1506, when he visited Recanati in June to sign the contract for the San Domenico polyptych, but then returned to Treviso to wind up his business there before settling in Recanati in October (p. 27). The assumption that Lotto was still present in central Italy during part of 1513–14 would also explain how he apparently knew the works painted by Raphael in these years, including the frescoes in the Stanza d'Eliodoro (p. 81).

The latter part of Lotto's first period in the Marches is customarily interpreted as one of trauma, in which self-doubts following his dismissal from papal service found direct expression in his works, especially in the *Entombment* and the *Transfiguration*. It is true that Lotto's own later writings reveal that he was a person prone to take deep offence and to nurse grievances; and, to an degree unusual among Italian Renaissance painters, the circumstances of his life and his state of his mind are closely reflected in his art. But with regard to the two altarpieces, it should be emphasised that Lotto would have been instinctively responsive to their respectively tragic and transcendental subjects, and probably also to the immediate fears among local communities in Jesi and Recanati of foreign invasion and schism; and significantly, there is no hint of trauma in the refined, jewel-like, semi-secular *Judith*, painted in the very same year. What is beyond doubt is that Lotto's exposure in High Renaissance Rome and Florence to an artistic culture quite different from anything he had previously experienced made an immediate and lasting impact on his own habits of style and composition. There is an obvious and dramatic contrast between the polyptych painted when Lotto first went to the Marches, which despite its enhanced Dürerism remains stylistically close to the earliest, Trevigian pictures, and the works painted after the return from Rome and Florence, with their highly personal adaptations from Raphael and Fra Bartolomeo. In the succeeding years in Bergamo, the sudden stylistic shifts characteristic of the Marchigian period quickly disappear, as the positive results of Lotto's central Italian experience fuse with new Lombard elements and a *rapprochement* with his Venetian background into a splendid new synthesis.

44 (*facing page*) Lotto. *Judith with the Head of Holofernes* (1512). Panel, 20 × 15 cm. Rome, Banca Nazionale del Lavoro.

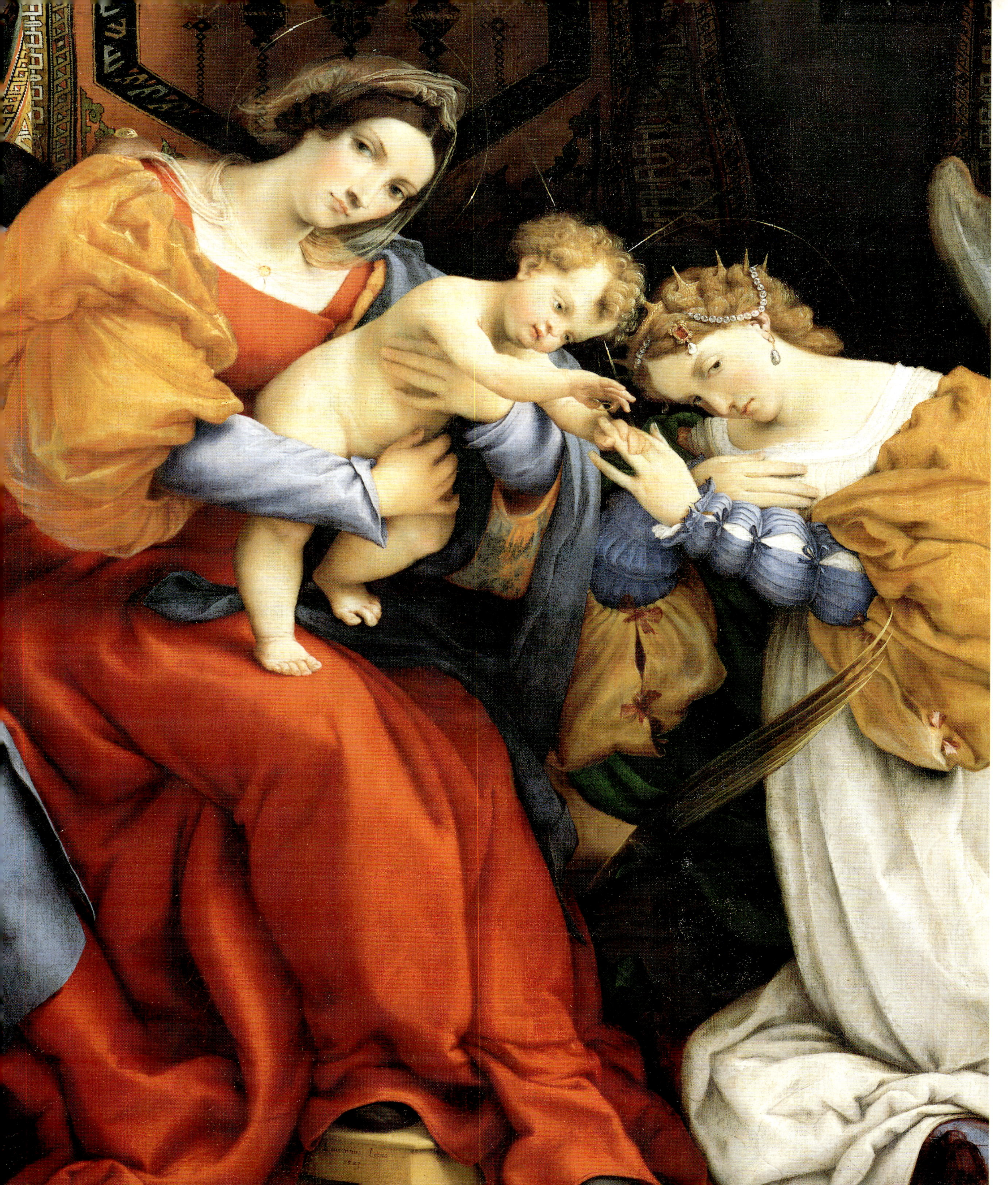

Chapter 3

BERGAMO 1513/14–1525

Lotto lived in Bergamo for eleven to twelve years, from 1513/14 until his return to his native Venice at the end of 1525. As in 1506, the immediate cause of his move to a distant new place of residence was the commission to paint the high altarpiece of an important Dominican church; but again, as in 1506, he must have hoped that other attractive commissions would flow from the initial one. This time he was not disappointed. During his Bergamask period Lotto was constantly in demand by local citizens and lay confraternities, as a painter not just of altarpieces, but also of frescoes, devotional pictures for the home and portraits. Towards the end of the period he undertook an unusual new challenge, to design the ambitious cycle of *intarsia* panels for the choir of the major city church of Santa Maria Maggiore. The broad scope of his activity was matched by a ceaseless inventiveness of artistic solution; and to judge from the rich exuberance of his Bergamask works, this was the happiest and most fulfilled decade of his life.[1]

Bergamo, with more than twice the poulation of Treviso and three times that of Recanati, was one of the principal cities of the extensive Venetian mainland empire. Situated near its western frontier, only thirty miles from Milan, it was of great strategic importance, and had suffered grievously during the recent War of the League of Cambrai. In the seven years following the Venetian defeat at nearby Agnadello in 1509, the city was successively captured by the French, recaptured by the Venetians, lost again to the French and occupied by Spanish, before finally being restored to the Venetians in 1515. The commission for the Colleoni Martinengo altarpiece in 1513 (pl. 47) coincided with the brief phase of the first recapture of the city by the Venetians, and the fact that Lotto did not complete it for another three years may in part be explained by the instability of the political and military situation. Thereafter, however, the more settled conditions, and a concerted will among local citizens for renewal, provided a favourable environment for artistic activity; and in fact, the decade of Lotto's residence in the city was to be the most glorious in the history of Bergamask painting in general. As has been mentioned (p. 41), Lotto was awarded the commission for the Colleoni Martinengo altarpiece in competition with a number of other distinguished painters ('quamplures egregii pictores');[2] and although the contract does not name these unsuccessful rivals, it is surely no coincidence that the native Bergamask Andrea Previtali chose this very moment to return home after several years' activity in Venice. Another expatriate, Giovanni Cariani, did not resettle in Bergamo until after the peace treaty of 1516; but he maintained close links with Bergamask patrons throughout his early career in Venice, and it is possible that he, too, was an unsuccessful competitor in 1513.[3] While both these painters were naturally responsive to the art of their colleague Lotto, he in turn was evidently highly stimulated by this renewed contact with the latest Venetian pictorial fashions. After about 1520, for example, he gradually abandoned the traditional panel support of his early works in favour of canvas and began to employ a freer manner of execution, one that was less dependant on

46 Detail of pl. 74.

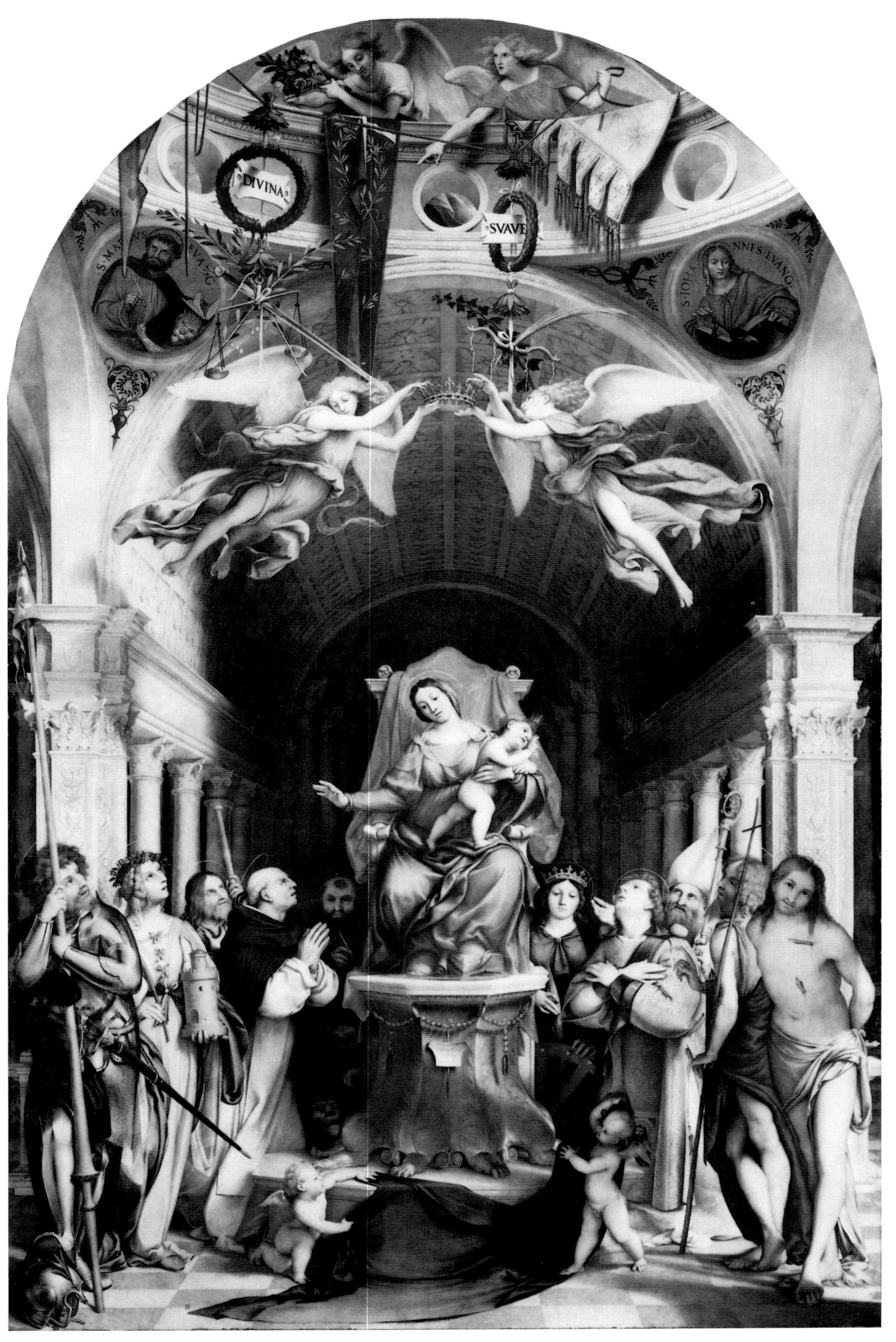
DIVINA
SVAVE

IVSTITIA RECTA AMICITIA ET ODIO EVAGINATA ET NVDA, ET PONDERATA LIBERALITAS REGNVM FIRMITER SERVAT

48 Hieroglyphic woodcut from *Hypnerotomachia Poliphili* (1499).

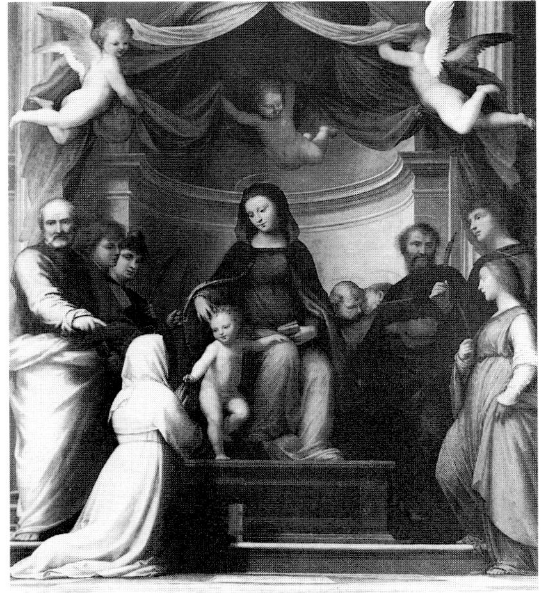

49 Fra Bartolomeo. *Mystic Marriage of St Catherine* (1511). Paris, Musée du Louvre.

47 (*facing page*) Lotto. Colleoni Martinengo altarpiece (1513–16). Panel, 520 × 250 cm. Bergamo, San Bartolomeo.

careful underdrawing and smooth finish, and more open to the use of expressive brushwork.

The Colleoni Martinengo altarpiece was painted for the high altar of the now demolished, but at that time recently rebuilt church of Santi Stefano e Domenico, in the upper city of Bergamo.[4] In 1504 patronage rights to the chancel had been granted to Count Alessandro Colleoni Martinengo, grandson and adoptive son of the celebrated *condottiere* Bartolomeo Colleoni, whose bronze equestrian monument by Verrocchio stood alongside the Dominican church of Santi Giovanni e Paolo in Venice, and whose equally striking mortuary chapel at Santa Maria Maggiore in Bergamo had been built and decorated during the 1470s and 1480s. Colleoni Martinengo clearly intended his own personal monument and burial place to be no less splendid; and after the installation of what turned out to be one of the largest altarpieces ever seen in northern Italy, he went on to commission a set of choirstalls expensively inlaid with wooden *intarsie*, and to bequeath to the chapel tapestries and liturgical furniture of silver and gold.[5] It is not known how Lotto in the distant Marches came to hear of the competition for the commission: perhaps he was informed by contacts within the Dominican order, by way of San Domenico in Recanati. Alternatively, he may have met Bergamask merchants with business interests in the Marches, such as members of the Cassotti and Marchetti families, both of whom were subsequently to employ him in his new home.[6] In any case, the painter would have been encouraged not only by the exceptionally generous fee of five hundred ducats being offered to the victor, but perhaps also by the consideration that the patron, while clearly seeking to give the maximum publicity to the commission, was likely to be predisposed to favour applicants who were Venetian-trained. Before the war of Cambrai, local Bergamask culture had been orientated towards nearby Milan; and characteristically, the commission for the high altar of the church of Santo Spirito had as recently as 1508 been awarded to the Milanese painter Bergognone (*in situ*). Colleoni Martinengo, however, who like his grandfather was a soldier, had taken a loyally pro-Venetian stance in the war, and there is good reason to suppose that when commissioning a grandiose altarpiece for his chapel he was concerned not simply with the welfare of his eternal soul, but also to make a statement that was overtly political.[7]

Whereas Bergognone's Santo Spirito altarpiece, in keeping with Lombard tradition, had consisted of a multi-compartmented polyptych, Lotto's painting conforms to the standard compositional formula of Venetian *sacra conversazione* altarpieces of the later fifteenth century. As in his own earlier *St Christina* altarpiece (pl. 24), he represents the Virgin and Child on a tall throne in a single vertical field, with saints at either side, and surrounded by a classicising architecture incorporating mosaics. But the Colleoni Martinengo altarpiece, besides being conceived on a much grander scale, alludes more explicitly to Venetian tradition by the contrasting placing of the miltary saint in armour in the left foreground – in this case St Alexander – and of the nude figure of St Sebastian on the right, exactly as in Antonello da Messina's San Cassiano altarpiece of 1475–6 (main fragment: Vienna, Kunsthistorisches Museum), or in Alvise Vivarini's Belluno altarpiece of about 1485–6 (formerly Berlin, Kaiser-Friedrich Museum). Among the rather large company of assembled saints, Dominic and Stephen naturally take pride of place as titulars of the church and altar, and Alexander is prominent as patron saint both of the donor and of the city of Bergamo. But it is also significant that Mark, patron saint of the Republic of Venice, is represented both in a position of honour at the Virgin's right hand, and in the spandrel mosaic at the top left. Perhaps similarly alluding as much to the benefits of Venetian rule as to the kingdom of Christ are the clusters of symbolic objects that hang like mobiles from the open vault at the apex. Arranged symmetrically across a vertical stalk and accompanied by cryptic inscriptions, these objects closely resemble the numerous pseudo-hieroglyphs that had appeared in the

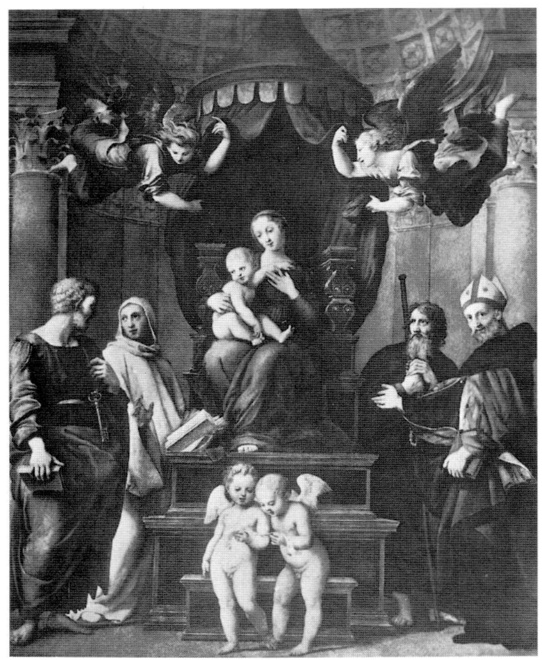

50 Raphael. *Madonna del Baldacchino* (1508). Florence, Palazzo Pitti.

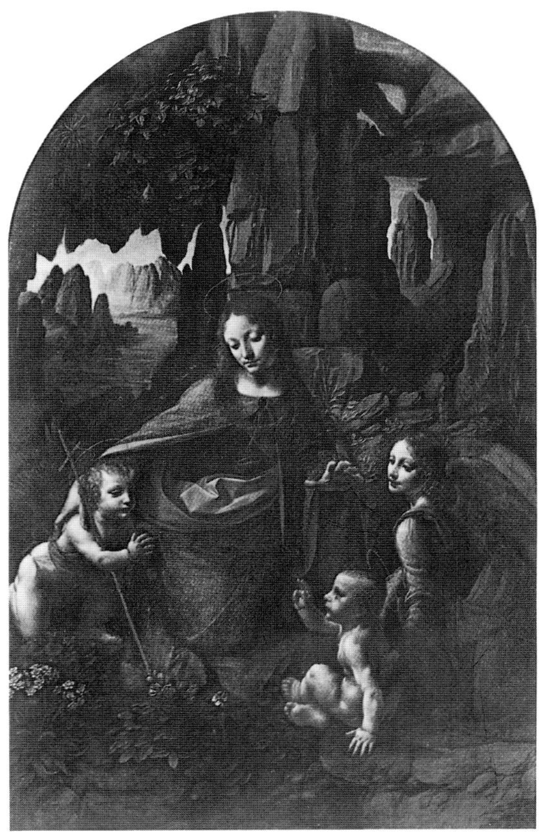

51 Leonardo da Vinci. *Virgin of the Rocks* (*c.*1495–1508). Panel, 189.5 × 120 cm. London, National Gallery.

Hypnerotomachia Poliphili of 1499 (pl. 48); and they mark a resurgence of an interest in hieroglyphic lore that had originated in Lotto's period in Treviso, and which was to reach a climax in the intarsia designs for Santa Maria Maggiore (pp. 90–92). Here, despite the unusualness of such cryptic, semi-profane imagery in the context of a church altarpiece, the combination of the inscription 'DIVINA' with the sword and scales at the left constitutes an easily legible rebus, signifying 'Divine justice'; and in combination with the olive branch symbolising wisdom (as an attribute of Minerva, as in the Rossi *Allegory* and the '*Maiden's Dream*'), it may well allude to standard concepts in Venetian political propaganda. Similarly, the combination of the inscription 'SUAVE' with the yoke, while clearly referring to the 'easy yoke' promised by Christ to his followers, may also carry a reference to the contentedly subjugated position of Bergamo in relation to Venice.[8]

Compared with the serenely immobile *sacre conversazioni* of Giovanni Bellini and Alvise Vivarini, Lotto's Colleoni Martinengo altarpiece is obviously much more animated in its figure composition, and in this respect it is closer to other High Renaissance Madonna and saints altarpieces, such as those by Fra Bartolomeo in Florence (pl. 49), or Raphael's *Madonna del Baldacchino* (pl. 50), or–and more problematically–Correggio's exactly contemporary *St Francis* altarpiece (Dresden, Gemäldegalerie), which Lotto is unlikely to have seen.[9] But the expression of reciprocal movement and spiritual ecstasy in all these parallel cases is more heroic and more mellifluous; whereas there is something approaching agitation, even neurosis, in the way in which Lotto's saints adore the central Virgin and Child. The impression that the saints are ordinary, frail, tormented human beings rather than champions of the Christian faith in a state of heavenly bliss, is exacerbated by their small scale in relation to the monumental barrel-vaulted architecture.[10] Similarly unheroic–although adding a characteristically Lottesque humour to the scene–is the effect of extemporisation created by the child angels in the foreground, who are still busy arranging the cloth of honour, and by their adolescent colleagues at the top, who likewise are still in the process of rigging up their complicated apparatus of ropes, banners and hanging mobiles.[11]

Another artistic relationship often noted in Lotto's altarpiece is that of Leonardo, whose Milanese works he would certainly have known. Particularly Leonardesque are the two male saints on the far right: the sweetly smiling, *contrapposto* figure of Sebastian; and the blonde, curly haired Baptist, whose gaze over his shoulder recalls that of the angel in the second version of the *Virgin of the Rocks* (pl. 51).[12] But beyond this, the way in which a volatile light and shade plays over the figures, while the background architecture disappears into a mysterious cavernous darkness, indicates a more general interest in the art of Leonardo.[13] Quite un-Leonardesque, on the other hand, is Lotto's continuing taste for clarity of line, glittering highlights and locally intense, enamel-like colours.

With the destruction in 1749 of its original, reputedly magnificent gilt and polychrome wooden frame, comprising huge fluted columns at the sides and a pediment at the top, Lotto's *Sacra conversazione* was reduced to a fragment of a once co-ordinated ensemble. Some idea of the spatial effect that would have been created by the association between the opening of the triumphal arch of the frame and Lotto's painted architecture can be visualised with the help of a photomontage, using a surviving frame designed by the Bergamask architect and colleague of the painter, Pietro Isabello.[14] But the original frame–which must have risen to a height of some eight metres–also incorporated at least four smaller panels, including an angel with a sceptre and orb in the pediment, and three narrative scenes in the predella (pl. 52), respectively representing a *Miracle of St Dominic*, the *Entombment* and the *Stoning of St Stephen*.[15] The last two in particular are masterpieces of narrative painting, and with their insistent compo-

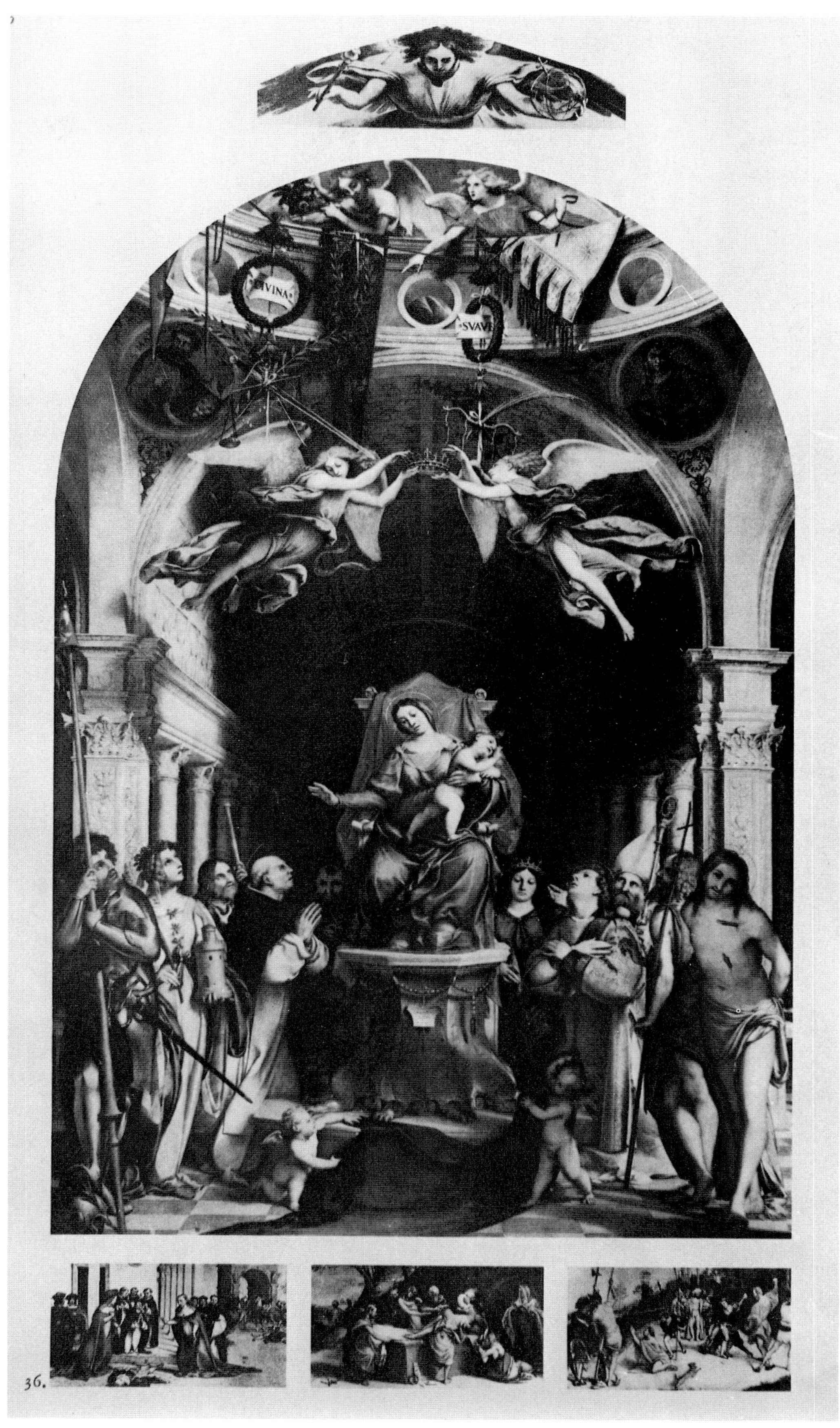

52 Reconstruction by G. Mascherpa (1978) of the Colleoni Martinengo altarpiece (pl. 47) with pinnacle and predella.

sitional diagonals and expressively energetic figures, they convey a vivid sense of the drama and religious pathos.

Of the various other altarpieces that Lotto painted for the city of Bergamo, the two finest are also symmetrically composed *sacre conversazioni*. Painted respectively for the churches of Santo Spirito and San Bernardino in Pignolo in the lower city, both remain in their original sites; both are near-square in format rather than tall and arched; and both show the holy figures against a background of landscape and sky rather than architecture. Both are also signed and dated 1521. The Santo Spirito altarpiece (pl. 54), which was probably the first to be commissioned and designed, occupies the fourth chapel on the right in the church, formerly belonging to the Augustinian canons;[16] and there is good reason to suppose that its donor was one Balsarino Marchetti Angelini, a member of a prosperous merchant family with business interests in the Marches, who himself later acted as a procurator for Lotto in his dealings with the Confraternity of Santa Lucia in Jesi (p. 85).[17] While the presence of St Augustine on the Virgin's right hand reflects the interests of the canons, and the dove at the apex of the composition clearly refers to the dedication of the church, the swarm of music-playing child angels may have been intended as an allusion to the family name of the chapel patrons. Lotto's choice of an open-air setting was probably inspired by the similarly composed altarpiece painted by Cariani for the church of San Gottardo in Bergamo in 1517–18 (pl. 53).[18] In many ways Cariani's picture may be seen as a deliberate critique of Lotto's own very recent Colleoni Martinengo altarpiece, which in its huge scale and dazzling quality must have appeared overwhelmingly impressive to the Bergamask public, but which to Cariani, recently returned from post-Giorgionesque Venice, would have seemed rather old-fashioned. Following the example of Giorgione, Titian and especially Palma Vecchio, whose Zerman altarpiece of about 1514 provides the most immediate compositional model,[19] Cariani abolished the traditional enclosing architecture, and set his *Sacra conversazione* in a pastoral landscape, with a view of woods, shepherd and sheep, and a distant hill-town. But despite the opening up of the background, Lotto was only partly seduced by the down-to-earth naturalism and chromatic warmth of Cariani. The experience of Raphael remains unmistakable, both in particular motifs such as the child Baptist, which is closely based on the foreground putto in the *Galatea* (Rome, Villa Farnesina) of about 1512, and in the firmly architectonic character of the design as a whole, which in its careful linking of the zones of heaven and earth, recalls that of the *Disputa*. Cariani's composition, by contrast, is casual to the point of formlessness. Lotto also retains his own characteristic taste for cool, dissonant colour and restless lighting, and for particularised gestures and expressions. The spiritual yearning of the saints is offset with characteristic wit by the mischievously grinning Baptist, who embraces his struggling lamb with over-impetuous affection, and by the antics of the flying angels, some of whom quarrel indecorously over their sheet music.

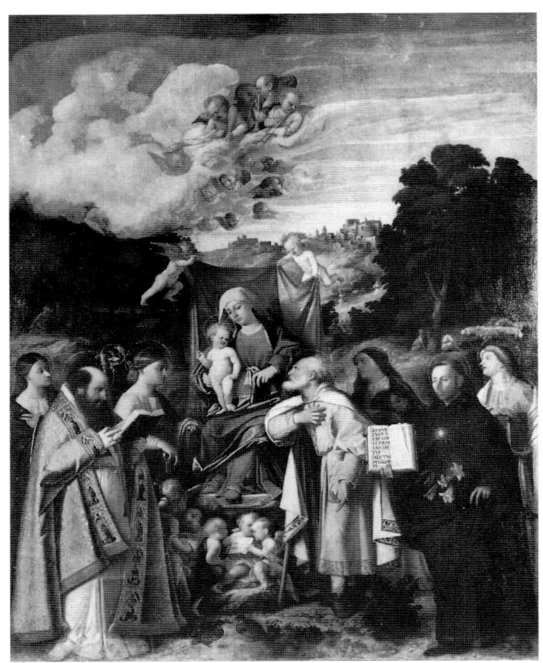

53 Giovanni Cariani. San Gottardo altarpiece (1517–18). Milan, Pinacoteca di Brera.

In spite of such details, the Santo Spirito altarpiece appears grand and formal compared with the more intimately conceived San Bernardino altarpiece (pl. 55).[20] Although the latter was painted for a main rather than a side-altar, San Bernardino in Pignolo is a small building, more of an oratory than a church, originally built to accommodate the devotions of a lay confraternity dedicated to the popular Franciscan saint. The fact that the membership of the confraternity comprised artisans as well as merchants also in part explains the simplicity of the setting and the accessories, and the choice of the humble carpenter Joseph on the left. Despite the reminiscences of Raphael's *Madonna del Baldacchino* (pl. 50) in the flying angels, and perhaps even more here of the altarpieces of Fra Bartolomeo (pl. 49), the comparison with these idealising Florentine prototypes again serves only to highlight the friendly informality and spontaneity of Lotto's solution. Even more than in the Colleoni Martinengo altarpiece,

54 (*facing page*) Lotto. *Virgin and Child with Saints* (1521). Canvas, 287 × 268 cm. Bergamo, Santo Spirito.

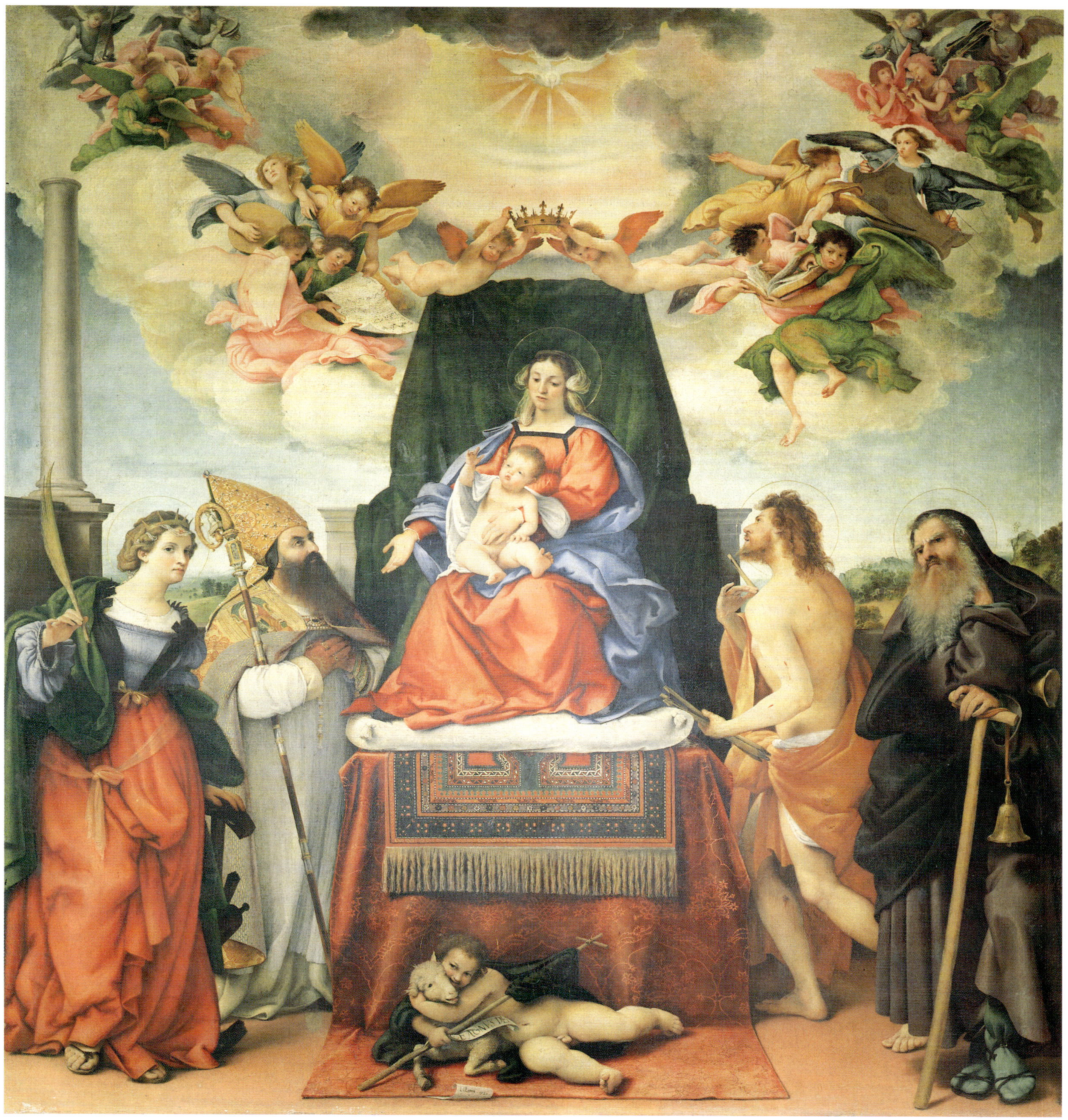

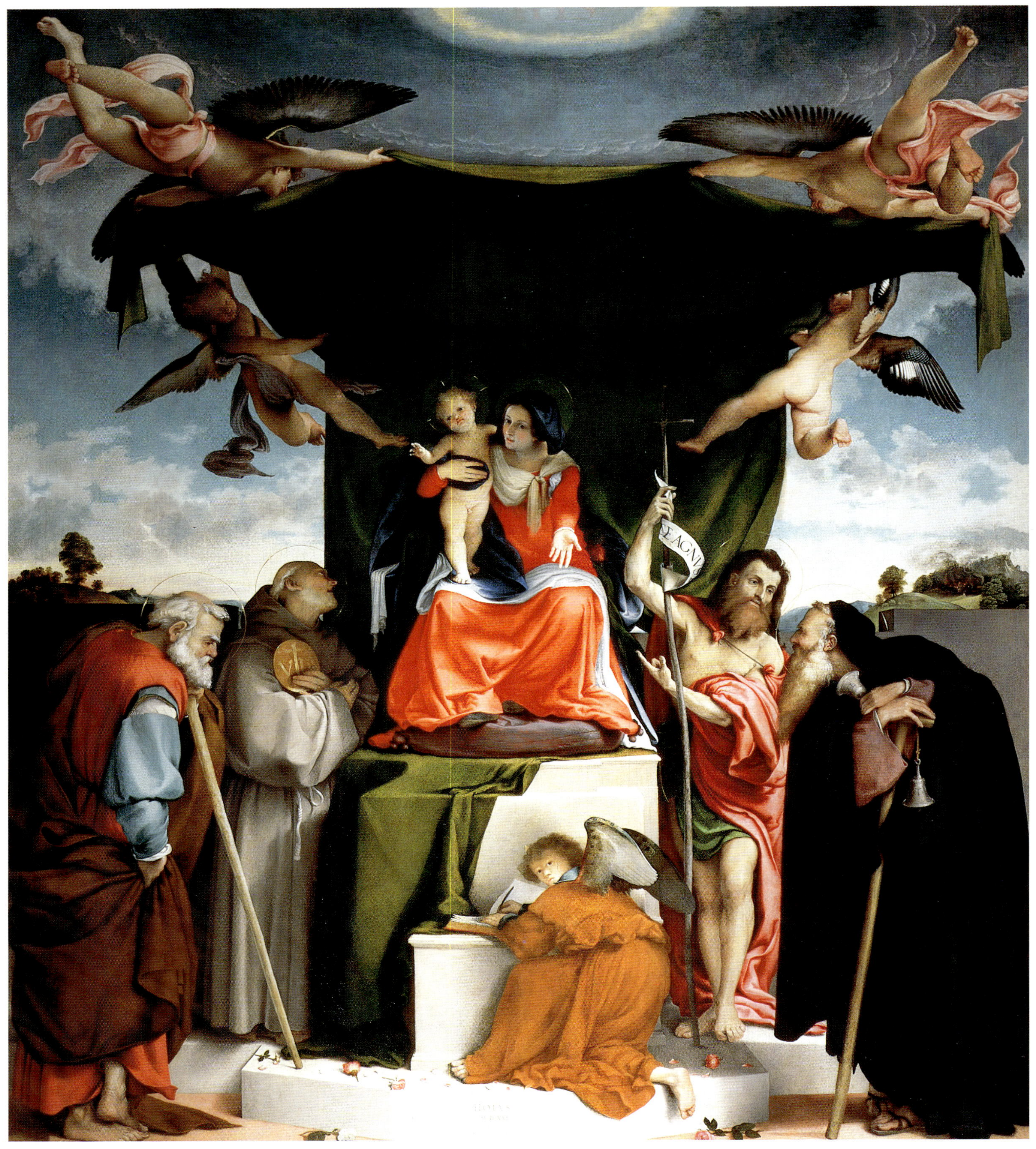

55 Lotto. *Virgin and Child with Saints* (1521). Canvas, 287 × 268 cm. Bergamo, San Bernardino in Pignolo.

56 (*facing page*) Detail of pl. 55.

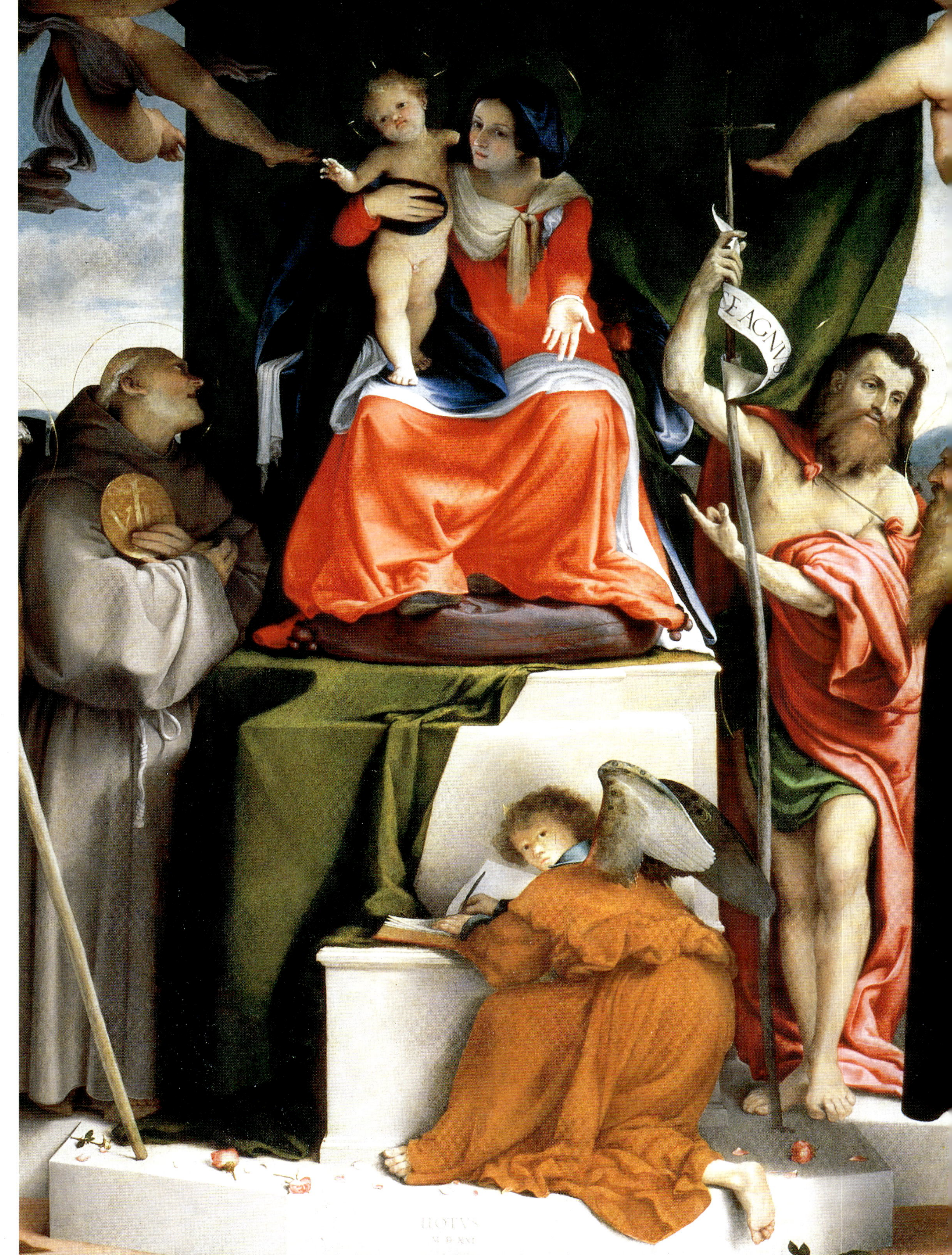
CE AGNVS
LLOTVS
M D XXI

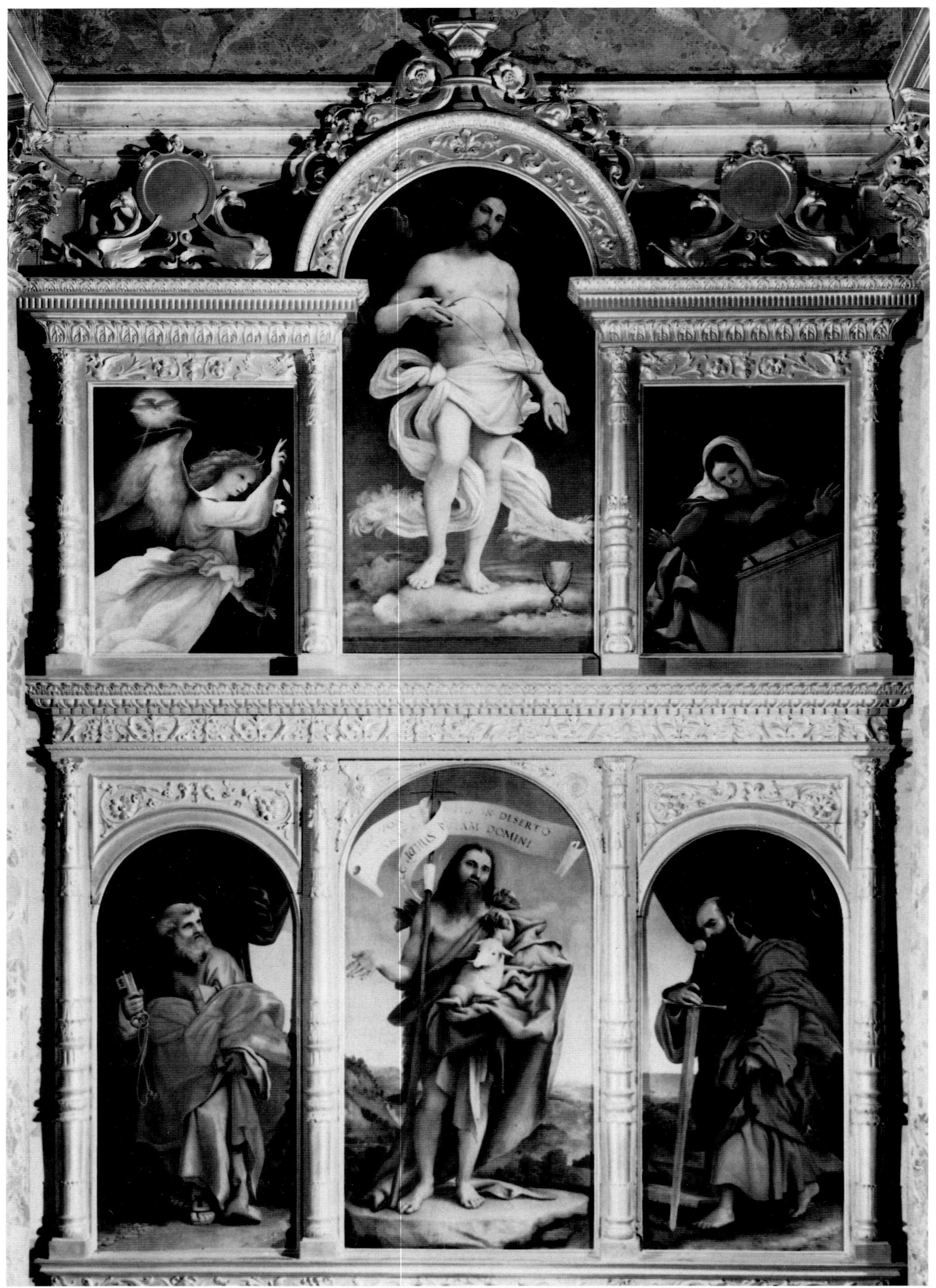
DESERTO
DOMINI

the accoutrements of majesty appear as if they are still hastily being put into place; and the child angel at the base of the throne turns to look at the spectator over his shoulder, as if caught unawares. The reddening above the horizon at the left and the extensive areas of deep shadow suggest that it is evening, in contrast to the brilliant daylight of the Santo Spirito altarpiece.

Very different in structure from these three *sacre conversazioni* is a fourth major altarpiece painted during the Bergamask period, the polyptych still in its original chapel in the village church of Ponteranica, a few miles north of the city at the entrance to the Brembo Valley (pls 57, 58).[21] The patron of this work has recently been identified as the Scuola del Corpo di Cristo, which in 1517 began a campaign to decorate its chapel and altar, dedicated to St John the Baptist.[22] From the wording of the documents it appears that the now lost original frame was carved and gilded by 1522; to judge from their style, however, Lotto's panels date from slightly later, and had perhaps only just been completed at the time of his departure from Venice in 1525.[23] The polyptych format chosen by the Scuola, although beginning to become old-fashioned by urban tastes of 1517/18, was ideally suited to the dual dedication of the altar to the Baptist and to the Corpus Christi, since each aspect is represented by images of equal size and importance in each of the two tiers. At the same time, the eucharistic devotion actively promoted by the Scuola, and so powerfully embodied in the figure of Christ pouring his blood into a chalice, is also expressed in the *Baptist* panel, in the centrally placed image of the lamb, which likewise displays a gaping red wound in its side. Following convention, the four full-length, arched panels are lit from the right, in other words, from the liturgical south; by contrast, the two smaller rectangular panels comprising the *Annunciation* are lit as if by the nimbus containing the dove of the Holy Spirit at the top left. The miraculous nature of this event is dramatically emphasised by the pink phosphorescence of the angel's garment, which glows magically against its background of dark green curtain. In their modern, pseudo-Renaissance frame the panels are clearly not placed quite in their intended relation to one another–particularly disturbing is the discontinuity of the seascape between the *Baptist* and the *St Paul* panels–and it may also be that originally the sides were placed obliquely to the centre rather than in the same plane.[24]

Both of the ample conventual churches for which Lotto worked in Bergamo, Santi Stefano e Domenico and Santo Spirito, were favourite sites for the private chapels of many of the leading local families, including respectively the Suardi and the Brembate, and the Tassi and the Cassotti.[25] All of these were to be important patrons of Lotto during his period in Bergamo; and, to a much greater extent than in the Marches, such patrons were interested in commissioning not just altarpieces, with their obvious public religious function, but also smaller pictures to admire and contemplate in the privacy of their homes. Two contemporary documents are of particular importance in recording this enlightened interest in domestic pictures, and especially in those of Lotto. The first is a list drawn up by the painter in 1524/5, itemising no less than eight pictures that he had recently painted for the wealthy cloth merchant Zanin (Giovanni) Cassotti.[26] While only two of these are certainly identifiable with surviving works, the list provides a valuable idea of the range of their subjects, of their approximate sizes, and of where in the house they were placed. Thus, the majority consisted of small-scale representions of the Virgin and Child with or without saints, presumably in half-length; but there were also a *Pietà*, a *St Jerome* (presumably full-length in a landscape), and several portraits, including the double portrait of Cassotti's son Marsilio and his wife (pl. 80).[27] Nearly all the pictures were hung–or were perhaps placed on furniture–in the privacy of the bedrooms of the various members of the family. The other important contemporary document is an account of private collections in Bergamo compiled by the Venetian patrician Marcantonio Michiel on a visit to the city in about 1525.[28] Since

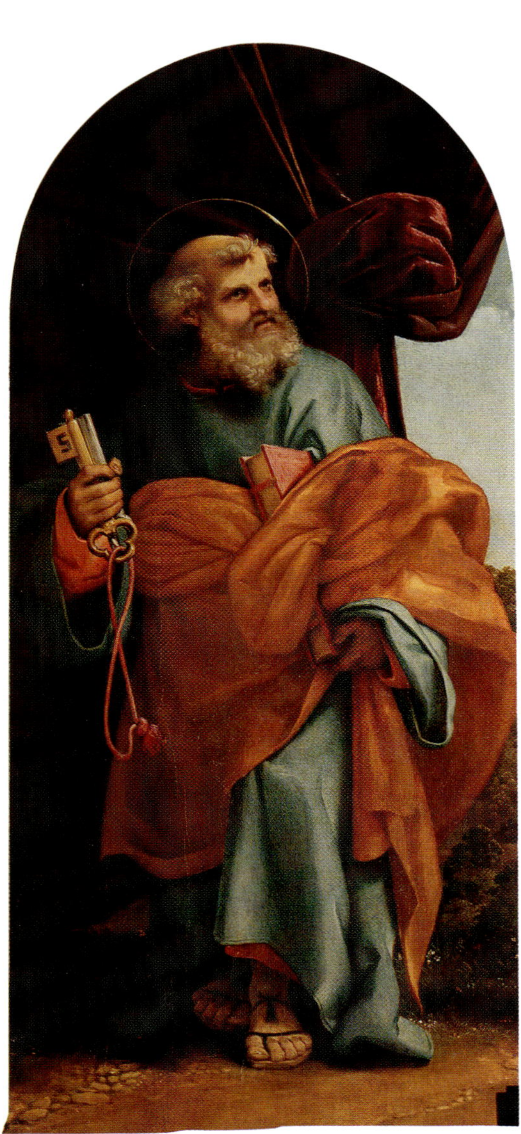

58 Lotto. *St Peter* (detail of pl. 57).

57 (*facing page*) Lotto. Ponteranica polyptych (*c.*1525). Six panels: 135 × 70 cm (each at centre); 75 × 35 cm (upper register, sides); 118 × 57 cm (lower register, sides). Ponteranica, parish church.

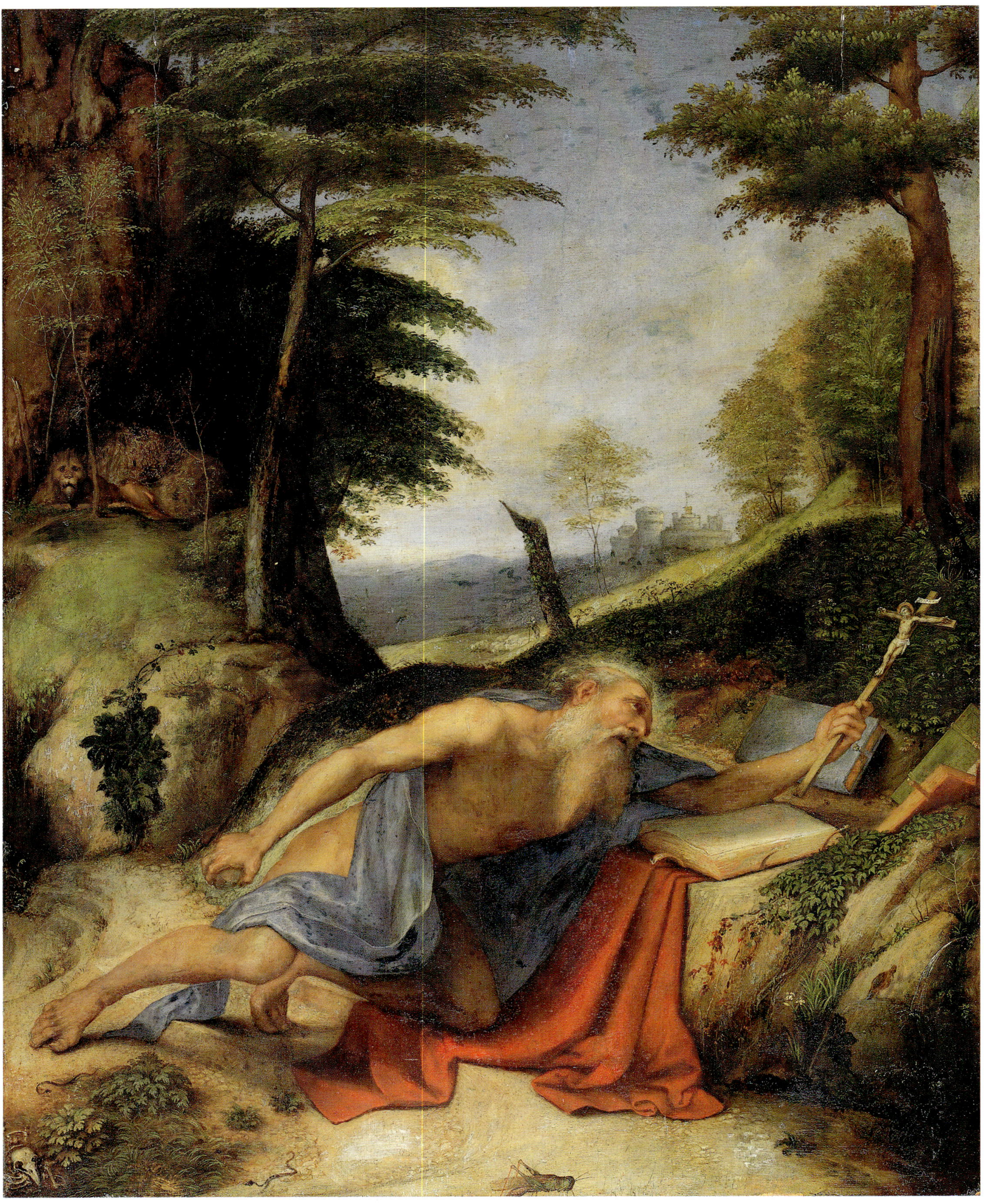

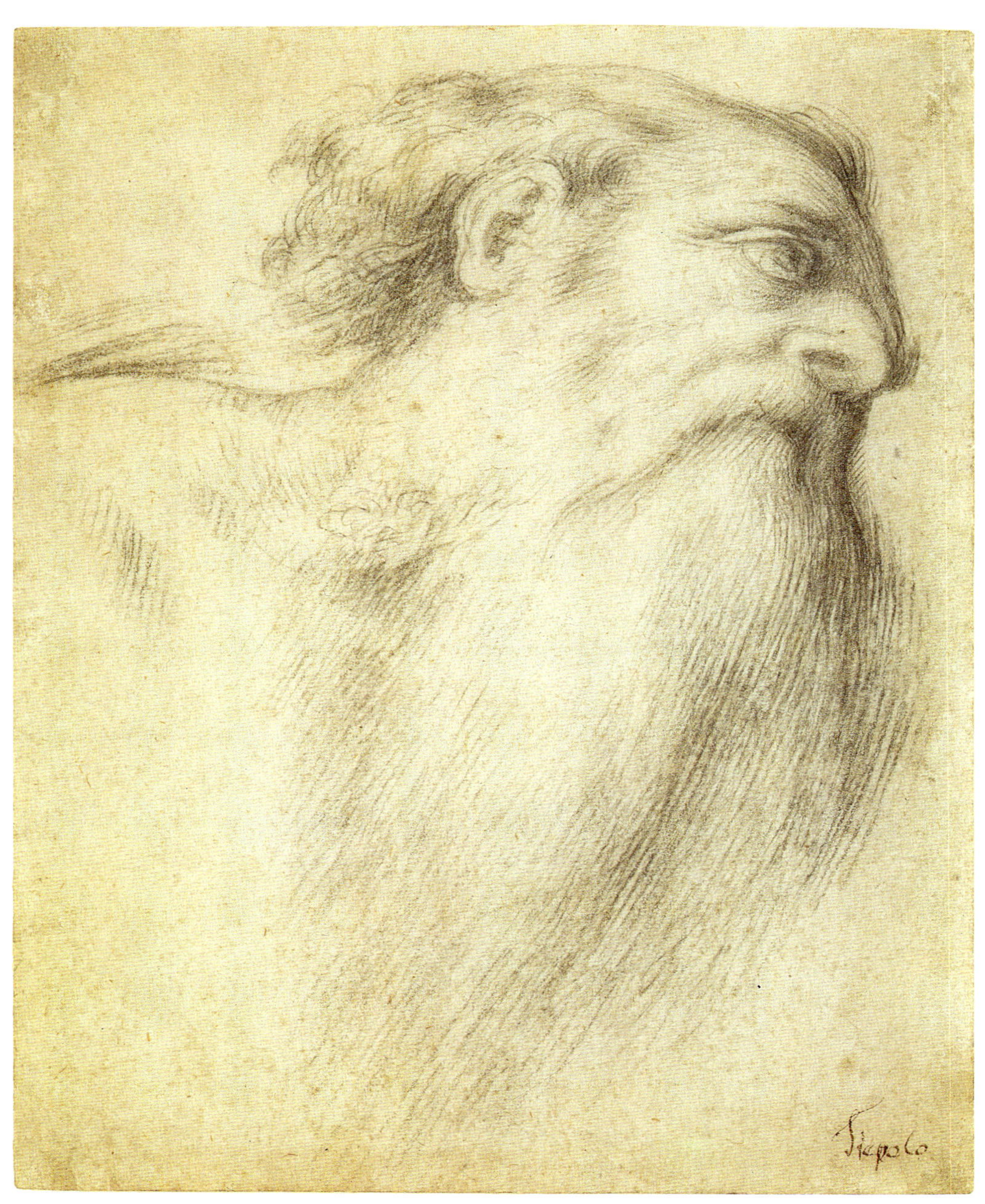

60 Lotto. Preparatory study for head of *St Jerome* (pl. 59). Black chalk, 16.8 × 13.5 cm. London, private collection.

59 (*facing page*) Lotto. *St Jerome* (*c.*1516–18). Canvas, 55.8 × 40 cm. Bucharest, Muzeul National de Arta al României.

he mentions (without describing) only two pictures in the house of Zanin Cassotti, it is clear that his account is far from complete; but he does usefully list two other houses with pictures by Lotto: that of the painter's landlord at the time, Niccolò Bonghi, who commissioned a *Mystic Marriage of St Catherine* including his portrait (pls 73, 74);[29] and that of Domenico Tassi dal Cornello, who owned a *Night Nativity*, another *Pietà*, and another *St Jerome*. It is further interesting to note that while two of these owners–Cassotti and Tassi–are known to have been active as patrons of art before Lotto's arrival in the city, both previously exhibited much more old-fashioned taste. Thus it was Tassi who in 1508 commissioned Bergognone's polyptych for the high altar of Santo Spirito; while Cassotti, together with his brother Paolo, had commissioned frescoes for their family chapel in Santa Maria delle Grazie from the very mediocre local painter Jacopo Scipioni.[30] In short, the arrival of Lotto, together with his fellow-Venetians Previtali and Cariani, created an aesthetic revolution in the city.

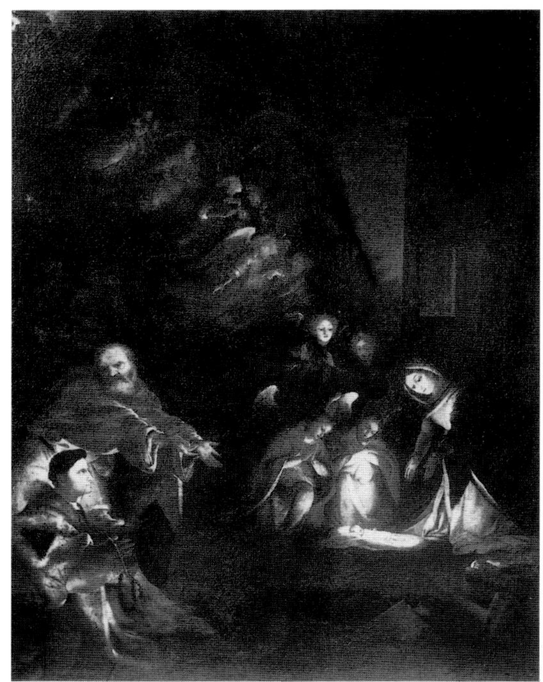

61 Copy after Lotto. *Night Nativity*. Canvas, 132 × 104 cm. Venice, Gallerie dell'Accademia.

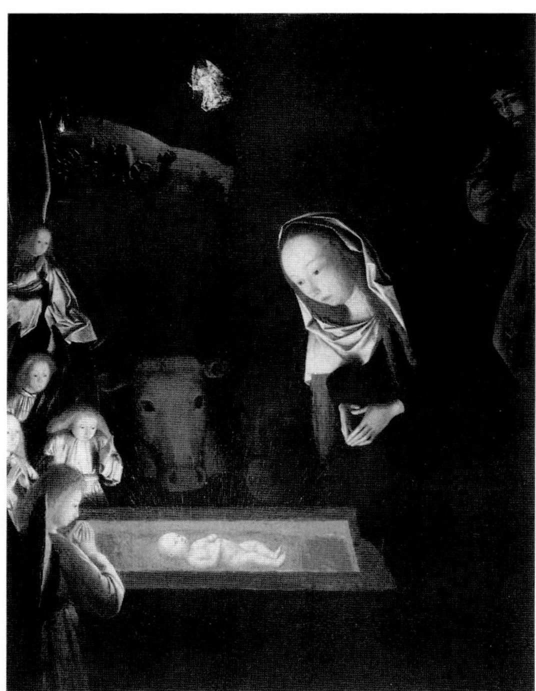

62 Geertgen tot Sint Jans. *Nativity* (*c*.1480?). London, National Gallery.

63 (*facing page*) Lotto. *Christ taking Leave of his Mother* (1521). Canvas, 126 × 99 cm. Berlin, Staatliche Museen.

A likely candidate for one of these two *St Jeromes* is the little canvas with a beautifully luminous, smokily atmospheric landscape now in Bucharest (pl. 59),[31] in which the lunging movement of the saint—so different from that in either of Lotto's two earlier versions of the subject (pls 22, 36)—has a counterpart in the predella of the Colleoni Martinengo altarpiece (pl. 52). Clearly made in preparation for the Bucharest picture, as a study for the saint's head, is a recently re-emerged drawing in black chalk (pl. 60),[32] in which the artist succeeds both in endowing the features with a portrait-like realism, and in suggesting the light, air and active pose to be developed in the painting. The re-emergence of the study is particularly fortunate, since despite the abiding importance of a clear, defining contour in Lotto's pictorial style, there survive relatively few drawings by him. The reason for this scarcity may be attributed in large part to the fact that he never maintained a stable workshop, and did not make consistent use of pupils and assistants who might have preserved his drawings for further use. But it is probably fair to assume that every picture he painted was carefully pre-planned, both with compositional sketches and with detailed studies of the heads, as here, and of the poses for the main figures.

As regards Domenico Tassi's *Night Nativity*, there is good reason to identify a much damaged and only semi-legible picture in the Accademia in Venice either as the drastically overpainted remains of the original, or more probably, as an early copy (pl. 61). Later sources add what Michiel failed to mention: first, that the *Nativity* was accompanied by a pendant, representing *Christ taking Leave of his Mother*; and second, that the two pictures included portraits respectively of the patron and of his wife, Elisabetta Rota.[33] The *Christ taking Leave* is certainly identifiable with the picture signed and dated 1521, now in Berlin (pl. 63), in which Elisabetta is prominently represented in the right foreground; and in the Venice picture the kneeling patron appears in a corresponding position to the left. The compositions of the two pictures as a whole are similarly complementary: thus in both cases, the figures are arranged along intersecting diagonals, which are then stabilised by a grid of background architecture.

Although not uncommon in southern Germany in the early years of the sixteenth century, the subject of Christ taking Leave was still very rare in Italian painting, and it is not entirely clear why it was chosen as a thematic pendant to the much more popular subject of the Nativity. But the themes are natural complements in the sense that one is joyful, celebrating the birth of Jesus, and the other sorrowful, treating a moment of high pathos, in which Christ bids a final farewell to his mother in Bethany before riding to Jerusalem to be arrested and crucified. The Virgin has crumpled into a deathly swoon, a motif commonly employed in representations of Passion scenes such as the Crucifixion and the Lamentation (see pls 127, 146), both to enhance a mood of bitter grief, and to express the theological concept of the Virgin as actively co-operative with her son in mankind's redemption. To emphasise the contrasting character of the two scenes, Lotto represents one in daylight and the other at night—although paradoxically, it is the joyful scene that takes place at night, with the darkness illuminated by the miraculously radiant figure of the infant in the manger. This motif, which had a literary source in the Revelations of St Bridget of Sweden, was well established in Netherlandish painting of the fifteenth century (see pl. 62); and, as in his various subsequent Night Nativities (pp. 58, 98–101), Lotto's treatment of it suggests that he was directly inspired by devotional panels or illuminated manuscripts imported from the Netherlands.[34] The inclusion of anachronistic donor portraits may be similarly Netherlandish in inspiration; at the same time, they provide a striking visual analogy with devotional handbooks of the period, which characteristically encourage their readers to imagine themselves physically present at the unfolding events of Christ's life, and to respond emotionally to them.[35]

According to a now illegible inscription recorded in an eighteenth-century inven-

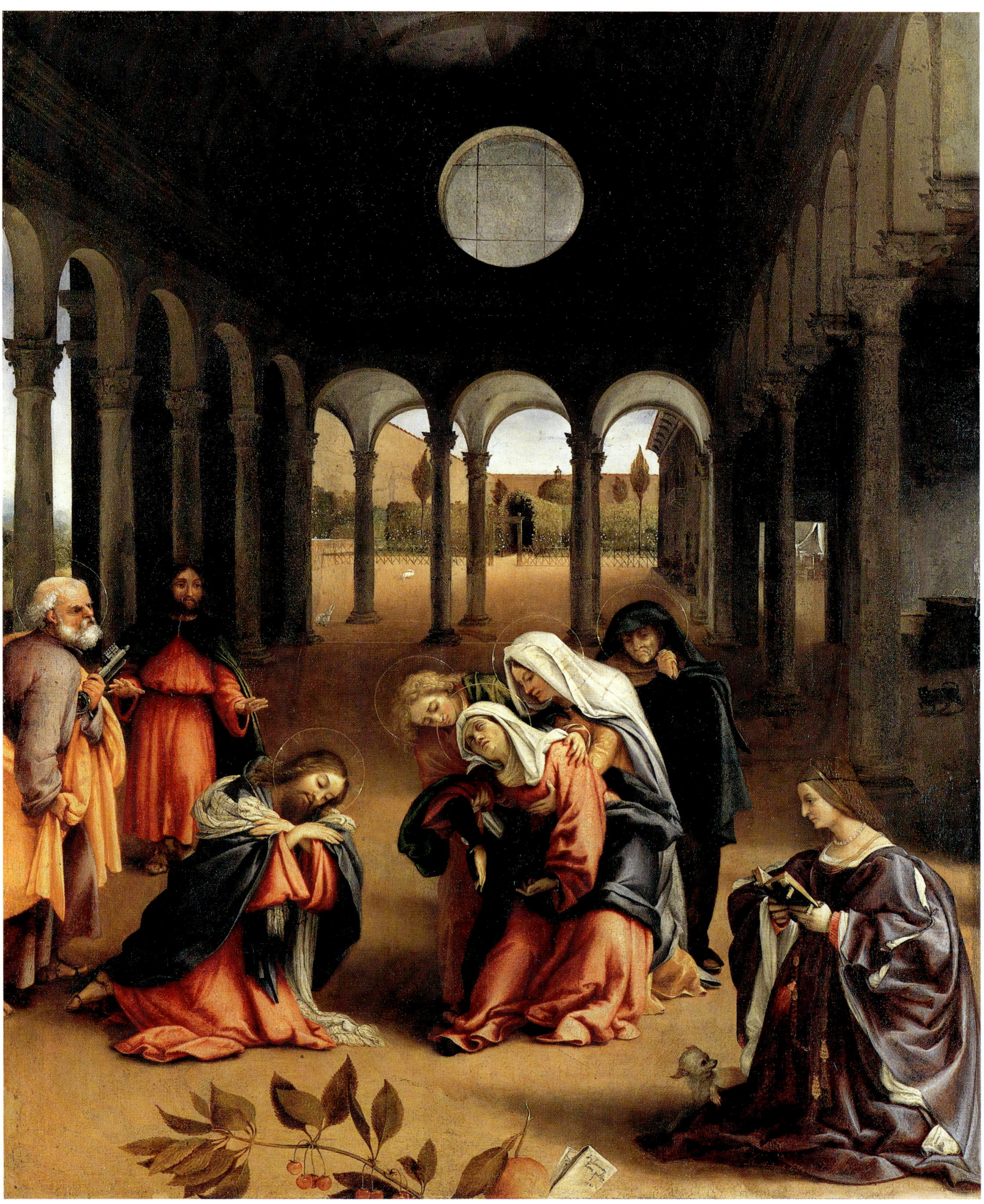

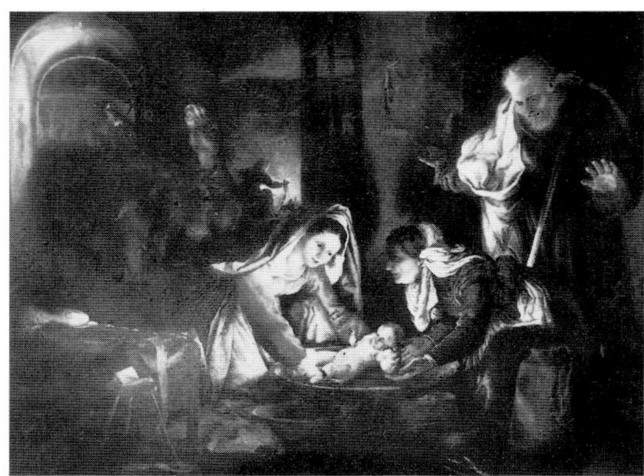

64 Early copy of Lotto's *Night Nativity* (pl. 66). Florence, Galleria degli Uffizi.

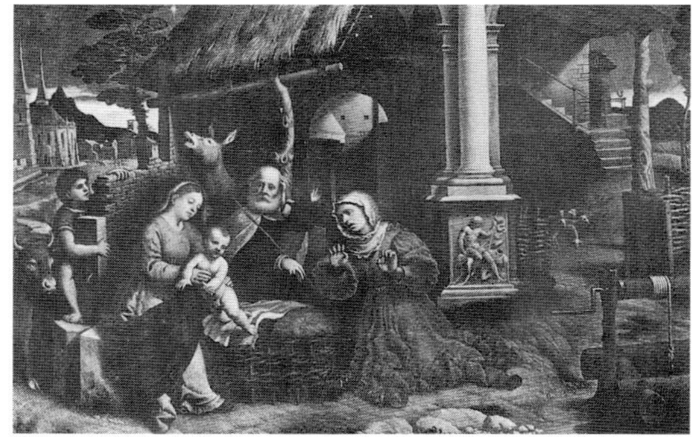

65 Domenico Capriolo. *Nativity* (1524). Treviso, Museo Civico.

66 (*facing page*) Lotto. *Night Nativity* (1521). Panel, 55.5 × 45.7 cm. Siena, Pinacoteca Nazionale.

tory, another *Night Nativity*, now in Siena (pl. 66), was similarly dated 1521.[36] As is evident from an early copy (pl. 64), this picture has been drastically cut down at the sides, and originally the format was horizontal rather than vertical. Although most modern critics have dated the work on stylistic grounds to about 1527, its style in fact seems perfectly consistent with that of the *Christ taking Leave* and of Lotto's other works of about 1521 (see pls 54, 55). Further confirmation of the reliability of the eighteenth-century reading of the date is provided by Domenico Capriolo's *Nativity* of 1524 (pl. 65), which appears to borrow a number of features from Lotto's picture.[37] These include the motif of the braying ass (more visible in the copy after Lotto than in the worn original), the crepuscular lighting and the view through the archway to a fire burning in the room in the background, and, perhaps most significantly of all, the incorporation of the traditional, but by that date rare motif of the incredulous midwife. According to both the *Golden Legend* and St Bridget, one of the two midwives present at Christ's birth was punished for her doubts about Mary's virginity by having her hand withered; but when bidden by an angel to touch the Child, she was miraculously healed. As in the Tassi *Nativity*, Lotto underscores the miraculous nature of the scene by means of the mysterious and poetic light emanating from the figure of the Christ Child, thereby transfiguring the humble interior of the stable, and filling potentially mundane details such as the Child's bath, or his still attached umbilical cord, with religious significance.[38]

If the Siena *Nativity* was indeed known to Capriolo, a Venetian painter working in Treviso, it follows that although painted in Bergamo, the picture is likely to have been destined for a patron in Venice or Treviso. From this it may further be inferred that not all the smaller-scale pictures executed by Lotto during his Bergamask period were necessarily commissioned by local patrons, and that some may have been painted for customers associated with his earlier areas of activity. On the other hand, there clearly did exist in Bergamo many more owners of domestic pictures by Lotto than those mentioned by Michiel, some of whom are identifiable, but several others of whom are not. It is likely to have been a Bergamask, for example, who commissioned yet another *Nativity*, this time on a much smaller scale, now in Washington and dated 1523 (pl. 67).[39] Although not a night scene, the Washington *Nativity* shares with the other two an intimacy of mood that encourages the emotional participation of the pious spectator and places a novel emphasis on the personality of Joseph. Traditionally Joseph had played a definitely subordinate role in Nativity scenes, and had appeared only very rarely in Madonna and saints altarpieces. But, partly under the influence of Franciscan preaching, Bergamo in the early years of the sixteenth century saw the growth of an enthusiastic cult of Christ's earthly father; and this is reflected in his prominence in two major altarpieces of the period: Cariani's San Gottardo altarpiece of 1517–18 (pl. 53), and Lotto's own San Bernardino altarpiece of 1521 (pl. 55). The former was commissioned by a devotional confraternity inaugurated in honour of Joseph in 1512, the Scuola di San Giuseppe; and the fact that Domenico Tassi was a founder member of the Scuola helps account for Joseph's exceptional importance as mediator between the kneeling donor and the newborn Christ in his *Night Nativity*.[40] But in the Washington *Nativity*, too, the figure of Joseph is virtually equivalent in compositional weight to that of the Virgin, and the picture is full of allusions both to the craft of carpenter (as in the unusual presence of a crucifix on the left, as well as in the jointed piece of wood carrying the artist's signature in the right foreground) and to Joseph's role as provider for the Holy Family in the forthcoming flight into Egypt. All this suggests that the unknown commissioner of the picture shared Tassi's special devotion to the saint.

Another, slightly earlier picture not mentioned by Michiel is the *Susannah and the Elders* of 1517 (pl. 70). As in a recent woodcut version of this hitherto unusual Old Testament subject by Girolamo da Treviso (pl. 69), Lotto's representation of the story

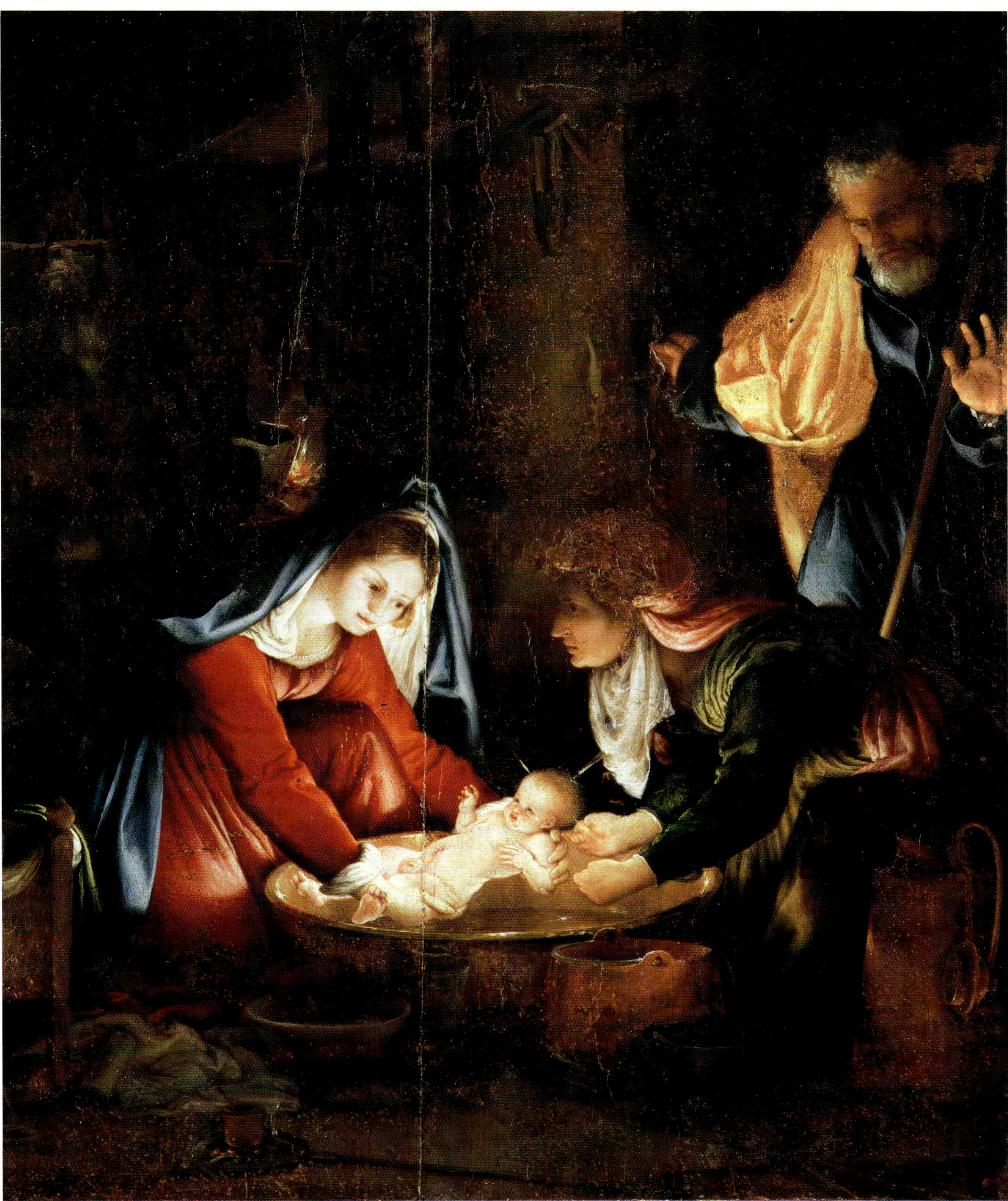

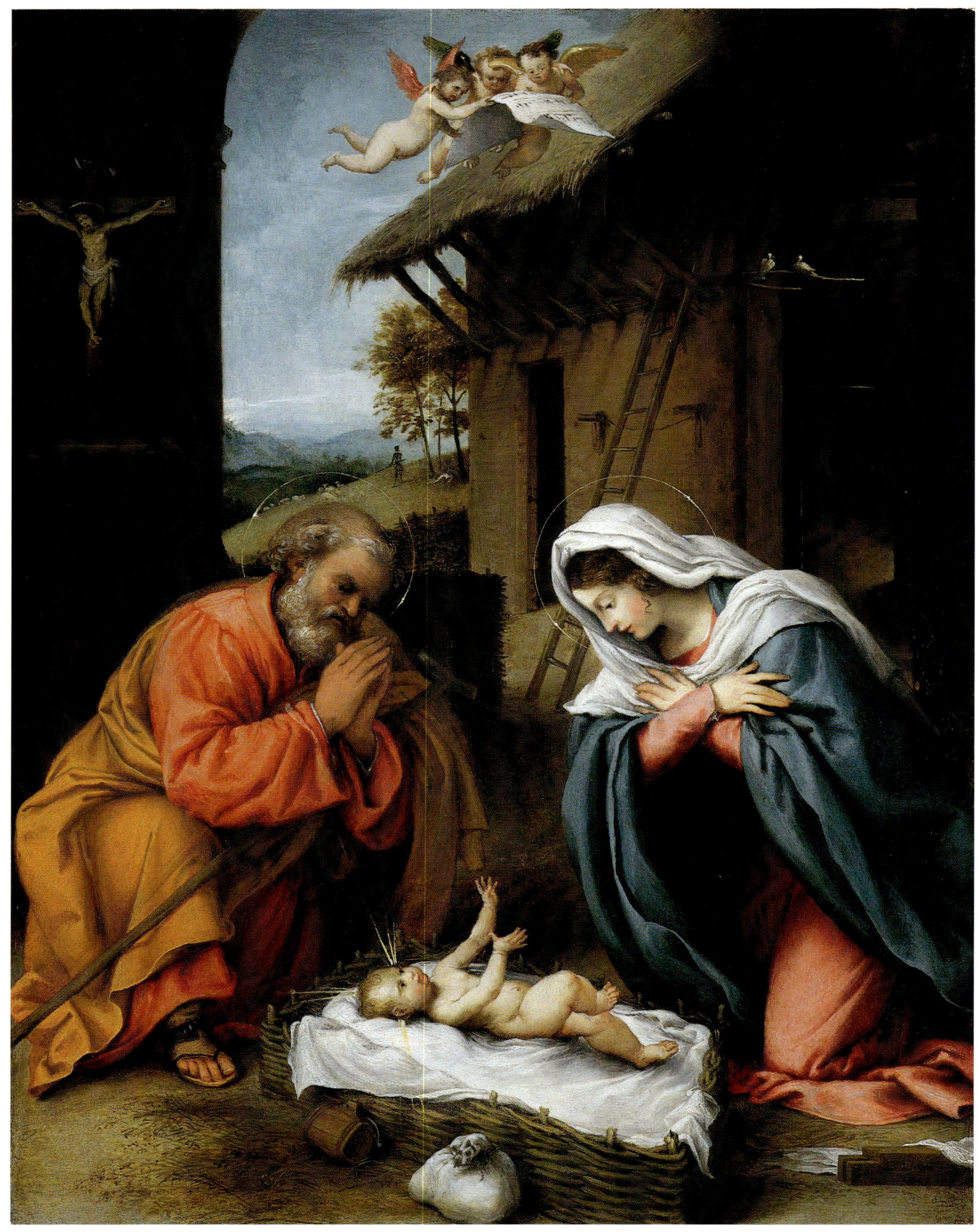

67 Lotto. *Nativity* (1523). Panel, 46 × 35.9 cm. Washington, DC, National Gallery of Art.

68 (*facing page*) Detail of pl. 67.

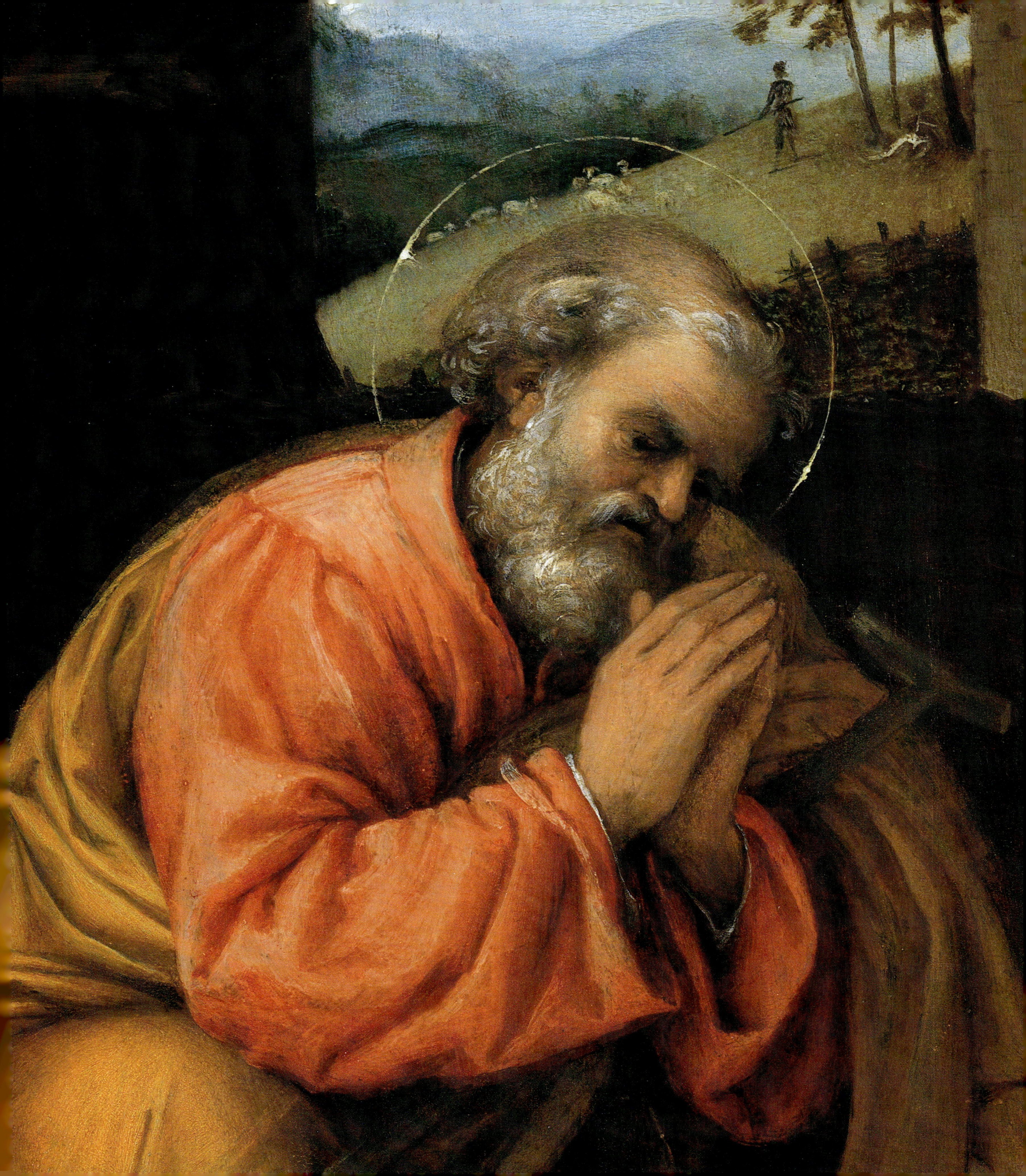

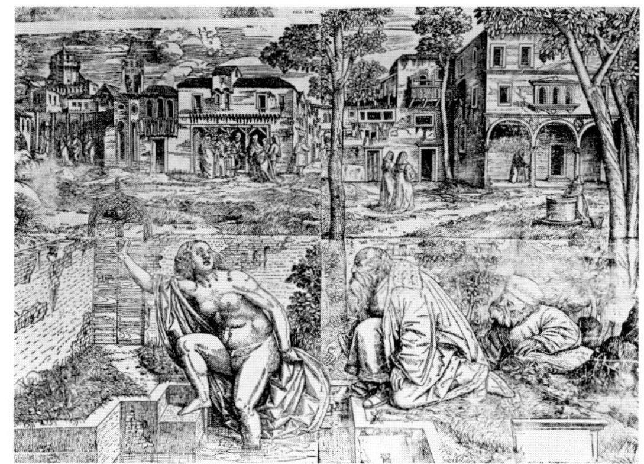

69 Girolamo da Treviso. *Susannah and the Elders* (1515). Woodcut. Copenhagen, Statens Museum for Kunst.

70 (*facing page*) Lotto. *Susannah and the Elders* (1517). Panel, 66 × 51 cm. Florence, Galleria degli Uffizi, Donazione Contini Bonacossi.

closely follows the biblical text.[41] As recounted in an apocryphal addition to the Book of Daniel, the story tells of how two elders conceived a lust for the virtuous married woman Susannah, and spied on her while she was bathing; and how when she indignantly rejected their advances, they took self-protective revenge by falsely and publicly accusing her of adultery with a young man, a crime punishable by death. In the foreground, Lotto portrays the moment in which the two elders, having been repulsed, call loudly for witnesses, and two servants of the house burst in to see what is happening. In the background, two earlier moments in the story are depicted: near the left edge, two maidservants go back to the house to fetch oil and balm for Susannah's bath, thus leaving her without witnesses; and in the enclosed garden—which, like the similar garden belonging to Martha and Mary at Bethany (pl. 63), sparkles with impressionistic dots of light—the still clothed Susannah is seen walking down the path towards her pool, watched by the two elders from the secrecy of the bushes. The story is obviously one of great erotic potential, and it was to be exploited as such by later Venetian painters, including Tintoretto and Veronese; even Girolamo da Treviso, whose woodcut Lotto would certainly have known, focuses attention on the spying episode, and shows Susannah in full nudity. Lotto concentrates rather on the moral of the story: the perversion of justice by unscrupulous officials, and implicitly the restoration of justice in a difficult situation by the just judge Daniel. The use of the archaic device of scrolls, inscribed with the words spoken by the actors,[42] further emphasises the didactic function of the picture. It is a reasonable deduction, therefore, that the unknown patron was a Venetian magistrate, or some other kind of official involved in the administration of justice in the subject city of Bergamo, and concerned to perform his duties in the manner of a new Daniel.[43]

Lotto's *Susannah* has often reminded critics of German art,[44] and in particular of the early work of Holbein. Indeed, several aspects of the foreground composition are remarkably Holbeinesque: the bold, bright planes of colour combined with touches of sharp detail; the dramatic but stilted gestures of the figure group, which resembles a ritual dance; the ornamental flourish of the curling scrolls. In 1517, however, Holbein was still aged no more than nineteen or twenty; and although it is not impossible that he had already visited Italy, including nearby Milan, it seems unlikely that at this stage he would have been well enough established as an artist to have come to the attention of Lotto. Any connections between the two painters may be rather by a common experience of the art of Dürer, whose prolific output of prints would certainly have continued to interest Lotto throughout his Marchigian and Bergamask periods. Particularly relevant for the *Susannah* are the various renderings of the *Flagellation* Dürer designed for his Great and Small Passion woodcuts (*c.*1497–1500; 1511) and for the Engraved Passion (1512), in which the torturers, many of them dressed in contemporary fashions, bear down with mincing, threatening gestures on the vulnerable, naked figure of Christ. A curious scrap of evidence that in this very year Lotto's thoughts were turned towards the other side of the Alps is provided by a legal document of 17 July 1517, in which he insists that a prospective apprentice be prepared to travel with him 'elsewhere in Italy, or else beyond Italy to Gallic lands or Germany'.[45] It is not known what the purpose of such a journey might have been; in any case, Lotto never actually undertook it.

Although Lotto was to represent the story of Susannah again many years later in a picture now lost (p. 140), the Cassotti and Michiel documents both indicate that the majority of domestic pictures he painted in Bergamo were much more traditional in subject, and included several representing the Madonna with saints. The commissioner of one of these, now in Ottawa and datable to about 1518 (pl. 71), has recently been identified as the painter's friend Battista Cucchi, also known as Battista degli Organi because of his part-time activity as an organist for the Consorzio della Misericordia. His

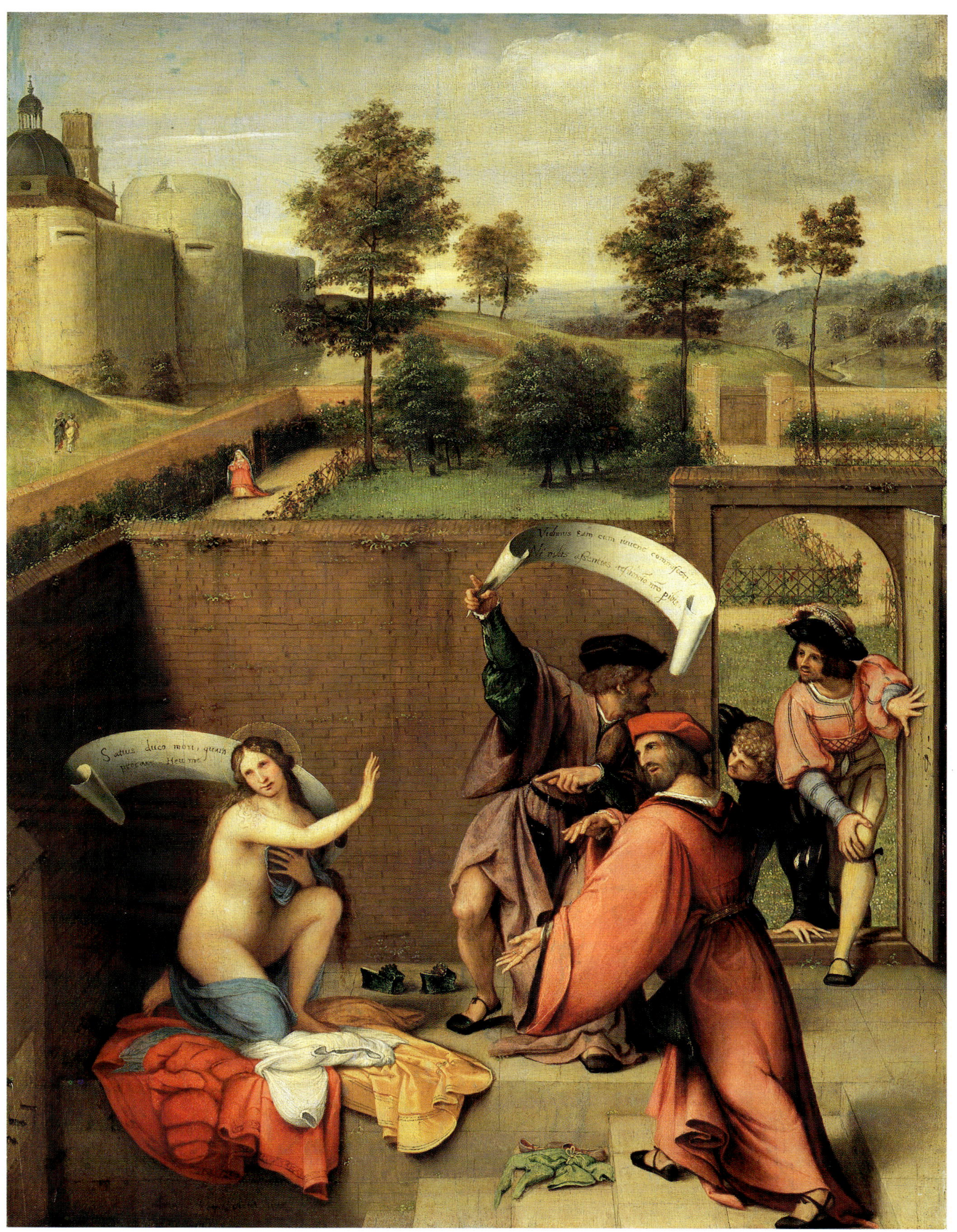
Vidimus eam cum iuvene commisceri
Satius duco mori, quam
peccare. Heu me

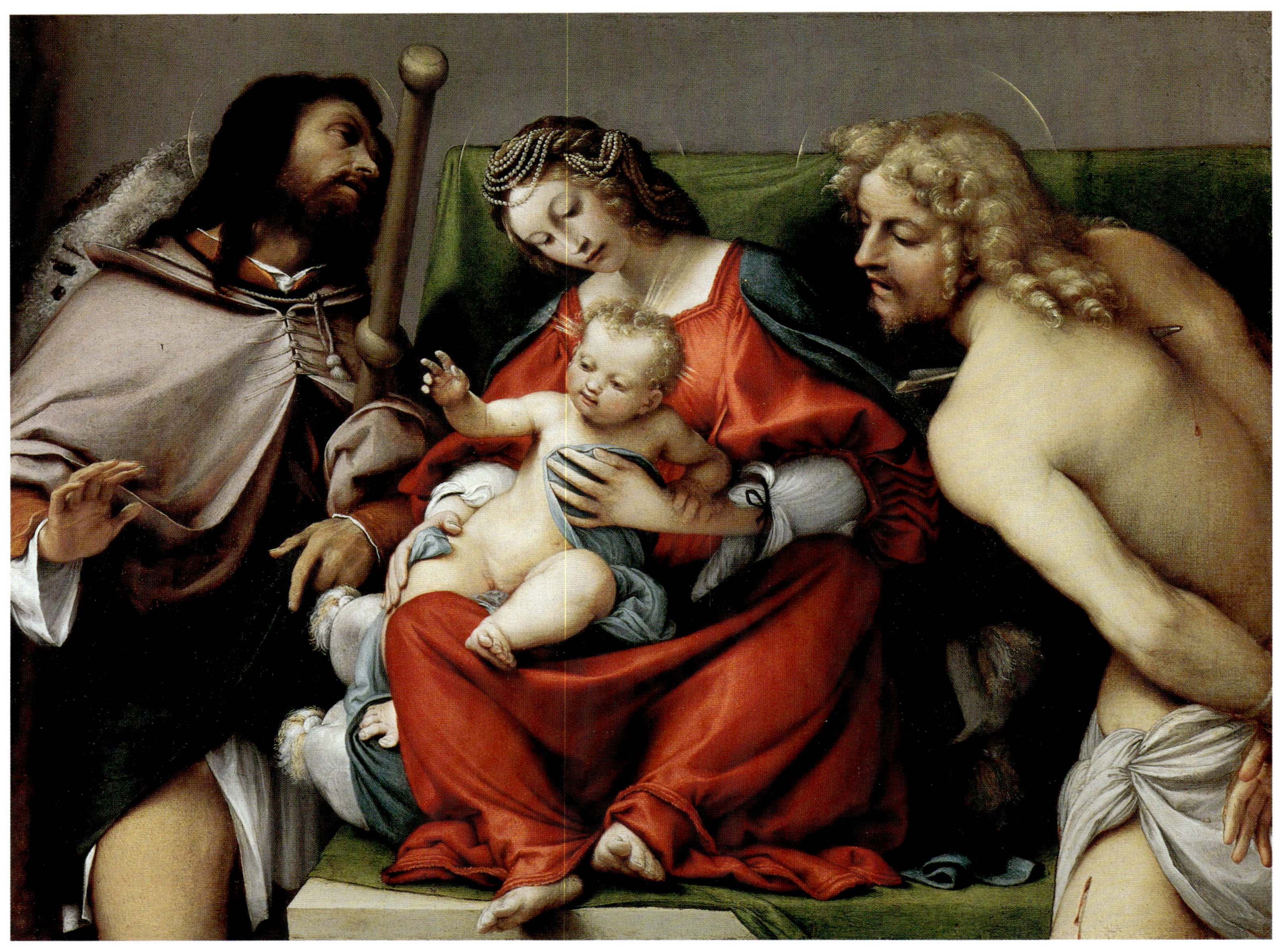

71 Lotto. *Virgin and Child with Sts Roch and Sebastian* (*c.*1518). Canvas, 81.8 × 108.5 cm. Ottawa, National Gallery of Canada.

true profession, however, was that of a surgeon, and this provides an obvious explanation for the presence in the picture of two saints closely associated with disease and its cure, Roch and Sebastian.[46] Compared with Lotto's earlier compositions of this type (see pls 27, 28), the Ottawa picture shows the figures in fuller length, with the Virgin's feet visible as she squats on her simple, improvised throne; and the insistent diagonals, combined with a complete disappearance of any vertical axis, create an effect of controlled dynamism. This process is taken further in the probably slightly later *Virgin and Child with Sts Jerome and Nicholas of Tolentino* now in Boston (pl. 72), painted for a patron so far unidentified, but certainly connected with the order of Augustinian hermits, or Austin friars.[47] Here the figures are smaller in relation to the field, and the use of diagonals is extended obliquely into the picture space. In both pictures, as in Lotto's contemporary altarpieces, the twisting, rhythmical poses are clearly inspired by those of Raphael and Leonardo, with the curly haired, self-consciously beautiful St Sebastian of the Cucchi picture again recalling in particular the angel of the *Virgin of the Rocks* (pl. 51). A climax of this expansion of the format of the domestic devotional

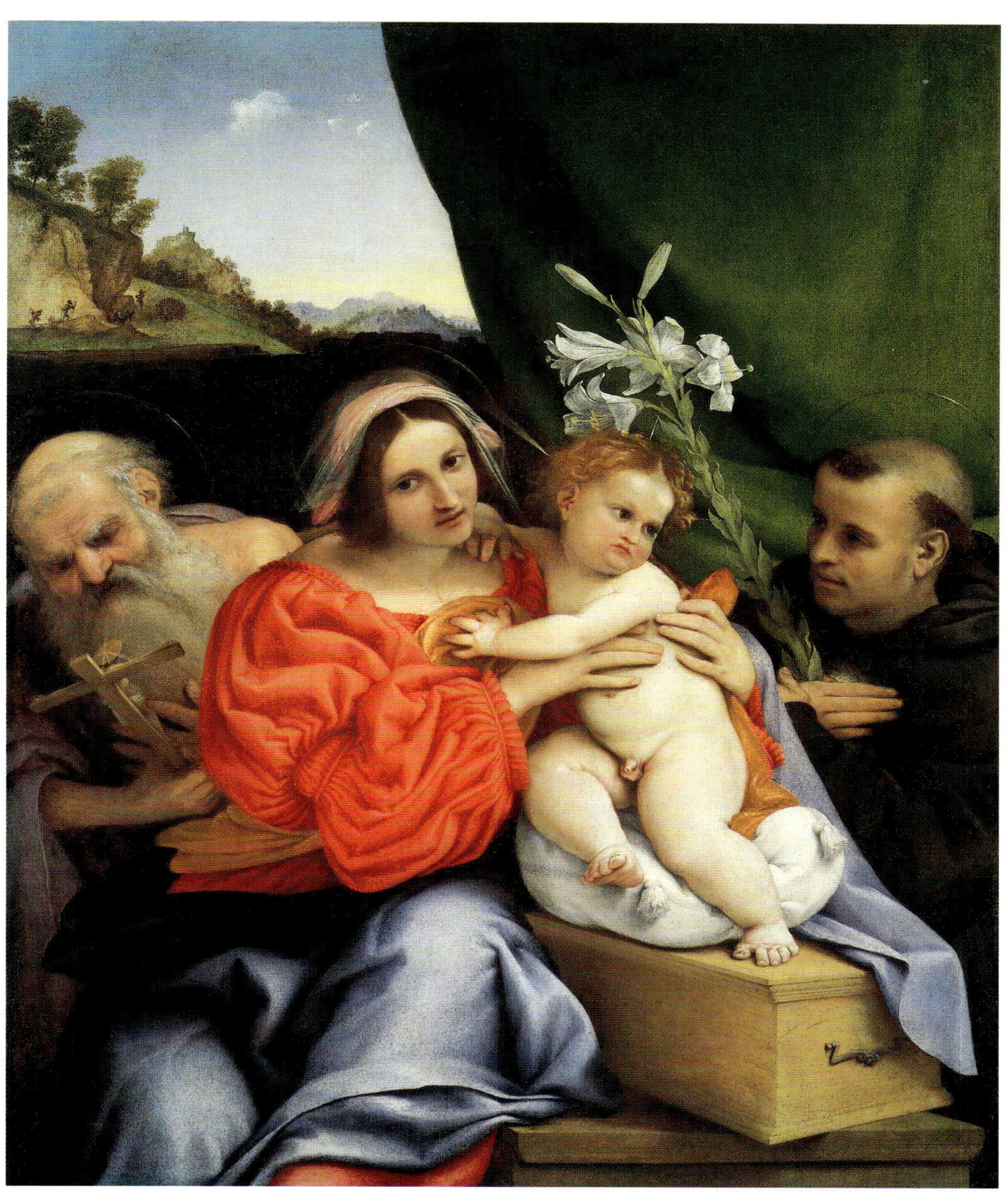

72 Lotto. *Virgin and Child with Sts Jerome and Nicholas of Tolentino* (*c.*1521). Canvas, 94.3 × 77.8 cm. Boston, Museum of Fine Arts, Charles Potter Kling Fund.

picture is then reached in the *Mystic Marriage of St Catherine with Niccolò Bonghi* of 1523 (pl. 74),[48] where the main figures are now represented in full length. Unfortunately this picture was mutilated at the top as early as 1528, reputedly by a French soldier;[49] and originally, as in the Boston picture but more extensively, a framed view of landscape was to be seen above the sill behind the saints' heads, in this case showing Mount Sinai as a symbol of St Catherine. Despite this damage, and despite the perished condition of the blue of the Virgin's mantle, this picture, with its broad contrasting planes of intense local colour, is one of the most pictorially magnificent of all Lotto's works. In its relative serenity of mood, as well as in its chromatic opulence, it shows striking affinities with the similarly full-length but intimate Madonna and saints pictures painted around this time by Palma Vecchio (see pl. 109). While no such examples are known to have existed in Bergamo, it is significant that Palma was a native Bergamask and from 1515 at the latest regularly sent altarpieces to churches in the region; it is not improbable, therefore, that he also painted domestic pictures for local patrons.

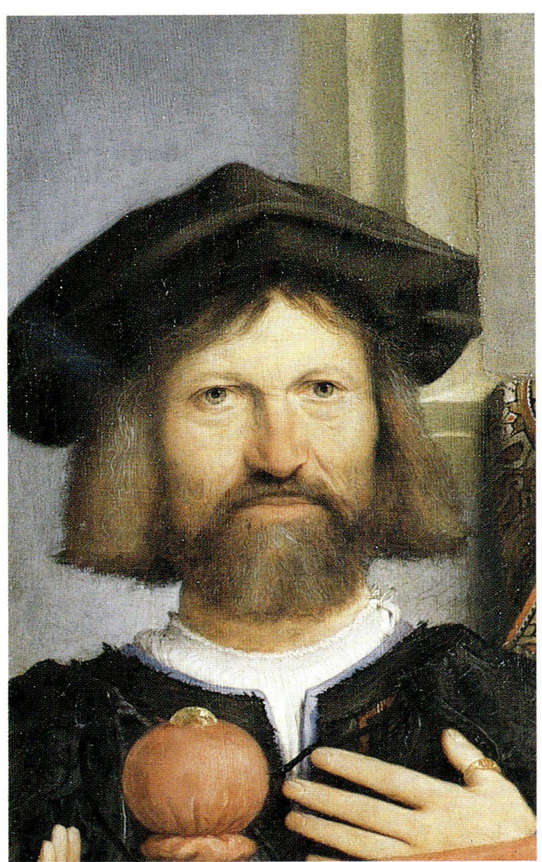

73 Detail of pl. 74.

74 (*facing page*) Lotto. *Mystic Marriage of St Catherine, with Niccolò Bonghi* (1523). Canvas, 172 × 134 cm. Bergamo, Accademia Carrara.

Lotto's landlord Niccolò Bonghi, who stands reverently behind the Virgin's throne at the left, is portrayed with vivid naturalism, his ruddy, craggy features contrasting with the pale refinement of the Virgin, St Catherine and the angel. A similar, unidealised immediacy is to be found in the various autonomous portraits, including three double portraits, that Lotto painted throughout his period in Bergamo. Despite the lack of any local tradition of portraiture, Lotto's presence in the city clearly stimulated a number of leading citizens to commission their portraits from him; and the painter seized the opportunity greatly to expand the compositional and expressive resources of the genre.

Probably the earliest of Lotto's Bergamask portraits is the *Giovanni Agostino and Niccolò della Torre*, signed and dated 1515 (pl. 75).[50] Both father and son had been leading members of the pro-Venetian faction during the recent troubles, and both were eminent physicians, Giovanni Agostino holding office as prior of the college of physicians from 1510 until his death in 1516. References to his professional and intellectual eminence are implied by the prominent inscriptions 'Galienus' (Galen) on the tome he holds open, and 'Medicorum Esculapio . . .' (to the Aesculapius of doctors . . .) on the letter in his right hand.[51] Compared with earlier portraits comprising more than one figure by Giorgione and Raphael, and even with later examples by Lotto himself, the formal composition is undeniably awkward; and from this it has often been inferred that Niccolò was included as an afterthought.[52] But the canvas would have been uncomfortably empty at the right without a second figure, and technical examination has not revealed the previous existence of a feature such as a window on the right, which would always have been needed to balance the still life on the left.[53] It may be concluded, therefore, that the picture was planned as a double portrait from the beginning, and in fact, the placing of the son and heir in a plane behind that of the father may be intended to express the idea of professional and family lineage. As with Lotto's Bergamask Madonna and saints pictures, the format has lengthened in comparison with the early Trevigian portraits, and the heads are smaller in relation to the frame; and room is accordingly created for at least the suggestion of a domestic interior, perhaps identifiable with Giovanni Agostino's study, furnished with a Savonarola chair and a table piled with books and papers. Despite the searching gazes of the two physicians towards the spectator, their prominence in the composition is somewhat compromised by the almost Flemish precision with which the various still-life details are rendered: from the ink-well spattered with ink to the penknife and quill, and to the *trompe-l'oeil* fly on the white handkerchief in the left foreground.[54]

In the *Lucina Brembate*, datable to about five years later (pl. 77), Lotto returns to a shorter, bust-length format, in which the face is even more dominant than in his earliest portraits. In a way that was to become characteristic of the painter's later and finest achievements in the field of portraiture, the accessories are used not so much to refer to the sitter's profession and position in society, as in the *Delle Torre* portrait, as to convey cryptic allusions to her name and private situation, as if the allegorical content of the *impresa*, formerly restricted to a separate image on the cover (p. 11), has now fully invaded the portrait itself. The identity of the female sitter – a member of the Bergamask nobility, and a close relative of Alessandro Colleoni Martinengo – was recognised earlier this century on the basis of the Brembate family escutcheon on the signet ring on her finger, and of the motif of the crescent moon at the top left. Inscribed with the letters 'CI', the motif constitutes a rebus, inviting the ingenious spectator to combine the two letters with the Latin and Italian word for the moon (*luna*) to spell out the sitter's name: 'LU-CI-NA'.[55] But the significance of the reference appears to extend further, because in classical mythology the goddess Juno Lucina was venerated as a protector of women in childbirth, and the placing of the

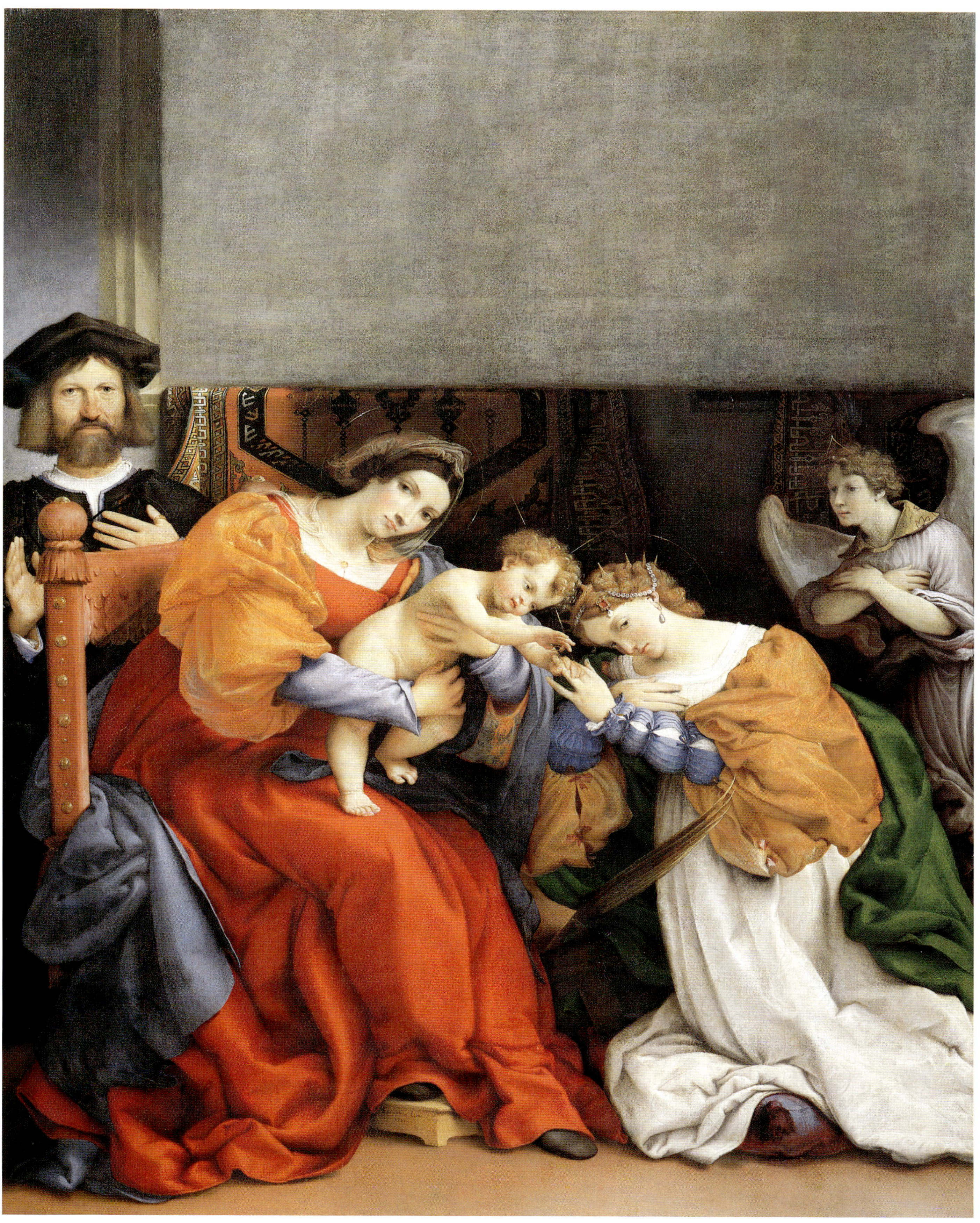

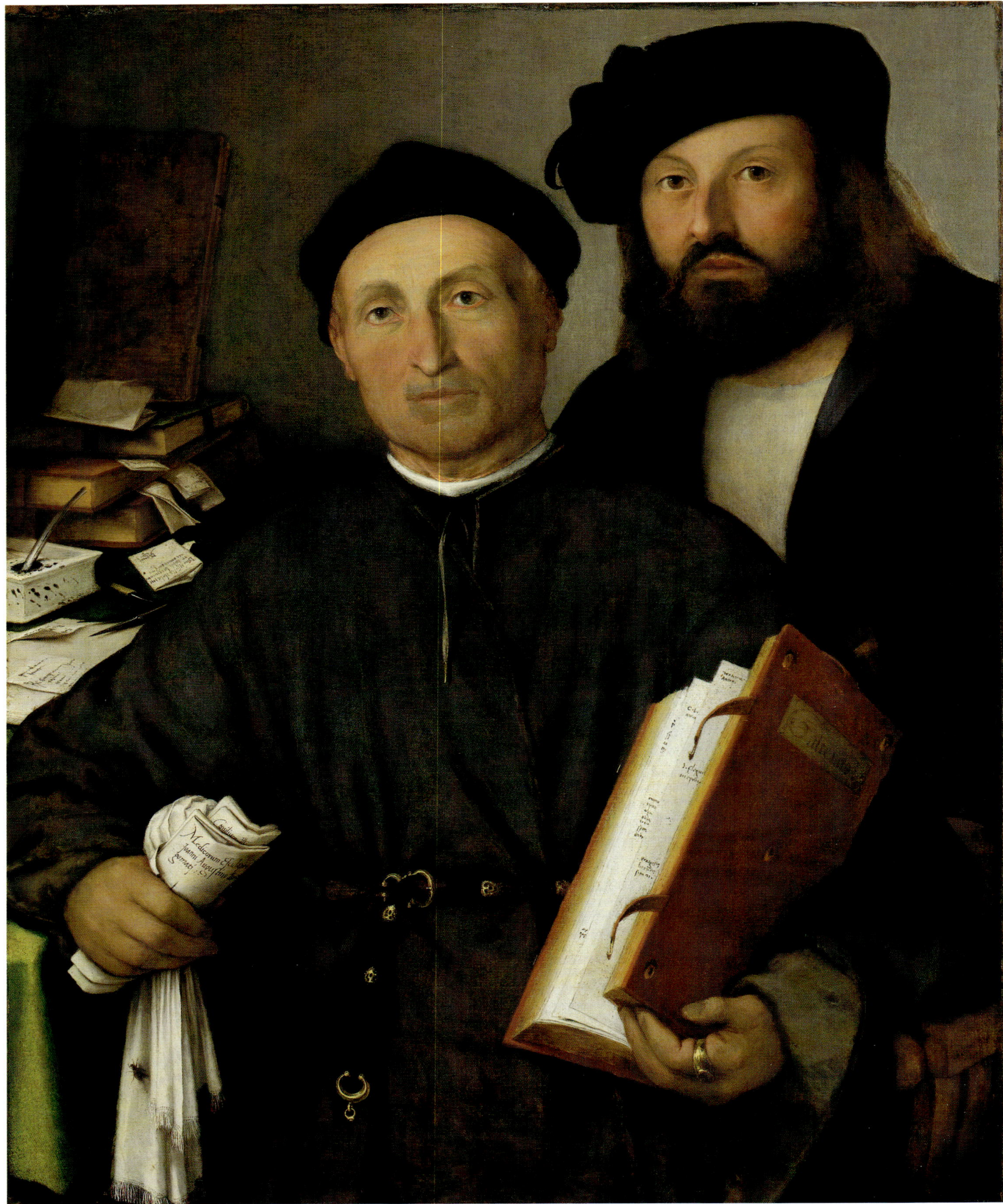

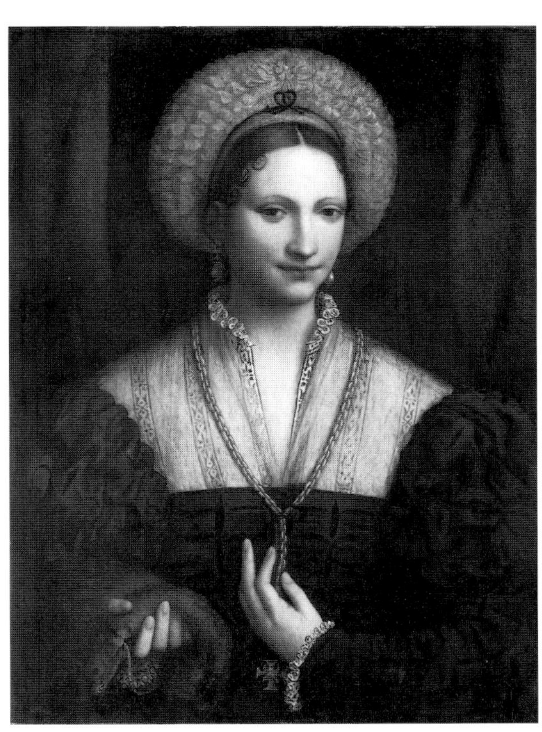

76 Bernardino Luini. *Portrait of a Lady* (*c*.1520–5). Washington, DC, National Gallery of Art. Andrew W. Mellon Collection.

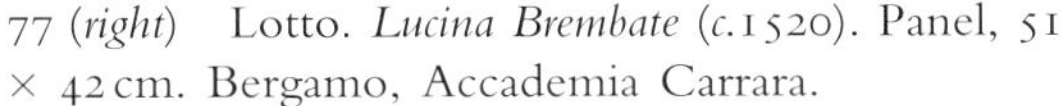

77 (*right*) Lotto. *Lucina Brembate* (*c*.1520). Panel, 51 × 42 cm. Bergamo, Accademia Carrara.

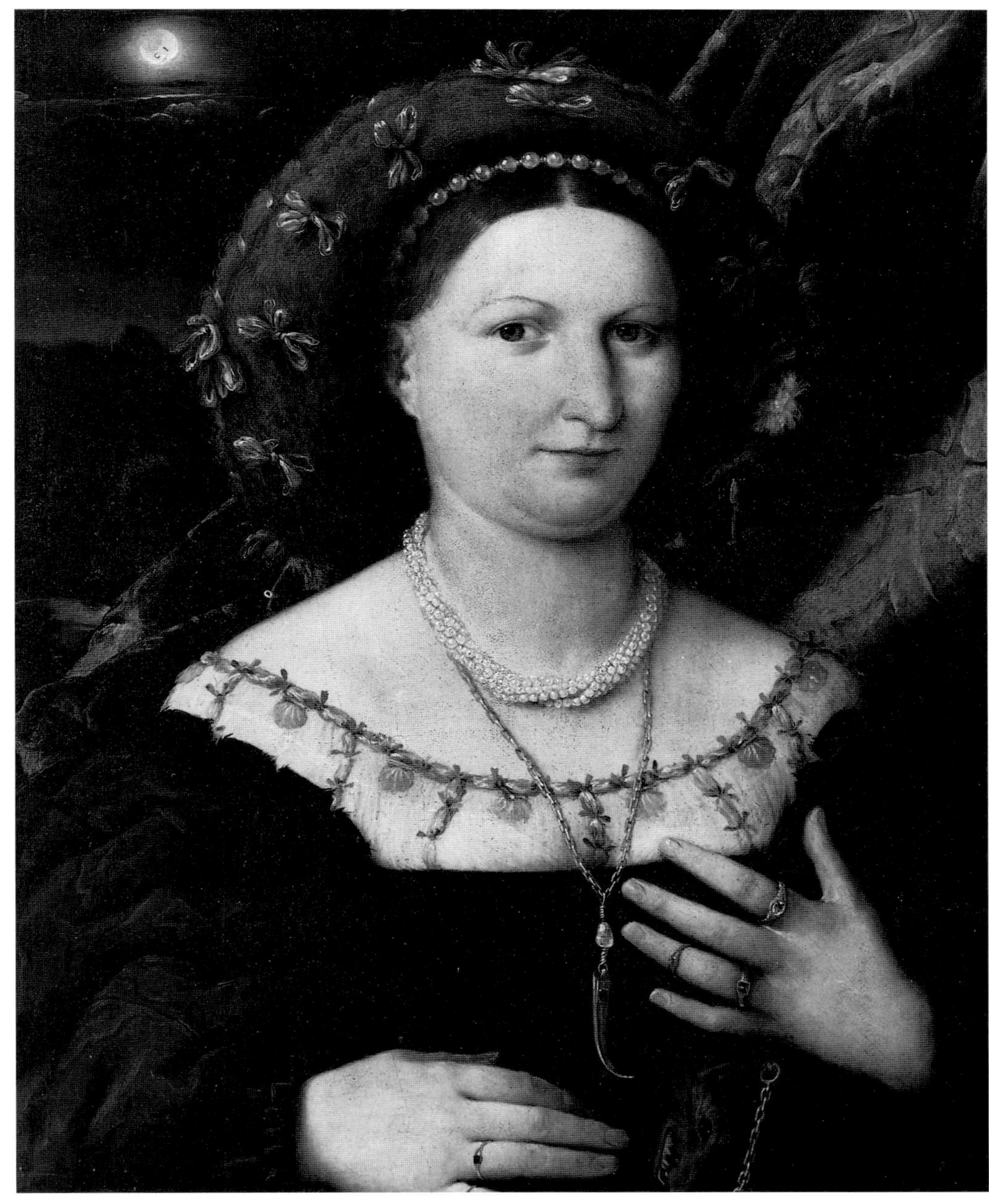

75 (*facing page*) Lotto. *Giovanni Agostino and Niccolò della Torre* (1515). Canvas, 84.4 × 68 cm. London, National Gallery.

sitter's hand across her stomach is consistent with the supposition that she is pregnant. The weasel-head and pelt, attached to the girdle by a golden chain, was a not uncommon accessory of feminine dress, and it recurs, for example, in Bernardino Luini's probably slightly later *Portrait of a Lady* now in Washington (pl. 76). But in Lotto's portrait it may also allude to the story of Galanthis, who, according to Ovid, was metamorphosed by the goddess Lucina into a weasel;[56] and if so, this and the horn amulet would constitute further references to Lucina Brembate's condition, and to her hopes for a successful outcome. Historical research has shown that she probably had good reason for anxious concern, since she had married her husband Leonino some twelve years earlier in 1508, and by 1520 was no longer young.

In metropolitan Venice, straightforward portraits of women were comparatively rare, and the female counterparts of the many male portraits tended to be the idealised, poeticised and often calculatedly erotic images of the type made popular by Titian and Palma Vecchio. By contrast with these, *Lucina Brembate*, although lacking the psychological profundity of Lotto's greatest portraits, is presented as frankly and directly as any of his male sitters; as in contemporary Milanese portraits, such as Luini's *Portrait of a Lady*, or Solario's *Lady with a Lute* (Rome, Palazzo Barberini), she is dressed in a circumstantially described costume that is clearly meant to appear both fashionable and very expensive. This willingness on Lotto's part to engage with the individual personality of a female sitter may be explained in part by his general independence of prevailing convention, but in part, too, by the differing social circumstances between Bergamo and the capital. In the patrician culture of Venice, great emphasis continued to be placed on lineage: that is, on the relation of the dominant male to his male ancestry, and to his peers in a cohesive, patriarchal society. Bergamo, by contrast, in common with other Italian cities including Milan and Florence, was affected by a new, middle-class emphasis on domesticity: that is, on the conjugal relationship between a man and his wife, and on the wife's role as a subordinate partner and mother to his children.[57] In keeping with this new emphasis, wives accompany their husbands in domestic devotional pictures much more commonly in Bergamo than in Venice, as in Previtali's *Virgin and Child with Sts Paul and Agnes, and Paolo and Agnese Cassotti* (pl. 78), or in Lotto's own *Night Nativity* and *Christ taking Leave*, with Domenico Tassi and Elisabetta Rota. Similarly, while independent conjugal portraits were to remain very rare indeed in Venice, Lotto painted at least two during the early 1520s in Bergamo.

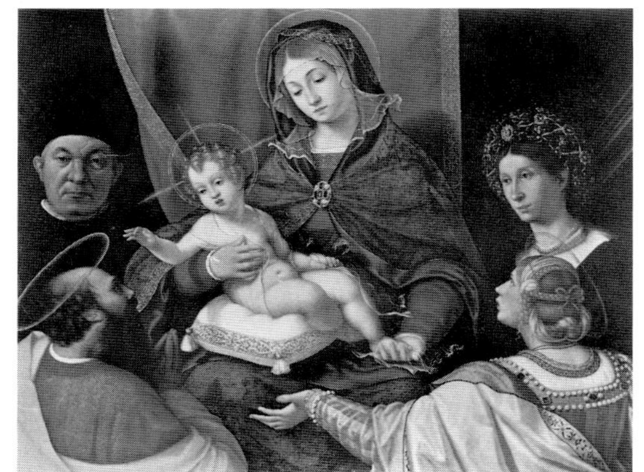

78 Andrea Previtali. *Virgin and Child with Sts Paul and Agnes, and Paolo and Agnese Cassotti* (*c.*1523). Bergamo, Accademia Carrara.

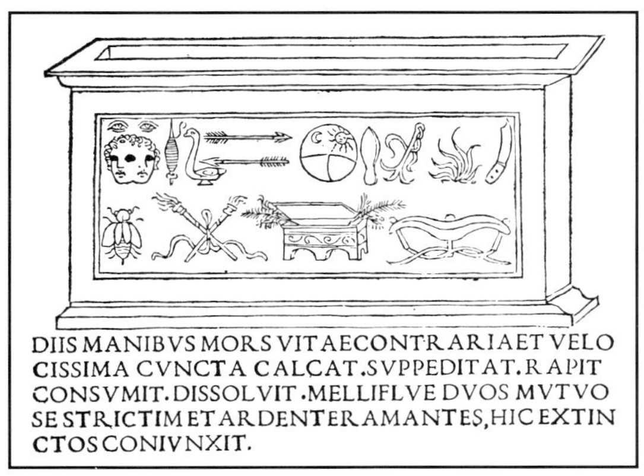

79 Hieroglyphic woodcut from *Hypnerotomachia Poliphili* (1499).

The first of these, the *Messer Marsilio and his Bride* (pl. 80), is dated 1523, and is one of the pictures listed by Lotto as having been painted for Marsilio's father, Zanin Cassotti (above, p. 53). As a double portrait it is compositionally much more sophisticated and symbolically much richer than the earlier *Della Torre* portrait. Presumably the work was commissioned to celebrate the couple's marriage: thus, while Marsilio tenderly places the ring on to his wife's middle finger, a smiling cupid binds them together with a symbolic yoke.[58] Marriage double portraits were virtually unknown in Italy, and Lotto's basic concept here was probably inspired by some northern European example, perhaps in the form of an engraving or woodcut.[59] On the other hand, the particular motifs of the cupid, the yoke and the laurel are more obviously classical, and like the symbolic motifs in the Colleoni Martinengo altarpiece (pp. 45–6), they have sources rather in the humanistic background of Lotto's early years in Treviso. Thus, according both to a pseudo-hieroglyph in the *Hypnerotomachia Poliphili* (pl. 79), and to Pierio Valeriano's *Hieroglifica*, the yoke signifies wedlock, while the evergreen laurel refers both to virtue and eternity. Together, then, symbolic accessories allude to a love between the couple that will endure beyond the grave. At the same time, in keeping with the social mores of the period, the compositional structure makes it clear that the loving relationship is not quite one of equals. Marsilio is significantly the more vertical in pose and the larger in bulk, with the top of his hat nearly touching the upper edge of the picture, and his left arm spreading well into the left half. His wife, by contrast, is made to appear demure and subservient by her smaller scale and by the tilt of her head towards his.

In Lotto's other conjugal portrait painted in Bergamo, now in St Petersburg and probably datable to a year or two later (pl. 82), the husband is seated on a lower level than his wife, yet he still dominates the composition by his more central placing. The couple has not yet been securely identified, but it has recently been observed that the luxurious headdress worn by the woman is the identical object to that previously worn by Agnese Cassotti in Previtali's *Virgin and Child with Saints* (pl. 78). Agnese was the wife of Paolo, brother of Zanin Cassotti, and it has accordingly been suggested that the St Petersburg wife represents a close relative of hers, perhaps Apollonia, daughter of Zanin, with her husband Antonio Agliardi.[60] If, however, the headdress was a family

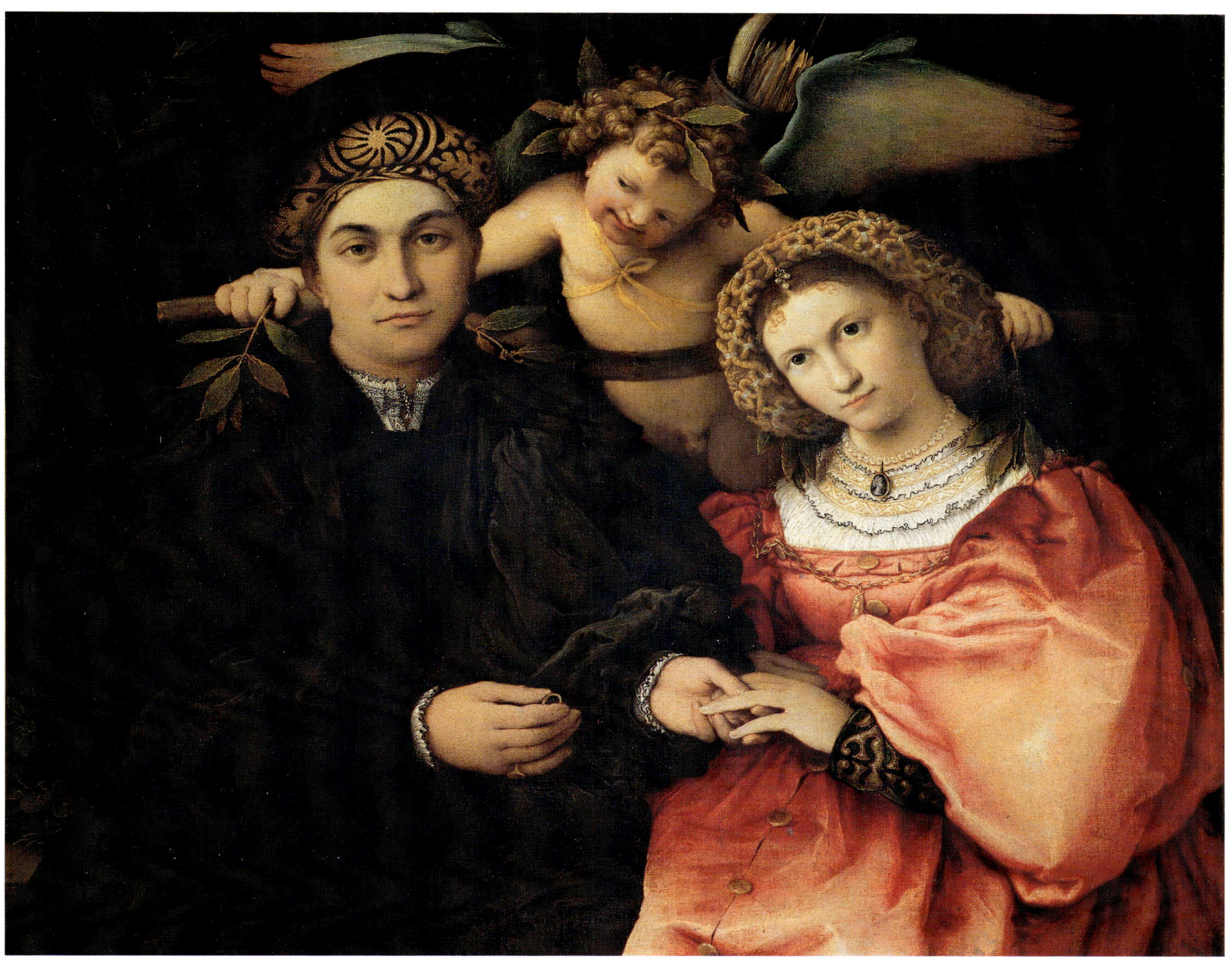

80 Lotto. *Messer Marsilio and his Bride* (1523). Canvas, 71 × 84 cm. Madrid, Museo del Prado.

possession, it is more likely that the husband, not the wife, is a Cassotti; in which case he may be identifiable with Marsilio's probably elder brother, Giovanni Maria, or even with Zanin himself.[61] Although clearly not a wedding portrait, the picture resembles the *Marsilio* in its demonstrative celebration of the conjugal relationship. The arms of the couple are entwined, the wife holds a small dog as a traditional symbol of fidelity, and the paper held up by the man is inscribed with the words 'HOMO NVM / QVAM'– an apparent reference to the words of Christ quoted in the marriage liturgy: 'What therefore God hath joined together, let no man put asunder' ('homo non separet') (Matt. 19:6; Mark 10:9).[62] At the same time, the man points to a sleeping squirrel on the table, an animal usually noted for its busy gathering of nuts in preparation for the hard times of winter–in other words, for its good husbandry[63]–but which here is shown fast asleep. The clear implication is that the man will never ('homo numquam') be similarly neglectful of his own responsibilities.

The St Petersburg picture is one of Lotto's very few works, and the only portrait,

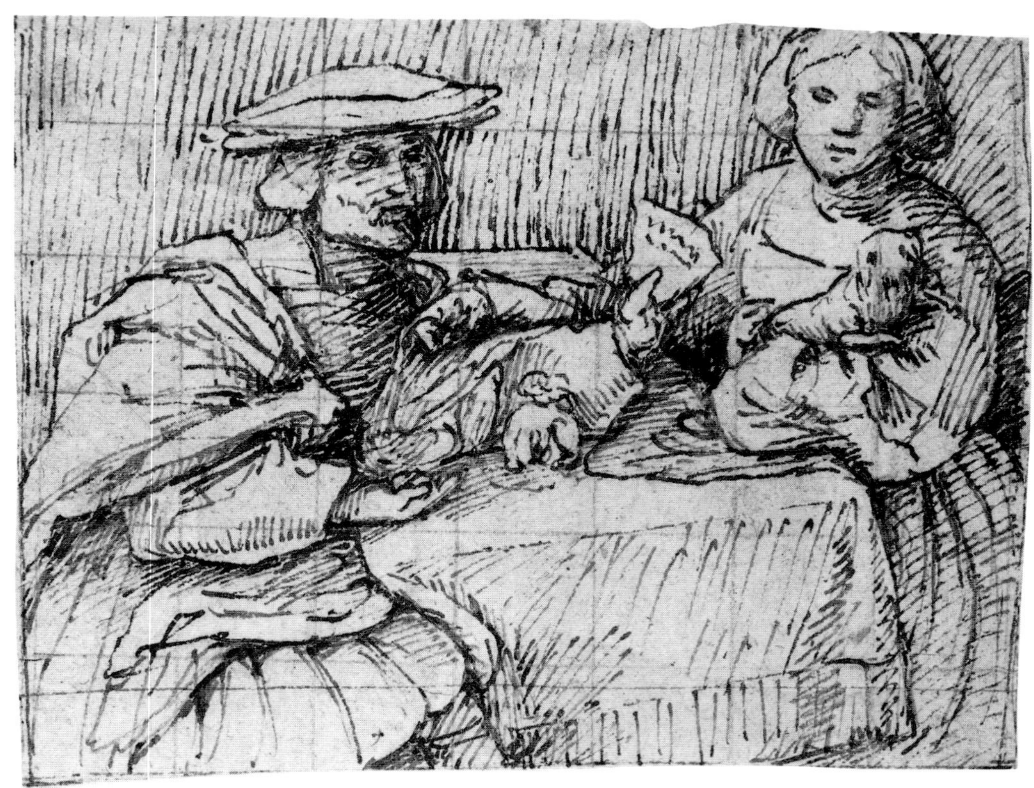

81 Lotto. Preparatory study for *Portrait of a Married Couple* (pl. 82). Pen and ink over red chalk, squared in red chalk, 16.9 × 21.5 cm. Amsterdam, Rijksmuseum.

for which a compositional drawing survives (pl. 81). This consists of a pen and ink sketch that, in keeping with its different function is much more rapidly and freely executed than the chalk study for the Bucharest *St Jerome* (pl. 60). The essentials of the design have already been formulated in the sketch, but the details of the surroundings, costumes (including the family headdress) and symbolic accessories have still to be elaborated. It has been observed that the poses appear much more natural and spontaneous than in the completed painting, where the need to introduce a philosophical gloss has resulted in an effect that is more selfconscious and stilted.[64]

The high demand among Bergamask patrons for easel pictures by Lotto was matched by a scarcely lesser demand for large-scale decorations by him in fresco. Soon after his arrival in the city in the spring of 1513, for example, he was commissioned to paint a cycle of scenes of the life of St Catherine for the church of Sant'Alessandro in Colonna.[65] Although it is not clear whether he ever actually executed these, he certainly did paint a *Martyrdom of St Catherine*—perhaps following on from the success of the Colleoni Martinengo altarpiece—on the rood-screen that straddled the nave of Santi Stefano e Domenico. This work was destroyed with the church as early as the mid-sixteenth century, but a record of the central section of the composition has been plausibly identified in a drawing now in Leipzig (pl. 83), carefully and sensitively modelled in light and shade.[66] The curve of an arch at the lower left would then correspond to the top of the archway leading from the nave to the choir and chancel, where St Catherine again appeared in Lotto's altarpiece, flanking the Virgin's throne. Of his surviving fresco cycles, two were painted in 1525, shortly before his final departure from Bergamo. The first of these, representing scenes from the life of the Virgin, was painted for the chapel of the Confraternity of the Virgin in the parish church of San Michele al Pozzo Bianco, close to where he was living in a property belonging to Niccolò Bonghi.[67] The second, apparently executed in a hurry, and now

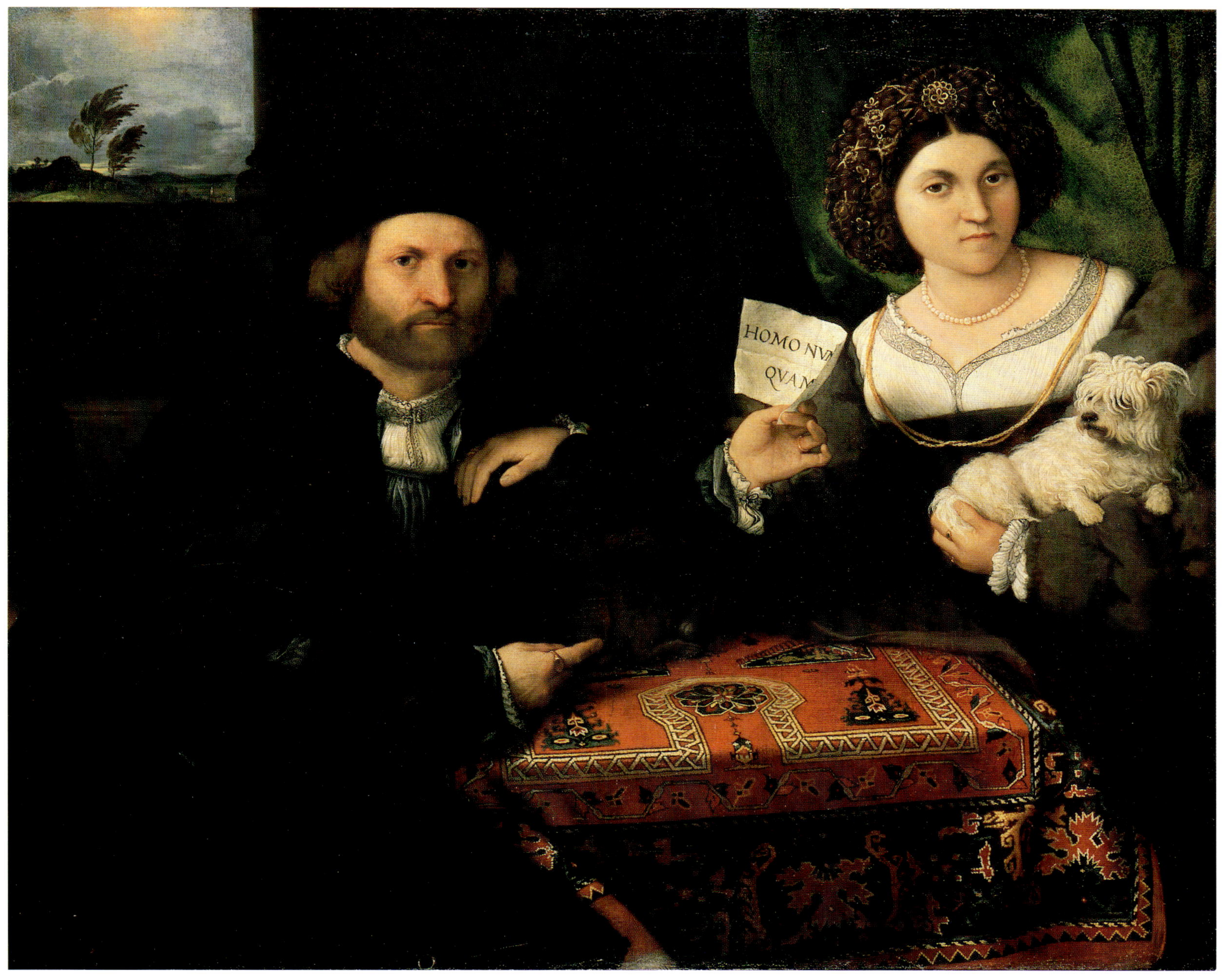

82 Lotto. *Portrait of a Married Couple* (*c.*1524–5). Canvas, 96 × 116 cm. St Petersburg, State Hermitage Museum.

much damaged, was painted for the village church of San Giorgio at Credaro outside Bergamo, and has as its principal scene a *Nativity*, with the figures of standing saints at the sides.

But Lotto's greatest and most comprehensive achievement as a fresco painter was probably always the cycle he executed in 1523–4 in the little oratory adjoining the property of the noble Suardi family, a few miles outside Bergamo near the village of Trescore.[68] Principally responsible for the commission, and probably also for devising its iconographical programme, was Battista Suardi, whose town house was also situated near San Michele al Pozzo Bianco. During the troubles of 1509–15 Suardi had made the mistake of supporting first the French and then the Spanish, and he was politically disgraced after the restoration of Venetian rule; but he remained active as a patron of art and letters, and in the life of a number of the city's most important devotional and

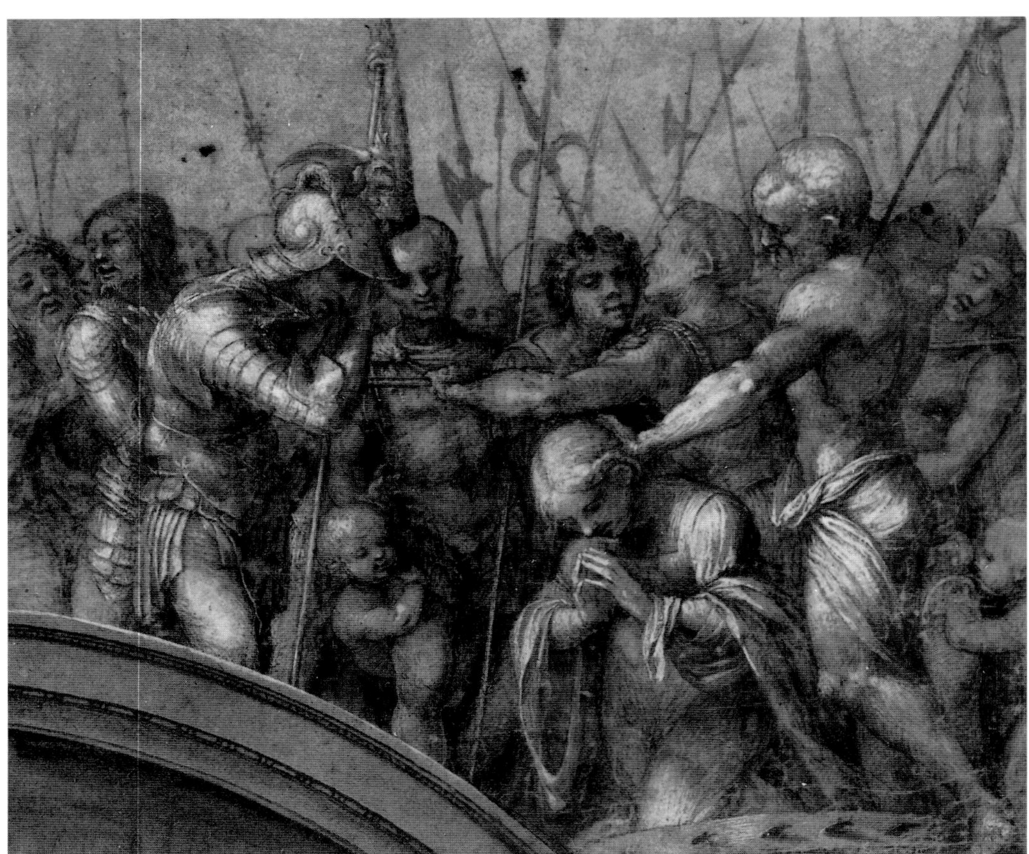

83 Lotto. *Martyrdom of St Catherine.* Pen with bistre wash over black chalk, squared in red chalk, 13.7 × 19.5 cm. Leipzig, Museum der bildenden Künste.

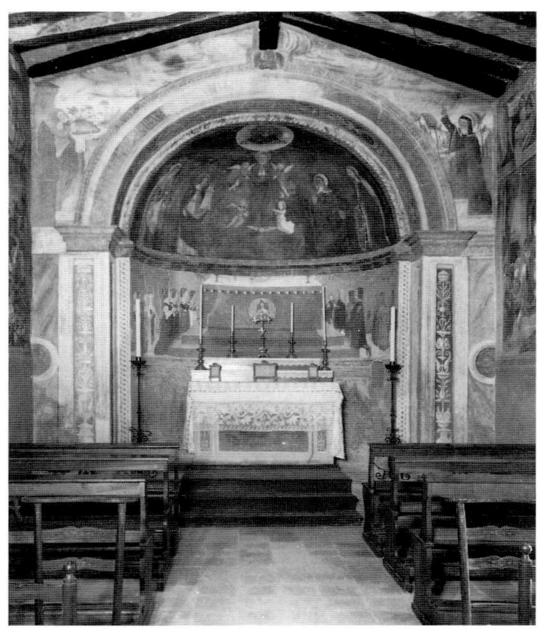

84 Trescore, Oratorio Suardi. View of east wall and apse with frescoes by anonymous Bergamask painter (*c.*1505).

85 (*facing page*) Trescore, Oratorio Suardi. View of interior looking west, with frescoes by Lotto (1523–4).

charitable institutions, including the Consorzio della Misericordia. He had built the oratory at Trescore as early as 1501–2, and immediately afterwards commissioned an unknown, modestly gifted local painter to decorate the east wall and apse (pl. 84). Represented in the apsidal half-dome is the Virgin of the Assumption flanked by the titular saints of the oratory, Barbara and Brigid of Ireland, together with Mary Magdalen and Catherine; while in the lower zone, Battista Suardi, his wife and numerous children kneel in adoration. In the spandrels of the arch Barbara and Brigid appear again, this time respectively to repel a thunderbolt and a shower of hail. This is the protective activity, so important for an agricultural community, with which each saint was particularly associated, and because of which each was chosen as a patron of the oratory.

Lotto's contribution was to paint the other three walls, and the areas between the thick wooden beams on the ceiling (pl. 85). Except for the framing arch of the apse and a dado moulding, the intimate and unpretentious interior of the oratory had no architectural articulation; and Lotto accordingly created two main horizontal zones on the south and west walls, the upper zone consisting of a frieze defined by fictive mouldings. In the frieze he painted a series of roundels, or illusionistic oculi, out of which project the alternating half-length figures of prophets and sybils. The south wall already had natural vertical subdivisions created by the entrance door and the two windows; and out of these Lotto created three principal fields, articulated at the sides by illusionistic Corinthian piers apparently supporting the frieze. In these fields he portrayed scenes from the life of St Brigid (pls 89, 90). Similar piers define two further fields on the west wall, which has been interrupted by a doorway only since the 1880s; and in these fields Lotto painted just one scene from the lives of each of the two, non-titular female saints represented in the apse, Catherine and Mary Magdalen (pl. 84).

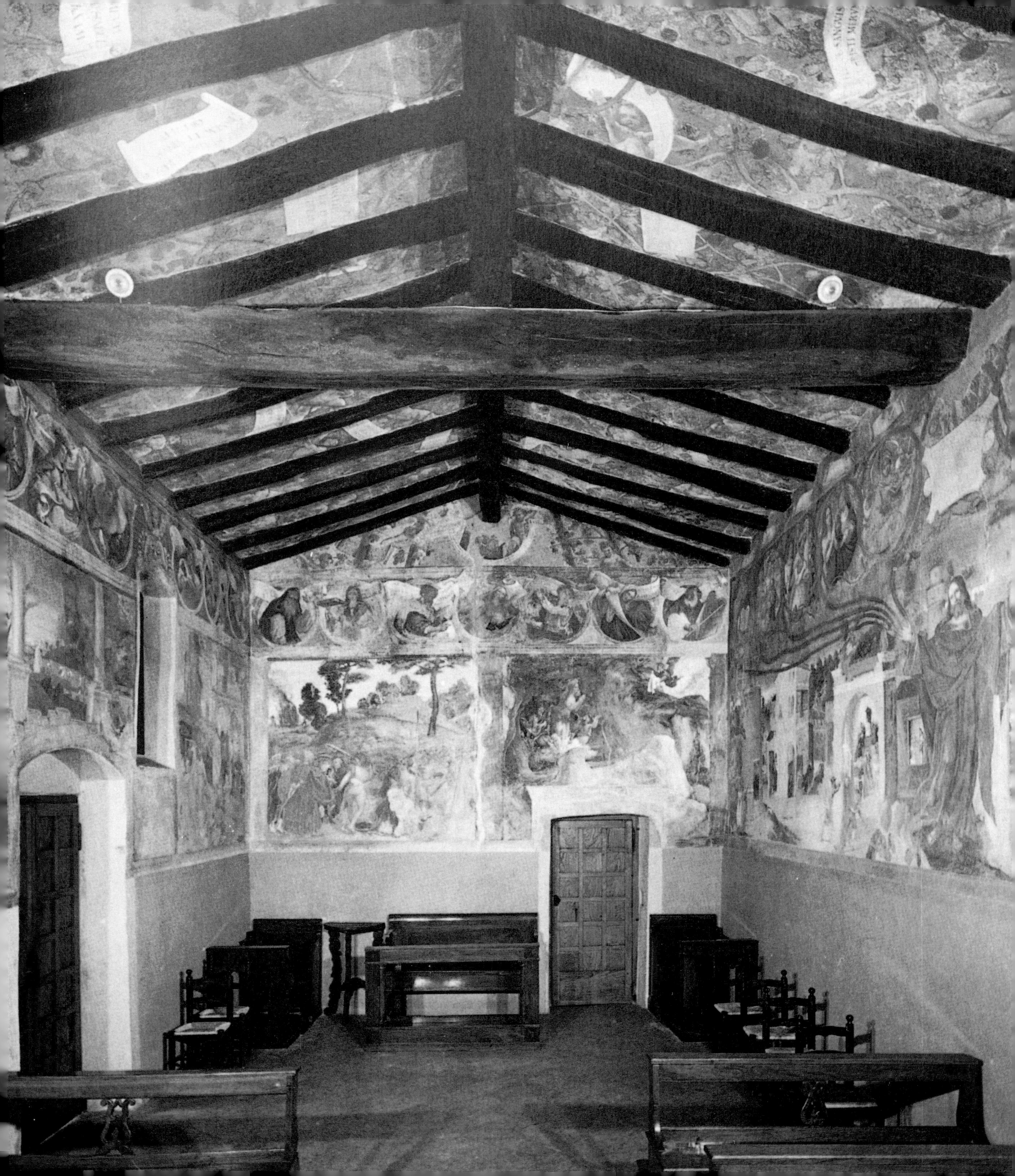

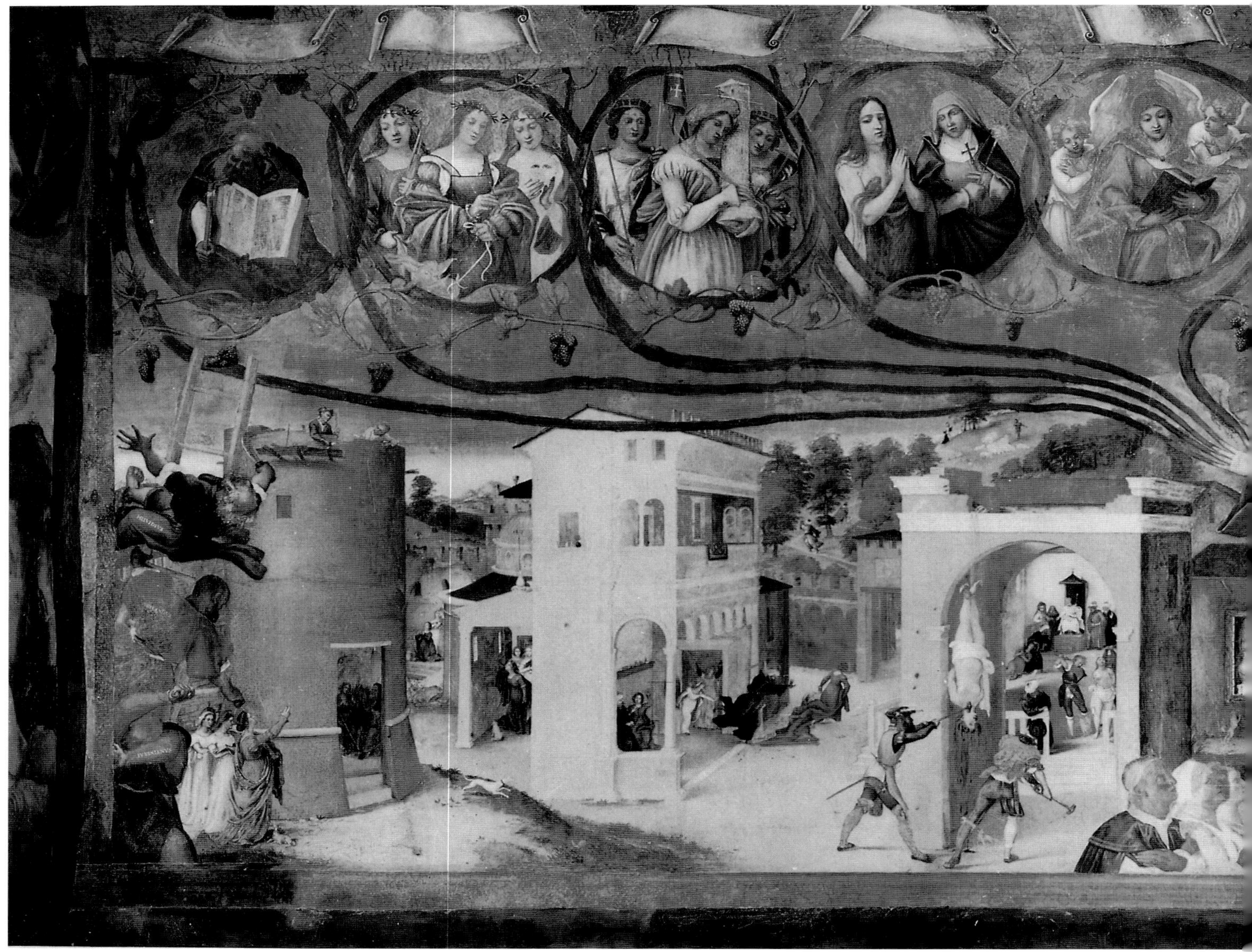

On the principal, north wall the painter abandoned his fictive architectural scheme (pl. 86). Instead, the entire wall is dominated by a monumental image of Christ as the Vine. Out of his outstretched fingers grow long branches that sprout vine-leaves and grapes, and which at the level of the frieze twist themselves into circular counterparts – this time containing saints – to the roundels containing prophets and sibyls on the south and west walls. The tendrils of the vine then spread upwards into the ceiling, and even across to the apex of the west wall, to provide a climbing frame for a band of playful putti. At either side on the north wall, heretics attempt to scale ladders that they have placed against the vine; but they are repulsed by St Jerome at the left and St Ambrose at the right, and most of them tumble to their fate into an abyss below the dado moulding. At the feet of Christ, the donor Battista Suardi, his wife and sister kneel in prayer. Beyond these large-scale foreground figures, in a background created by a mixture of landscape and buildings, the life of the other co-titular, St Barbara, unfolds in a sequence of numerous episodes.

As is particularly evident from the north wall, the iconographical programme of the

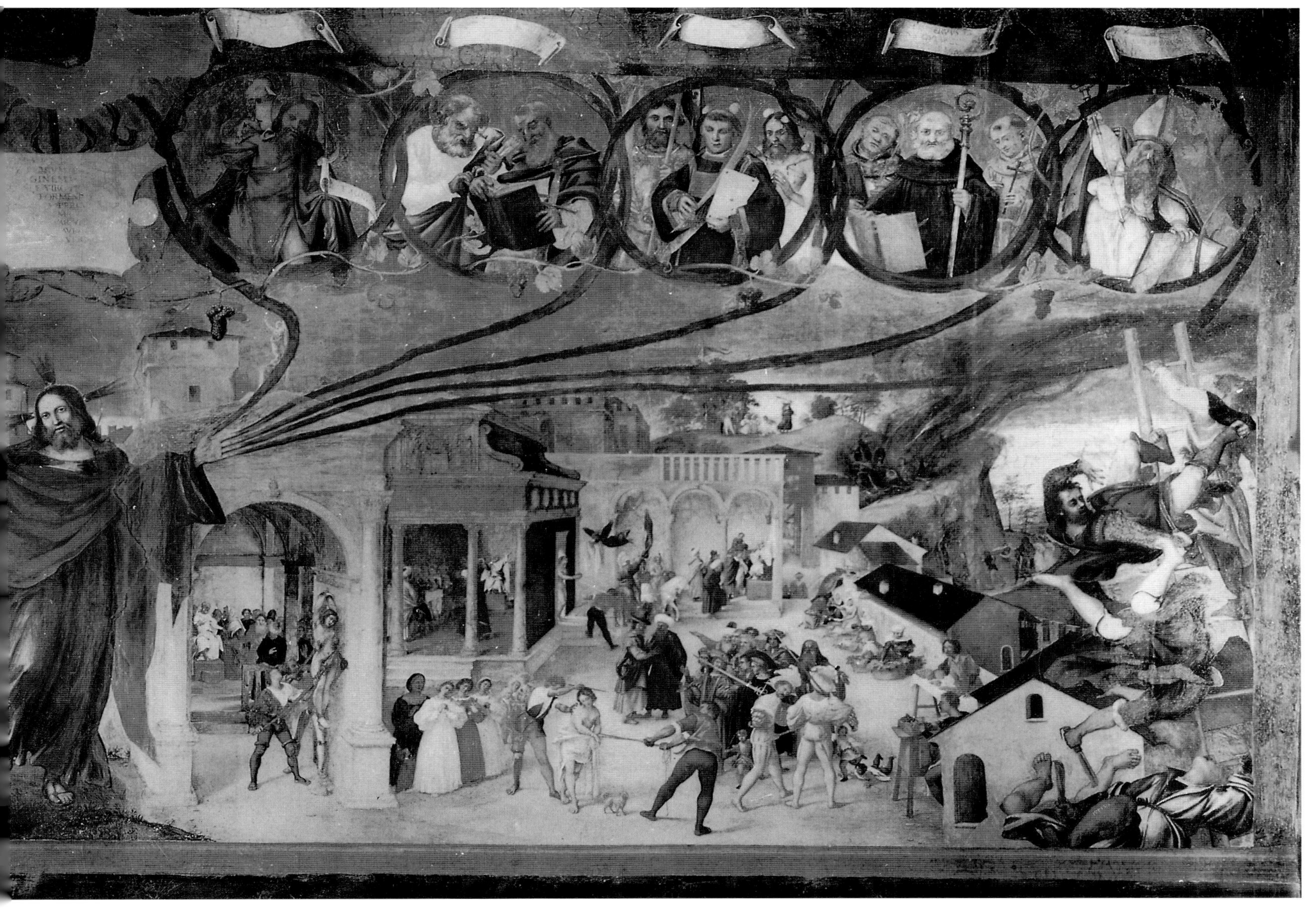

86 Trescore, Oratorio Suardi. View of north wall, with *Christ the Vine and Life of St Barbara* by Lotto (1523–4).

Oratorio Suardi comprises two distinct strands. The first is focused on the Christ as Vine image, which has its textual source in John 15: 5–6: 'I am the vine, and ye are the branches: he that abideth in me, and I in him, the same bringeth forth much fruit: for without me ye can do nothing. If a man abide not in me, he is cast forth as a branch and is withered; and men gather them, and cast them into the fire, and they are burned.' Apart, therefore for its obvious appropriateness to a country oratory surrounded by vineyards, this viticultural image was clearly designed to convey a message of grand theological import: that salvation is attainable only through Christ and the teachings of his Church; and that whoever rejects them is doomed to everlasting damnation. The unusual emphasis given to the tumbling heretics, all of whom carry identifying labels (Helvidius, Vigiliantius, Arianus, Sabellianus, etc.) suggests that the patron was much preoccupied by the growing threat of Protestantism; certainly, as a pious and learned Catholic, Suardi would have been well aware that several of the doctrines expounded by these early Christian heretics (including the denial of the perpetual virginity of Mary, and the opposition to the cult of the saints and to priestly

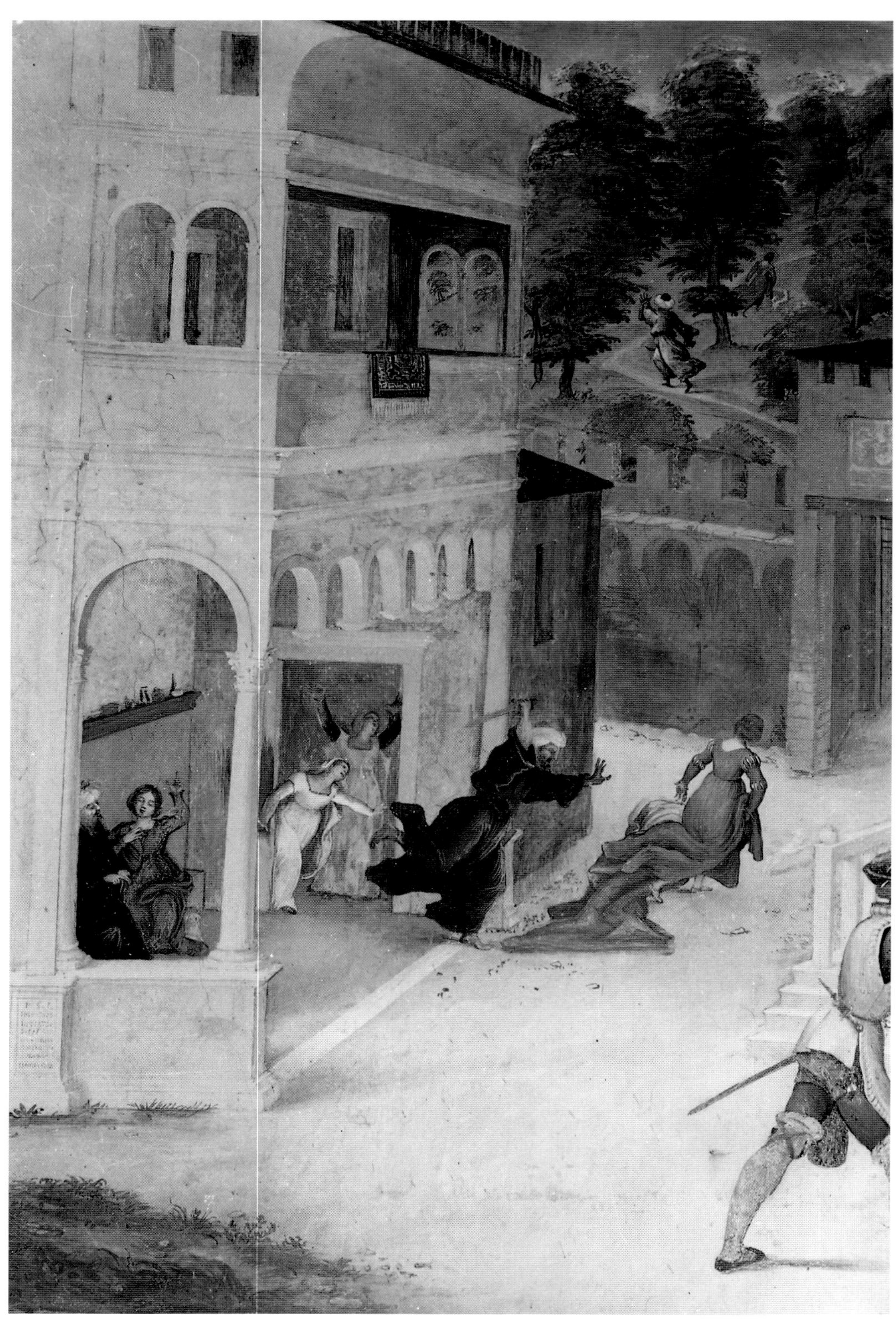

87 Lotto. Detail of *Life of St Barbara* (pl. 86).

88 (*facing page*) Lotto. Detail of *Life of St Barbara* (pl. 86).

celibacy) were in these very years being actively revived by Luther in Saxony and by Zwingli in not very distant Switzerland.[69]

The second main strand of the programme expands on the expression of devotion to the two titular saints of the oratory already adumbrated in the apse decoration of 1502. The scenes from the life of St Barbara follow the text of the *Golden Legend* (4

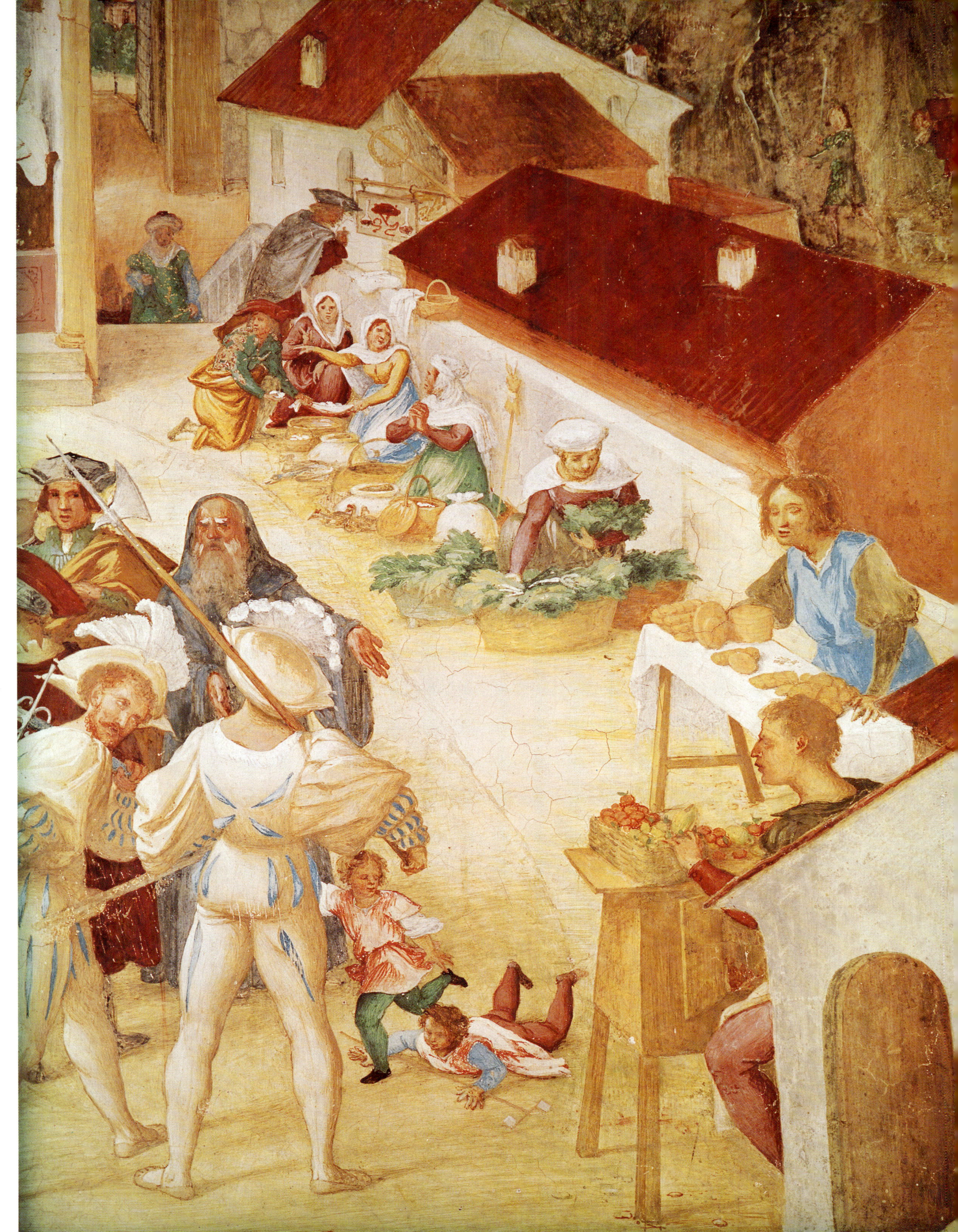

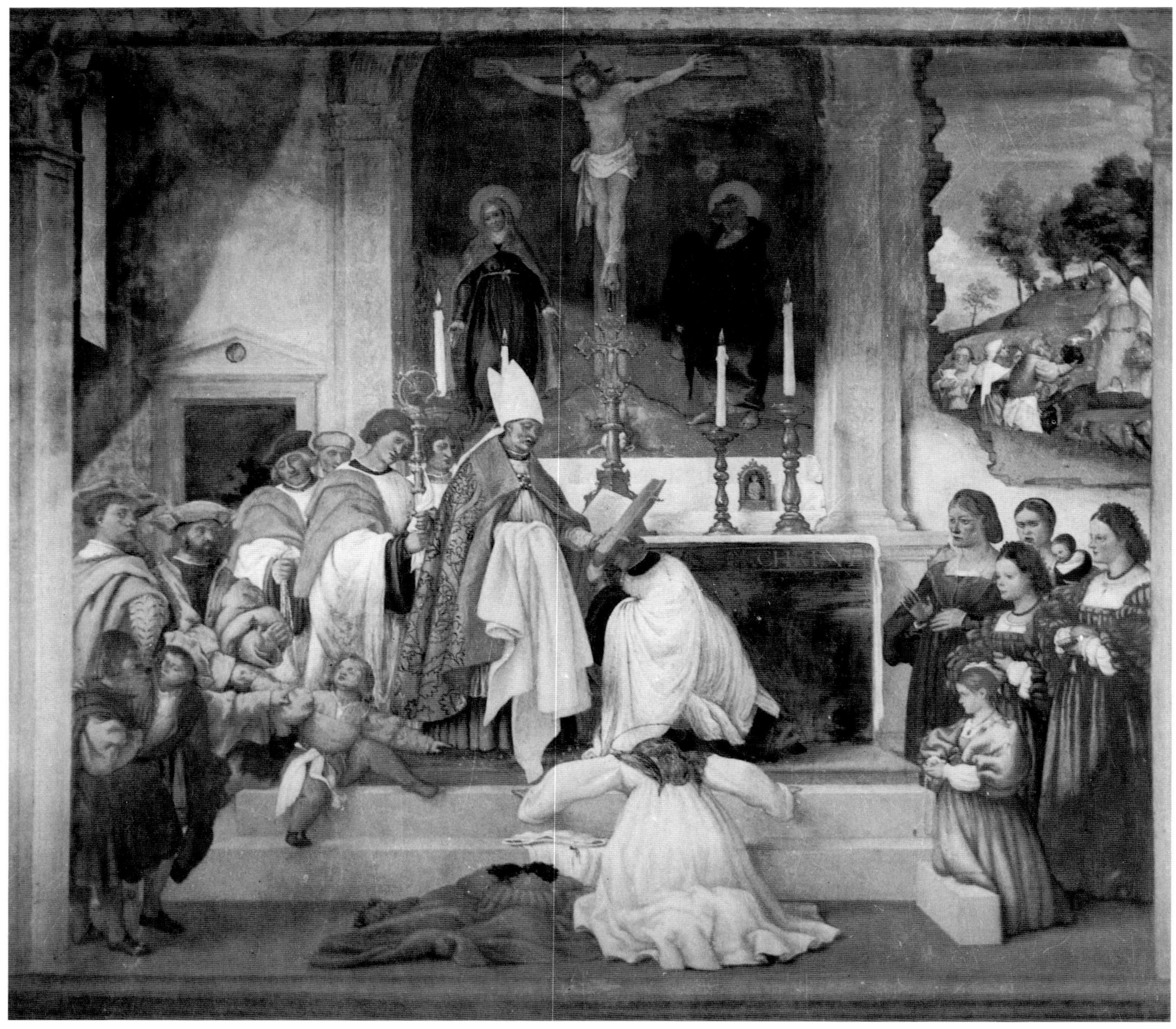

December), and show how the virtuous maiden was first imprisoned in a tower by her pagan father (at the far left); how she was converted to Christianity in his absence; how he chased her out of his house into the fields, and, having caught her, handed her over to the authorities to be tortured (pl. 87); how she was visited in prison by a vision of Christ (to the left of the Christ-Vine); how, after enduring further terrible tortures, she was beheaded by her own father (on the hill in the right background); and how, finally, he was killed by a thunderbolt from heaven. It was as a result of this final event that Barbara became associated with thunderbolts, and with protection from them.

Lotto's compositional structure and pictorial style are perfectly attuned to the naive piety of the legend. Barbara and her father, who appear repeatedly, are clearly recognisable by their costumes and accessories: she (before being stripped naked) by her blue robe and yellow cloak, and by her constant companion, a little white dog; he by his crimson gown, white turban and outlandish scimitar. It is their meandering progress

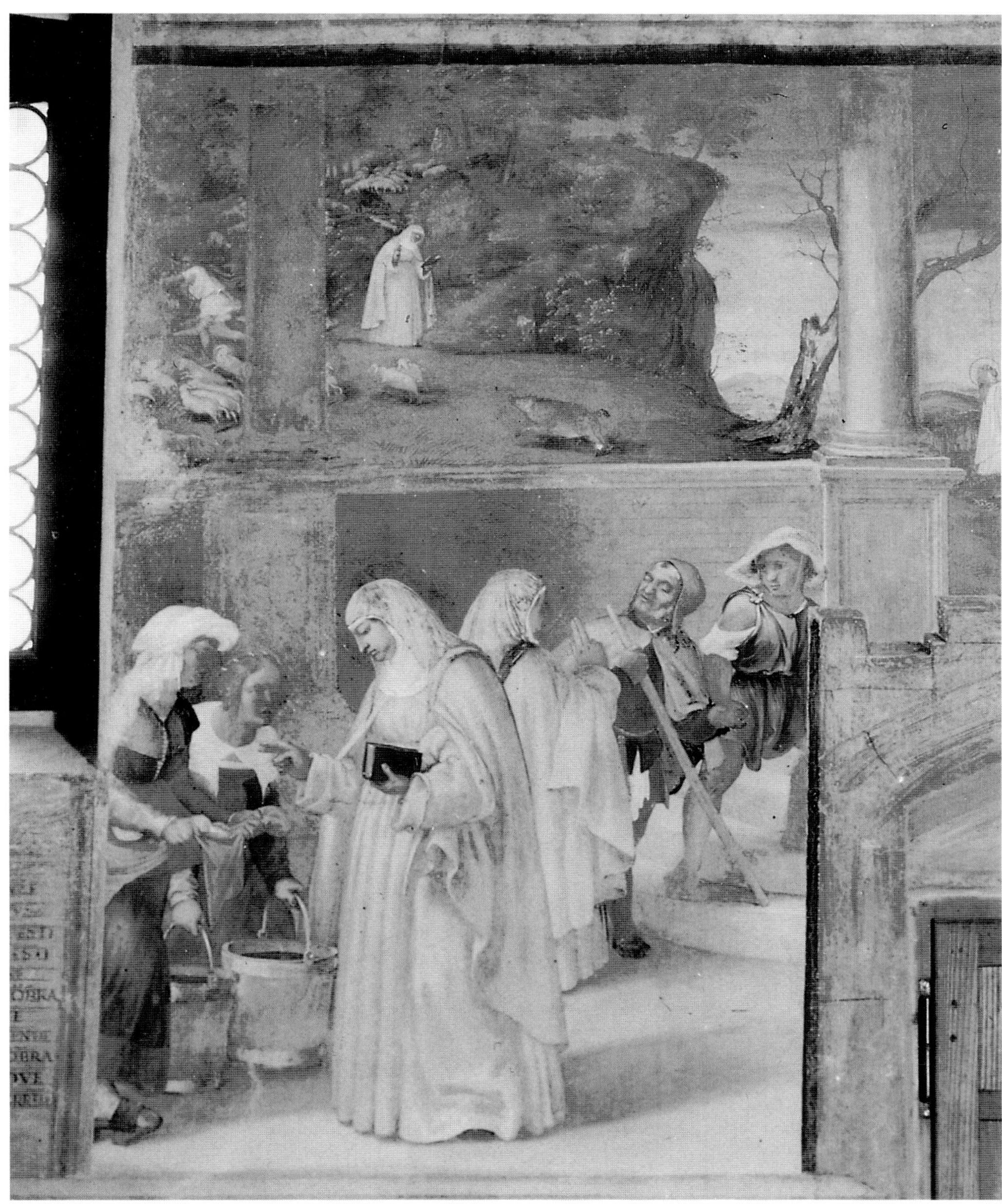

89 (*facing page*) Lotto. *Investiture of St Brigid* (1523–4). Trescore, Oratorio Suardi, detail of south wall.

90 (*right*) Lotto. *St Brigid ministering to the Poor and St Brigid saving the Sheep* (1523–4). Trescore, Oratorio Suardi, detail of south wall.

across the picture field, rather than any effect of spatial unity, that draws the various compositional elements together. The accumulation of picturesque and toy-like houses, loggias and piazzas do not, in fact, cohere perspectivally into a credible townscape, but serve as a series of self-sufficient little stages for the successive moments of the action. Although it has been pointed out that several of the poses adopted by the actors have sources in Raphael's Stanza d'Eliodoro,[68] their inelegant proportions and facial types, and their contemporary costumes, relate them rather to the world of the familar and everyday. Witnesses to the scene of Barbara's torture in the right foreground are street vendors with their stalls, selling fruit, bread, vegetables and poultry (pl. 88). Equally unheroic, but similarly contributing to the anecdotal vividness of the scene are the incongruous touches of humour: Barbara's undignified flight up the hillside in the left background (pl. 87); the children playing in the crowd in the right foreground. Finally, as is apparent from close inspection of the frescoes, the freshness and vividness of the narrative is further enhanced by the lightness of Lotto's palette, and the extraordinary freedom of his technique. Abandoning the carefully crafted, meticulous finish characteristic of his easel pictures, he applies the paint sketchily and suggestively, allowing the rapid strokes and touches of his brush to remain everywhere visible.

The story of the Irish nun Brigid–whose cult in Italy was much less widespread than that of Barbara–does not appear in the *Golden Legend*, and Lotto's scenes were drawn instead from a number of other compendia of saints' lives.[71] All relate to miracles, including the first large scene on the left, when Brigid's investiture as a nun is accompanied by the sprouting of flowers from the wooden altar-step, an event that is noticed only by the restless small boys. These, together with the adult laymen on the left and the group of women and girls on the right, represent portraits of the family of Maffeo Suardi, cousin to Battista and co-sponsor of the commission. Above the women the wall has opened to reveal a scene of St Brigid in her most popular guise: serving the needs of humble peasants by bringing them gifts of bread and milk (pl. 89). The theme of charity to the poor is extended across the following scenes in the foreground, while in the background the saint continues her good works in the woods and fields: first by saving a flock of sheep from a wild boar (pl. 90), and then by warding off a storm that threatens the harvest. As in the St Barbara scenes, these unsophisticated stories are told with an engaging simplicity, naturalness and humour.

To prove more onerous in the long run than any of his fresco cycles was a cyclical commission of a different kind: that to provide designs for sixty-eight wooden *intarsia* panels for the choir-screen and choirstalls of the church of Santa Maria Maggiore (pls 91, 92).[72] The painter received the commission in the early spring of 1524, probably while the Trescore frescoes were still in progress, but he had apparently made little headway before his departure for Venice in December 1525. Thereafter the commission was pursued at long range, with the painter sending his designs at regular intervals by courier, and requesting further advice from his employers by letter. Lotto did not finally complete his share of the project until 1531, close to the probable end of his first Venetian period; and although the resulting work may be regarded as a major masterpiece of its genre, the painter's letters reveal that over the years the commission was to cause him considerable frustration and trouble.

Santa Maria Maggiore, situated in the heart of the upper city, was probably the most important church in Bergamo, and it certainly represented a more popular focus for civic religion than did the neighbouring cathedral. Since 1449 the church had been administered by a devotional confraternity, the Consorzio della Misericordia, the members of which included some of the city's wealthiest and politically most influential citizens. After the restoration of Venetian rule in 1515, the governors of the Consorzio resolved to redecorate the choir and chancel with fitting splendour. Their first priority was to replace the previously modest high altarpiece with a more magnificent one in silver and gilt bronze, and in 1520 Lotto was one of number of local experts consulted on its design. Although progress on this project was slow (and was in fact to end in failure), the governors decided as soon as 1522 to complement it with the scarcely less ambitious *intarsia* project. As has been seen (p. 45), the installation of Lotto's Colleoni Martinengo altarpiece in the chancel of Santi Stefano e Domenico in 1516 was followed by the commission there for choirstalls inlaid with *intarsie*; and the craftsman responsible for that project, the Dominican friar Fra Damiano Zambelli, was the obvious candidate for the Santa Maria Maggiore commission as well. But on the advice of Lotto, the Consorzio chose instead Fra Damiano's fomer assistant, Giovanni Francesco Capoferri–advice for which the friar never apparently forgave him. Curiously, when a year later the governors came to select a painter to design Capoferri's *intarsie*, they at first decided to exclude Lotto as well, in favour of the otherwise completely unknown Nicolino Cabrini. But Cabrini suddenly died in January 1524,

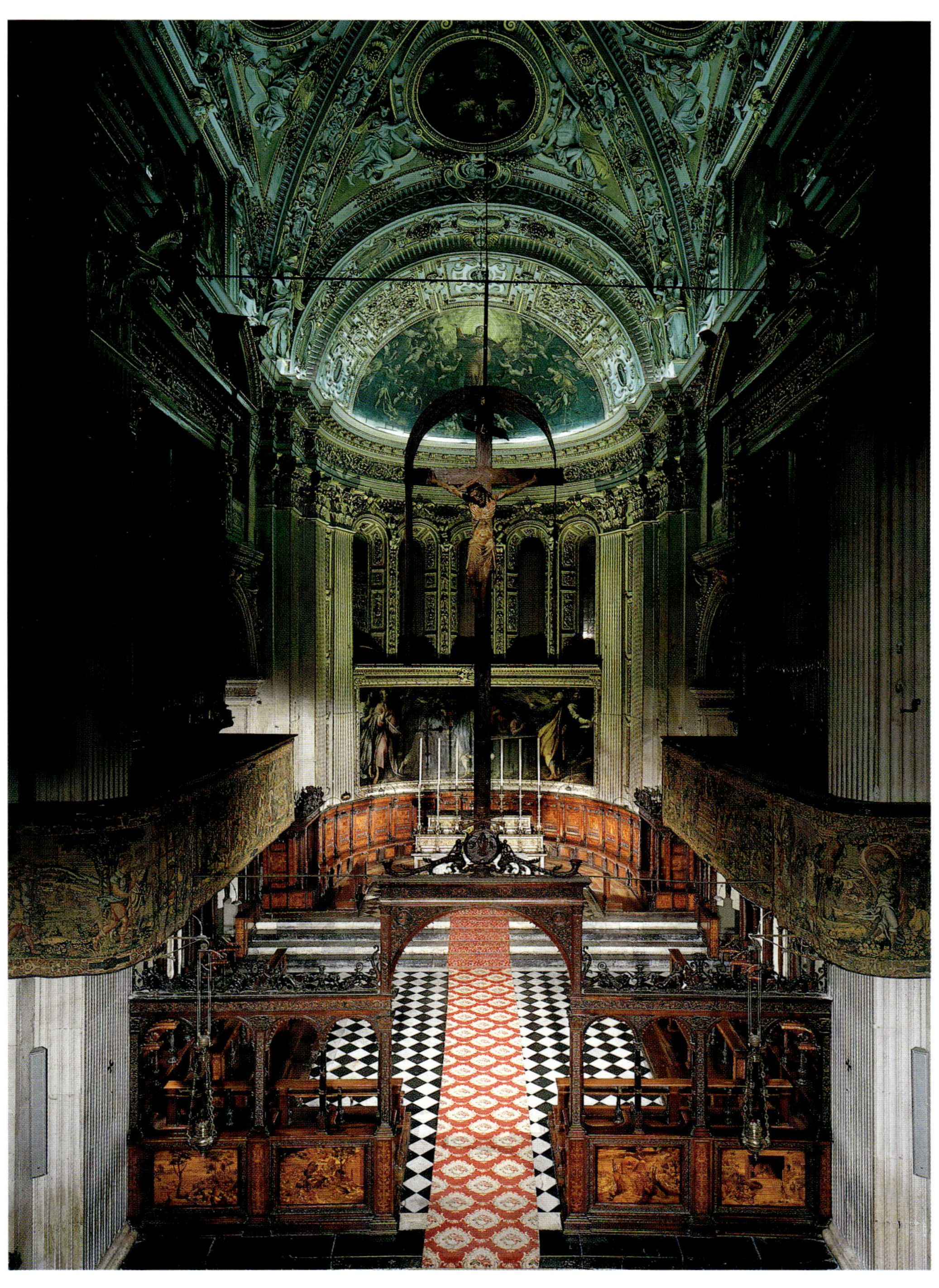

91 Bergamo, Santa Maria Maggiore. View of choir, with screen and stalls.

and in March the commission was transferred to Lotto. The iconographical programme of the cycle, which had been devised by an expert theologian, Fra Girolamo Terzi, consisted of scenes drawn from the Old Testament. Of these, four were to be on a larger scale than the others and were to adorn the exterior of the wooden choir-screen, while a further twenty-eight were to be inlaid into the stalls. In June of the same year, however, the cycle doubled in size when it was decided to equip each of the narrative scenes with a protective cover, likewise inlaid with an *intarsia.* The iconography of the covers, which is symbolic rather than narrative, was apparently devised not by Fra Girolamo, but by Lotto himself (below, pp. 90–92).

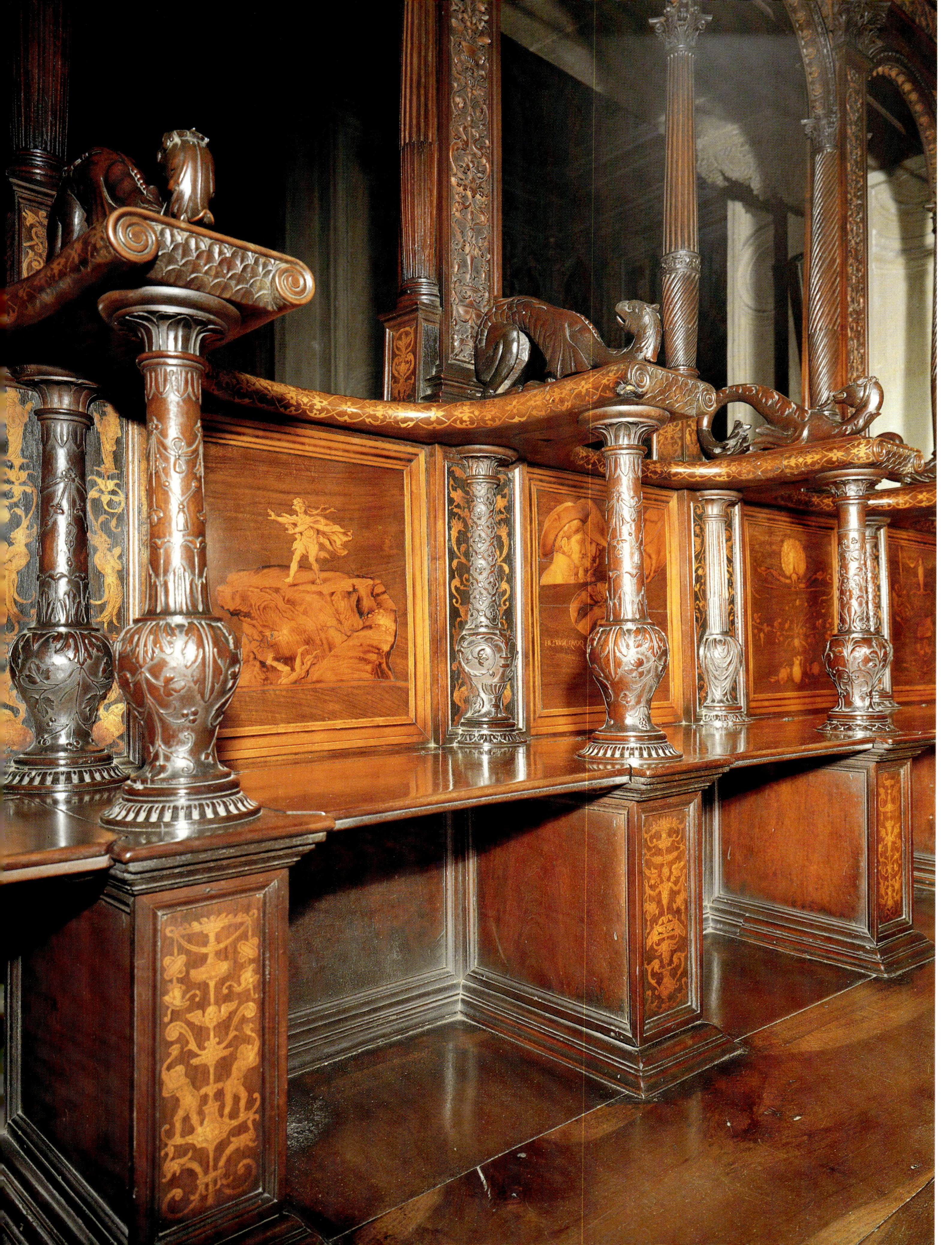

Lotto must have been exceptionally busy during the last two years of his Bergamo period. At the end of 1523, perhaps after having stopped work on the Trescore frescoes for the winter months, he paid a brief visit to the Marches to sign the contract to paint an altarpiece for the Confraternity of Santa Lucia in Jesi. As far as is known, this was the first time he had left the Bergamo area since his arrival there in 1513/14. But he obviously continued to maintain links with his earlier base of operations, probably again by way of the Cassotti and Marchetti families (p. 45). Indeed, in a document attached to the contract for the *St Lucy* altarpiece, Balsarino Marchetti – the probable donor of the Santo Spirito altarpiece of 1521 (p. 48) – and his brother Giovanni, then present with Lotto in Jesi, are named as the painter's legal representatives, or procurators.[73] Presumably Lotto's route to the Marches took him first overland to Venice, from where he would have continued by sea down the Adriatic coast; and it may well have been on this occasion that he began to think about returning to his native city to settle. Back in Bergamo in the spring of 1524, he undertook the commission for the Santa Maria Maggiore *intarsie*; later in the same year he completed the Trescore frescoes; and in 1525 he painted the two cycles for San Michele al Pozzo Bianco and San Giorgio in Credaro, and probably also the Ponteranica polyptych. In the same years he may also have undertaken the commission for another altarpiece for a country parish, this time for the village of Celana; but, like the *intarsia* designs, this was not executed on the spot, but was later sent from Venice (p. 93). In his letters to the Consorzio Lotto occasionally mentioned plans to revisit Bergamo (see Appendix A, p. 176), but, in fact, after his departure in December 1525 he was never to see the city again.

92 Bergamo, Santa Maria Maggiore. Choirstalls, with *intarsie* designed by Lotto.

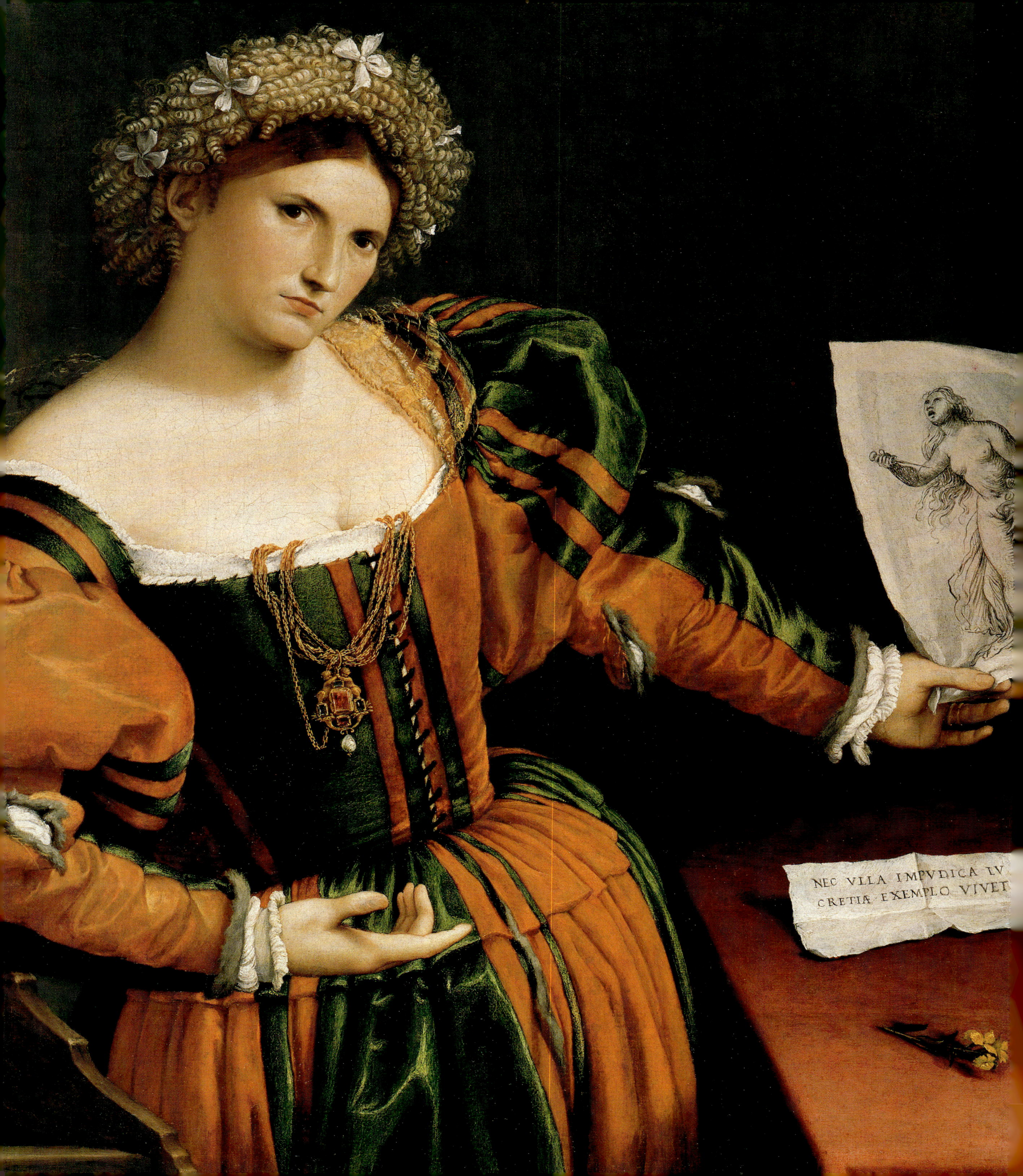
NEC VLLA IMPVDICA LV
CRETIÆ EXEMPLO VIVET

Chapter 4

VENICE 1525–1533

As emerges from his letters to the Consorzio della Misericordia, Lotto arrived back in the city of his birth on 20 December 1525, and began living in the Dominican convent of Santi Giovanni e Paolo. By this date he was aged well over forty, and probably planned to spend the rest of his life in Venice. Indeed, a central provision of the will made twenty-one years later was that he should be buried in the Dominican cemetery (p. 151). But the traditional supposition that—except for a brief spell in Treviso in the early 1540s—Lotto continued to live in Venice more or less uninterruptedly until 1549, has had to be revised in recent years by growing evidence that for most of the 1530s he was in the Marches. It seems, then, that his first and longest period of residence in Venice lasted no more than seven years, and ended in the spring of 1533.

Besides being one of the largest cities in the Christian world and the capital of an extensive empire, Venice was already internationally famous for its school of painting. Since Lotto's years as an apprentice in the 1490s the artistic scene had changed dramatically. Alvise Vivarini, Giovanni Bellini, Cima and the other members of the fifteenth-century generation were all dead; and so, too, was the short-lived Giorgione. The dominant figure was now Lotto's probably slightly younger contemporary Titian, whose unrivalled supremacy as a painter of large-scale public commissions was displayed above all by the monumental *Assunta*, installed above the high altar of the church of the Frari in 1518 (pl. 94). But there were a number of other highly talented and productive painters working in Venice, chief among whom were Palma Vecchio (who, however, was to die prematurely in 1528, not long after Lotto's return), Savoldo, Bonifacio de' Pitati and Paris Bordone. Then in 1527 the Friulian Pordenone, who previously had had an even more peripatetic career than Lotto, followed his example and also settled in Venice.

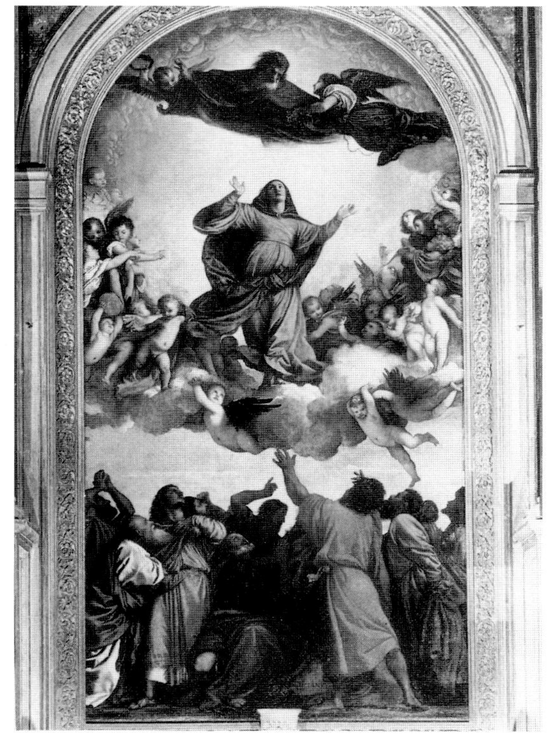

94 Titian. *Assumption of the Virgin* (*L'Assunta*) (*c.*1515–18). Venice, Santa Maria Gloriosa dei Frari.

93 (*facing page*) Detail of pl. 118.

Critics have sometimes expressed surprise that having reached middle age, Lotto should have chosen to abandon Bergamo, where he had apparently been happy and successful, for the keenly competitive artistic world of Venice, where by now he would have been a virtual stranger. But whereas Bergamo was situated on the periphery of the Venetian empire, at the edge of the Alpine foothills, Venice occupied the centre of highly developed system of communications by both land and sea. Lotto cannot have been indifferent to the prospect of receiving attractive commissions from within metropolitan Venice. But, perhaps even more importantly, Venice served an ideal base for continuing contacts with both Bergamo in the west and the Marches in the south. At the time of his return, in fact, he held at least one major commission from each of the two centres, and during the following seven years he undertook several more for both of them.

In addition, however, to these general considerations of business advantage, there is reason to suppose that Lotto's decision to return was clinched by the offer of one important Venetian commission in particular: that to paint an altarpiece in honour of St Antoninus, Archbishop of Florence, for the transept of Santi Giovanni e Paolo. This

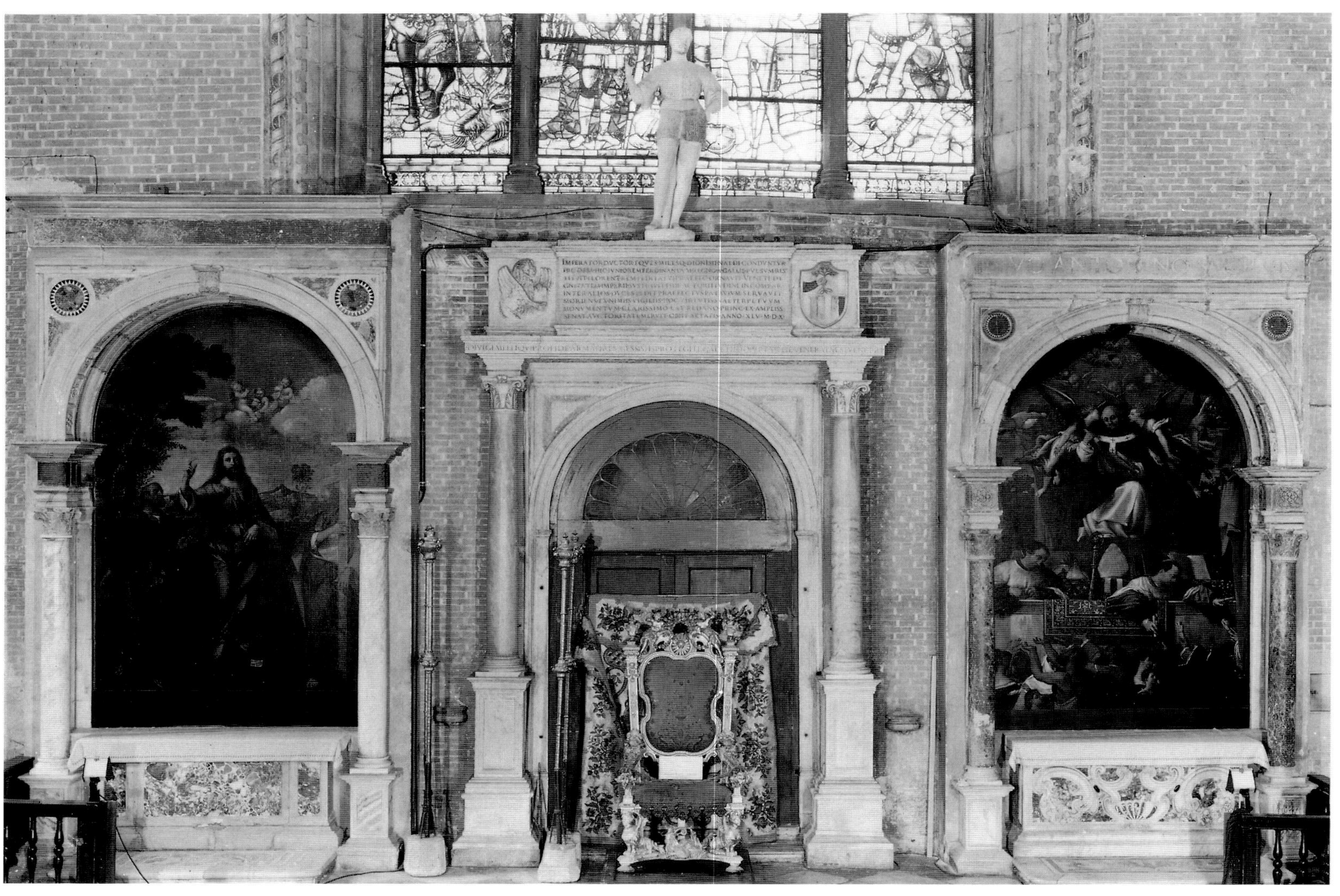

95 Venice, Santi Giovanni e Paolo. View of south transept with Rocco Marconi's *Christ with Sts Peter and Andrew* (*c.*1526–8) and Lotto's *St Antoninus* altarpiece (pl. 141).

supposition is somewhat contentious, since the completed altarpiece is dated 1542 (pl. 141), and Lotto's account-book shows that he did not begin the task of painting it until December 1540, a full fifteen years after his return from Bergamo.[1] But in favour of the supposition, three very suggestive items of circumstantial evidence have been advanced. First, Antoninus was canonised in May 1523, and to celebrate this elevation of a member of the Dominican order to the ranks of the saints, a temporary altar dedicated to him was erected in Santi Giovanni e Paolo in January 1526. Plans for a permanent altar and altarpiece are very likely, therefore, to have been laid at this time. Second, unless Lotto was already involved in these plans, it is hard to explain why he immediately took up residence in the convent on arrival in Venice a month earlier. It is significant in this connection that his earlier residence at San Domenico in Recanati (p. 27), and his later one at San Francesco alle Scale in Ancona (p. 158), were both directly related to commissions for altarpieces for the respective churches. Third, the reference in the account-book of 8 December 1540 speaks of transporting to his workshop an existing canvas, already nailed to its stretcher, and of restretching and renailing it before painting.[2] To these three arguments a fourth may be added: in its dimensions and in the architectural style of its stone frame, Lotto's altarpiece closely matches those of Rocco Marconi's *Christ with Sts Peter and Andrew*, which is placed in a pendant position on the other side of the doorway to the convent cemetery (pl. 95).

The latter work is undated, but it is universally accepted as a late work by the painter, who was dead by 1529;[3] and the pre-Sansovinesque style of the two frames would also be consistent with a date of about 1526–8. It would appear, then, that the two altarpieces were commissioned as a pair in 1525/6, and that the framed *Christ with Saints* and the *St Antoninus* frame were punctually installed soon afterwards; but that for some reason, the execution of Lotto's painting became severely delayed. The reason is surely connected with the fact that in July 1526 Lotto was forced to move out of the convent after a quarrel (see below). The commission would then have lain dormant during the painter's absence in the Marches in the 1530s, and would have been revived on his second return to Venice in 1539/40 (p. 137).

For six of the seven years of his residence in Venice Lotto worked continuously on the sixty-eight designs for the *intarsie* for Santa Maria Maggiore. Indeed, it was the completion of this major project in 1531 that finally liberated him from all his commitments in Bergamo, and enabled him to travel to the Marches in the following year. The progress of the commission is documented in detail by the sequence of letters written by Lotto either directly to the governors of the Consorzio della Misericordia, or to their representative, the notary Girolamo San Pellegrino (p. 2).[4] As is evident from just one of these letters, dated 18 July 1526 (Appendix A, pp. 176–7), they are very revealing not only about the practicalities of the commission, but also about Lotto's personal circumstances and state of mind. In the letter he mentions that he is currently engaged on the designs for one large panel (the *Crossing of the Red Sea*) and two smaller ones for the pilasters of the screen, and asks to receive details of the further scenes he is to represent. He is very insistent – here and throughout his correspondence – that his cartoons be looked after carefully by the craftsmen, and be returned to him after use. He stresses his commitment to the success of the enterprise by telling how he has publicised the commission for the high altarpiece throughout Venice, and by proposing that he visit Bergamo in the near future, to check progress on the execution and to help iron out practical problems. He complains that he has been badly treated by the governors, and seeks to enlist the notary's assistance in persuading them to alter some of the clauses in the contract. He expresses irritation with the *intarsiatore* Capoferri – whom, however, he says he loves dearly and will forgive – for not responding to his letters. By contrast, he expresses real anger with Fra Damiano Zambelli, the Dominican *intarsiatore* who apparently blamed him for his exclusion from the commission (p. 82), and whom Lotto now accused of stirring up trouble for him at Santi Giovanni e Paolo, and of forcing him to move out of his room in the convent. He implicitly compares what he calls Fra Damiano's ignorance and lack of true religion with the seriousness of his own Christian commitment ('perché sono di natura et religion christiana').

Although some critics have surely gone too far in interpreting this last phrase as an expression of sympathy with Protestantism,[5] other passages in Lotto's letters suggest that he did indeed have a direct and personal interest in the content of the *intarsie*, and a confidence in his own independent judgement in religious matters. On 9 May 1527, for example, he wrote suggesting that the story of Joshua and the stilling of the sun (Josh. 10: 12–13) would be suitable for inclusion, since he had recently heard a sermon on the subject; and even more tellingly, on 10 February 1528 he ventured to criticise the programme devised by the Consorzio's theological expert, Fra Girolamo Terzi, adding that certain worthy theologians and preachers in Venice agreed with him.[6] By this time Lotto was clearly becoming disillusioned with the commission. His complaints about the dilatoriness of the governors' responses to his queries, and of their payments to him, become increasingly insistent; and in the same letter of February 1528, and again in May of the following year, he speaks of his troubled state of mind.[7] It may have been this souring of relations between the painter and his employers that made him decide not, after all, to revisit Bergamo to inspect progress.

Despite Lotto's eventual disillusionment, the *intarsie* themselves bear witness to the spirit of fertile inventiveness, in both form and iconography, with which he approached the commission. The *David and Goliath*, for example (pl. 96), one of the four large panels destined for the exterior of the choir-screen (pl. 91) and sent with the letter of 18 July 1526, has little in common with the static, perspectivally conceived designs hitherto traditional for Renaissance *intarsie*. Instead, it has all the narrative liveliness of the Trescore frescoes, and similarly combines three different types of setting, from the landscape at the left, to the interior in the centre and to the townscape at the right. As at Trescore, the protagonist of the story reappears repeatedly as the story unfolds from left to right (1 Sam. 17–18). Thus, in the left background the shepherd-boy David protects his father's sheep from a lion and a bear; further forwards, he is sent by Jesse to Saul's camp; in the throne-room in the centre he kneels before the king, and undertakes to fight Goliath; in the centre foreground he slays Goliath with a stone from his sling; in the left foreground he decapitates the dead giant; and finally, in the right background he carries Goliath's head to the city, where he is met by singing, dancing and rejoicing women. Again as at Trescore, spatial ambivalence does not compromise the perfect narrative clarity, which is achieved partly through expressive pose and gesture, and partly through the distribution of light and shade. Indeed, despite the intransigent nature of *intarsia*, Lotto and Capoferri succeeded in introducing unprecedented luministic and pictorial effects into the medium, as is apparent above all in the subtle play of light and penumbra in Saul's throne-room.

In contrast to the narrative character of the Old Testament scenes, the imagery of their covers is essentially symbolic, and was apparently devised by Lotto himself on the basis of a long-held interest in the language of *imprese* and in hieroglyphic lore.[8] This interest, which had its roots in his early experience of the humanistic culture of Treviso, had resurfaced during Lotto's years in Bergamo, as has already been seen in works such as the Colleoni Martinengo altarpiece (pp. 45–6) and the *Marsilio* portrait (p. 70). According to the contract for the work, the covers were 'to correspond in meaning to the panels over which they will be respectively placed';[9] in other words, as in the early *Rossi* portrait (p. 11), the images on the covers were to consist of *imprese* that would provide an allegorical commentary on the more factually descriptive narratives below, in a way that would explicate their inner meaning. The precise significance of the visual symbols devised by Lotto for this purpose is often now difficult to interpret; indeed, there is evidence that even then, his employers had some difficulty in deciphering them. This emerges from a letter of 10 February 1528, in which he attempts to clarify his approach by explaining, 'As for the designs of the covers you should know that since they do not follow any written programme, they must be interpreted by the imagination'.[10] In other words, the key is not to be found in any pre-existing source; rather, the artist wants his viewers to use their ingenuity to work out the hidden meaning for themselves.

In the case of many of the covers, including that of the *David and Goliath* (pl. 97), the meaning is relatively accessible. Like the hanging mobiles in the Colleoni Martinengo altarpiece, the symbolic objects in the upper part of the composition are suspended from ribbons in a flat, symmetrical arrangement recalling that of the pseudo-hieroglyphs of the *Hypnerotomachia* (pl. 48). At the centre is David's sling, full of stones; above are two palms of victory; at the sides are tablets bearing the inscription 'MAXI / MI / CERTAMINIS / VICTO / RIA' ('Victory in the very great struggle'). On a base below are grouped Goliath's weapons, in an only slightly less symmetrical arrangement: his cuirass, helmet, sword, spear and shield. The imagery of the cover thus constitutes a distillation of the essence of the story beneath, using objects selected according to the principle of synecdoche. In this condensed form, the story loses the character of a mere historical episode and acquires one of a universal truth.

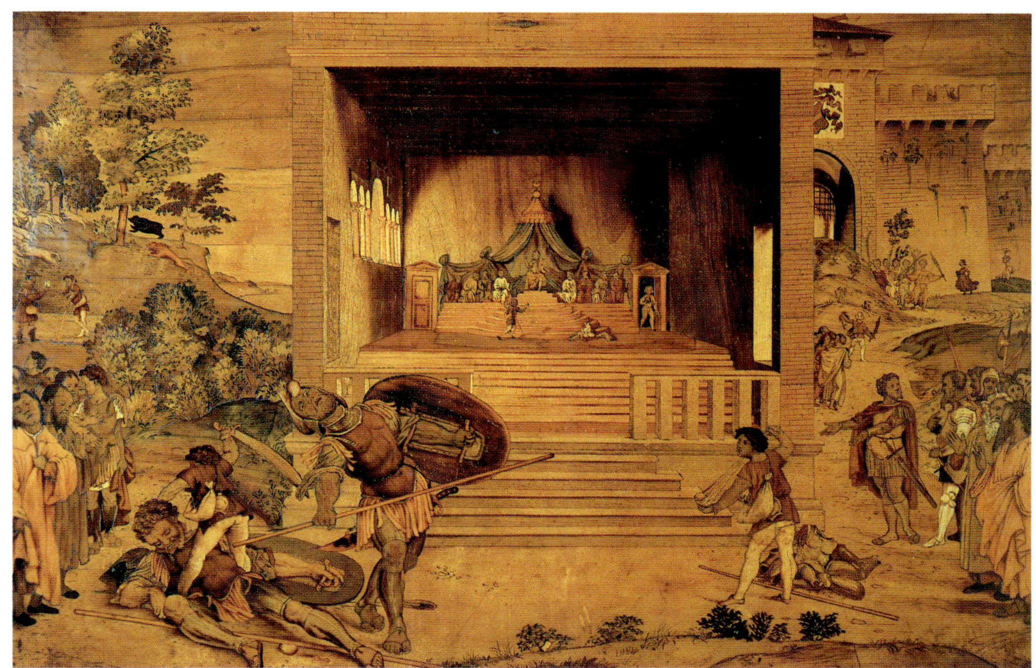

96 Giovanni Francesco Capoferri (after a design by Lotto). *David and Goliath* (1526–7). *Intarsia*, 67.5 × 100.5 cm. Bergamo, Santa Maria Maggiore.

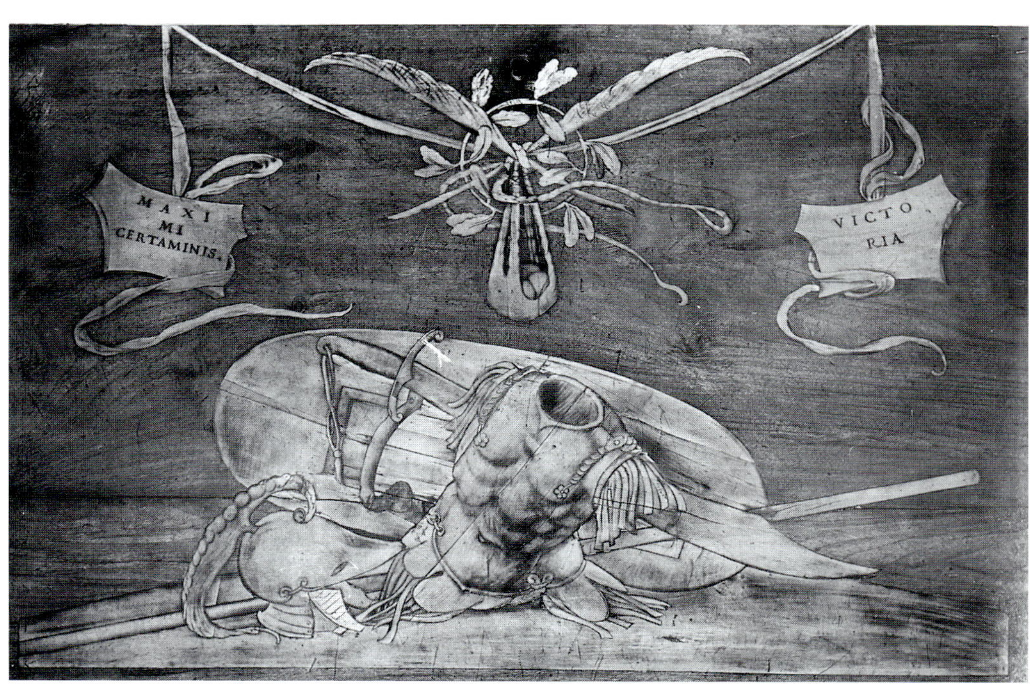

97 Giovanni Francesco Capoferri (after a design by Lotto). Cover to *David and Goliath* (1527–30). *Intarsia*, 70 × 109 cm. Bergamo, Santa Maria Maggiore.

The symbols devised by Lotto for some of the other covers are less transparent. In the cover to *David mourning Absolom*, for example (pl. 98), the meaning of the clasped hands and the inscription 'HEV FILI MI' ('Alas, o my son'–an abbreviation of David's words in 2 Sam. 18:33 and 19:4) are clear enough; and so, too, is the meaning of the three arrows at the bottom, which obviously refer to the three darts ('lanceas') with which Joab killed Absolom as he hung trapped in the oak-tree (18:14). Less clear, on the other hand, are the symbolic objects–again suspended symmetrically from a ribbon–in the upper part of the composition. But as has been seen, Lotto had already employed a yoke to signify marriage or subjugation (p. 70; p. 46); and in the present

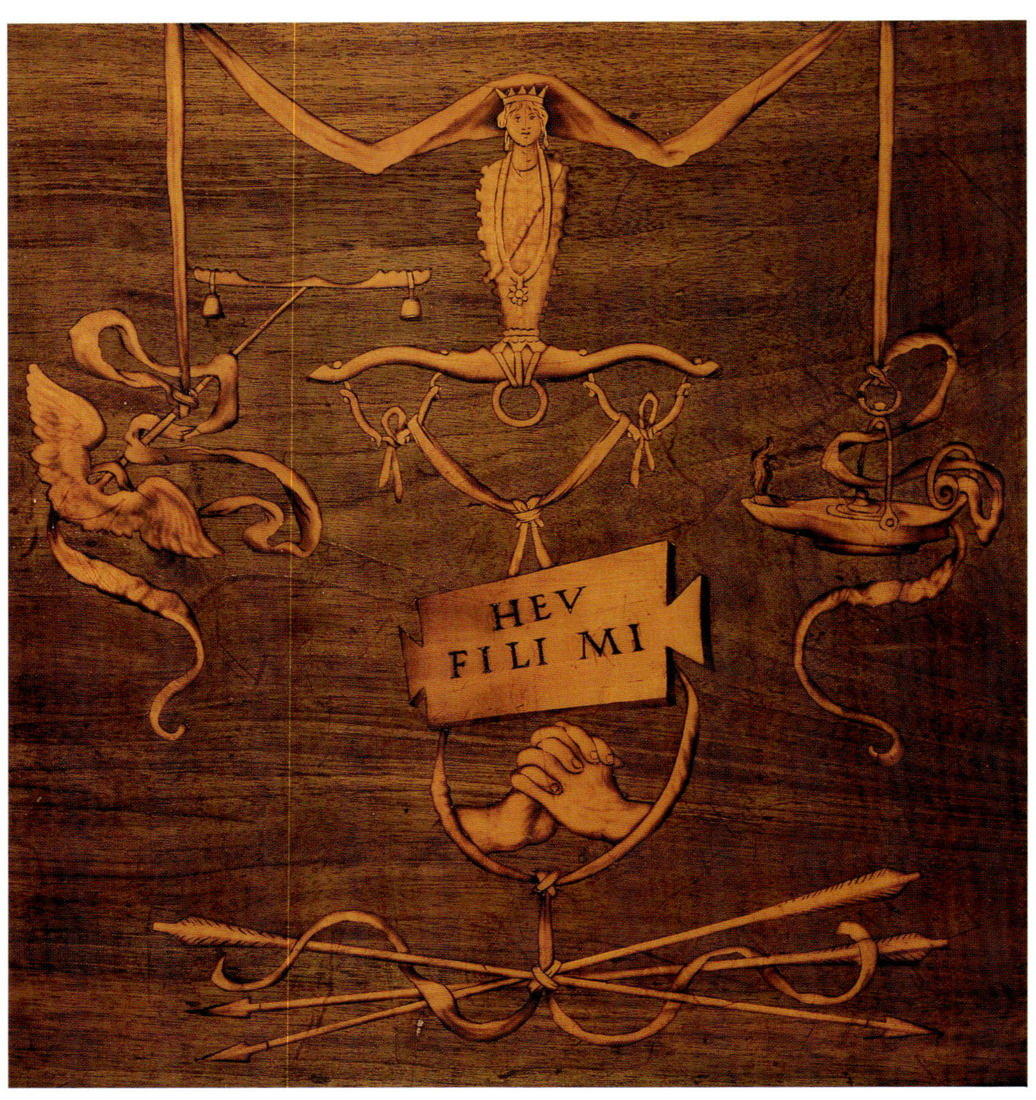

98 Giovanni Francesco Capoferri (after a design by Lotto). Cover to *David mourning Absolom* (1527–30). *Intarsia*, 43 × 40 cm. Bergamo, Santa Maria Maggiore.

context, where it is combined with a many-breasted idol, it probably refers to David's sinful enthralment and subsequent marriage to Bathsheba, for which God punished him with the rebellion and death of his son.[11] The significance of the flickering lamp on the right is even less clear, but perhaps it refers, as in the early portrait *Young Man with a Lamp* (pl. 26), to the uncertainty and transience of human life (p. 21). Once again, therefore, Lotto is seeking to provide the ingenious viewer with a crystallisation of the Old Testament story, retold in an invented language of hieroglyphs. Contrary, however, to much of current critical opinion,[12] the use of this language need not imply that any typological reference is intended (comparing, for example, David with Christ); nor does it even necessarily imply any wider moralising message.

Lotto's letters to the Consorzio are disappointingly uninformative about the various other commissions with which he was involved during the first Venetian period. A letter dated 12 August 1527 contains a rare and laconic reference to 'two recently completed altarpieces with their frames', which he had just had sent off to the Marches;[13] these are probably identifiable with two commissions for Jesi, the *Virgin and Child with Sts Joseph and Jerome* dated 1526 (p. 94), and a *St John the Evangelist* triptych (the flanking *Annunciation* group of which is preserved in the Pinacoteca Civica).[14] Surprisingly, however, the painter makes no mention of a second triptych, dated 1531,

99 Lotto. *Assumption of the Virgin* (1527). Canvas, 250 × 210 cm. Celana, parish church.

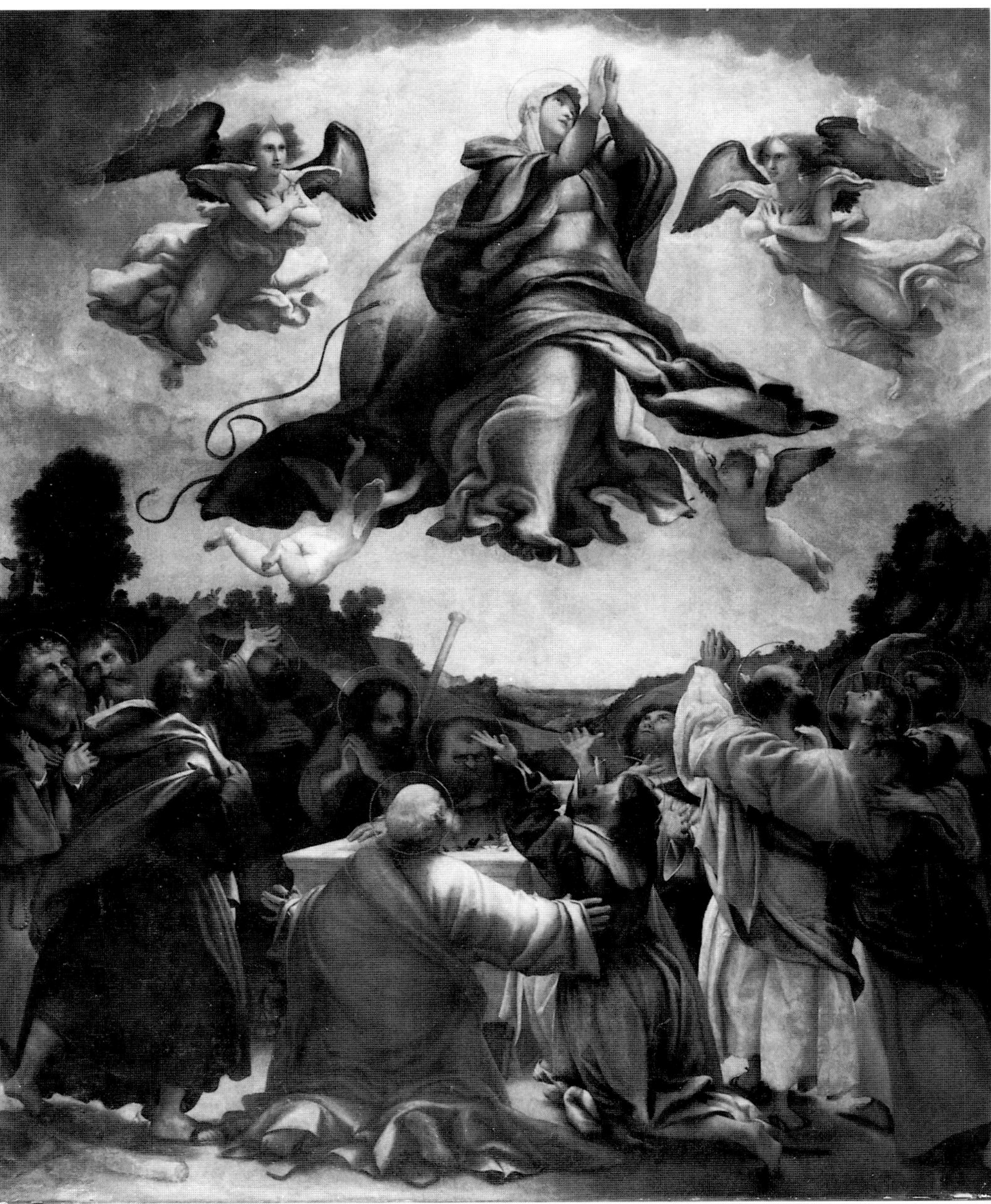

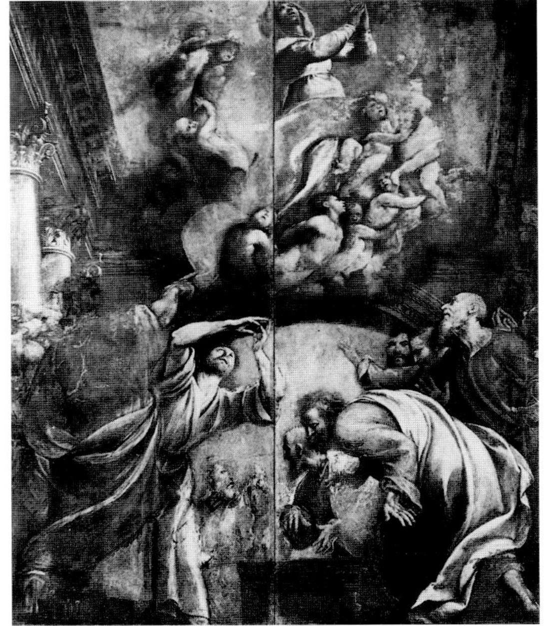

100 Pordenone. *Assumption of the Virgin* (1524). Spilimbergo, Duomo.

this time for the village of Castelplanio near Jesi (flanking saints in Berlin, Staatliche Museen);[15] and nor does he mention an important altarpiece sent from Venice to the province of Bergamo. This last work, an *Assumption of the Virgin*, which is signed and dated 1527 (pl. 99), remains in place above the main altar of Santa Maria Assunta in the village of Celana, to the west of the city of Bergamo, on a tributary of the river Adda.[16] Although a canvas of only moderate size, and so not particularly heavy, the completed picture would still have been sent from Venice most conveniently by water westwards up the Po from the Adriatic. The commission is undocumented, but it has been pointed out that Celana is in the district of Caprino, from which the family of Lotto's patron Balsarino Marchetti originated;[17] and it may be, therefore, that the painter received the commission fom the parish shortly before his departure from Venice on the recommendation of the Marchetti. In his representation of the subject–an obvious choice by his patrons, given the dedication of the church–Lotto lays greater emphasis than in his two earlier versions at Asolo (pl. 25) and in the Brera (pl. 40) on the episode of the *cintola*, the Virgin's girdle, which according to the *Golden Legend* she let fall as she ascended to heaven, as a way of giving tangible proof of the miracle to the incredulous Thomas, who arrived late at the scene. In the Brera predella panel, Thomas is clearly to be seen in the right background, hurrying to catch up with the other eleven apostles. In the Celana *Assumption* he is probably similarly to be recognised in the figure on the hill in the left background; but since this time all twelve apostles are present in the foreground, Thomas may also be the prominent figure on the left, looking and gesturing straight up to the falling girdle. Compared with the highly static Asolo *Assumption*, and even with the rhythmical fluency of the predella panel, the Celana *Assumption*, with its active poses and windswept draperies, is much more obviously dramatic in its treatment. Yet it is remarkable, despite Lotto's recent first-hand experience of Titian's *Assunta* (pl. 94), how independent he remains of that overwhelmingly authoritative prototype; and the twisting, foreshortened figure of the Virgin, with her arms uplifted in prayer, betrays a closer interest in the version of the subject painted by Pordenone in 1524 for the organ shutters of the cathedral of Spilimbergo (pl. 100).[18] Seasoned traveller as he was, Lotto is unlikely to have made an expedition to the Friuli just to see this work; but he may well have seen drawings. Where, however, Pordenone's compositional rhythms are broad and sweeping, those of Lotto wriggle restlessly; and in the frantic gesticulation of the figures, too, the altarpiece retains much more in common with certain of Lotto's own *intarsia* designs, such as the *Flood* of 1525. Typical, too, of Lotto himself is the mildly humorous treatment of the bespectacled apostle at the centre, who peers into the empty tomb as if searching for the departed Virgin.

Dating, according to a prominently placed inscription, to a year earlier than the Celana *Assumption* is the *Virgin and Child with Sts Joseph and Jerome, Sts Francis and Clare*, originally above a side-altar in the now destroyed church of San Francesco al Monte in Jesi (pl. 101).[19] In keeping with this destination is the presence in the lunette of St Francis himself, shown receiving the stigmata, together with his disciple St Clare displaying the monstrance; and, as has been mentioned, the cult of Joseph was likewise championed with particular enthusiasm by the Franciscan order, not just in Bergamo but throughout Italy. Both in its format, comprising a squarish main panel capped by a semicircular lunette, and in its modest scale, the altarpiece resembles that painted twenty years earlier for Santa Cristina al Tiverone (pl. 24). But although already by 1526 the format would have seemed old-fashioned by Venetian standards, Lotto succeeds in reanimating it by infusing the main panel with a highly original effect of human warmth and intimacy. Compared with the *St Christina* altarpiece, and also with the more recent *sacre conversazioni* for Bergamo (pls 47, 54, 55), the Jesi altarpiece shows a much reduced cast of saints, a minimum of honorific trappings, and an enlarged scale of the holy figures in relation to their surroundings, so that they acquire closer physical contact with one another. Thus the Virgin lays the fingers of her outstretched left hand on St Jerome's book, while the elderly Joseph tenderly, and with touching diffidence, raises his gnarled, carpenter's hands towards the happily responsive Christ Child. X-ray photographs show that the Virgin's head was originally posed more vertically, and centrally to the shell-niche behind;[20] and Lotto's decision to tilt it into a diagonal was clearly made for the sake of greater informality. The mood of humble devotion and domestic affection is heightened by Joseph's homely attributes: his rustic staff, and the sack and water-bottle on the throne-step. The solid, heavy-boned, peasant-like figures of both Joseph and Jerome are new to the art of Lotto; and together with the meandering, tubular folds of the Virgin's robe, they suggest that on his return to Venice he was particularly struck by his first contact with the art of Savoldo. As in the *St Christina* altarpiece, the daylit *sacra conversazione* below is complemented by a darker

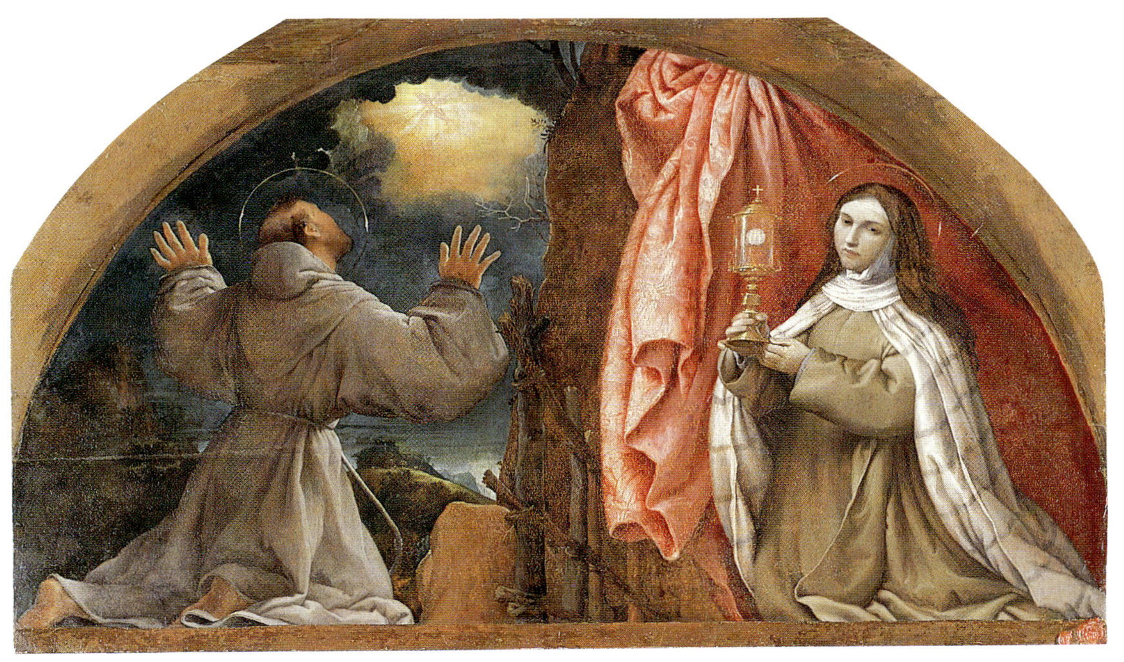

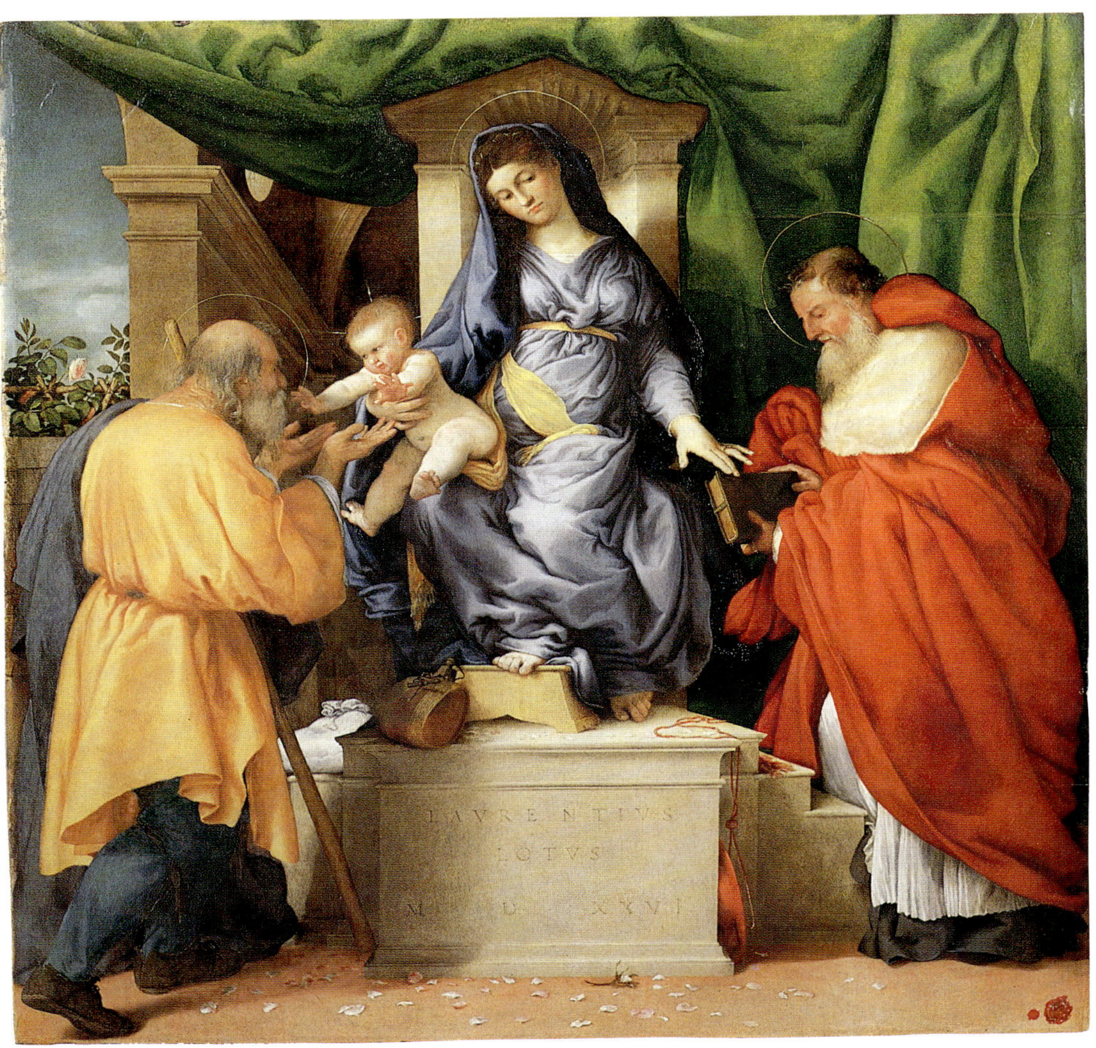

101 Lotto. *Virgin and Child with Sts Joseph and Jerome, Sts Francis and Clare* (1526). Two panels: 155 × 160 cm (main field); 85 × 160 cm (lunette). Jesi, Pinacoteca Civica.

scene in the lunette above; but in this case, the earlier neutral black background is replaced on the left by a mysteriously supernatural moonlit landscape, in which St Francis is seen receiving the stigmata from a radiant opening in the night sky. In his interest in unusual light effects, Lotto again has much in common with Savoldo; in the development of the nocturne in particular, however, it appears that it was Lotto who was the leader (p. 101).

More conventional in its format, although scarcely less original in its approach to altarpiece design, is the only altarpiece that Lotto painted for a Venetian church during this phase. This is the *St Nicholas in Glory*, still in its original stone frame above its original altar in the former Carmelite church of Santa Maria dei Carmini (pls 102, 103).[21] According to the early sources,[22] the picture once bore the date of 1529, two years later than the date of the commission recorded on the base of the frame. Also inscribed on the frame are the names of the two confraternity officers – Giovanni Battista Donati and Giorgio de' Mundis – who commissioned the altarpiece on behalf of the Scuola dei Mercanti, a confraternity of merchants dedicated to St Nicholas.[23] This explains the inclusion of the officers' name saints in the picture: John the Baptist, prominently seated on a cloud next to the central St Nicholas; and George, represented instead on a tiny scale, in the act of slaying the dragon, in the landscape at the bottom right. In his first public work for his native city, Lotto clearly made a special effort to conform to local traditions and tastes. As well as adopting the standard local format of the tall arched rectangle, he modified his pictorial style to resemble that of Titian, using a rather warmer palette than in his Bergamask works, with softer transitions and more pronounced contrasts of light and shade. Similarly, the composition is much more self-consciously grandiose than that of the Jesi altarpiece, and the saints are more idealised, with more rhetorical gestures and conventionally pious expressions. Yet Lotto remains unable to restrain his own individuality, and the juxtapositions of cool emerald greens, crimsons, oranges and violets in the draperies are characteristically dissonant. And although Titian had already provided authoritative prototypes for a compositional formula in which the upper part of the arched field is occupied by holy figures enthroned on clouds, he was always to retain large-scale saints in the lower foreground. Lotto, by contrast, combines his airborne saints with a panoramic landscape below dotted with tiny figures, in a way that looks back to his own *St Vincent Ferrer* fresco of the previous decade (pl. 43), and beyond that to prints by Dürer, such as the *St Michael and the Dragon* (pl. 42).[24] The landscape itself, which was singled out for admiring mention by Vasari (p. 4), is strongly Netherlandish in character, and seems to have been inspired by works by painters such as Patinir and Scorel, several of which are known to have existed in Venetian collections.[25] Lotto's highly poetic evocation of a passing sea-storm, which is still dark and oppressive on the right but which has cleared to leave brightness on the horizon at the left, is eloquently expressive of the merchants' devotion to St Nicholas as a protector of their cargoes on the open seas.

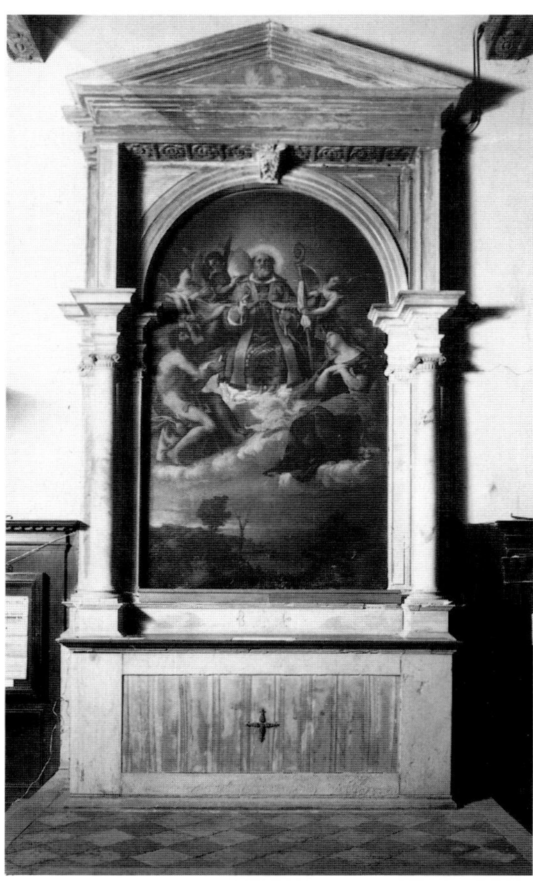

102 View of Lotto's *St Nicholas* altarpiece (pl. 103) in its original frame.

Thirty years later, after Lotto's death, Lodovico Dolce was to be openly critical of the *St Nicholas* altarpiece, describing it as a 'very notable example of a bad use of colour'.[26] But as has been seen (p. 4), this comment was made in the context of a polemical eulogy of the art of Titian; and it is not necessary to infer from it, as some contemporary art historians have done, that anyone at the time regarded the *St Nicholas* altarpiece as a failure. It is true that Lotto did not receive any further altarpiece commissions for Venetian churches until after his return to the city in 1540; and despite his previous experience as a large-scale decorator, he was never to be employed on any of the various pictorial cycles for the Doge's Palace or the Scuole Grandi. But progress on these was in any case in the doldrums in the later 1520s and the early 1530s; and during this period Lotto's colleagues Palma, Savoldo and Paris Bordone – and even to some extent Titian – similarly tended to concentrate on Venetian commissions that

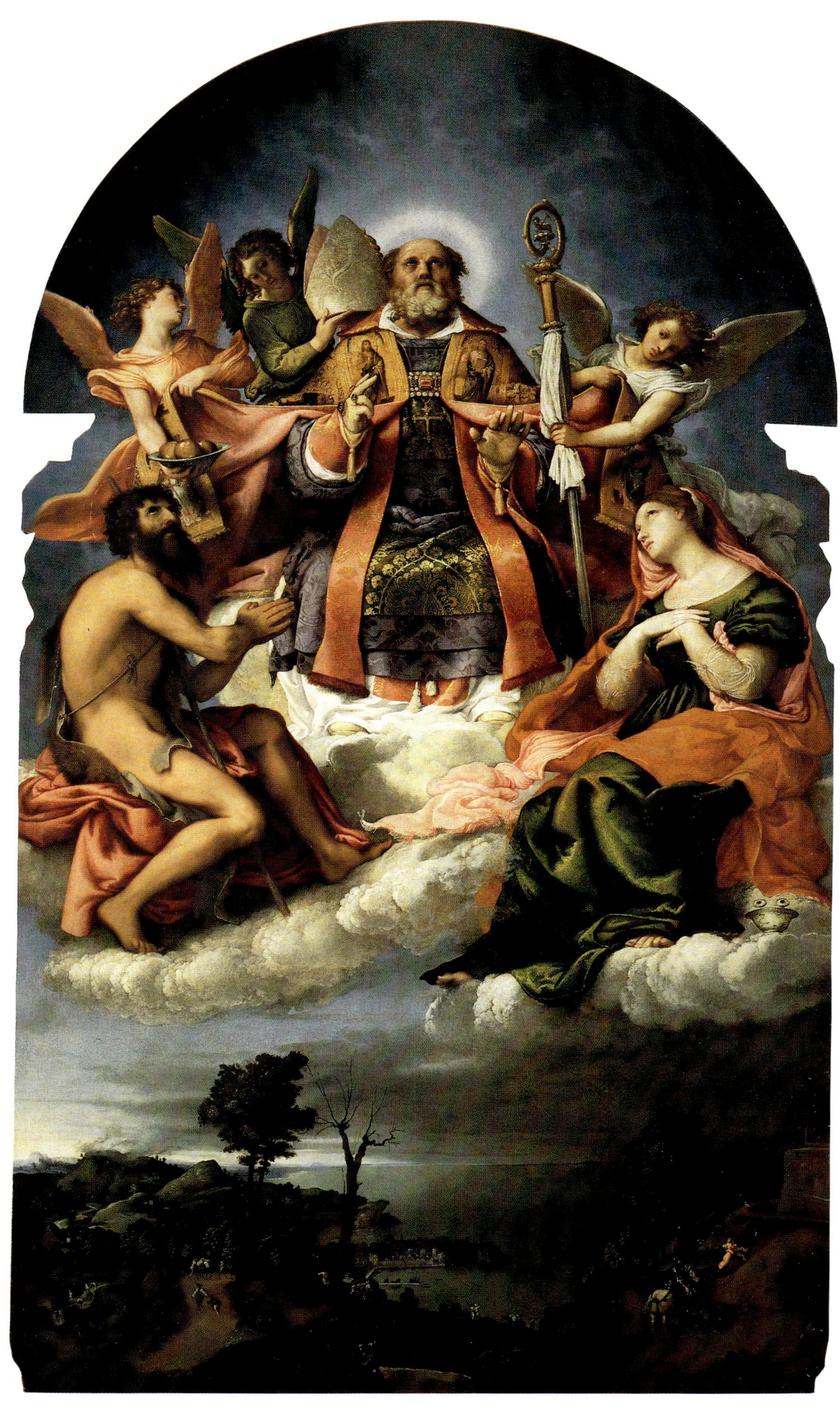

103 Lotto. *St Nicholas* altarpiece (1527–9). Canvas, 335 × 188 cm. Venice, Santa Maria dei Carmini.

106 (*facing page*) Lotto. *Christ carrying the Cross* (1526). Canvas, 66 × 60 cm. Paris, Musée du Louvre.

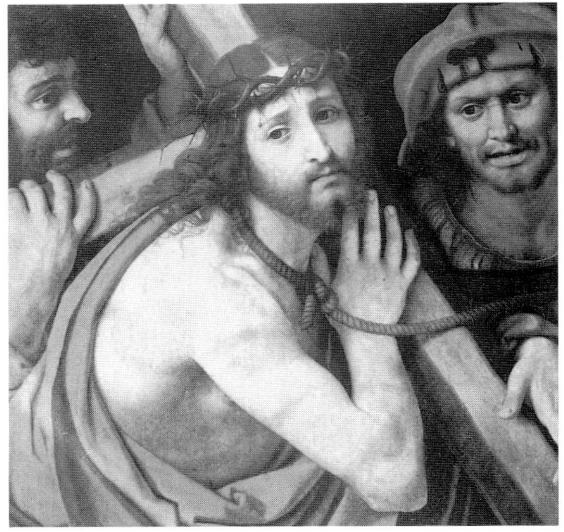

104 Andrea Solario. *Christ carrying the Cross* (1521). Rome, Galleria Borghese.

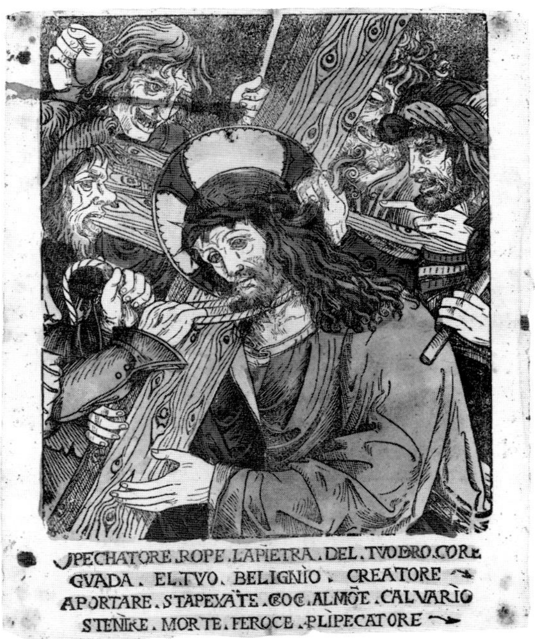

105 Anon. Lombard artist. *Christ carrying the Cross* (?*c.*1500–10). Washington, DC, National Gallery of Art. Pepita Milmore Memorial Fund.

were private rather than public in character. Unfortunately, the account of Venetian private collections given by Marcantonio Michiel is rather disappointing as regards Lotto, by whom only one picture – the splendid portrait of Andrea Odoni (pl. 115) – is mentioned (pp. 106–7). But that Lotto enjoyed considerable success in the private sphere is implied by Vasari, who speaks of the 'many pictures and portraits' by Lotto to be seen 'in the houses of gentlemen'; and in the mid-seventeenth century Carlo Ridolfi similarly recorded several works of this kind by him, which had clearly been in Venetian palaces from the beginning.[27] From these sources – and also from contemporary inventories – it may further be deduced that while Lotto's Venetian patrons seem to have comprised chiefly members of the prosperous citizen class, such as Andrea Odoni, they also included members of the ruling patriciate.

One of the domestic pictures recorded by Ridolfi, in his day in the collection of one Jacopo Pighetti, a Bergamask living in Venice, is almost certainly identifiable with the *Christ carrying the Cross* dated 1526, and now in the Louvre (pl. 106).[28] The theme had been a favourite one in both Venetian and Lombard painting since the later fifteenth century; and in Venice a particularly famous example was represented by the miracle-working image in the church of San Rocco (now in the Scuola), attributed by some to Giorgione and by others to the young Titian. As in this earlier treatment, the suffering Redeemer is shown in half-length surrounded by ugly, leering tormentors, and looking out as if in direct appeal to the pious spectator. But Lotto's composition differs from that of the San Rocco version in its more frontal and central placing of Christ, and in the similarly frontal placing of the tormentors, so that instead of confronting him in profile they encircle him; and in this respect Lotto's version is more closely related to certain of the variations of the theme by the Lombard followers of Leonardo. A relevant example is that of about 1521 by Andrea Solario (pl. 105), which Lotto could have seen in Milan before his return to Venice;[29] but the characteristically Leonardesque motif of the tormentor's clenched fist brutally tugging at Christ's hair shows that Lotto must have known other Lombard versions as well. An innovation by Lotto himself is the compositional device, found in a number of his other devotional pictures, of cutting some of the forms – in this case of the tormentors – at the edges, thereby suggesting a larger crowd than is actually portrayed (see pl. 123), while also focusing the spectator's attention more exclusively on the central image of Christ. The text accompanying a popular Lombard woodcut of a similar iconography provides an apt illustration of one of the principal functions of Lotto's picture, which is to stir the pious emotions of the viewer: 'O sinner, break the stone of your hard heart. See your loving Christ carry the heavy cross to Mount Calvary and suffer terrible death for the sake of sinners' (pl. 105).[30] At the same time, there is obviously a huge qualitative gap between a popular woodcut of this kind and the pictorial sophistication of Lotto's picture, with its infinitely subtle play of light and shade; and this contrast indicates the degree to which the latter was simultaneously conceived as a object of beauty, for the appreciation of connoisseurs.

Another important religious picture recorded by Ridolfi is a *Night Nativity*, which in 1646 had recently been taken from Venice by the wealthy Dutch merchant and collector Jan Reynst to one of his houses in Amsterdam. The picture is unfortunately lost, but at least its composition is recorded in an engraving made by Jeremias Falck when it was in the collection of Jan's brother Gerrit (pl. 107).[31] It has been reasonably supposed that the picture was also identical with a *Night Nativity*, in which the Christ Child likewise provided the source of light, recorded by Vasari in the house of Tommaso da Empoli, a Florentine jeweller resident in Venice;[32] it should be pointed out, however, that according to Vasari, Tommaso's picture contained the full-length, kneeling figure of the patrician Marco Loredan – whereas the two shepherds on the right in the Falck engraving are both stooping rather than kneeling, and are hardly

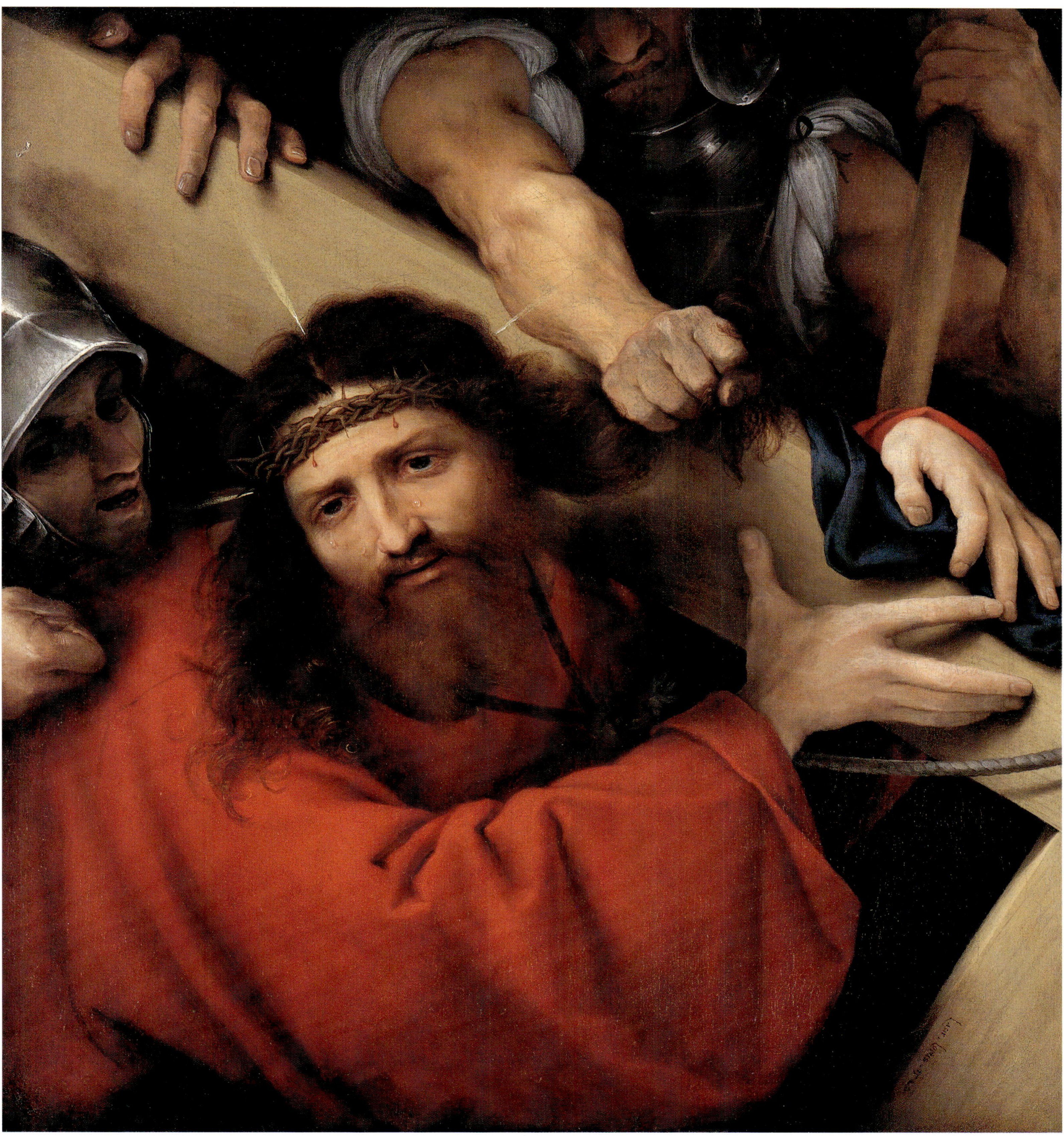

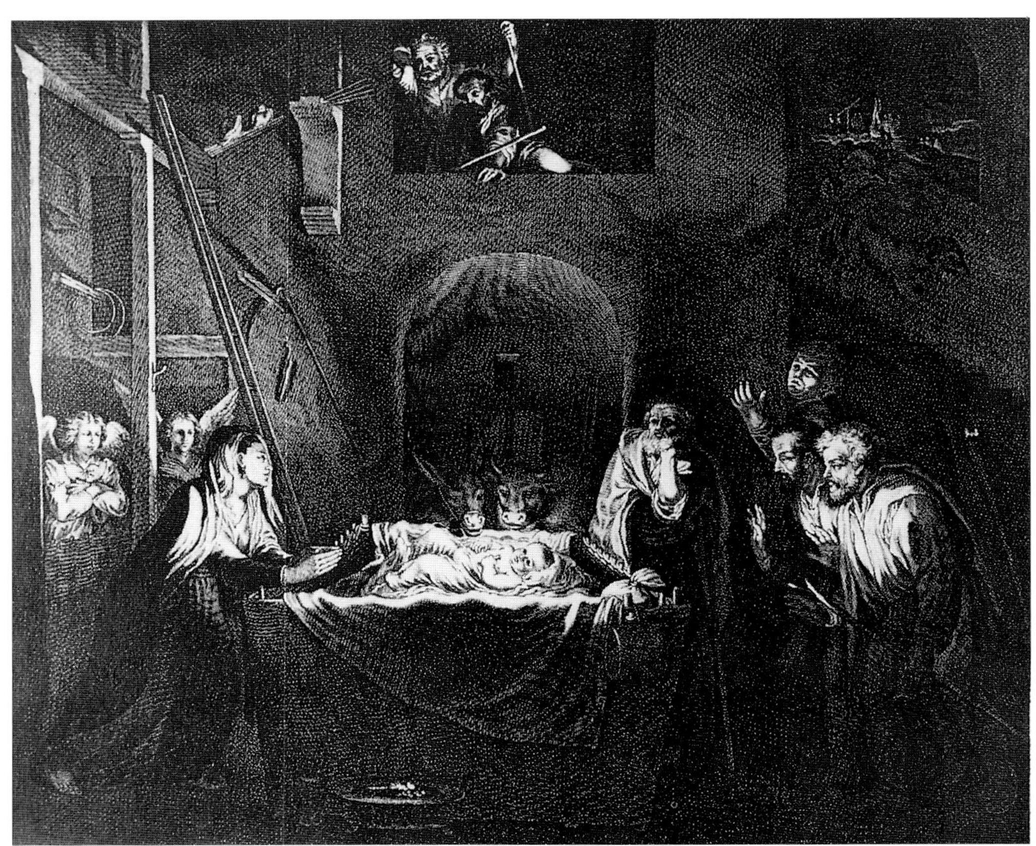

107 Jeremias Falck. Engraving after *Night Nativity* by Lotto.

differentiated from one another. In any case, it seems reasonable to date the ex-Reynst picture to this phase of Lotto's career, partly because of its Venetian provenance, and partly because of certain formal correspondences between the Falck engraving and works of the later 1520s, such as the *St Nicholas* altarpiece (pl. 103). Thus the angels on the left have close counterparts in the angels that hover around St Nicholas, while the types of Joseph and the Virgin closely resemble those of Nicholas and Lucy. This tentative dating of the lost work to about 1527–9 again raises the question of Lotto's artistic relation to Savoldo, a painter who made even more of a speciality of night scenes, special light effects, casually naturalistic poses, and rustic figure types and settings (see pl. 108).[33] It is not easy to answer the question of priority categorically, since so few of Savoldo's pictures are dated, and his chronology is still far from firmly established. But according to current critical opinion, all of Savoldo's true nocturnes date from after about 1530; whereas, as has been seen, Lotto had already painted at least two Night Nativities while in Bergamo in 1521 (pls 61, 66). As in these earlier contributions to the theme, the Reynst *Nativity* continues to reflect the inspiration of Netherlandish examples, now also evident in motifs such as the intimate proximity of the animals' muzzles to the Christ Child (see pl. 62), and the placing of several of the shepherds outside the main space of the stable, so that they look through gaps in the walls or round corners. As far as it is possible to tell from the engraving, the treatment of light was more subtle and suggestive than in the earlier works: thus, in addition to the main source in the Christ Child, which casts dramatic shadows of the animals' heads on the back wall, there was a series of lesser sources, in the foreground brazier, in a torch at the right and in the angelic apparition to the shepherds in the right background. It is possible that Lotto was stimulated to develop luministic subtleties of this kind by his new acquaintance with works by Savoldo in Venetian collections—especially since, as

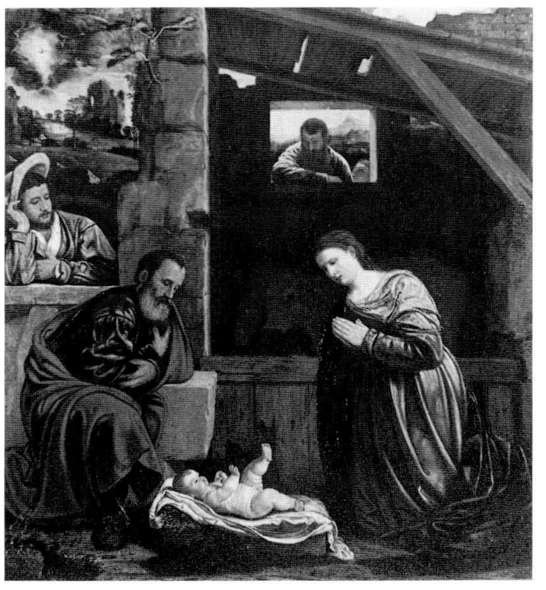

108 Giovanni Girolamo Savoldo. *Nativity* (*c.*1538–40). Brescia, Pinacoteca Tosio Martinengo.

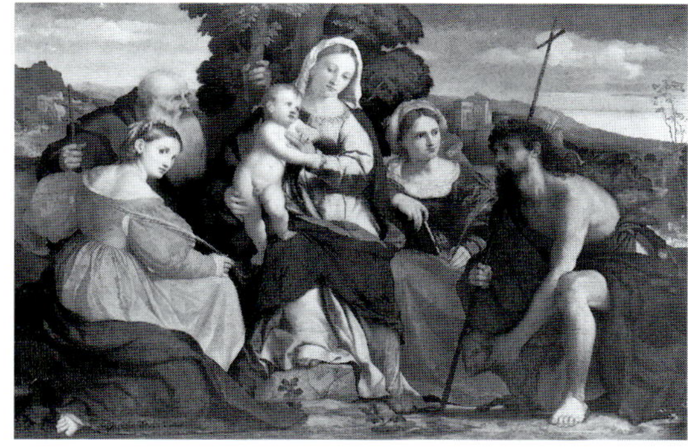

109 Palma Vecchio. *Virgin and Child with Saints* (*c.*1518). Vienna, Kunsthistorisches Museum.

110 Lotto. *Virgin and Child with Sts Catherine and Thomas* (*c.*1528–30). Canvas, 113.5 × 152 cm. Vienna, Kunsthistorisches Museum.

has already been seen, there are clear signs that he was interested in other aspects of Savoldo's art (p. 94). But it is equally clear that Savoldo was in turn profoundly impressed by the art of Lotto; and the Reynst *Nativity* must have represented a particularly important source of inspiration for Savoldo's subsequent *Nativity* altarpieces for San Barnaba in Brescia (pl. 108) and San Giobbe in Venice (*in situ*). It is significant in this context that Vasari, as well as correctly recording Tommaso da Empoli's *Night Nativity* as by Lotto, elsewhere – and mistakenly – recorded it as a work by Savoldo.[34]

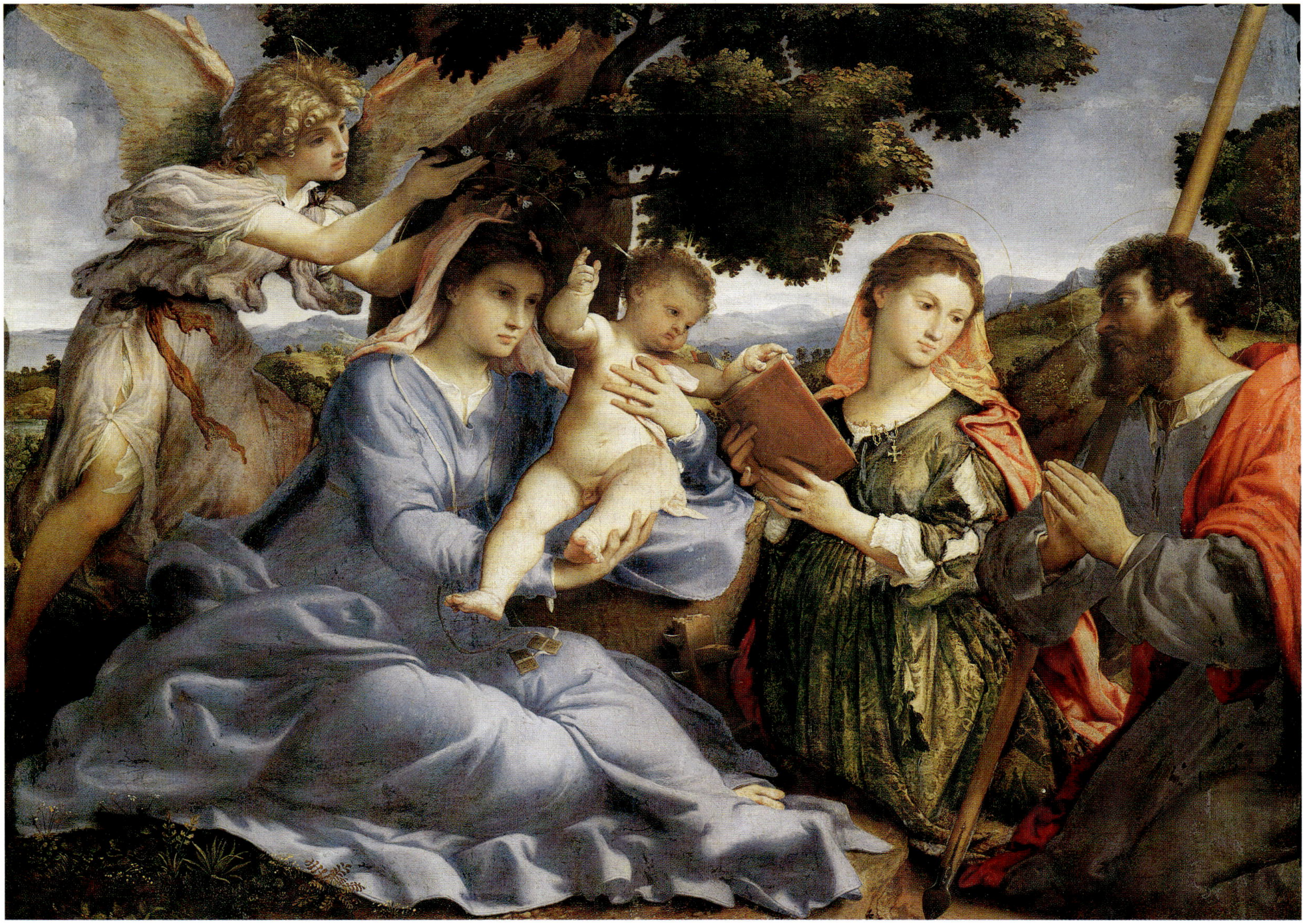

Probably dating from slightly later than the Reynst *Nativity* is the *Virgin and Child with Sts Catherine and Thomas* in Vienna (pl. 110).[35] This exquisitely beautiful picture – hailed by Marco Boschini in 1660 as 'un vero razo de splendor', a true ray of splendour[36] – may be seen as marking a climax in the series of informal Madonnas and saints that had begun with the half-length format of the early picture in Edinburgh (pl. 27), and had gradually expanded by way of the three-quarter lengths in Ottawa and Boston (pls 71, 72), to the full-length of the Bonghi *Mystic Marriage* of 1523 (pl. 74). In keeping with a characteristically Venetian compositional type, already made popular by Titian, Paris Bordon, Bonifacio and, especially, Palma Vecchio (pl. 109), Lotto now also represents his holy figures sitting and kneeling in a pleasant sunlit landscape. Where, however, Palma typically arranged his figures into a compact and restful pyramid, Lotto's formal composition is based on intersecting diagonals that lend it an effect of instability consistent with the volatile play of light. No less different from Palma are the cool brilliance of the colour and the restless rhythms of the draperies, with the gauzy tunic of the angel looking almost Hellenistic in its chiselled swirls. The exceptional refinement of the pictorial handling suggests that Lotto was making a special effort here to impress a patron either of the highest social rank, or of the greatest aesthetic sophistication, or of both. Although unfortunately nothing is known of the identity of this patron, it is significant that by the time of Boschini the picture had already been acquired for the imperial Habsburg collection.

Lotto's first Venetian period was probably also the most productive of his entire career in the field of portrait painting.[37] Although the demands of metropolitan patrons provided him with little opportunity to develop further his earlier innovations in double and female portraiture (but see pl. 118), he continued to experiment with a range of different compositions and formats, while always holding his distance from the example of Titian. During the earlier 1520s, in fact, Titian's portraits had temporarily settled into something of a formula, with the sitter, almost invariably male, represented waist or thigh length, dressed in a rich but unostentatious dark costume with a white shirt, and posed with elegant simplicity against a shadowy, neutral background (pl. 4). By contrast, the Venetian portraits of Lotto offer a deliberate, almost showy variety of solutions. Although the identity of most of Titian's sitters of this phase is unknown, the relaxed dignity of their bearing declares them to be noblemen; and they require only a minimum of props–a glove, a sword, a chain–with which to confirm their elevated rank. With some notable exceptions, Lotto's portraits similarly tend to be anonymous; but from their dress, and perhaps also from their more personalised accessories, they appear to comprise members of the citizen class rather than those of the patrician class: merchants, professional men, prosperous master craftsmen. As earlier in Bergamo, and again quite unlike Titian, he typically surrounds his sitters with objects that are clearly charged with a highly personal symbolic significance, alluding in the manner of an *impresa* to the sitter's name, particular circumstances or aspiration. Typically, too, the sitter adopts an active, although somewhat stilted pose, which is designed to draw the spectator's attention to one key-object in particular. As with the *intarsia* covers, the precise meaning of Lotto's picture language is often deliberately veiled, challenging the educated viewer to decode it; and also as before, it may be assumed that the painter himself played a leading role in devising the symbolic programme. At the same time, this clearly must also have reflected the ideas and wishes of the sitter, who would naturally have expected at least his family and friends, if not a wider circle of privileged viewers, to be able to unravel the coded allusions. The problem for modern viewers is that we too often do not possess sufficient information about the sitter and his situation to enable us to read Lotto's portraits as fully as his contemporaries could; and although in many cases art historians have suggested interpretations that seem consistent with Lotto's general approach to symbolism, it is rarely possible, without more concrete historical evidence, to accept them as proven.

Uncharacteristically lacking in symbolic accessories is probably the earliest of Lotto's Venetian portraits, the unusually small, intimate and immediate *Portrait of a Youth with a Book*, now in the Castello Sforzesco in Milan (pl. 112).[38] Also unusual for Lotto is the fashionable, even courtly elegance of the sitter's attire, with his striped violet doublet, gloves and beret adorned with a golden chain. The glance outwards over the shoulder betrays the inspiration of Giorgionesque portraiture, and probably in particular of Sebastiano del Piombo's highly Giorgionesque *Shepherd with a Flute* of about 1508–10 (pl. 113). Despite its pseudo-rusticity, from this model Lotto clearly derived not just the

111 Detail of pl. 110.

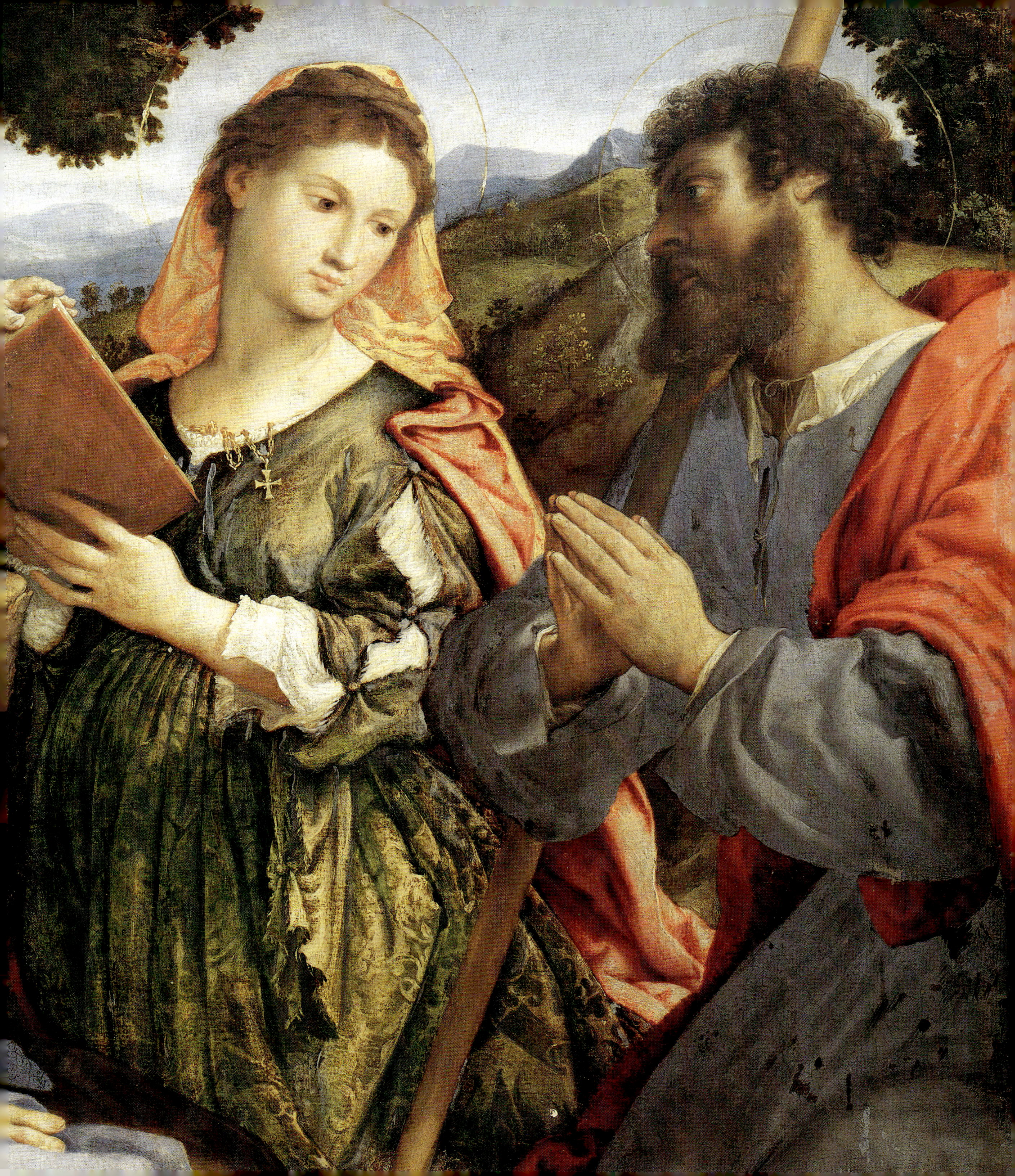

112 Lotto. *Portrait of a Youth with a Book* (*c.*1526). Panel, 35 × 28 cm. Milan, Castello Sforzesco.

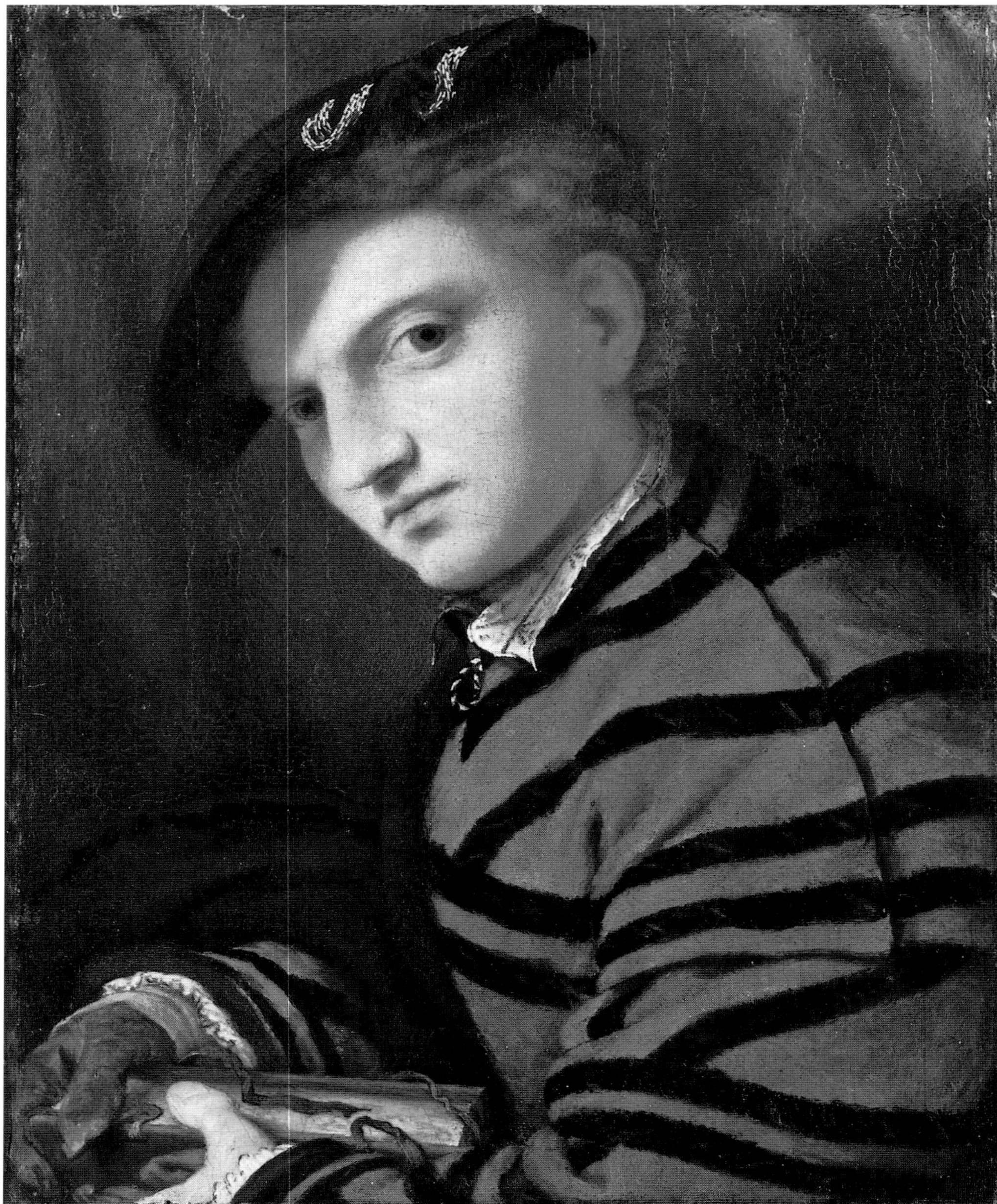

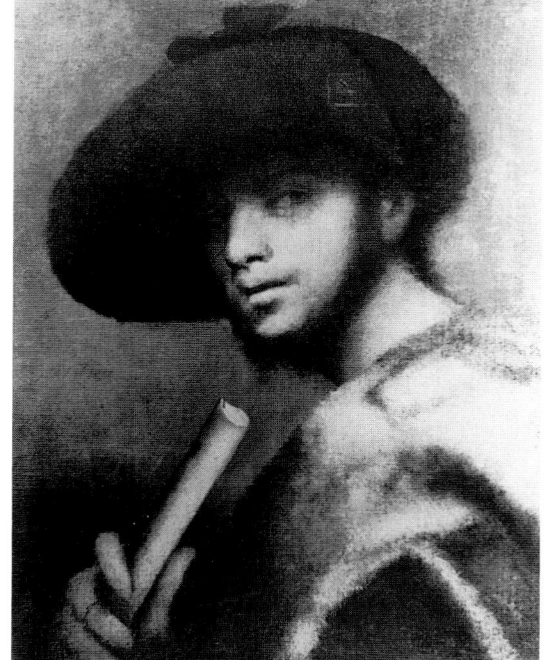

113 Sebastiano del Piombo. *Shepherd with a Flute* (*c.*1508–10). Wilton House (Wiltshire), the Earl of Pembroke.

pose with the principal curving diagonal of the head and the back balanced by the contrasting diagonals of the hat and collar, but also the suggestive shadow thrown by the hat over the upper face. It is as if on his return to Venice Lotto sought to counter the prevailing portrait style of Titian by first catching up on a phase of local development that had taken place during his long absence.

Approximating more closely to Titian is the *Man with a Golden Paw* (pl. 114), datable, perhaps, to the same year as the Castello Sforzesco portrait. As well as adopting the fashionable three-quarter-length format and the dark costume, Lotto also adopts here an unusually warm palette, and sets the figure against a foil of intensely saturated complementaries of red and green. But the slanting, unclearly articulated pose is inherently unstable, and further contributes to the expression of diffidence and sentimental appeal conveyed by the sitter's face and gesture. The key to a full understanding of the portrait is obviously provided by the golden paw that he holds out towards the viewer; and although this detail has not yet been satisfactorily explained, it seems likely that it refers in some way to the sitter's name. According to one suggestion along these lines, he is to be identified with the Bergamask nobleman Leonino Brembate, husband of Lucina, whose portrait by Lotto (pl. 77) similarly contains a reference to her name in the form of a rebus (p. 66).[39] But a problem with this identification is that it implies a dating of the portrait to the Bergamask period, whereas its self-consciously Venetian style and composition indicate rather that it was painted after Lotto's return to Venice in 1525.[40] Furthermore, the choice of attribute seems to refer not so much to a small lion ('leonino') as to a small paw ('zampina', or in Venetian dialect 'zattina'). In this

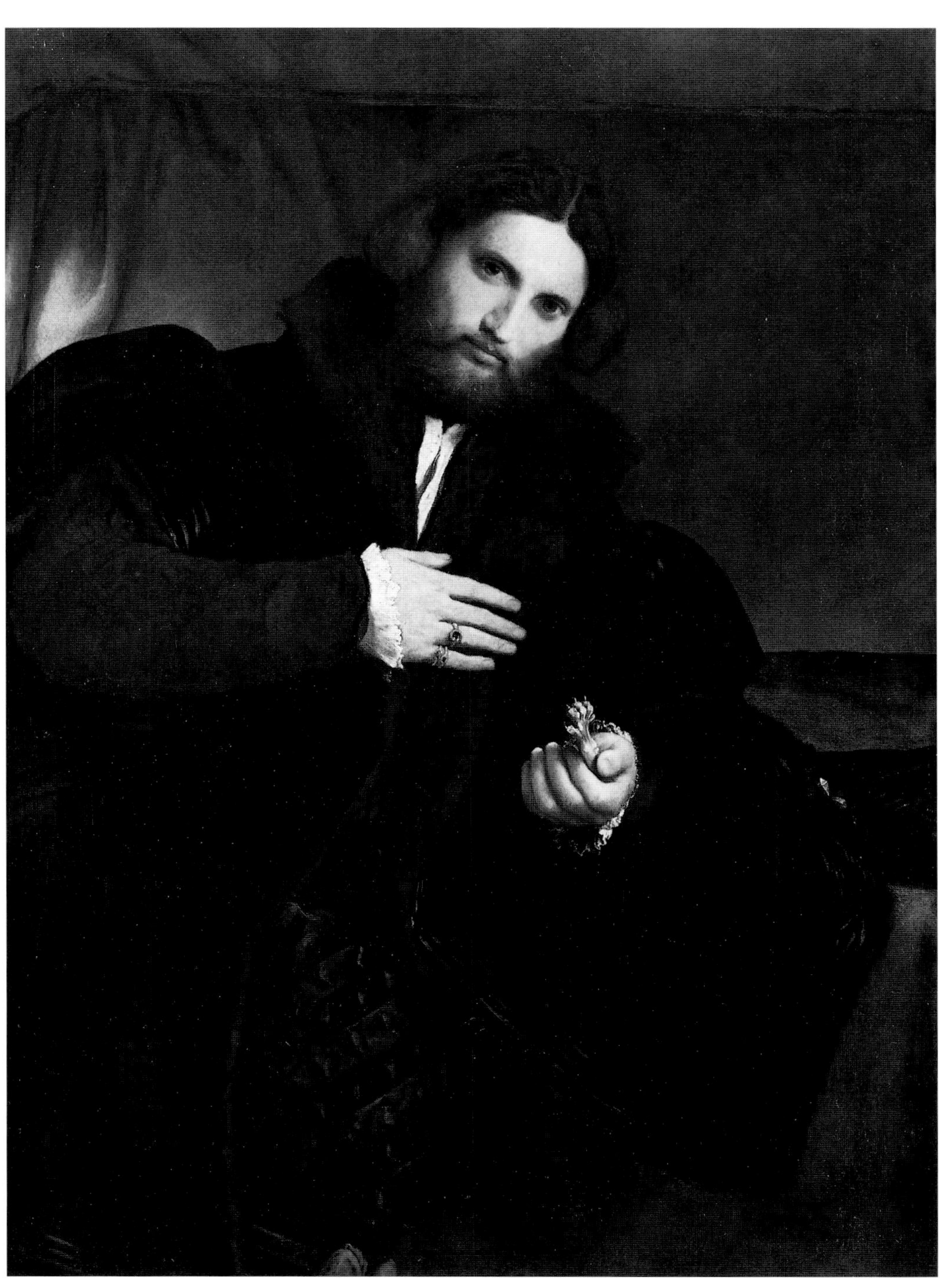

114 Lotto. *Man with a Golden Paw* (*c.*1526–7). Canvas, 95.5 × 69.5 cm. Vienna, Kunsthistorisches Museum.

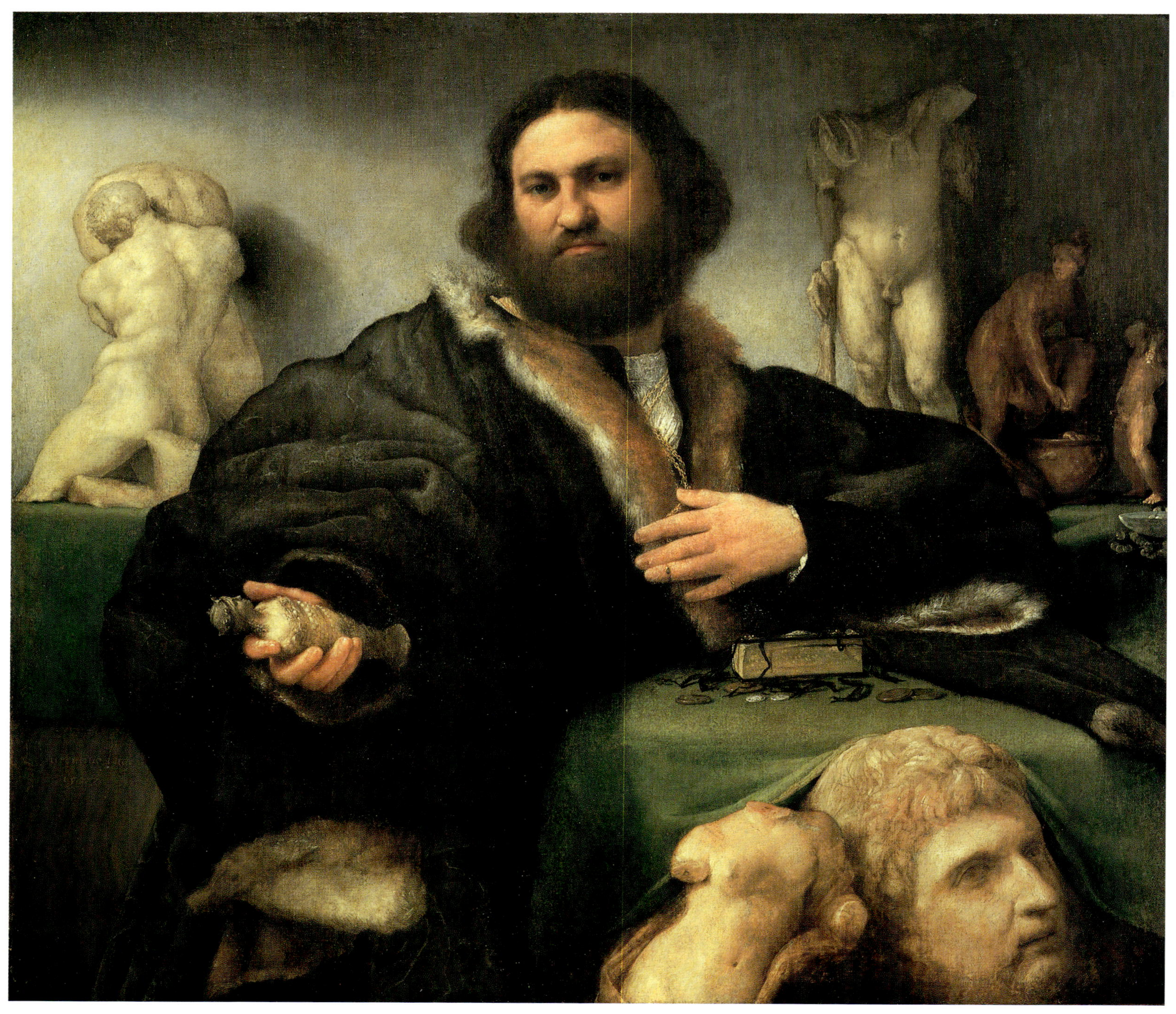

115 Lotto. *Andrea Odoni* (1527). Canvas, 104 × 116.6 cm. The Royal Collection © Her Majesty the Queen.

connection it is worth quoting Ridolfi's mention of a now lost portrait of a woman, which he attributed to Palma Vecchio: 'a member of the Zatta family ('La Zattina'), of gracious aspect with blond hair, who holds in her hand a little gilded paw, alluding to her surname.'[41] It seems reasonable to conclude from this that Lotto's portrait likewise represents a member of the Venetian citizen family of Zatta, especially since the *stemma* (escutcheon) of this family displays at its centre the paw of an indeterminate feline.[42]

Signed and dated 1527, so perhaps painted within a year of the *Man with a Golden Paw*, is one of the finest and most ambitious of all Lotto's portraits, that of *Andrea Odoni* (pl. 115).[43] As in the earlier work, the richly dressed sitter is seen in three-quarter length

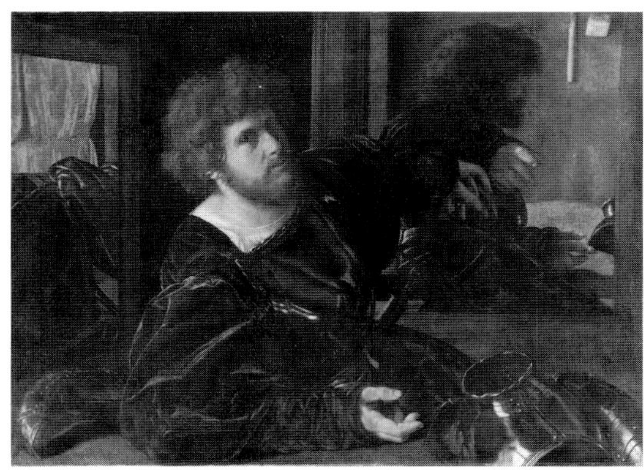

116 Giovanni Girolamo Savoldo. *Portrait of a Man* ('Gaston de Foix') (*c.*1527–30). Paris, Musée du Louvre.

and in a diagonal pose, leaning against a table covered with a green cloth. He makes similar gestures, while similarly fixing a questioning gaze on the viewer, and once more, the space is shallow and enclosed. The pictorial handling is again relatively soft and fused, and more than in the *Man with a Golden Paw* Lotto adopts a carefully restricted palette, concentrating, as if in emulation of Titian, on subtle modulations of tone. But the *Odoni* is quite unlike the portraits of Titian in the plenitude of the still-life detail, and in the highly original adoption–prompted, perhaps, by the need to accommodate such detail–of a broad format. Lotto had previously used a horizontal field for his double portraits in Bergamo, but following the successful experiment with the *Odoni*, he was to re-use it on several further occasions for single portraits in the later 1520s and early 1530s (pls 117–19).[44] His example was imitated in turn by a number of other Venetian painters, most notably Savoldo, as in his so-called '*Gaston de Foix*' (pl. 116).[45]

Lotto's sitter can be identified thanks to Marcantonio Michiel, who visited Odoni's splendidly decorated palace on the Fondamenta del Gaffero in Venice in 1532, and recorded the portrait together with other artistic treasures.[46] Andrea Odoni (1488–1548) was a wealthy merchant of Milanese origin, who held a number of minor appointments in the Venetian civil service and was a friend of several leading figures in the city's intellectual and artistic life, including the writer Pietro Aretino and the architect Sebastiano Serlio. From Michiel's description of the palace–and also from an inventory of the owner's possessions made after his death[47]–it is clear that he owned a exceptionally fine collection, which included paintings by Giorgione, Titian, Palma and Savoldo, and a number of antique sculptures–or at least, copies or casts after the antique. By having himself portrayed in the midst of choice pieces of statuary, Odoni clearly wished to present himself as a man of wealth and culture; and it is surely no accident that the large marble head prominently placed in the right foreground corresponds to the portrait bust of a celebrated patron of the arts in ancient Rome, the Emperor Hadrian. In this particular case, it appears from Odoni's inventory that he actually possessed a copy in stucco of the bust, a good surviving version of which is now in Museo Nazionale, Naples.[48] The various other pieces, however, which include three different representations of Hercules and two of an antique goddess, perhaps identifiable as Venus, do not correspond to items in Odoni's collection; and they must, therefore, have been included in the portrait for purely symbolic rather than documentary reasons. Despite the abundance of the visual evidence, the precise message of the picture remains elusive; but critics are generally agreed in identifying the key to it, as in the *Man with a Golden Paw*, in the object held out by the sitter towards the viewer. The object in this case is a statuette representing the multi-breasted Diana of Ephesus, an image previously used by Lotto in the *intarsia* covers to signify lust, or enthralment to the senses (pl. 98; p. 92), but which here seems to carry the more positive connotation of nature, or fecundity. It may be, therefore, that Odoni wishes to philosophise on the contrast between the enduring power of nature, and the transitoriness of art and of human endeavour.[49] Or according to another reading, his self-identification with Hadrian may also have been based on the fact that, like Odoni himself, the emperor was childless, despite his devotion to the cult of Venus; but Odoni still hopes that his own marriage will be fruitful, and that he will have children to inherit his wealth and possessions.[50]

Very similar in size and shape to the *Odoni*, and equally rich in symbolic allusion, is the *Portrait of a Young Man* in the Accademia Gallery in Venice (pl. 117). Also as in the *Odoni*, the dark costume of the sitter is complemented by a restricted palette; but the fact that the relatively soft handling of the *Odoni* and of the *St Nicholas* altarpiece has returned to an analytic precision, suggests that it slightly postdates these works.[51] The anonymity of the sitter makes it even more difficult to know how to interpret the

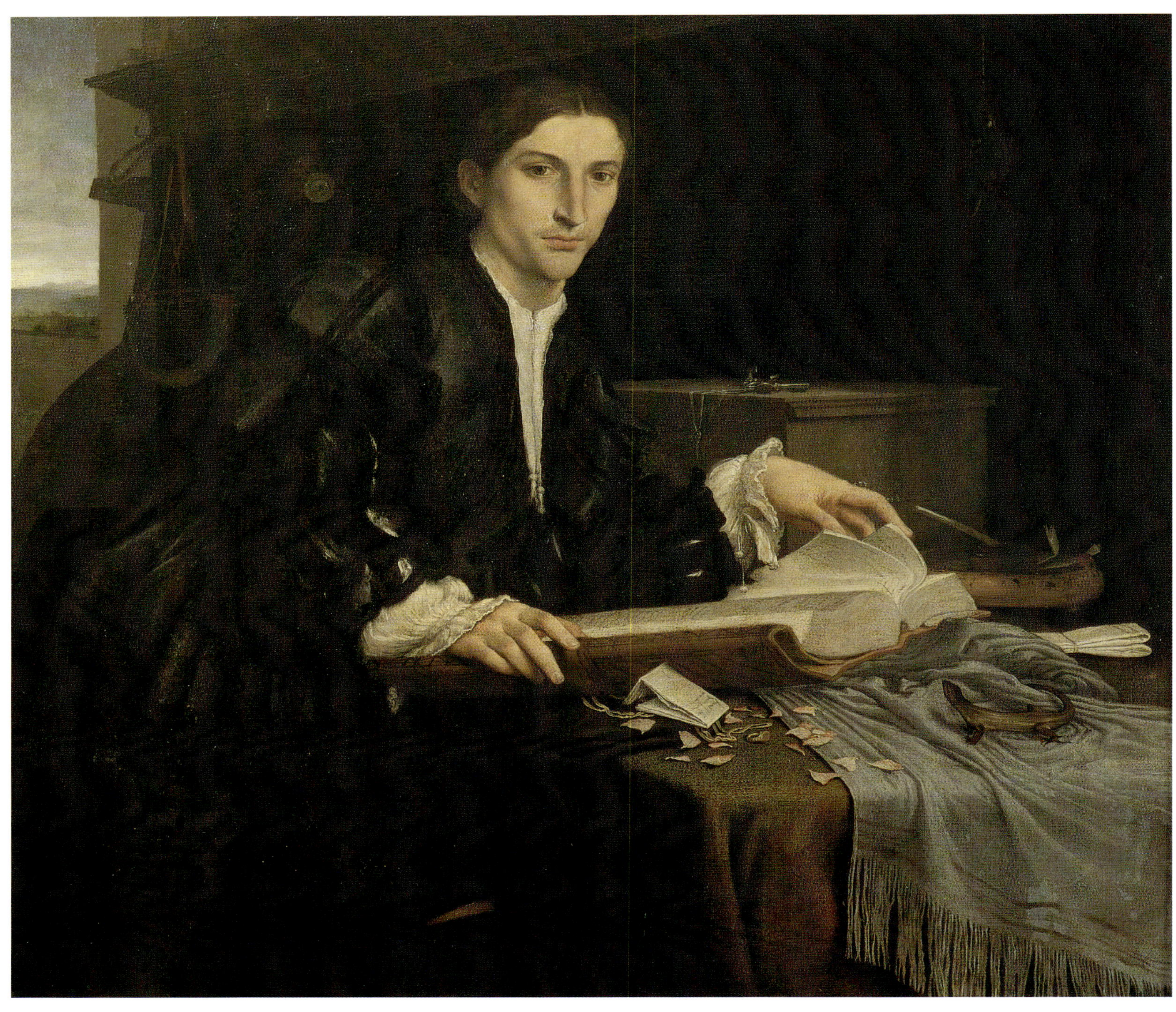

117 Lotto. *Portrait of a Young Man* (*c.*1530). Canvas, 98 × 111 cm. Venice, Gallerie dell'Accademia.

obviously highly personalised symbols: the lizard on the pale blue cloth in the right foreground; the rose-petals scattered on the table; the discarded ring; the letters; the horn in the left background. But this last object has been plausibly recognised as a reference to the pleasures of the hunt and of music; and since the sitter seems to be turning his back on it in favour of the book on the table, it has been proposed that the portrait commemorates a turning-point in his life, at which the frivolity of his youth is abandoned for more serious and intellectual pursuits. The scattered petals would then serve as a warning, to the viewer as well as to the sitter, against placing too much trust in objects of only fragile and transient beauty.[52] According to an elaboration of this

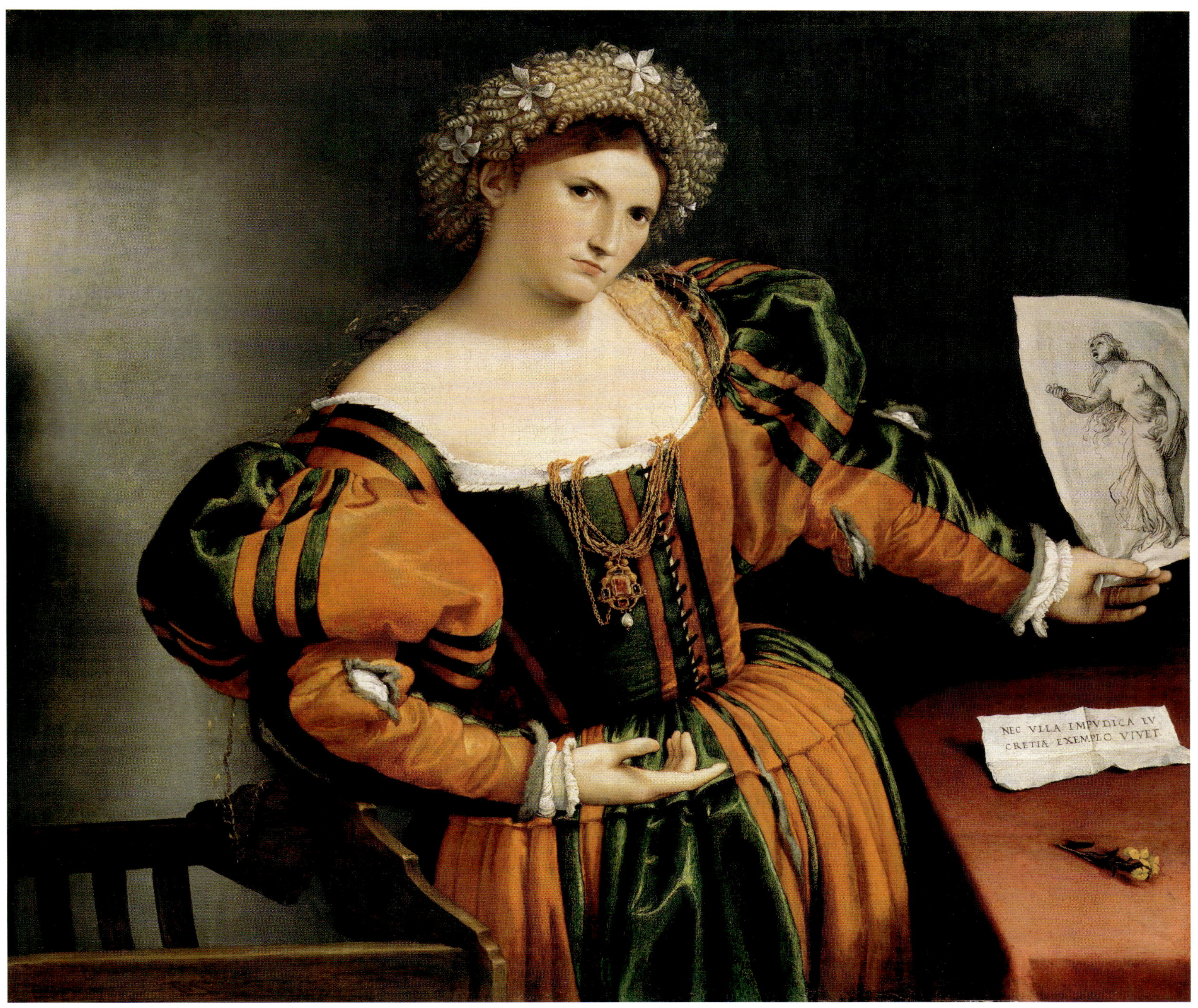

118 Lotto. *Lucrezia Valier* (*c*.1533). Canvas, 95.9 × 110.5. London, National Gallery.

reading, the ring, the letters and the lizard, the cold nature of which makes it insensitive to love, all suggest that the young man has wasted his time in an unhappy love affair; while the large size of the book, more characteristic of a ledger than of a work of literature or philosophy, would imply that the sitter has returned from an errant youth to the mercantile profession of his family.[53] But so detailed a reconstruction of an event in the life of a completely unknown sitter is hardly warranted by the visual evidence; furthermore, as has been seen (p. 92), there is no evidence that Lotto's repertory of symbols was meant to carry any strong moralising or admonitory message. Rather, it may be seen here as a way of summarising the soberly clad sitter's general personality: pensive, averse to frivolous pleasure, perhaps prone to melancholy. The lizard would then serve as an entirely appropriate symbol of the dry, cold nature of the melancholic temperament. It is worth noting in this connection that in the sixteenth century a widely recognised remedy for the relief of melancholy was to scatter the sufferer's room with the petals of various flowers, including roses.[54]

A third Venetian portrait of a similar format to the *Odoni* and the *Young Man*, but unusually representing a woman and a patrician, is the *Lucrezia Valier* in the National Gallery, London (pl. 118). The sitter, who has been convincingly identified on the basis of the picture's provenance, married Benedetto di Girolamo Pesaro on 19 January 1533, and as her hair is tied up, indicating that she is no longer a fiancée or a bride, the picture probably slightly postdates the wedding.[55] This time the symbolic accessories are reduced to an easily interpretable three: a drawing of the Roman heroine Lucretia, who preferred death to a loss of her marital honour; a paper inscribed with a quotation from Livy's account of her virtuous suicide;[56] and a sprig of wallflower. The obvious message is that like her namesake, Lucrezia would rather die than ever betray her noble husband; and it is reinforced by the didactic clarity of her somewhat ungainly pose, displaying the drawing in one hand and pointing to it with the other. Although, as in Lotto's male portraits of the period, the range of colours remains limited, the magnificence of the sitter's green and orange dress lends the picture an exceptional chromatic splendour, which is further heightened by the effects of texture created by the surface sheen, by the fur trimmings and by the detailed display of costly jewellery on her breast. Wonderfully sensuous, too, is the way in which Lucrezia's transparent veil has become partly untucked from her bodice, and caresses her bare right shoulder before trailing down on to the chair-back.

As revealed by numerous entries in his account-book, Lotto had a particular taste for jewellery and goldsmith-work, and his will of 1546 mentions his collection of cameos, as well as a gold ring inset with an engraved antique cornelian (Appendix C, p. 181). The same documents also reveal his friendship with a number of goldsmiths, and most notably with Bartolomeo Carpan, who had his workshop on the Ruga del Sole in Venice, and with his brothers Antonio and Vettore, who continued to practise their craft in their native Treviso. On this evidence, it has been suggested that the portrait of a *Goldsmith in Three Views*, datable on stylistic grounds to about 1529–30 (pl. 119), represents Bartolomeo.[57] The identification cannot be proved, especially since it is not certain that Lotto knew the brothers before the 1540s;[58] but in favour of it—apart from the fact that the sitter is identified as a goldsmith by the case of gold rings at the centre of the lower edge—are the unpretentious costume, and the combination of the broad picture field with a reversion to an intimate, bust-length format. According to an ingenious variation on this identification, the portrait may represent rather a triple-portrait of all three Carpan brothers, in which case the presentation of their faces from different viewpoints might constitute a typically Lottesque rebus, referring to their native city (*Tre-visi*).[59] Although ultimately this suggestion has to be discarded, because the three heads resemble one another too closely even to represent brothers, it does have the merit of accounting for the otherwise curious idea of portraying the same sitter three times in the same field. The true explanation, however, probably lies in Lotto's wish to contribute to the *paragone* debate, current both among aestheticising humanists and practising artists, on the relative merits of painting and sculpture.[60] This issue was first raised in Venice at the beginning of the century, in the wake of Leonardo's visit to the city in 1500; and since then, painters had constantly sought different ways of countering the principal argument made by sculptors for the superiority of their own art: namely, that a sculpted object can be seen from all sides, whereas a painted one can be seen from only one. An almost programmatic counter-argument by a painter was provided by Savoldo's closely contemporary '*Gaston de Foix*' (pl. 116), a portrait that, as has been mentioned (p. 107), owes much to the example of Lotto in

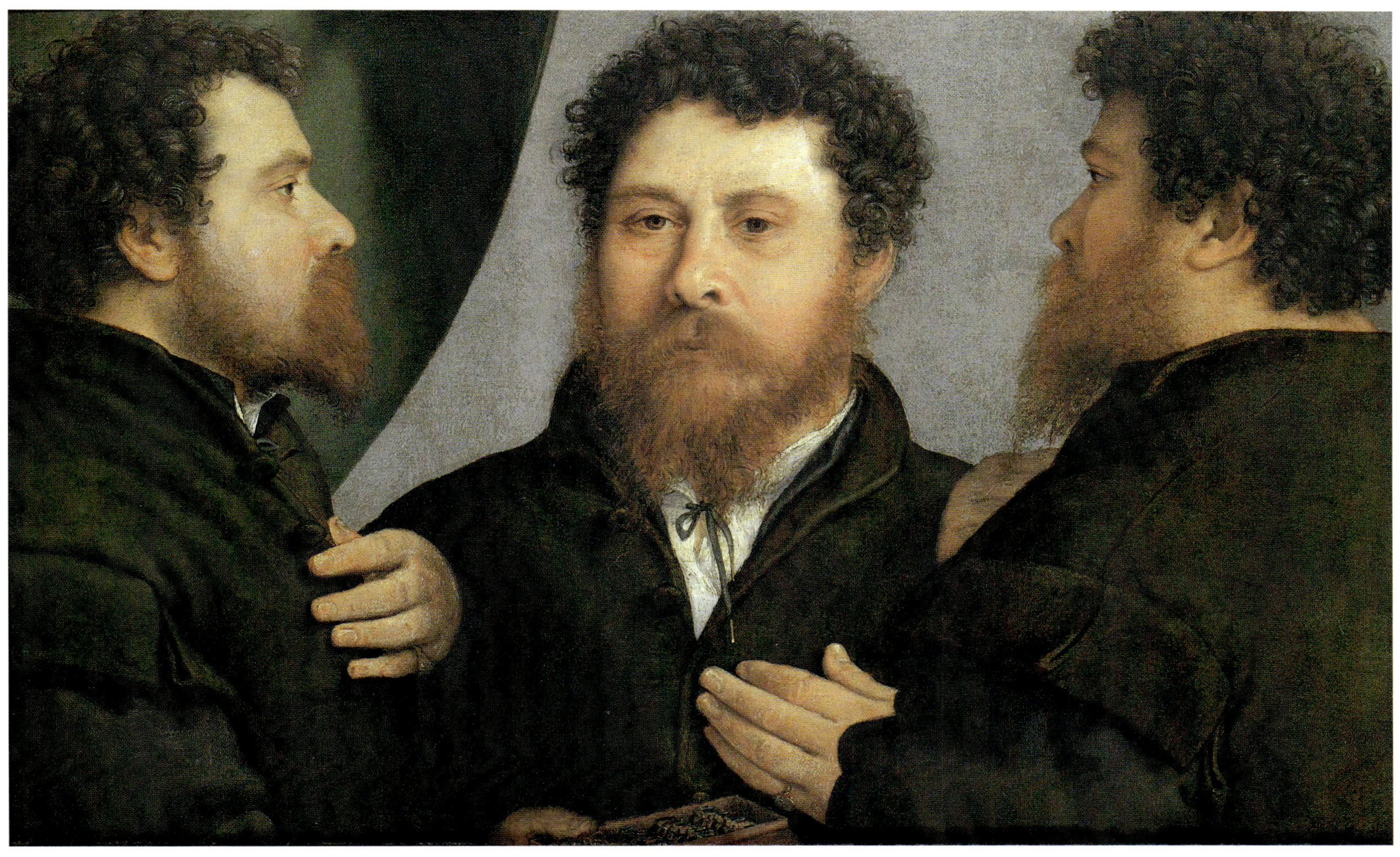

119 Lotto. *Goldsmith in Three Views* (*c.*1529–30). Canvas, 52 × 79 cm. Vienna, Kunsthistorisches Museum.

120 and 121 (*following pages*) Details of pl. 119.

its format and composition, but also develops the Leonardesque and Giorgionesque idea of surrounding the figure with reflective surfaces (the armour, the mirror), so that it can be seen from the sides and back as well as from the front. Although there are no mirrors in Lotto's *Goldsmith*, the Leonardesque inspiration behind the use of a triple viewpoint is evident from a comparison with Leonardo's so-called *Cesare Borgia* drawing (Turin, Biblioteca Reale), apparently executed shortly before 1500, and perhaps left behind by the artist in Venice.[61] It was perhaps the very fact that his sitter was a goldsmith – a craftsman whose special skill was closely related to that of a sculptor – that prompted Lotto to allude in his portrait to the *paragone*, in a spirit of wit and of friendly rivalry between colleagues.

Rather little is known of Lotto's personal relations with his fellow-painters in Venice. But according to Vasari he was a 'companion and friend' of Palma Vecchio,[62] and, indeed, despite the clear differences of temperament between the two artists, there are traces of reciprocal influence between them. Lotto was apparently also actively involved in the affairs of the Arte dei Depentori, the painters' guild, since in 1531 he served on a committee appointed to implement a bequest by the recently deceased Vincenzo Catena, granting dowries to the daughters of impoverished masters.[63] He would certainly, therefore, have been at least acquainted with all the leading figures, including Titian, who was appointed to the same committee, and who in 1548 passed on greetings to him by way of an open letter from Pietro Aretino (pp. 156–8). On the other hand, the lack of any reference at all to his great contemporary among the many

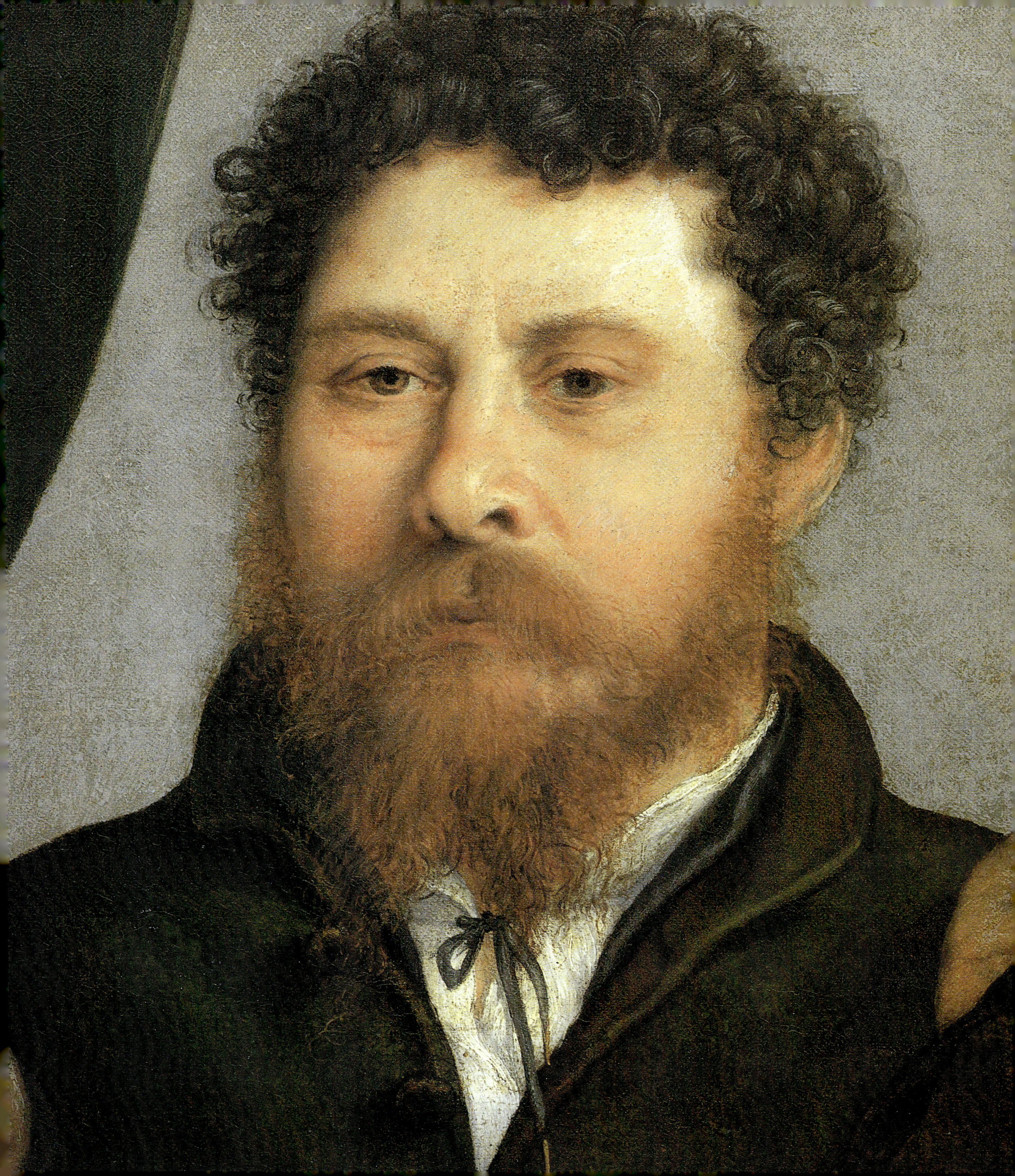

artists and craftsmen later named in the account-book suggests that the relationship between the two painters was not particularly warm or close. By contrast, Lotto certainly did enjoy friendly personal relations with two leading practitioners of the arts of sculpture and architecture, both of whom came to Venice in 1527 as refugees from the Sack of Rome: the Florentine Jacopo Sansovino, who was soon also to become a close mutual friend of Titian and Aretino; and the Bolognese Sebastiano Serlio.[64] Thus, many years before Sansovino lent Lotto a helping hand on several occasions during the 1540s, as recorded in the account-book (p. 142), the painter enthusiastically recommended the Florentine to the Consorzio della Misericordia as the sculptor best qualified to undertake the projected silver altarpiece for the choir of Santa Maria Maggiore (p. 82).[65] Indeed, Lotto's advocacy of his friend's talents may in part have stimulated the interest in the *paragone* so evident in the *Goldsmith* portrait. His relationship with Serlio is less well documented, since the latter moved to France in 1540. But the painter acted as a witness to the architect's will, made in 1528 soon after his arrival in Venice;[66] and that the two formed part of a particular circle of artists and patrons is suggested by the fact that, according to Michiel, Lotto's patron Andrea Odoni owned a picture by Cariani, with buildings designed by Serlio.[67]

Lotto's association with craftsmen working in different media is also reflected in another work datable to the beginning of the 1530s, but of a very different type: the handsome woodcut frontispiece for the Italian translation of the Bible made by the Florentine exile Antonio Brucioli, and first published by Luc'Antonio Giunta in Venice in 1532 (pl. 122). Not all scholars accept the attribution of the design to Lotto;[68] and indeed, the hallmarks of his drawing style are obscured by the transfer to the medium of woodcut. But there are a number of convincing parallels of motif and composition between the woodcut and several of the Bergamo *intarsie*, which were nearing completion at this time; and the *impresa*-like cartouche and the scene of the Night Nativity are likewise characteristically Lottesque in conception. Closely connected with the question of attribution is the hotly debated issue of Lotto's religious stance. Following extensive travels in France and Germany, Brucioli had been expelled from Florence on accusations of heresy; and during the next two to three decades, before it was placed on the Index in 1559, his Bible was to provide a major source of inspiration for the movement of popular Evangelism in Italy.[69] A characteristically Evangelical sympathy towards the Protestant position is reflected in the iconographic programme, presumably devised by Brucioli himself, in its emphasis on St Paul at the expense of St Peter; and that Lotto shared this sympathy may be inferred from the fact that several of his closest friends—including Bartolomeo Carpan, and perhaps also Sansovino and Serlio[70]—are known to have had Evangelical tendencies (p. 153). Lotto's knowledge of Latin was poor,[71] and the evident seriousness of his religious temperament, and his interest in textual accuracy when representing biblical narratives (pp. 2, 89), would naturally have attracted him to Brucioli's translation. This is not, however, to conclude that he would have regarded his involvement in the production of the Italian Bible as in any way inconsistent with being a faithful member of the Roman Church. At this date leading advocates of ecclesiastical reform, such as the Venetian patrician and humanist Gasparo Contarini—to be made a cardinal in 1535—still hoped for a reconciliation with the Protestants and for a reunification of the Church, once institutional abuses contrary to the true spirit of Christ had been eradicated. It was to be another decade, following the failure of the Colloquy of Regensburg in 1541 and the death of Contarini in 1542, before such views were condemned as heretical by the Church; and it was not until 1547—two years before Lotto's final departure from Venice—that the Venetian authorities reconstituted the local Inquisition, and began more systematically to investigate individuals accused of heterodox religious beliefs.[72]

Something of Lotto's religious outlook—probably reformist, yet remaining perfectly

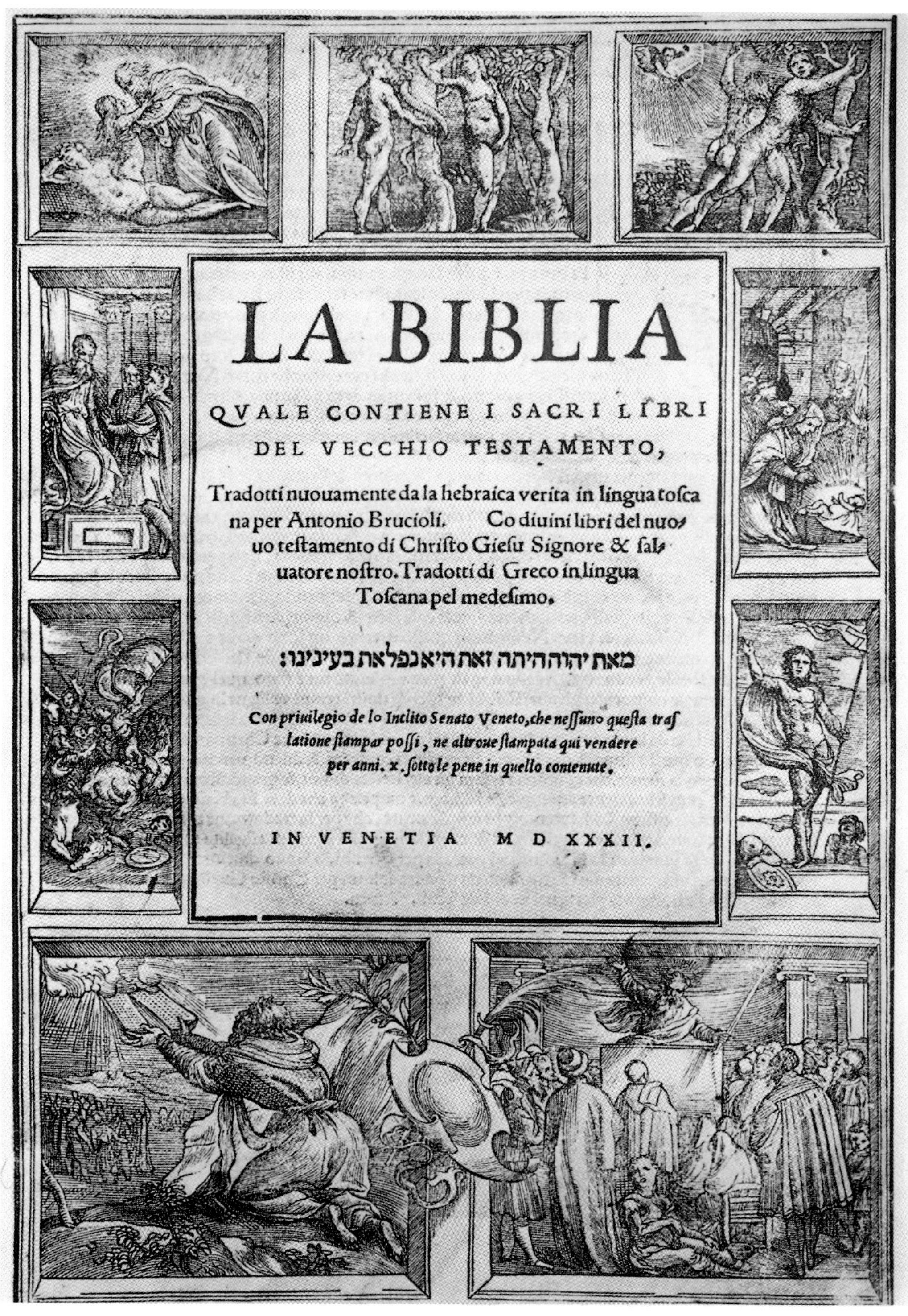
LA BIBLIA

QVALE CONTIENE I SACRI LIBRI
DEL VECCHIO TESTAMENTO,

Tradotti nuouamente da la hebraica verita in lingua toſca
na per Antonio Brucioli. Co diuini libri del nuo
uo teſtamento di Chriſto Gieſu Signore & ſal
uatore noſtro. Tradotti di Greco in lingua
Toſcana pel medeſimo.

מאת יהוה היתה זאת היא נפלאת בעינינו:

*Con priuilegio de lo Inclito Senato Veneto, che neſſuno queſta traſ
latione ſtampar poſſi, ne altroue ſtampata qui vendere
per anni. x. ſotto le pene in quello contenute.*

IN VENETIA M D XXXII.

122 Woodcut frontispiece for Antonio Brucioli's Italian translation of the Bible (1532).

orthodox[73]—may be deduced from the *St Lucy* altarpiece, which he completed after a long delay in the last year or two of his period in Venice (pl. 123).[74] As has been seen, this had been commissioned nearly a decade previously in 1523, for the same church of San Floriano in Jesi for which he had earlier painted the *Entombment*; and at that time he travelled from Bergamo to the Marches to sign the contract with his employers, the Confraternity of Santa Lucia (p. 85). As the document mentions an approved drawing, the subject-matter and the composition of the altarpiece and of its predella must already have been worked out; but, presumably because of his existing commitments in Bergamo, and then because of new commitments undertaken in Venice, Lotto neglected to make further progress on this comparatively large and taxing project. In 1528 the Confraternity even reallocated the commission to another painter, but Lotto must have persuaded his employers to remain patient, and he finally completed the work and signed it in 1532.

The iconographic programme of the *St Lucy* altarpiece is highly unusual, and there is every sign that Lotto himself made an important contribution to devising it. At this date it was common practice for the principal field of an altarpiece in honour of a saint to show an iconic assembly of saints, or *sacra conversazione*, and for any narrative episodes from the titular's life to be assigned to the smaller scale of the predella. Lotto's own Colleoni Martinengo altarpiece, painted for a altar dedicated jointly to Sts Stephen and Dominic, provides a clear illustration of this convention (pl. 52). In the *St Lucy* altarpiece, however, the principal field is occupied by a narrative scene – *St Lucy before Paschasius* – which belongs to the same narrative sequence as the various scenes in the predella. Thus the story of Lucy's virtuous life, based closely on the account in the *Golden Legend* (13 December),[75] begins in the left panel of the predella. Here, accompanied by her invalid mother, she performs a series of pious Christian acts in several episodes. For this she is denounced by her fiancé, a 'dull-witted, greedy fellow', and is arrested and brought before the Roman consul Paschasius. The two enter into vigorous debate, witnessed by Paschasius's counsellors and Lucy's fiancé (dressed in green and yellow, and like her, wearing a laurel crown; to the left of the next predella panel). The story then continues on a large scale in the main panel.[76] Paschasius orders Lucy to be removed to a brothel; 'but when the panders tried to carry her off, the Holy Ghost made her so heavy that they were unable to move her. Paschasius called for a thousand men, and had her hands and feet bound; but still they did not succeed in lifting her.' The fiancé reappears at the right of the composition, and Paschasius and his counsellors have become more animated in their anger. The action then moves back down to the central and right panels of the predella, where teams of oxen are lined up to do what the thousand men failed to accomplish; but again to no avail. At the top left of the central panel the Holy Ghost intervenes on Lucy's behalf, while the rage of Paschasius below is expressed by his now even more horizontal pose.[77]

It is perhaps only to be expected that the narrative technique employed in the predella panels, with their highly animated, small-scale figures, and their picturesque variety of architectural settings, should closely resemble that used for the story of St Barbara in the Oratorio Suardi. There, too, the succession of heinous assaults on the Christian heroine had closely followed the text of the *Golden Legend*; and at the time of undertaking the Jesi commission, Lotto would have been about half way through the execution of the *St Barbara* frescoes. Highly original, however, is his treatment of the two episodes represented in the central and right-hand panels, with one tightly compressed into a narrow space to the left of the green curtain, and the other, by contrast, generously extended across both panels, allowing an expressive multiplication of the impotent teams of oxen. Even more original is Lotto's application of a similar narrative approach to the principal panel of his altarpiece, making the figures unusually small in relation to the field, and showing them involved in turbulent action. Such an approach carried its risks, for it was important for devotional reasons that the titular saint of the altar and confraternity should remain as prominent as in any *sacra conversazione*. But Lotto achieves this by placing Lucy, the only truly vertical figure in the composition, on the central vertical axis, and by making her bright yellow and white dress shine out against the shadowy environment. Furthermore, the figures in the main panel are not as numerous as they at first seem; and by cutting those at the edges

123 Lotto. *St Lucy* altarpiece (completed 1532). Four panels: 243 × 237 cm (main field); 32 × 69 cm (each of predella panels). Jesi, Pinacoteca Comunale.

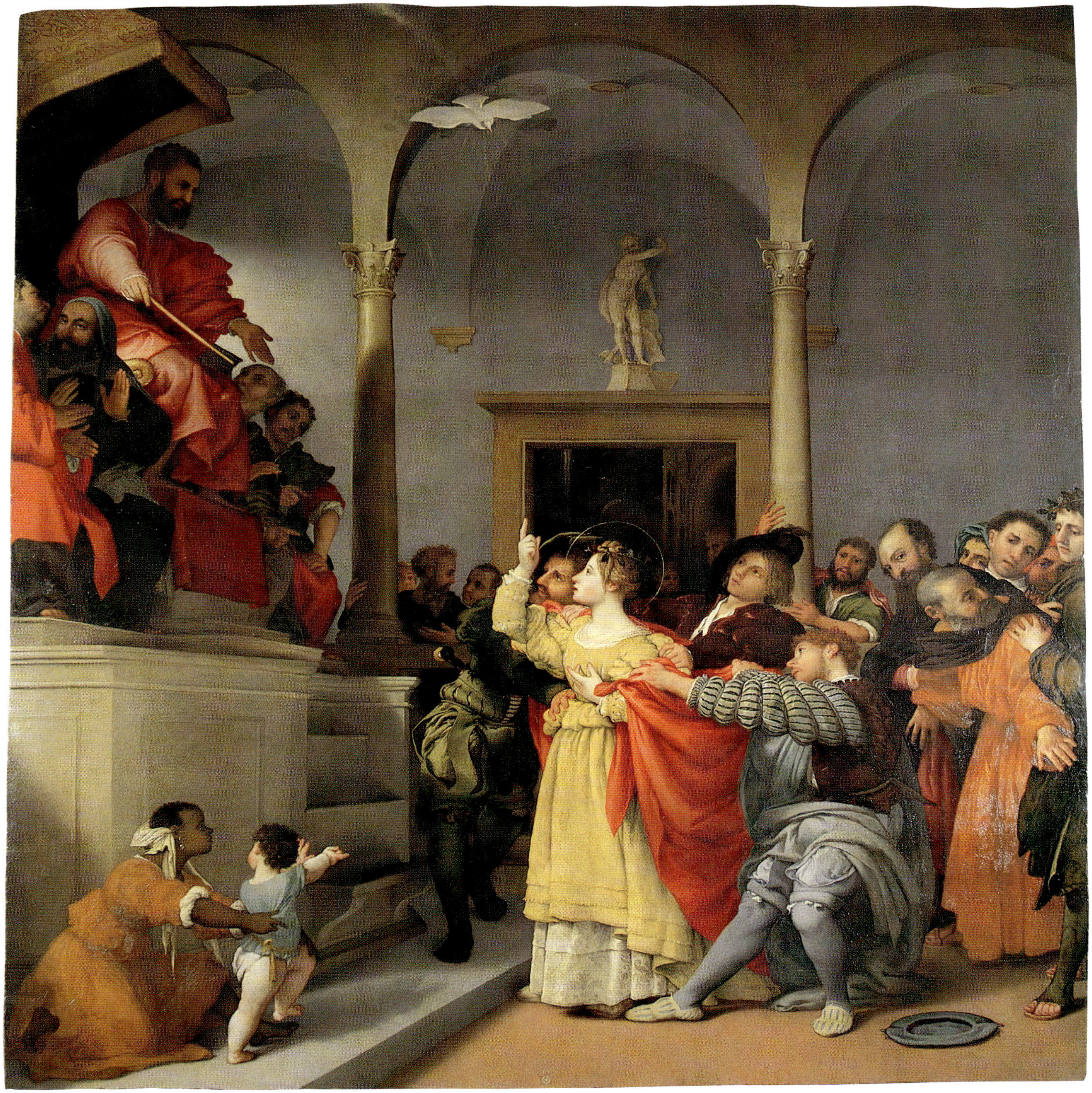

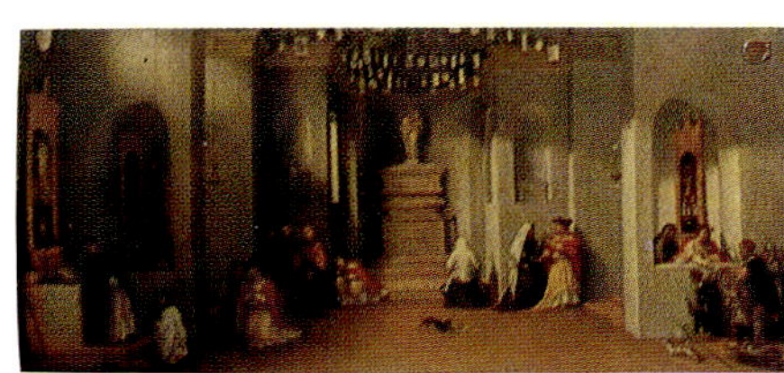

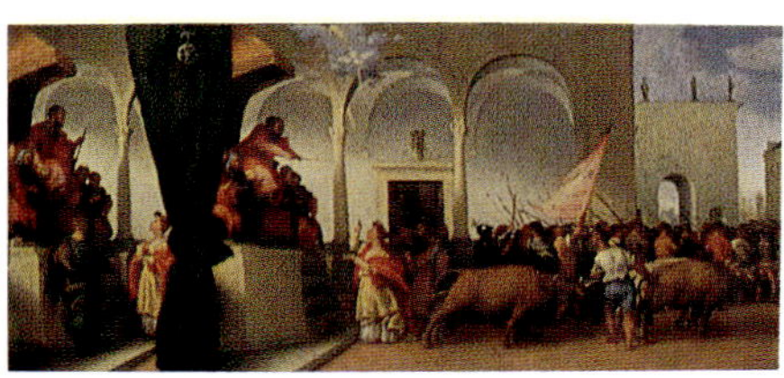

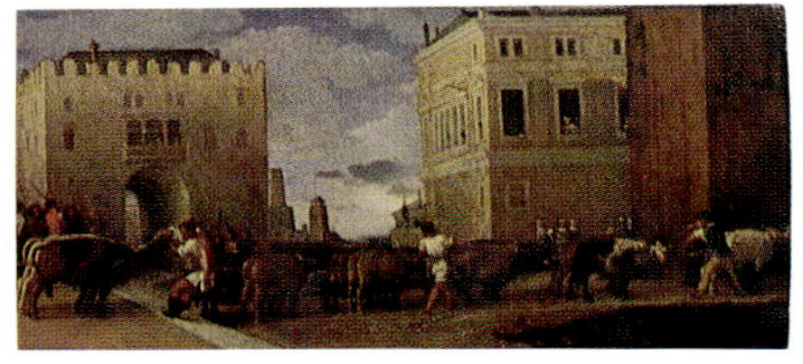

by the frame (see p. 98), the painter succeeds in suggesting the vast numbers called in to remove Lucy, without swamping the composition.

Lotto's interest in aesthetic experiment generally, and in introducing novel expressive effects into the genre of the altarpiece in particular, would certainly have played a part in this unusual choice of a hagiological narrative for the central panel. But although the use of the *Golden Legend* in some ways represents an old-fashioned adherence to the popular, semi-superstitious devotional tastes of the later Middle Ages, the new emphasis on the steadfast courage displayed by a Christian martyr may also be seen as consistent with reforming currents within the Church. Traditionally, the cult of the saints was inspired by the devotee's wish to cultivate powerful allies in heaven, who would help ease his or her path through the many difficulties of this life, and on to salvation; and the primary religious function of the *sacra conversazione*, as of the polyptych, was similarly to provide a visible array of such supernatural helpers and intercessors, to whom the devotee could pray.[78] But according to reformers such as Erasmus, such passivity was unworthy of the followers of Christ, and the true way for Christians to honour the saints was to adopt them as role models, and to imitate the practical example afforded by their lives. It is significant that as the sixteenth century developed, it became increasingly common for morally heroic events in the lives of saints, and especially their martyrdoms, to be chosen as the principal subjects of altarpieces; and in this sense, Lotto's dramatic portrayal of Lucy's defiance of evil in the name of Christ may be seen – like Titian's closely contemporary *Death of St Peter Martyr* (destroyed; formerly Venice, Santi Giovanni e Paolo) – as representing a historic milestone.

According to the terms of his contract, Lotto was required to deliver the heavy panel to Jesi in person, supervising its unloading at a landing-stage on the Adriatic coast, and then its carriage by ox-cart overland to its destination. It is possible that he did this immediately after finishing the work in 1532, before briefly returning to Venice to paint the portrait of *Lucrezia Valier* (pl. 118). It is more likely, however, that he kept the Confraternity of Santa Lucia waiting another few months, until after Lucrezia's wedding on 19 January 1533; and this supposition seems confirmed by the fact that on 28 January he made a will. Although this document is now unfortunately lost,[79] the timing of it suggests that he had decided temporarily to abandon Venice for the Marches. The reason for this decision is not clear, but it is a fair guess that with the project for the Bergamo *intarsie* finally complete, and with no immediate obligations at home, he felt free to concentrate on another major Marchigian commission, which for practical reasons was most conveniently executed on the spot: the huge *Crucifixion* for the hilltop city of Monte San Giusto.

Although during his seven-year residence in Venice Lotto remained essentially an independent spirit, his art was nevertheless enriched in a number of ways by the experience of working in the metropolis. As has been seen, the almost inescapable influence of Titian is apparent in the relative breadth of handling and warmth of palette in works such as the St *Nicholas* altarpiece (pl. 103) and the *Andrea Odoni* (pl. 115), especially as compared with the works of the preceding Bergamask period. At the same time, Lotto seems deliberately to have sought inspiration from sources other than Titian in his continuing taste for sharp formal definition and for unorthodox expressiveness. An interest in Pordenone, for example, may be detected not just in the Celana *Assumption* (pl. 99; p. 94), but also in the ungainly muscularity of the giant in the *intarsia* of *David and Goliath* (pl. 96). Similarly, Lotto seems to have been instinctively attracted to the combination of homely realism and magical light effects in the work of Savoldo (pp. 94–6), another painter who remained remarkably independent of the classicising, normative art of Titian. This unwillingness by Lotto to accommodate himself to the prevailing Titianism of Venetian painting of these years may, perhaps, have compro-

124 Detail of pl. 123.

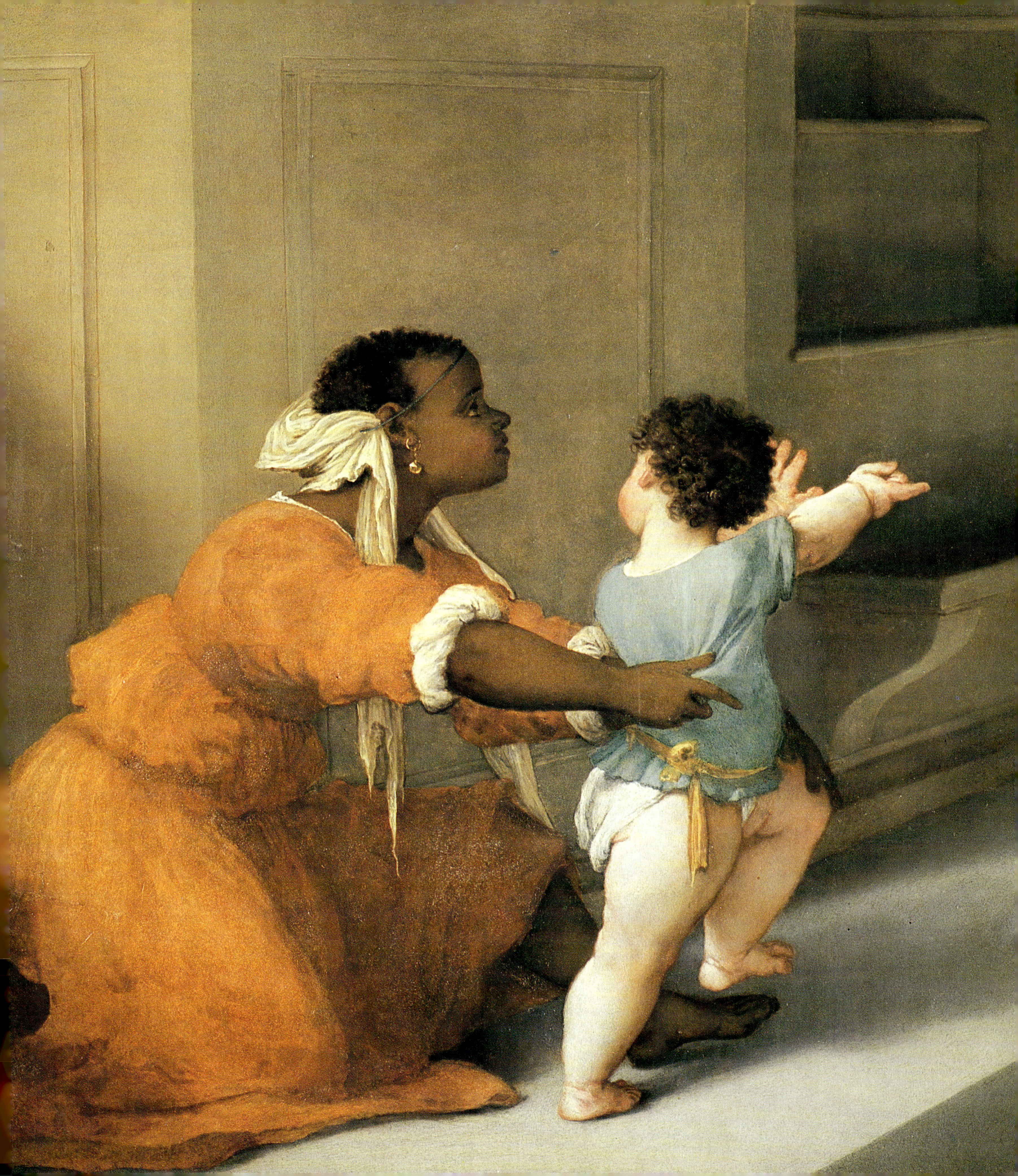

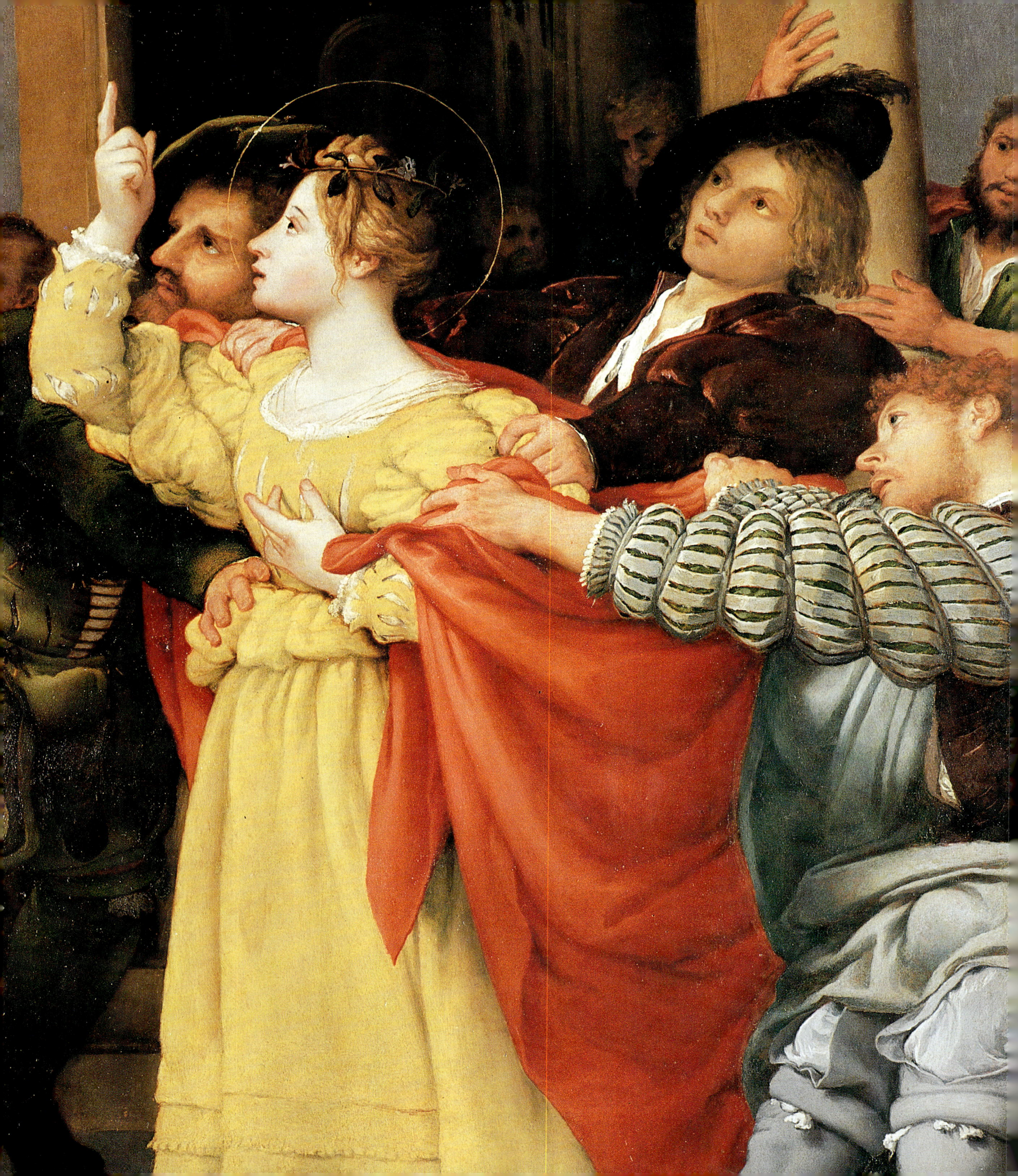

mised his chances of greater success in the public arena; certainly, his presence in the city seems to have made rather little impact on his fellow-painters. The great exception to this generalisation is again Savoldo, whose horizontal portrait formats of the late 1520s and whose development of the nocturne were deeply indebted to the example of Lotto (p. 101). To a lesser extent Palma, in the final two years of his abbreviated career, also seems to have been struck by the distinctiveness of Lotto's work. It has been pointed out, for example, that the composition of the *Seastorm* for the Scuola di San Marco (Venice, Accademia) is closely derived from Lotto's design for the *intarsia* of *Jonah and the Whale*; while Palma's *St John the Baptist* (Vienna, Kunsthistorisches Museum) is apparently based on the two central figures of the Ponteranica polyptych (pl. 57).[80] Yet it is unlikely that Palma, who as a native Bergamask would in any case have known Lotto's work long before 1526, would ever have absorbed more than superficial features from so very different an artistic personality; and other close disciples of Titian, such as Paris Bordone and Bonifacio, remained completely impervious to Lotto. Likewise Titian himself, although still remarkably open to diverse artistic experiences in his full maturity and at the height of his public success, must have found Lotto's art too personal, and his sense of beauty too odd and unheroic, to be of any relevance for his own work. It is worth noting, however, that in his old age, forty years after the execution of the *Odoni* portrait, Titian paid a handsome tribute to it in the composition of his *Jacopo Strada* (Vienna, Kunsthistorisches Museum), in a way that suggests, after all, a secret, longstanding admiration for an art so different from his own.

125 Detail of pl. 123.

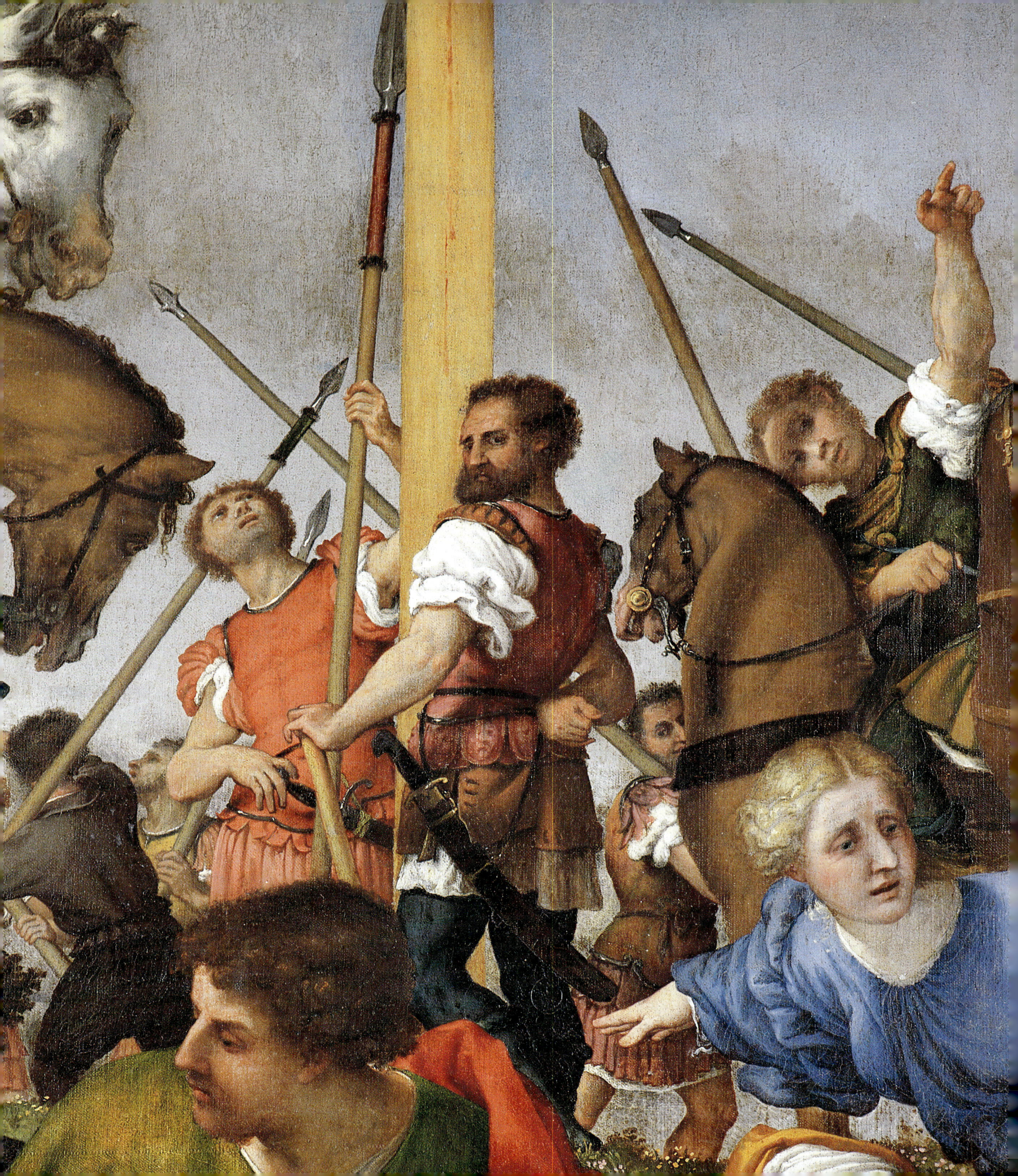

Chapter 5

BACK TO THE MARCHES, VENICE AND TREVISO 1533–1545

LOTTO'S MOVEMENTS DURING MOST of the 1530s are only imprecisely recorded. In August 1535 he undertook a short journey to Jesi in connection with a commission to decorate the chapel of the local Palazzo dei Priori – a work that he never in fact executed. In August 1538 he was in Ancona; and in October 1539 he was in Macerata, having recently spent some months in Cingoli. On the evidence of these few documentary references, but also of at least seven surviving altarpieces, it may be deduced that Lotto spent the period between 1533 and 1539 moving from one small Marchigian town to another, executing altarpieces *in situ*. By contrast, the period from 1540 to the painter's death in the mid-1550s is very well documented indeed, thanks above all to the remarkable survival of Lotto's account-book for these years, the *Libro di Spese Diverse* (p. 2).[1] This shows that by January 1540 he was back in Venice, where he took up residence with his 'nephew' – actually a younger cousin – Mario d'Armano and his family. Then in 1542 Lotto moved to Treviso, to the house of Giovanni dal Saon, a mutual friend of the painter and of the Carpan brothers; but in 1545 he returned once more to his native city, where he had now decided to end his days. Both the *Libro* and the will he made in 1546 after his return shed considerable light on the personal circumstances that prompted these various changes of residence in the early 1540s.

As has already been suggested (p. 118), the principal reason for Lotto's transfer to the Marches, probably in the spring of 1533, was to undertake the execution of the *Crucifixion*, still in its original place above the high altar of the church of Santa Maria in Telusiano at Monte San Giusto (pl. 127).[2] Although painted on canvas and so not heavy, the work is one of the largest of Lotto's altarpieces, and it would have been awkward to transport from Venice to its hilltop destination. Furthermore the donor, Niccolò Bonafede, was one of the socially most eminent of all Lotto's patrons, and planned to have himself portrayed in the picture. There was every incentive, therefore, for Lotto to come and live in Monte San Giusto for the duration. It is not known when and under what circumstances the altarpiece was commissioned, but the church had recently been renovated at Bonafede's expense, and rededicated in 1529; and since the donor would certainly already have known of Lotto by reputation, he may well have sent a representative to Venice about that time to engage him. Given the inclusion of the donor portrait, the altarpiece is likely to have been substantially complete at the time of Bonafede's death in January 1534.

Niccolò Bonafede (1464–1534), ennobled in 1503 and Bishop of Chiusi since 1504, had spent a lifetime as an administrator for successive popes, and in promoting the political authority of the Holy See in its Marchigian territories.[3] He devoted his final years to the architectural embellishment of his personal fiefdom of Monte San Giusto, building himself a handsome palace as well as renovating the neighbouring church, and preparing his mausoleum there. It was according to his wish that the church was

126 Detail of pl. 127, with probable self-portrait by Lotto.

rededicated to the Virgin of the Pietà; and although the principal event portrayed in Lotto's altarpiece is the Crucifixion, it is appropriate that the central foreground is occupied by the figure of the swooning Virgin, with the bishop kneeling in prayer to her at the left. As in the more intimate *Christ taking Leave* of a decade earlier, in which the sorrowful scene is similarly witnessed at close quarters by a kneeling donor, the motif of the death-like swoon refers to the Virgin's role as co-Redeemer (pl. 63; p. 56); it is significant that as well as being placed on the same vertical axis as Christ on the cross, her forearms are raised into a horizontal, as if she too is undergoing crucifixion. This duality of narrative and devotional interest, and the dramatisation of the event with crowds of active figures, make the *Crucifixion* one of Lotto's most complex and ambitious compositions. On the one hand, the distance that separates the group of mourners in the foreground from the Crucifixion in the middleground is emphasised by the spatial thrust of the poses and gestures of the two women at the right. But on the other, a tightly knit unity of surface design is created by the dominant saltire cross created by the figure grouping, the arms of which intersect on the vertical axis; and also by the large, brightly lit patches of repeating colour, which shine out against broader areas of darkness. This almost abstract patterning of light, shade and colour was to become a characteristic feature of the works painted by Lotto in the Marches during the 1530s.

On the same central axis that links Christ with the Virgin is placed a Roman soldier, physically isolated from his companions, and made especially prominent by the turn of his head over his shoulder to look out at the spectator (pl. 126). This portrait-like treatment lends credence to the suggestion that the figure constitutes a self-portrait of the fifty-year old painter.[4] Although a number of other candidates for self-portraits of Lotto have been proposed in the past, including the *Goldsmith* (pl. 119) and the Borghese *Portrait of a Man* (pl. 5), all have turned out for one reason or another to be unacceptable. Ultimately there is no way of proving this new identification either; but in further support of it, as has been pointed out, is the close physical association of the soldier with Christ's cross. There is evidence from various phrases in his writings that Lotto shared with many Evangelising Catholics a special devotion to the person and sufferings of Christ; and in a small-scale *Mystic Crucifixion*, later apparently painted for his own private use (pl. 145; p. 142), he closely adapted the main figure from the Monte San Giusto altarpiece.

Very close in style to the *Crucifixion*, and presumably also in date, is the *St Christopher with Sts Roch and Sebastian*, recorded by Vasari in the right aisle of the basilica of the Santa Casa at Loreto (pl. 128).[5] It is possible that Lotto received his first commission for the holy city where he was to spend his final years through Niccolò Bonafede, in his role as papal vice-legate to the Marches. But Loreto is in any case not far from Monte San Giusto, and in the absence of any local painter of more than mediocre talent, the news of Lotto's return to the central Marches would have spread quickly among discriminating patrons. The identity of the particular donor of the *St Christopher* altarpiece is unknown, but the three saints represented are entirely appropriate to the shrine of the Holy House as a destination for pilgrims, and especially for those seeking protection from the plague.[6] Probably related to the prophylactic function of the saints is the motif in the central foreground, comprising a paper scroll inscribed with an eye and the painter's signature, wound round a snake. Although its precise meaning remains to be elucidated, this characteristically Lottesque hieroglyph refers in some way to the conquest of evil (the snake) through the power of God (the all-seeing eye).[7] As in the *Crucifixion*, a dramatic tension exists between the effects on the one hand of space, here exemplified by the dynamic contrapposto of the disproportionately huge St Christopher, and on the other of silhouette and of colour pattern, dominated by the intense red of the fluttering cloak and the yellow of the loincloth.

127 Lotto. *Crucifixion* (*c.*1533–4). Canvas, 452.5 × 248 cm. Original frame. Monte San Giusto, Santa Maria in Telusiano.

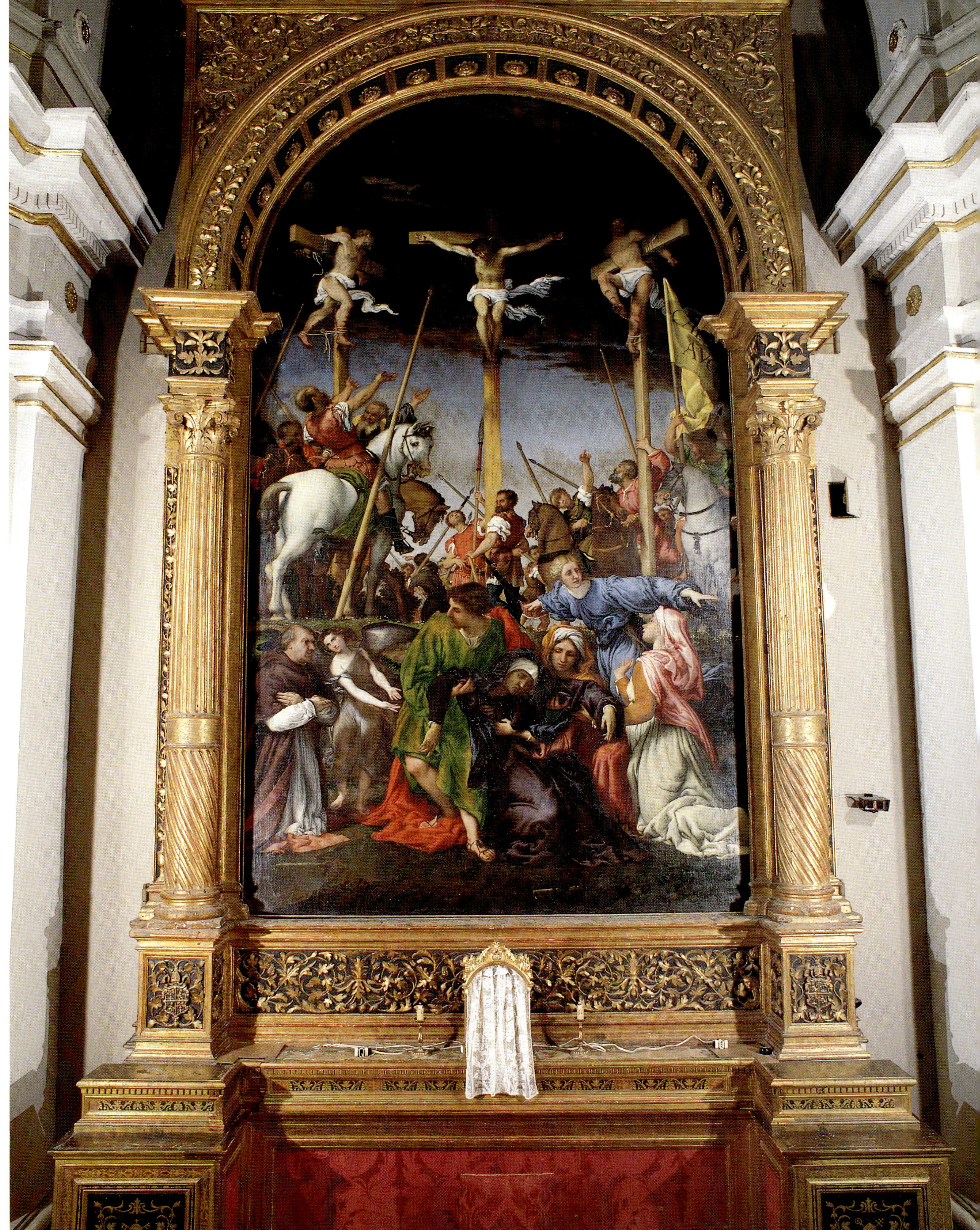

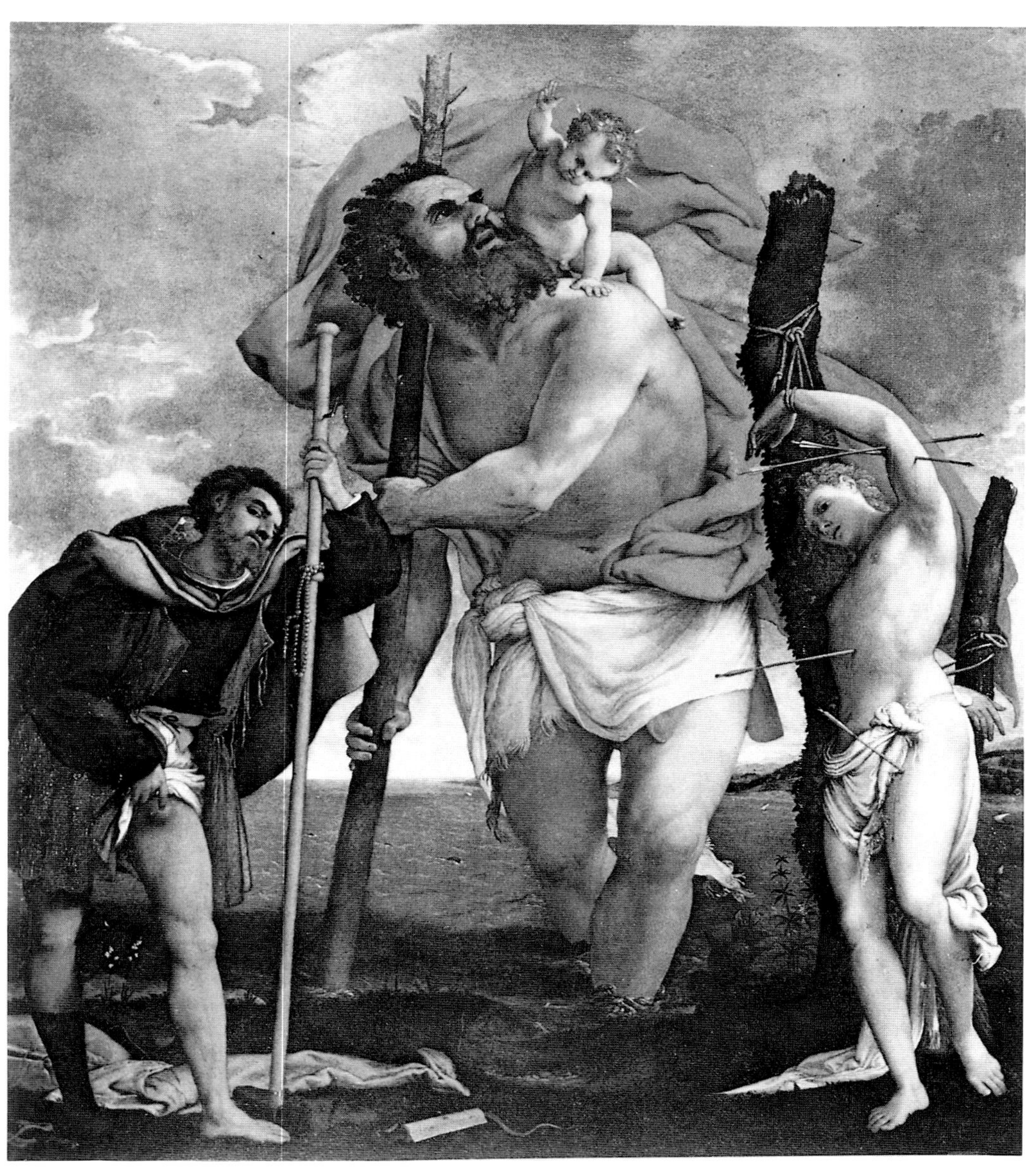

128 Lotto. *St Christopher with Sts Roch and Sebastian* (*c.*1534). Canvas, 275 × 232 cm. Loreto, Palazzo Apostolico.

Lotto's work at the basilica of Loreto would naturally have focused his attention on the monumental programme of relief sculpture that encased the relic of the Holy House; and in the *Annunciation* (pl. 2), painted for the Confraternity of Santa Maria sopra Mercanti in nearby Recanati, several pictorial ideas – the cat, the shelf with still-life objects, the curtained bed behind the Virgin – seem to have been loosely adapted from Andrea Sansovino's relief of the same subject, prominently placed at the front of the shrine, immediately behind the high altar.[8] Lotto's altarpiece, which has already been discussed in the Introduction (pp. 1–2), has in the past consistently been dated to about 1527–8,[9] and has often been connected with a reference in Lotto's letter to Bergamo of August 1527, in which he mentions that he has just sent off two framed altarpieces to the Marches. But as has been seen (p. 92), both of these works are likely to have been destined rather for Jesi; and stylistically, the Recanati *Annunciation* does not particularly resemble the *St Nicholas* altarpiece of 1527–9 (pl. 103), with its comparatively rich colour, bold chiaroscuro and painterly handling. The *Annunciation* is characterised, rather, by a limited colour range, pale shadows, rigid gestures and by relatively slender figures with small heads—all features typical of the works Lotto painted when in the Marches in the mid-1530s.[10] If the picture can indeed be convincingly redated to about 1534–5—in other words to the phase immediately after the *Crucifixion* and the *St Christopher* altarpiece—the commission may be linked to a document of July 1533, in which the Bishop of Recanati gave official permission to the Confraternity to move its oratory to a new building.[11]

During his second stay in the Marches, Lotto painted three Madonna and saints altarpieces, respectively for the towns of Fermo, Ancona and Cingoli. The badly damaged Fermo altarpiece, which carries the date 1535 (pl. 129), follows the iconography of Titian's altarpiece of 1520 for San Francesco ad Alto in nearby Ancona (now Pinacoteca Civica) in showing the Virgin and Child seated on clouds in the upper part of the composition, with two male saints gazing up from the ground below.[12] Although this proto-Baroque scheme was to become very popular indeed in Italian altarpieces in the period after the Council of Trent, Lotto characteristically does not exploit its potential for grandiose glorification, and concentrates rather on the humble devotion and rustic realism of the Savoldo-like saints. The altarpiece was originally placed in the sacristy of the church of Sant'Agostino in Fermo, and it may be that such details as the use of a landscape setting, the penitential fervour of the nude St Jerome, and the display of St Andrew's bare, dusty feet, were inspired by the ideals of the local order of Augustinian Hermits. The Fermo altarpiece is also of special interest because although it is a painting of high, clearly autograph quality, it helps document the presence in Lotto's workshop for the first time of a young pupil, by the name of Durante Nobili. This painter, later recorded as an assistant to Lotto in Ancona and Loreto in 1548 and the early 1550s, is chiefly known for a series of mediocre and not even particularly Lottesque altarpieces executed for small towns in the Marches between 1549 and 1575. But his earliest known work, a *Virgin and Child in Glory with Sts Cosmas and Damian* (Caldarola, San Martino) painted for his home town of Caldarola in 1535 when he was only seventeen, is stylistically very close to Lotto, and compositionally represents a close variant of the Fermo altarpiece of the same year.[13] From the visual evidence, therefore, it may be deduced that Durante first became associated with Lotto as an apprentice soon after his arrival in the Marches in 1533, and perhaps remained with him until his departure in 1539.

The Ancona altarpiece (pl. 130), which perhaps not coincidentally was commissioned, like the Fermo altarpiece, for a church of Sant'Agostino officiated by the Hermits, shows the much more conventional scheme of the Virgin and Child enthroned in an architectural setting. According to the recently rediscovered contract, the work was commissioned on 1 August 1538 by one Simone di Giovannino Pizoni, a nobleman of Ancona, for his side-altar; and this information has in turn led to the correct identification of the figure with the inverted halberd, looking out at the spectator, as the donor's name-saint Simon Zelotes.[14] His counterpart, the elderly John the Evangelist, clearly refers to the donor's father; while the two outer saints, Stephen and Lawrence, both patrons of the city of Ancona, must have owed their inclusion rather to patriotic considerations. The rediscovery of the contract has also led to the convincing identification of a segmental canvas, hitherto unnoticed in a local church, and representing the dove of the Holy Spirit above a semicircle of seven winged cherub-heads, as the original lunette of the altarpiece;[15] a third constituent part of the altarpiece, however, a predella scene representing St Ursula and the Eleven Thousand Virgins, has not so far re-emerged. Compared with Lotto's earlier *sacre conversazioni*, such as the splendidly rich and varied pair painted in Bergamo in 1521 (pls 54, 55), or the Jesi altarpiece of 1526 (pl. 101), the Ancona altarpiece shows a greater formality, combined with a simplification of detail and texture, and a use of more veiled and muted colours. In some ways, this development may be seen as foreshadowing the

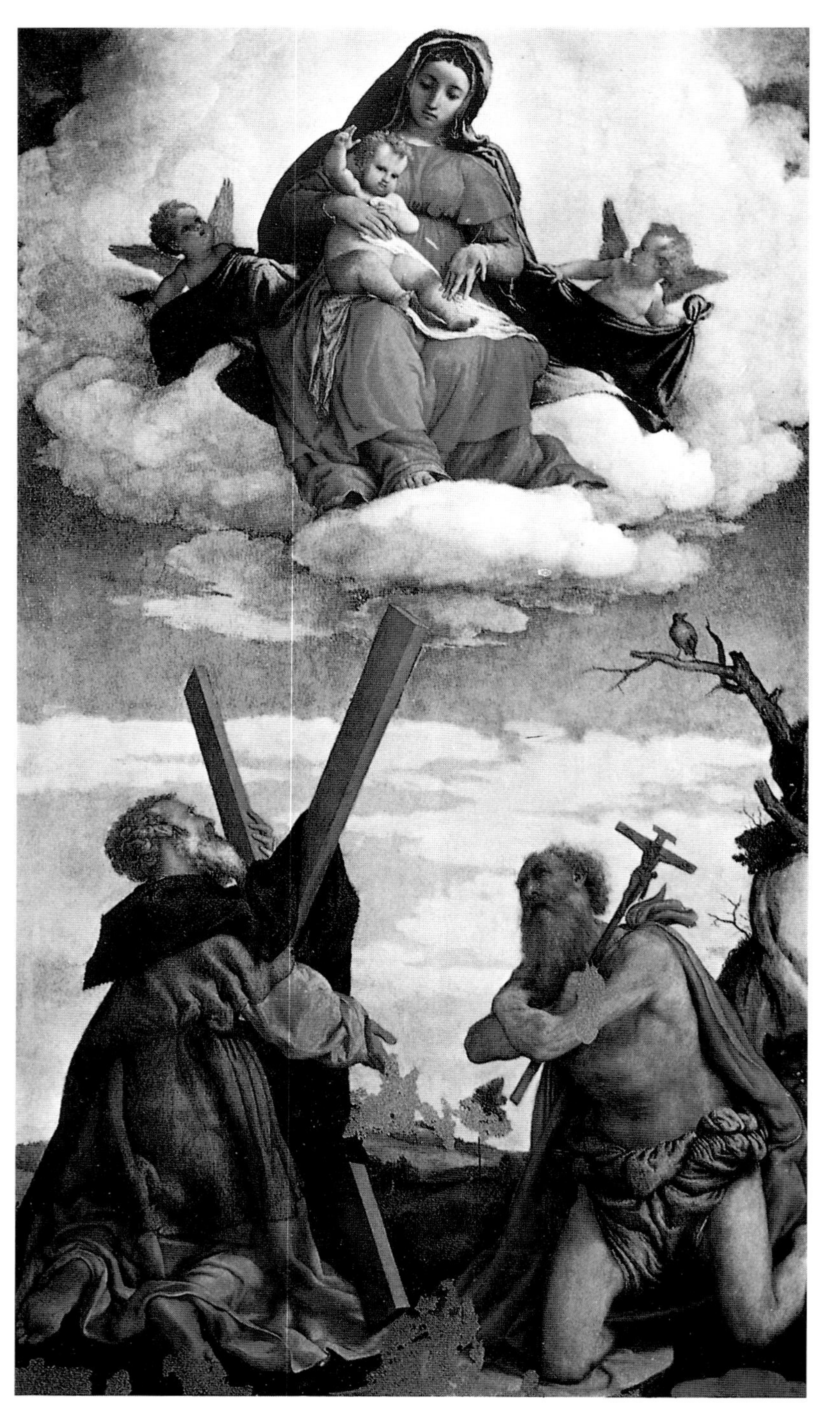

129 Lotto. *Virgin and Child in Glory with Sts Andrew and Jerome* (1535). Canvas, 250 × 141 cm. Rome, private collection.

impoverishment of inspiration that was to characterise many of the large-scale works of Lotto's final years; on the other hand, the use of dramatic, and often apparently arbitrary spotlighting still serves to provide great pictorial interest and to heighten the expressiveness of the interaction between the holy figures. Technically, the altarpiece may be regarded as characteristic of Lotto's practice throughout the later part of his career, with the paint applied relatively thickly and swiftly, and highlights achieved with dry, opaque touches with the tip of the brush (as in the broadly painted hair of St Simon) rather than with the carefully blended strokes and luminous glazes of the early works.

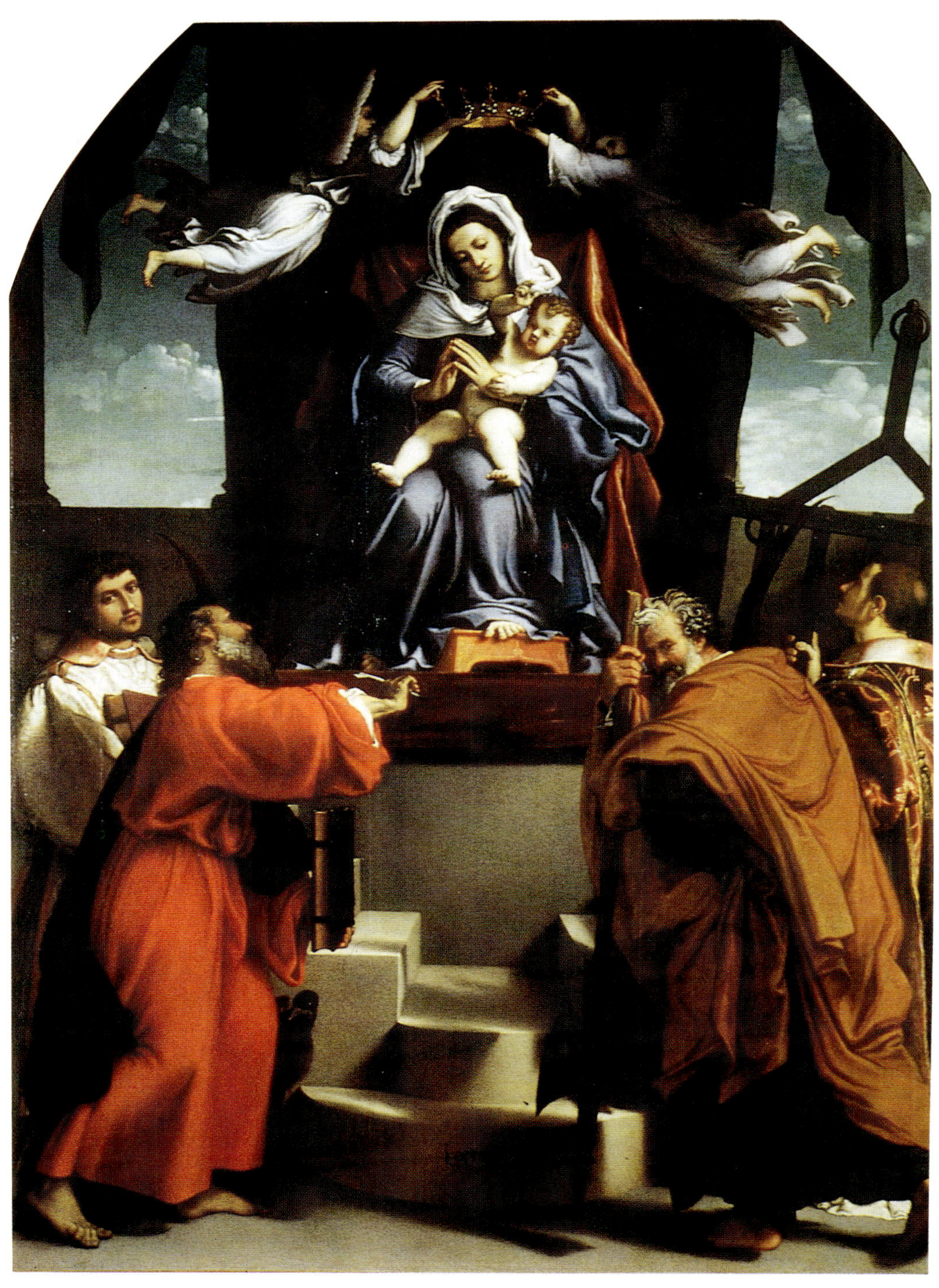

130 Lotto. *Virgin and Child with Saints* (1538–9). Canvas, 294 × 216 cm. Ancona, Pinacoteca Civica.

There is certainly no hint of any decline in Lotto's powers of invention or execution in the altarpiece he painted for the church of San Domenico in Cingoli, in the hills between Jesi and Macerata, in the same year as the Ancona altarpiece (pl. 131).[16] The central element of the composition, consisting of a Virgin and Child on a tall throne set against a high wall, is similar to that of the Ancona altarpiece, and the crimson damask of St Lawrence's dalmatic recurs in the cloth slung over the Virgin's throne. But the composition of the Cingoli altarpiece as a whole is much more complex, both because of the greater number of more fervently animated figures, and especially also because of the extraordinary way in which the fifteen narrative roundels, representing

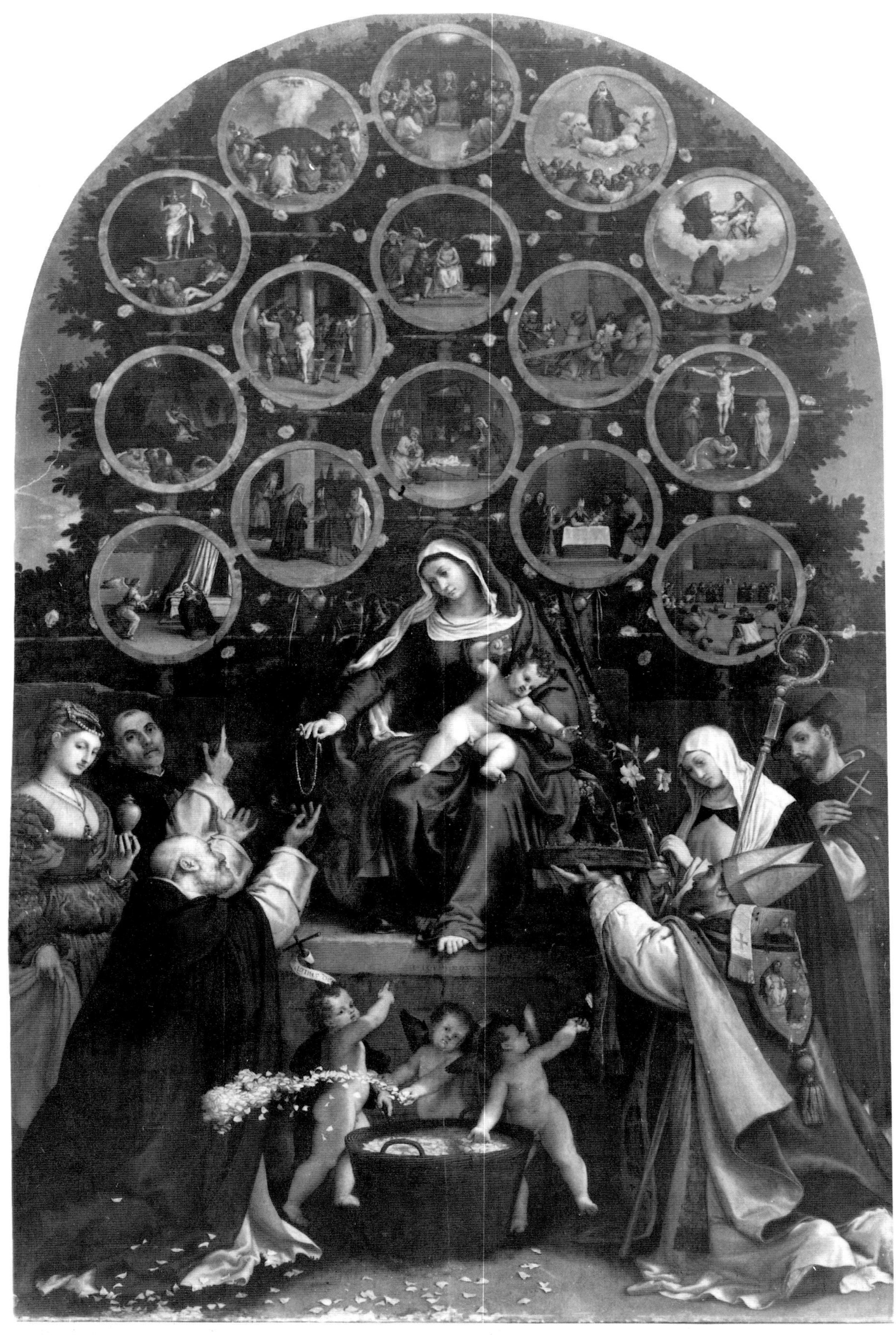

131 Lotto. *Virgin and Child with Saints* (1539). Canvas, 384 × 264 cm. Cingoli, Pinacoteca Civica.

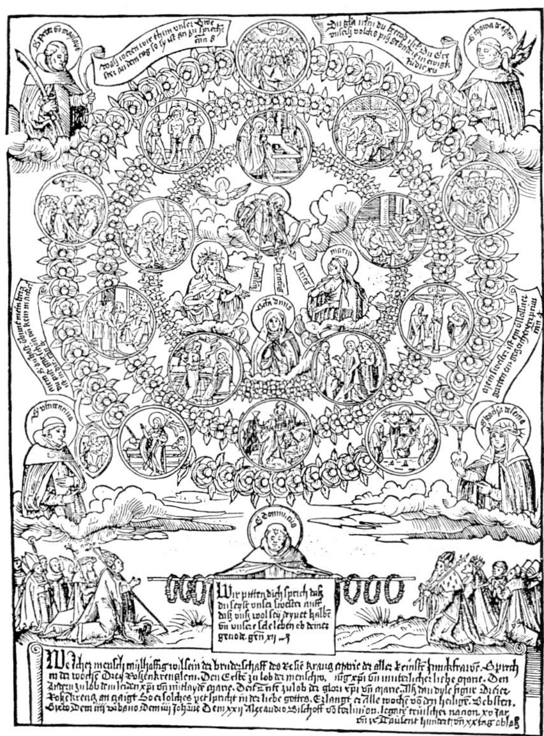

132 Wolf Traut. *Virgin of the Rosary* (*c.*1510). Woodcut.

the fifteen mysteries of the rosary, are displayed on a wooden trellis placed between the wall and the rose-hedge behind it. This method of display, which was presumably devised by Lotto in consultation with his patrons, a local Confraternity of the Rosary, was clearly in large part inspired by German prints celebrating the cult of the Virgin of the Rosary, such as that by Wolf Traut of about 1510 (pl. 132). A common feature of such prints was the combination of narrative roundels, representing the fifteen standard scenes from the lives of Christ and the Virgin, with images of the principal Dominican saints. The four represented here – Dominic, Vincent Ferrer, Catherine of Siena and Peter Martyr – had already appeared in Lotto's first altarpiece for the Marches, the polyptych for San Domenico in Recanati (pl. 31); and as before, the titular saint of the church, shown kneeling on the left, is the object of the Virgin's special attention. His counterpart on the right is St Exuperantius, a patron saint of Cingoli, who holds up a model of the town to be blessed by the Christ Child; and there is good reason to suppose, again as at Recanati (p. 28), that the prominent presence of this civic saint signifies that the town council made some contribution to the cost of the altarpiece.[17] Finally as at Recanati, the religious seriousness of the saints is expressively complemented by the amusing antics of the two child angels, who present their own variation on the rosary theme by gathering petals from the rose-hedge into a tub, and showering them like confetti over the robes of St Dominic. With characteristic wit Lotto represents their companion, the child Baptist, alerting the spectator not merely to the presence of the Christ Child on the Virgin's lap, but simultaneously also to the painter's signature on the step of her throne.

Lotto's activity as a painter of smaller-scale religious pictures and portraits during the mid- to late 1530s is even more poorly documented than in the previous Venetian phase. But it is likely that he was equally highly regarded by Marchigian patrons – or at least, by patrons in the papal states generally – as a painter of domestic pictures as of altarpieces; and indeed, there are a number of such pictures, which although customarily dated to the later 1520s, may more reasonably be dated to the Marchigian period.

One such example is the *Virgin and Child with Donors*, now in the Getty Museum (pl. 133), the style of which has often been compared with that of the Vienna *Virgin and Child with Saints* (pl. 110).[18] But the limbs of the holy figures in the Getty picture are more elongated than in the Vienna picture, and the treatment of surface textures, of the fall of light and shade, and of detail has all become simpler and more perfunctory, in a manner that parallels other works of the early to mid-1530s (see pls 2, 128). Similarly, the landscape background is more schematic than in the Vienna picture, and may be compared rather to that of the Fermo altarpiece (pl. 129). Quite exceptionally for the mature Lotto, the Madonna group is based closely on the work of another painter, Catena's *Holy Family with St Anne*, formerly in the Mexborough Collection (pl. 134),[19] and this circumstance has understandably been seen as confirming the supposition that the Getty picture dates from the period of Lotto's residence in Venice. But as has already been seen (p. 111), he served as one of the executors of Catena's will in 1531, and in this office he would naturally have acquired a close familiarity with the contents of his deceased colleague's studio; indeed, he may even have owned the ex-Mexborough picture, or another version of it. A further argument that the Getty picture was painted in the Marches may be found in the presence of the donor portraits. As has also been seen (p. 70), conjugal portraits, while not unusual in northern and central Italy as a whole, were for sociological reasons virtually unknown in Venice.

Another picture for private devotion usually dated to the later 1520s, close to the Vienna *Virgin and Saints*, is the *Adoration of the Shepherds* in Brescia (pl. 135). In its touching intimacy, with Holy Family, shepherds, animals and angels all brought close together in quietly meditative worship, the *Adoration* indeed resembles the Vienna picture as a perfect expression of Lotto's finely attuned religious sensibility. Although

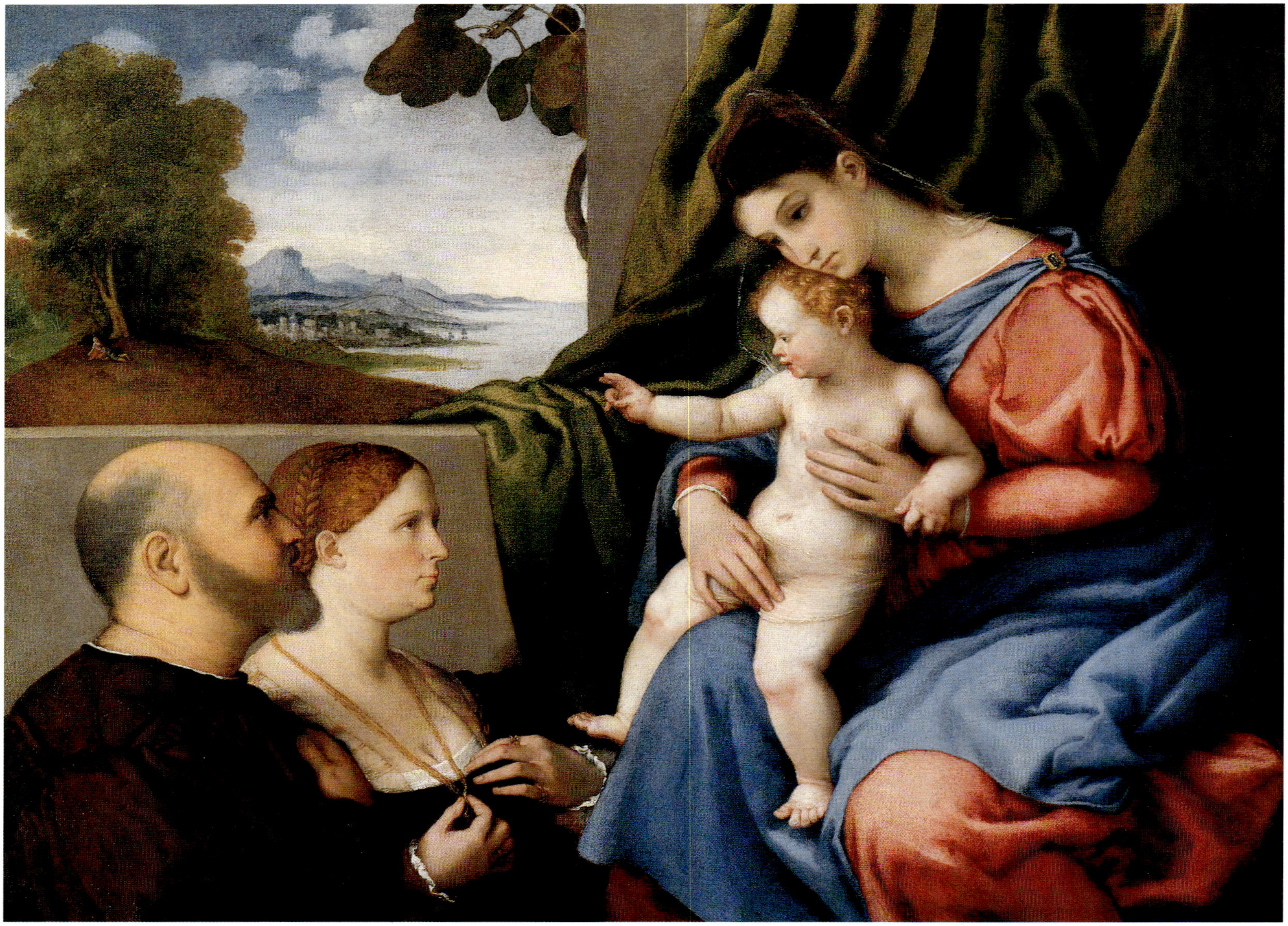

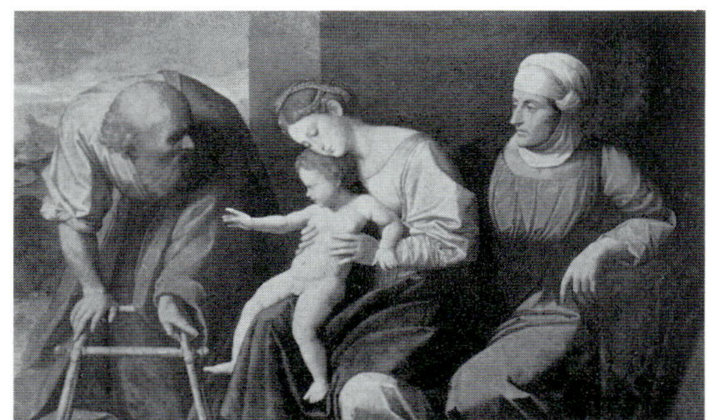

134 Vincenzo Catena. *Holy Family with St Anne* (*c.*1518–20). Formerly London, the Earl of Mexborough.

unlike the Reynst *Nativity* and its Bergamask predecessors this is not a true nocturne, the magically illuminated evening sky outside the stable–presumably alluding to the glory of the angelic host–and the deep shadows inside, endow the scene with a comparable effect of poetic enchantment. It is probably the unmistakable affinity of such features with the work of Savoldo (see pl. 108)–reinforced, perhaps, by the circumstance that the picture is housed today in Savoldo's native city of Brescia–that has encouraged the dating to Lotto's Venetian period.[20] But stylistically the Brescia *Adoration* resembles less the Vienna picture and other works of the late 1520s, than the Getty *Virgin and Child with Donors*, as is especially evident in the recurrence of the swan-necked Virgin, but also in the similar compression of the foreground space and the use of bold silhouette. It may also be pointed out that a very similar patterning of the angels' wings recurs in the *Virgin and Child with Angels*, formerly in Osimo (between Recanati and Ancona) and universally accepted as having been painted in the Marches in the mid- to late 1530s.[21] Furthermore, according to the earliest report of the picture's provenance,[22] it was painted for the ruling family of Perugia, the Baglione–for a patron, in other words, living not in northern Italy but in the Papal

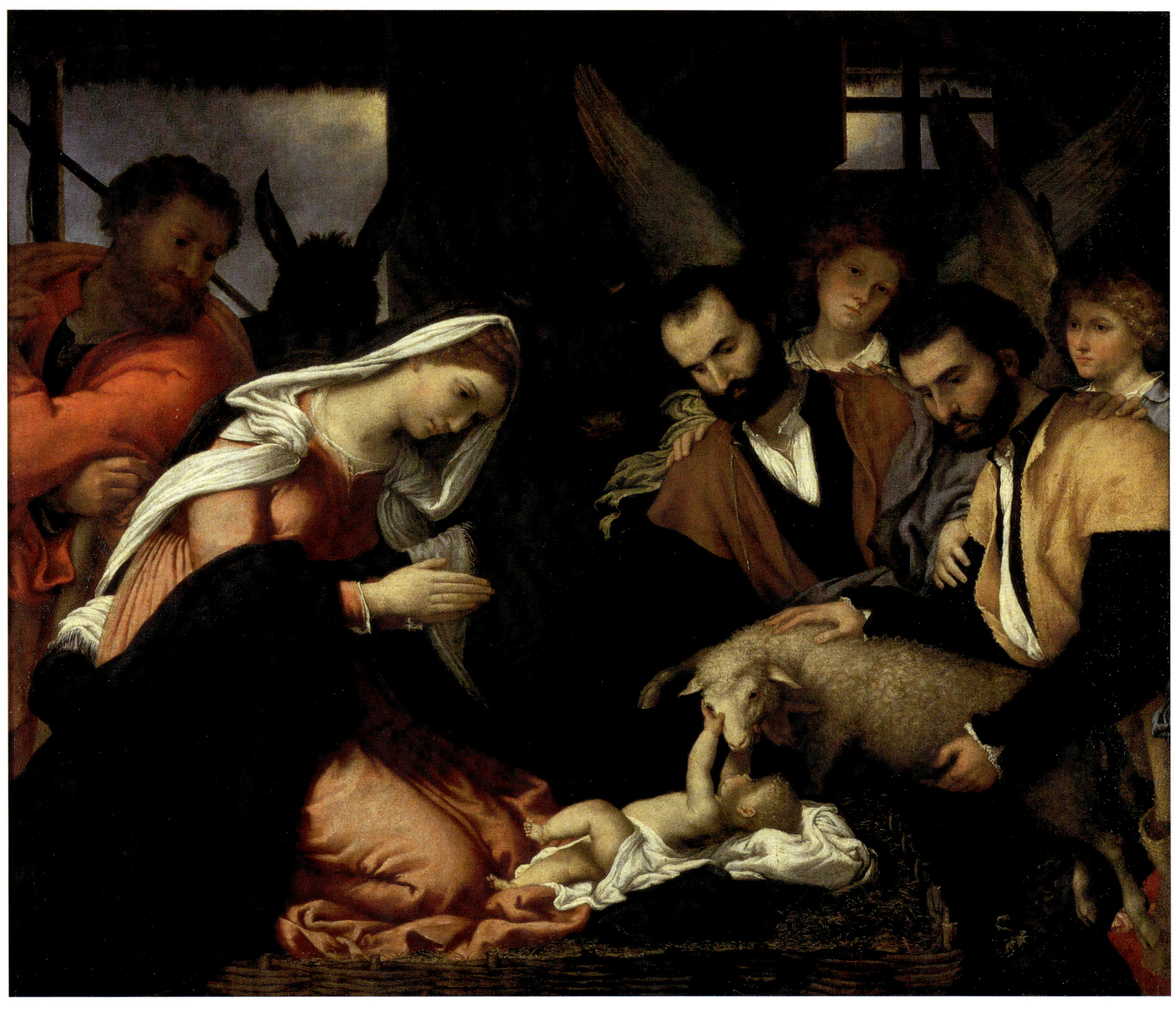

135 Lotto. *Adoration of the Shepherds* (*c.*1534). Canvas, 147 × 166 cm. Brescia, Pinacoteca Tosio Martinengo.

133 (*facing page top*) Lotto. *Virgin and Child with Donors* (*c.*1533–5). Canvas, 85.7 × 115.5 cm. Malibu, California, Collection of the J. Paul Getty Museum.

States, just across the Apennines from Lotto's area of operations in the Marches. Admittedly this report, made by an early nineteenth-century Florentine dealer, cannot automatically be accepted as reliable, and it may yet turn out to be mere romantic fantasy. But at least consistent with it are two further circumstances: first, that the two shepherds, apparently brothers, are clearly portraits of gentlemen, wearing elegant black silk doublets and quilted red and blue breeches under their rustic jerkins;[23] second, that the subject, with emphasis on Joseph and the Holy Family, would have been highly appropriate for Perugia, where special veneration was accorded to the relic of the Holy Ring. Supposedly the very object used for the Marriage of the Virgin, this relic had been housed since 1473 in a chapel dedicated to Joseph in the Cathedral of San

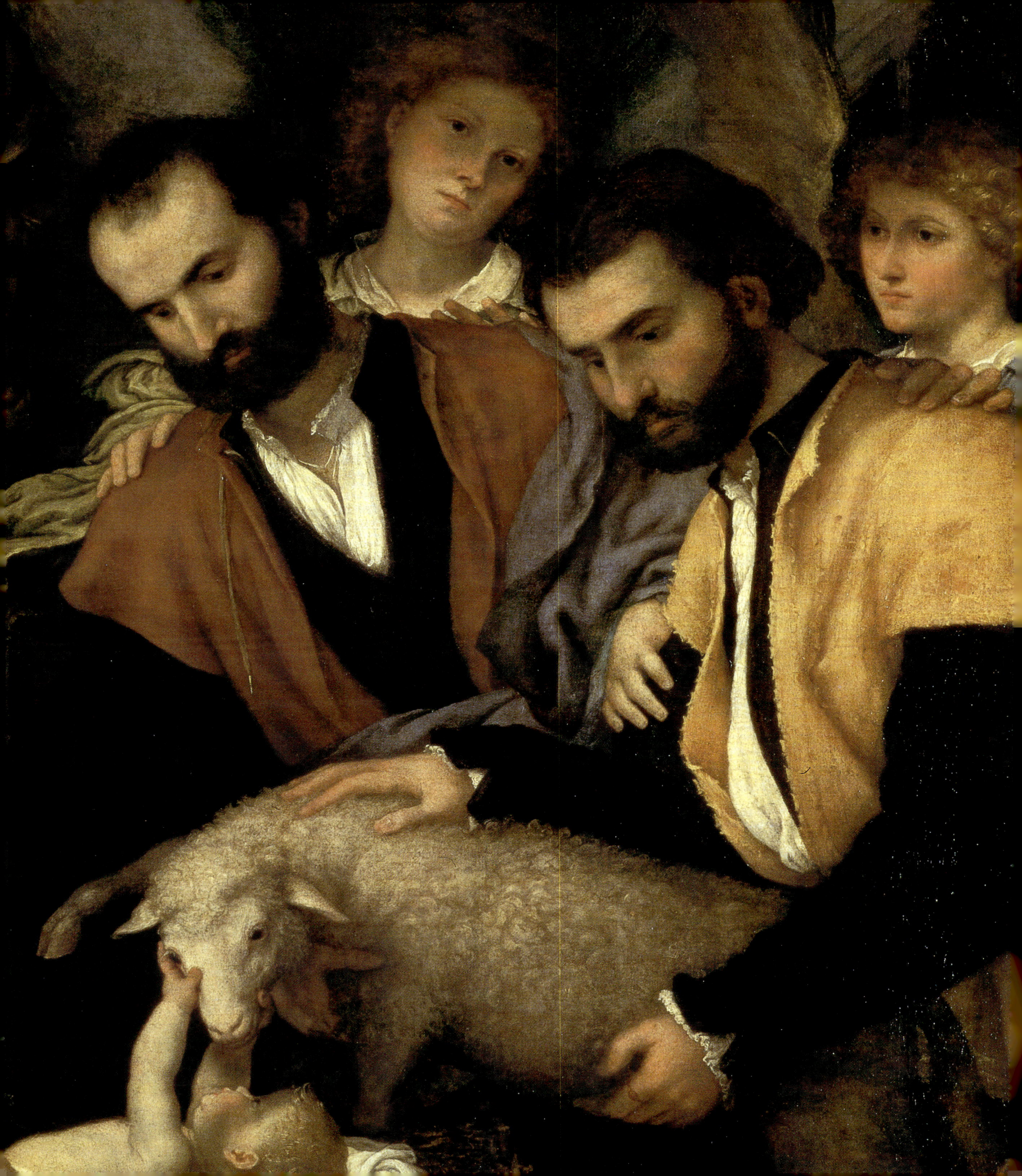

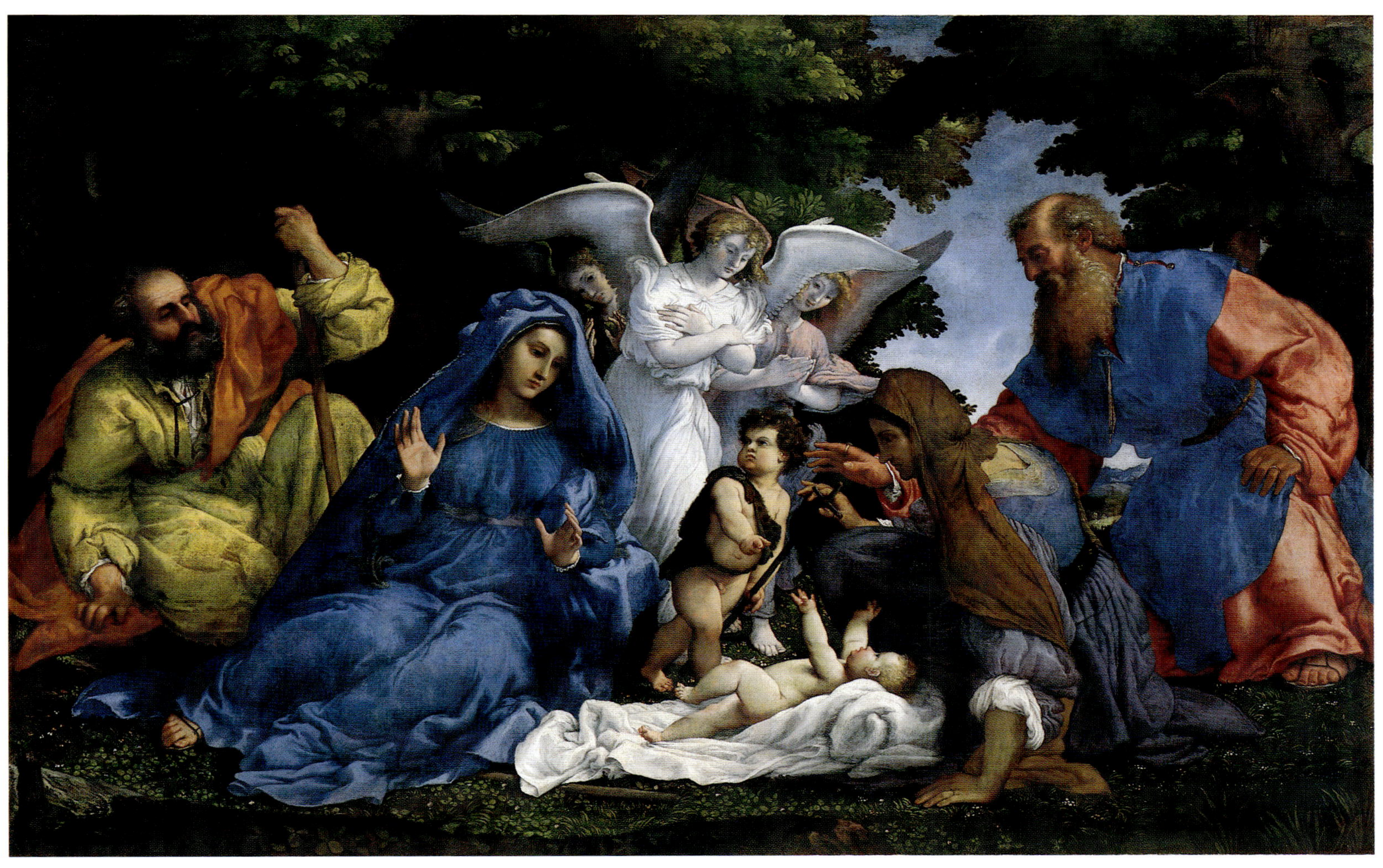

137 Lotto. *Holy Family with Angels* (*c.*1536–7). Canvas, 150 × 237 cm. Paris, Musée du Louvre.

136 (*facing page*) Detail of pl. 135.

Lorenzo;[24] and it may be significant, therefore, that, unusually in a Nativity scene, Lotto's Virgin displays a ring on the fourth finger of her right hand.

Similar in format and content to the Brescia *Adoration*, and incorporating an almost verbatim repetition of the Christ Child, is the Louvre *Holy Family with Angels* (pl. 137), a work that, by contrast, has always been dated to the 1530s.[25] With its magnificently intense (although characteristically dissonant) colour and its meticulous execution, this, too, must have been painted for a patron of importance; this unidentified person seems, however, never to have taken delivery, since the picture remained in Lotto's possession and was later one of those put up for auction in Ancona in 1550. As a pastoral idyll, in which an informally posed Holy Family relaxes in a verdant landscape with adoring saints and angels, the subject is obviously related to that of the Vienna *Virgin and Saints* and similar works by such Venetian painters as Palma (pl. 109). But here the scene has been enriched by narrative associations, and the presence of the child John the Baptist with his parents Elizabeth and Zacharias recalls the various apocryphal accounts of meetings between the two holy children as described by late medieval devotional writers such as the Franciscan Pseudo-Bonaventure and the Dominican Domenico Cavalca. The two most relevant episodes are those of the visit to Bethlehem by the six-month-old Baptist with his parents soon after the birth of Christ, and the meeting between the two children in the desert during the Holy Family's Flight into Egypt.[26] Yet neither of these episodes is portrayed with textual literalness, since the first supposedly took place in the stable at Bethlehem, and the second when the Baptist had

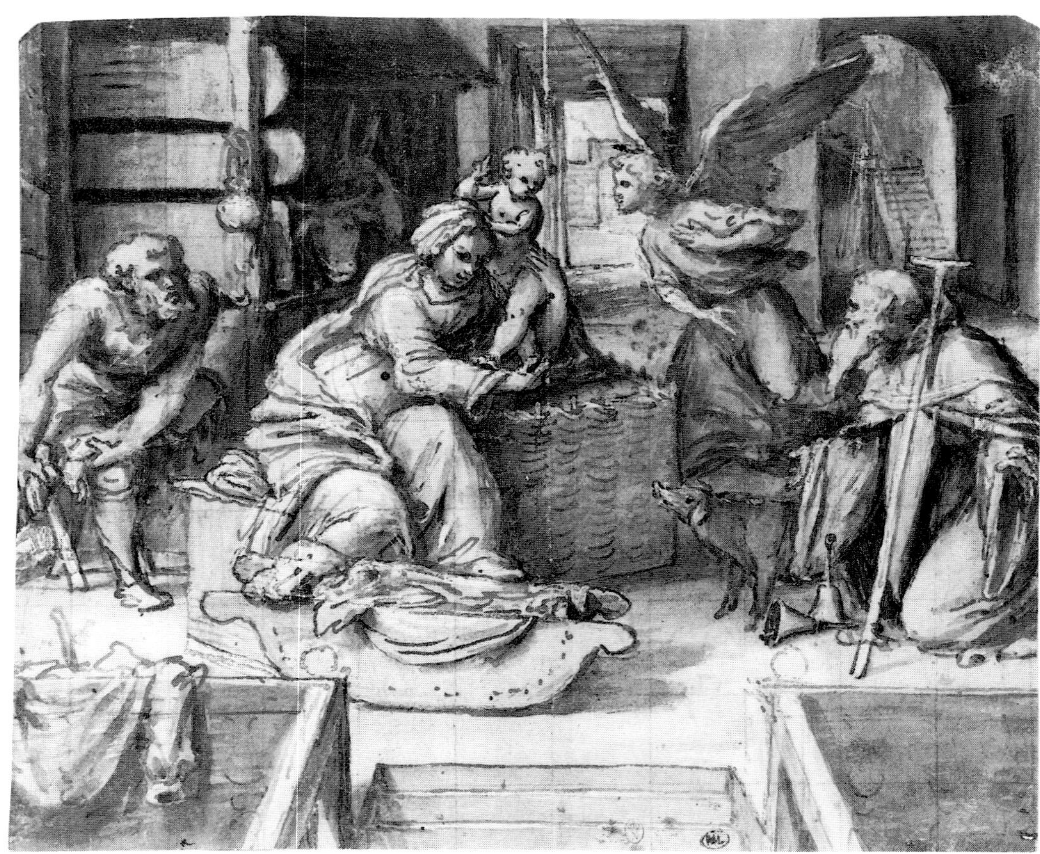

138 Lotto. *Holy Family with an Angel and St Anthony Abbot* (*c*.1534–6). 16.8 × 20 cm. Pen and brown ink with grey wash, heightened with white, squared with red chalk. Paris, Musée du Louvre.

already begun his career as a hermit, watched over by the Archangel Uriel, but in the absence of Elizabeth and Zacharias. Lotto's subject thus consists of an ideal conflation of these legends, the emotionally affective power of which is all the greater for not being limited to a single event.

Unconnected with any known painting, but close in mood and motif to both the Brescia *Adoration* and the Louvre *Holy Family with Angels*, is one of Lotto's most appealing drawings, a *Holy Family with an Angel and St Anthony Abbot* (pl. 138).[27] Probably likewise dating from the mid-1530s, and also therefore executed in the Marches, the drawing portrays the stable at Bethlehem, which to a greater extent than in the Brescia painting is evoked spatially, offering enticing glimpses through openings in the background, as well as in terms of a subtle and poetic illumination. Completely characteristic of Lotto is the ability to combine, as in the Recanati *Annunciation* (pl. 2), a sincerity and directness of religious expression with a delight in amusing detail, as in that of St Anthony's pig who acts as a full participant in the presentation of its master by the angel to the welcoming Virgin and Child.

Although few or no portraits have been traditionally assigned to Lotto's second Marchigian period, there is no external reason why his extraordinary talents as a portraitist should not have been as much in demand in the Marches as in Venice or Bergamo. As we have seen, there are good stylistic reasons for supposing that the Getty *Virgin and Child* with its donor portraits (pl. 133) was painted during this second period; furthermore, the earliest record in his account-book, dated 16 November 1538, refers to a commission to paint the portrait of the protonotary Giovanni Maria Pizoni, a member of a noble family of Ancona, and presumably closely related to the Simone di Giovannino Pizoni who had commissioned the Ancona altarpiece on 1 August of that year.[28] Probably dating from slightly earlier, perhaps about 1535, is the *Portrait of a Man*

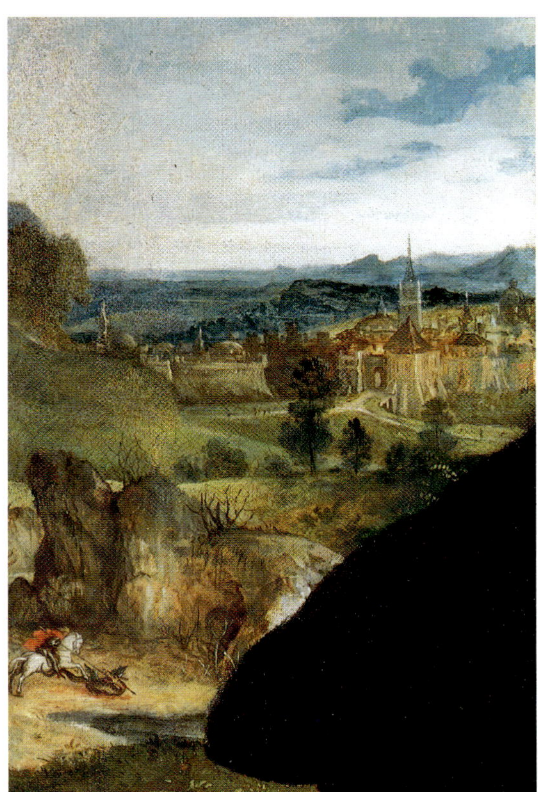

139 Detail of pl. 5.

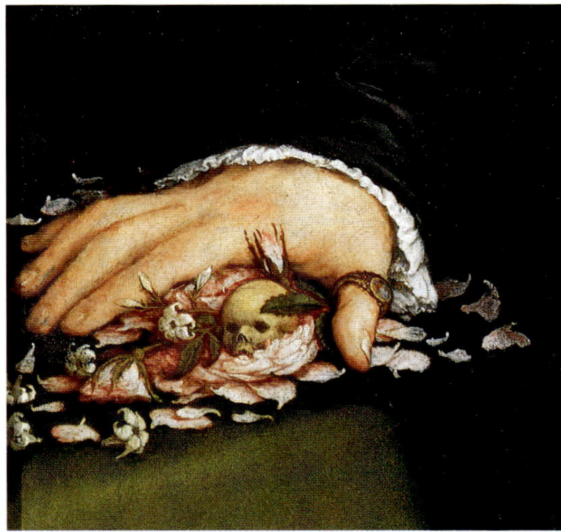

140 Detail of pl. 5.

in the Galleria Borghese (pl. 5), recently but inconclusively identified as a certain Mercurio Bua.[29] This Bua was a *condottiere* of Albanian origin, who, when not in Venice, lived in Treviso, where he founded a funerary chapel dedicated to St George. Although this saint is indeed to be seen slaying the dragon in the landscape background, central to the identification of the sitter as Bua is the recognition of the walled city beyond as Treviso (pl. 139). But the city is only very generically represented, with a standard display of towers and fortifications; and it is surely more probable that a professional soldier would have chosen to be portrayed in a military aspect than in plain black. It is likely, then, that the diminutive figure of St George, as in the similar detail in the *St Nicholas* altarpiece (pl. 103; p. 96), refers simply to the unknown sitter's name-saint. The identification of him as Bua is based also on the assumption that the portrait was painted before Lotto's departure for the Marches in 1533. But compositionally the Borghese *Man* is very different from Lotto's Venetian portraits, such as the *Odoni*, the *Young Man* and even *Lucrezia Valier*, with their broad formats, circumstantially described environments, and spatially dynamic poses based on diagonals. Instead the emphasis here, as in the works of the mid-1530s generally, is on silhouette, with the unstable outline of the black costume serving to underline the sitter's state of mind. Even more than the sitter of the *Young Man*, this older sitter, who similarly resorts to the relief provided by rose-petals (pp. 108–10), seems in the grip of a deep melancholy; and the gesture of his left hand appears to point explicitly to his spleen, traditionally regarded as the seat of his debilitating humour. The presence of a tiny skull among the rose-petals suggests that his black mood has been prompted by thoughts of death (pl. 140); it remains a matter of speculation, however, whether he has suffered a recent bereavement, as apparently in the case of the sitter of Lotto's later Doria portrait (pl. 154; pp. 154–5), or whether such thoughts were simply characteristic of the sitter's temperament.[30]

As has just been mentioned, the earliest entry in the *Libro* dates from November 1538, when he was in Ancona working on his altarpiece for Sant'Agostino (pl. 130). This, however, is an isolated reference, and he did not start making consistent use of this extant account-book until his return to Venice, probably at the very end of 1539 or the beginning of 1540. From now onwards his movements and commissions are recorded in meticulous detail. The principal project undertaken in the two and a half years before he moved on to Treviso consisted of the much-delayed *St Antoninus* altarpiece for the friars of Santi Giovanni e Paolo (pl. 141). Although this was apparently commissioned as far back as 1525/6 (pp. 88–9), Lotto began the actual task of painting only in December 1540, and delivered the completed work in May 1542. As has been seen, a likely impetus for the original commission was the canonisation of Antoninus in 1523, and the subsequent erection of an altar in his honour. Although the fifteenth-century Archbishop of Florence was prolific as a theologian, his popular cult was due above all to the saintly poverty of his way of life and to his generosity to the poor. In 1442 he founded a confraternity for the assistance of the so-called *poveri vergognosi*–that is, respectable persons in reduced circumstances, who were ashamed to beg. In 1537 a similar confraternity had been founded under his influence in Venice; and this received strong official backing from the government, which in its efforts to reduce beggary and vagabondage after a series of terrible famines on the Venetian *terraferma* in 1527–9, had instituted a more systematic method of poor relief, whereby provision was made for the 'shamefaced' poor, but parasitical beggars were made to work for their living. Against this background, it is perhaps no accident that Lotto's altarpiece was completed to coincide with the centenary of the foundation of Antoninus's confraternity. In keeping with the ideal of organised charity promoted by Antoninus, Lotto depicts him under the inspiration of a pair of flying angels, instructing his deacons to receive petitions from, and to give alms to the poor–some of whom clearly comprise respectable

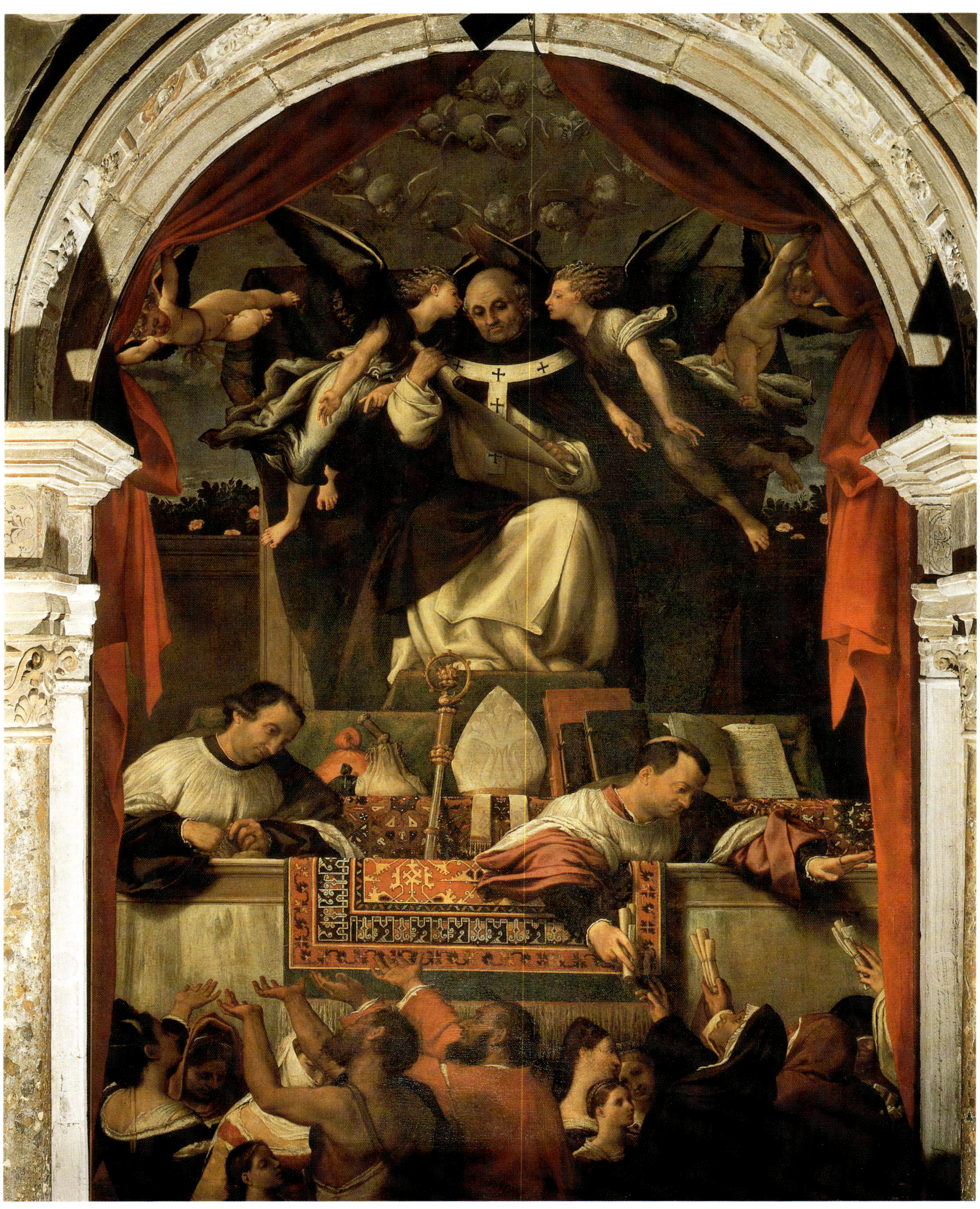

widows and orphans, as well as beggars proper. The apparent hesitation with which the deacon on the left dips into his purse may be intended to convey the message that the saint's charity is not to be dispensed indiscriminately, but according the principles of informed pity and justice.[31]

In this hitherto unusual choice of a scene from a saint's life for the main field of an altarpiece–as opposed to showing him or her as part of a timeless *sacra conversazione*–the work may be compared with the *St Lucy* altarpiece (p. 116). Here, too, the stress is laid on the example of practical virtue set by the saints rather than on their supernatural powers; and again, this shift of emphasis in official religious imagery may be related not simply to the social policies of the Venetian government, but also to the ideals of such Evangelical reformers as Gasparo Contarini.[32] Much more than in the *St Lucy* altarpiece, however, and perhaps as a way of imposing a sense of timeless order on to this scene of pitiful human distress, Lotto's composition retains much in common with traditional altarpiece design; indeed, it closely resembles that of his recent *sacre conversazioni* for Ancona and Cingoli (pls 130, 131) in its placing of an enthroned figure at the apex of a symmetrical triangle, and in its use of a shallow, layered space, closed off by a high wall. But also, as in the Cingoli altarpiece, the traditional scheme is then successfully reanimated by the use of highly expressive heads and gestures–studied from life, using real paupers, according to the *Libro*[33]–and by the arresting technical brilliance of the still-life detail.

During the execution of the *St Antoninus* altarpiece Lotto lived in the house of Mario d'Armano, his closest living blood-relative. As a specially itemised list of expenses inserted into the *Libro* makes clear (Appendix B, pp. 177–8), Lotto contributed to household expenses by regularly providing bulk purchases of food, including olive oil, vinegar, wine, cheese and ham, as well as other domestic necessities such as soap, and seemingly endless pairs of shoes for Mario's little daughter Lauretta. Lotto also painted a number of pictures for his cousin and for the various members of his family, some of them portraits, but most of them small-scale Madonnas or other devotional subjects. Although all of these are now lost or unrecognised, a rare mythological subject, a *Venus* commissioned by Mario in September 1540, and originally equipped with a gilt frame in walnut and a black cloth bearing an inscription, may well be identical with the *Venus and Cupid* now in the Metropolitan Museum, New York (pl. 142). This recently rediscovered picture has been dated rather earlier, to the late Bergamask or to the beginning of the first Venetian period;[34] stylistically, however, it seems consistent rather with the *St Antoninus* altarpiece, and with other works of the later 1530s or earlier 1540s, such as the Ancona altarpiece or the *Laura da Pola* (pl. 148). The colours are duskier and more muted than in the earlier period and the forms more rigid; indeed, the complicated artificiality of Venus's pose, and the elongation of her smooth, marbly limbs, suggests a certain interest on the part of Lotto in the activity of the Florentine Mannerist Francesco Salviati, who worked in Venice for two years from the summer of 1539. Somewhat incongruously, however, the abstractly ornamental nude body is combined with the homely, gently amused features of the portrait-like head; while the uninhibited merriment of the urinating Cupid has nothing at all in common with central Italian *maniera*. Although mythological subjects were always to be a rarity in Lotto's own oeuvre, representations of the reclining Venus, usually accompanied by Cupid, had constituted a popular genre in Venetian painting ever since the time of Giorgione (see pl. 143). Most of them, if not all, were probably commissioned as wedding gifts; but in Lotto's contribution, which is characteristically laden with hieroglyph-like symbolism, epithalamic allusions are particularly overt. Most obviously, the stream of urine from Cupid to Venus's lap alludes to sexual union, and to the hope for fertility; but the vulva-like sea-shell above her head, while also referring to the myth of her own birth, carries no less obvious sexual connotations. Significantly, too,

141 (*facing page*) Lotto. *St Antoninus* altarpiece (1541–2). Canvas, 332 × 235 cm. Venice, Santi Giovanni e Paolo.

142 (*following page top*) Lotto. *Venus and Cupid* (1540(?)). Canvas, 92 × 111 cm. New York, Metropolitan Museum of Art. Purchase, Mrs. Charles Wrightsman Gift, in honor of Marietta Tree, 1986.

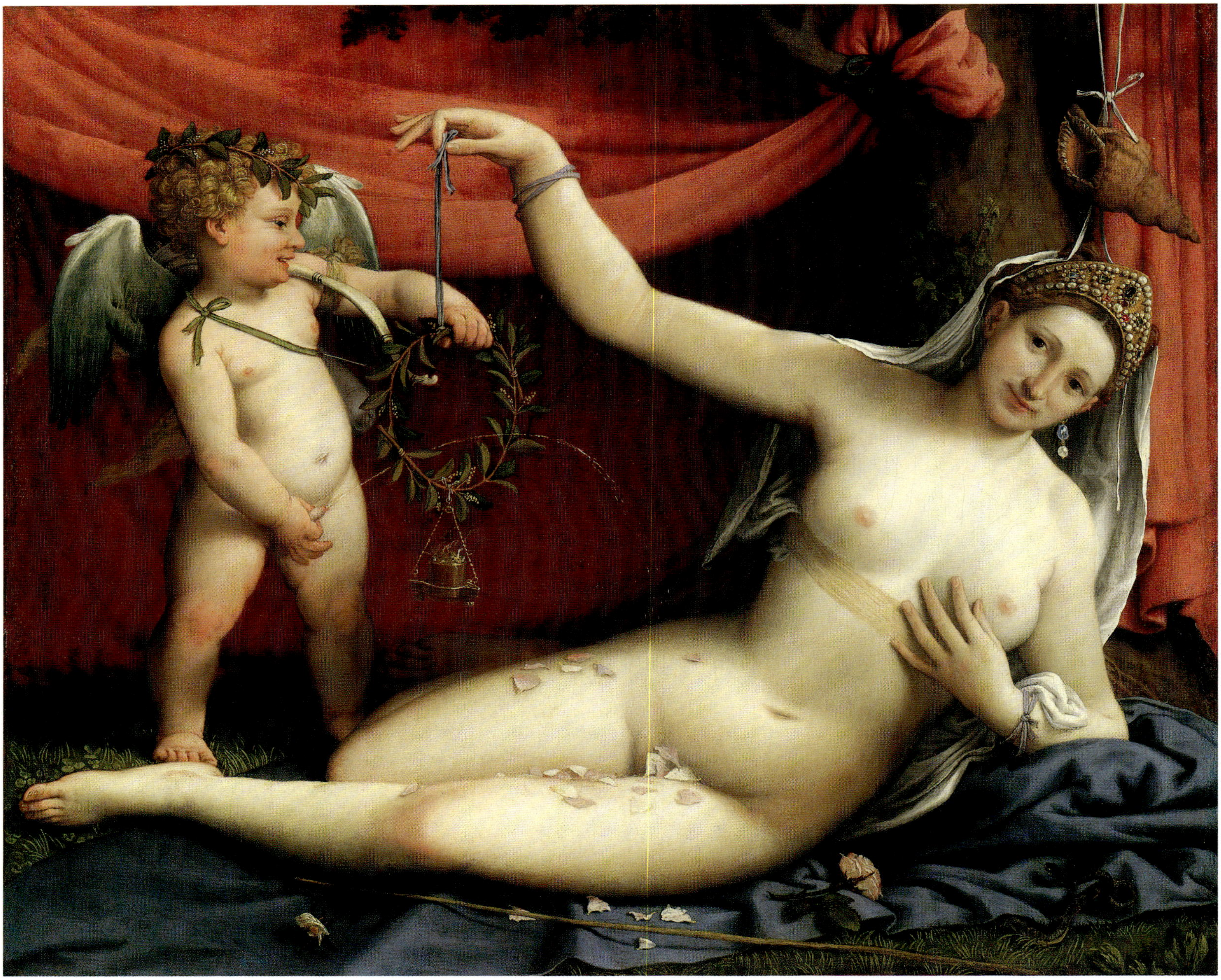

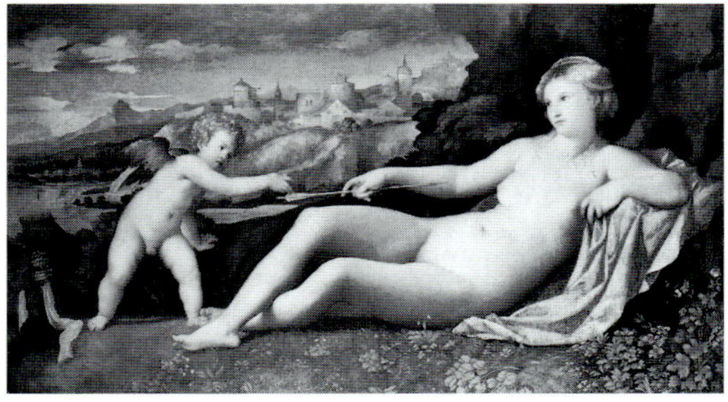

143 Palma Vecchio. *Venus and Cupid* (*c.*1520–25). Cambridge, Fitzwilliam Museum.

and again unusually among Venetian pictures of this time, Venus wears a head-dress with veil of a type worn by a bride. Presumably the meaning of these visual symbols was originally summed up, as in the Bergamo *intarsie*, by the inscription placed on the cover. Mario d'Armano himself had long been married, and must have commissioned the picture to celebrate the wedding of a friend; and in this connection it is interesting to note that nine months later, in May 1541, he commissioned from Lotto a now lost pendant representing *Susannah and the Elders*—as an exhortation, perhaps, to his friend's wife to preserve her chastity for her husband.

In October 1540 Lotto painted another pair of pictures for Mario to give to a friend: portraits, presumably copied from German prints, of Martin Luther and his wife Catharina von Bora (Appendix B, p. 177).[35] This reference has naturally excited much speculation among scholars about the painter's attitude towards the Protestant reli-

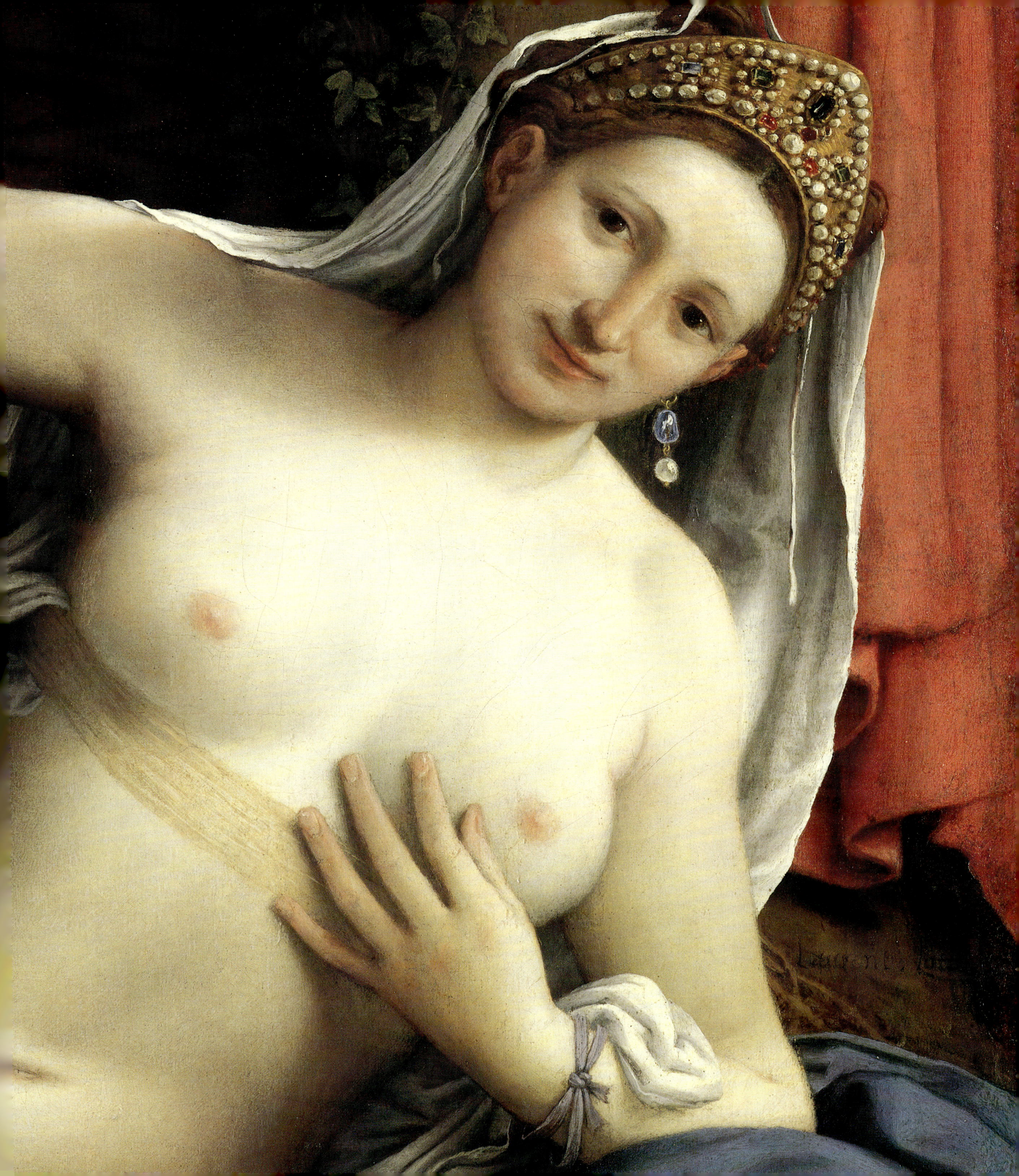

gion.[36] Luther had been excommunicated from the Catholic Church as early as 1521, and one of the many crimes for which he stood condemned was the fact that he had broken his monastic vows by marrying. That Mario d'Armano, together with a number of his friends and relatives, was at least sympathetic to Lutheran teaching is confirmed by the fact that in 1559 he and his nephew Marcantonio are known to have been under investigation by the Venetian Inquisition.[37] Lotto's personal, independent approach to religious imagery suggests that he might have shared this sympathy; and as has been seen (p. 114), a decade earlier he had been involved in the production of Brucioli's Italian Bible. But although time was beginning to run out for the Evangelicals, in 1540 – a year before Contarini's ill-fated mission to Regensburg – there still existed high hopes for a reconciliation with the Protestants; and philo-Protestant literature such as the highly popular *Beneficio di Cristo* (1543) continued to pour from the Venetian printing-presses without official hindrance.[38] There was still no need, in other words, for Lotto to sense any contradiction between copying the portrait of an admired spiritual leader and continuing to work for Catholic institutions, including for the ultra-orthodox Dominican order. Thus, on the one hand, he could paint for his own personal devotion on Good Friday a tiny *Mystic Crucifixion* (pl. 145),[39] the deep Christocentricity of which accords perfectly with the spirit of the *Beneficio* and also with Luther's emphasis on a direct, unmediated relationship between man and God, while on the other hand, the sincerity of his continuing loyalty to the Dominicans is demonstrated by the fact that when he delivered the *St Antoninus* altarpiece in 1542, he renounced a proportion of his fee, on the understanding that when he died he would be buried in the cemetery of Santi Giovanni e Paolo, dressed in the habit of a friar.[40]

In October 1542 Lotto moved from Venice to Treviso, the city where forty years earlier he had achieved his first successes as a painter.[41] As he explains in his will of 1546 (Appendix C, p. 179), he had now decided to spend the rest of his life in the house of Giovanni dal Saon, a mutual friend of Lotto and the goldsmith Antonio Carpan, brother of Bartolomeo (p. 110). Saon had been an admirer of Lotto's art since at least 1532, when he had bought a number of pictures from him,[42] and part of the arrangement was that he should give instruction in painting to his host's sons. It is not completely clear why Lotto decided to leave the house of his cousin Mario d'Armano, with whom he was still apparently on perfectly friendly terms. At the end of his list of expenses for 1540–42 he noted that he wished 'to go and live a more quiet life in Treviso, because of the many disturbances in the house'. But Saon's family similarly included young children, so Lotto's explanation cannot represent the whole truth; and there is more than a hint in the same paragraph that he was embarrassed at seeming to the outside world to be financially dependent on his nephew. Further evidence that his earnings in Venice were precarious is provided by an entry in February 1542, when he borrowed money from his friend Jacopo Sansovino.[43] Lotto may, therefore, have wanted to move as much for professional as domestic reasons, perhaps calculating that he would face no serious competition from local artists. Indeed, despite the occasional presence in the city during the 1520s of major artists such as Titian (see pl. 3), Pordenone, Savoldo and the native Trevigian Paris Bordone, Treviso during the course of the 1530s had declined into a provincial backwater. But if Lotto imagined that he would find a more appreciative clientele in Treviso than in Venice, where a sophisticated Mannerism inspired by the Florentine visitors Salviati and Vasari was now the prevailing fashion, he was quickly to be disillusioned. True, the account-book shows that during the next three years he did not lack customers, and soon after his arrival he came to the attention of the Venetian *podestà* Francesco Giustinian, who commissioned him to paint his portrait.[44] But the account-book also shows that he was rather poorly paid for his work by his Trevigian patrons, and that, as in Venice, the extraordinary quality of his talent was often not properly appreciated. In January 1545, for example,

144 (*previous page*) Detail of pl. 142.

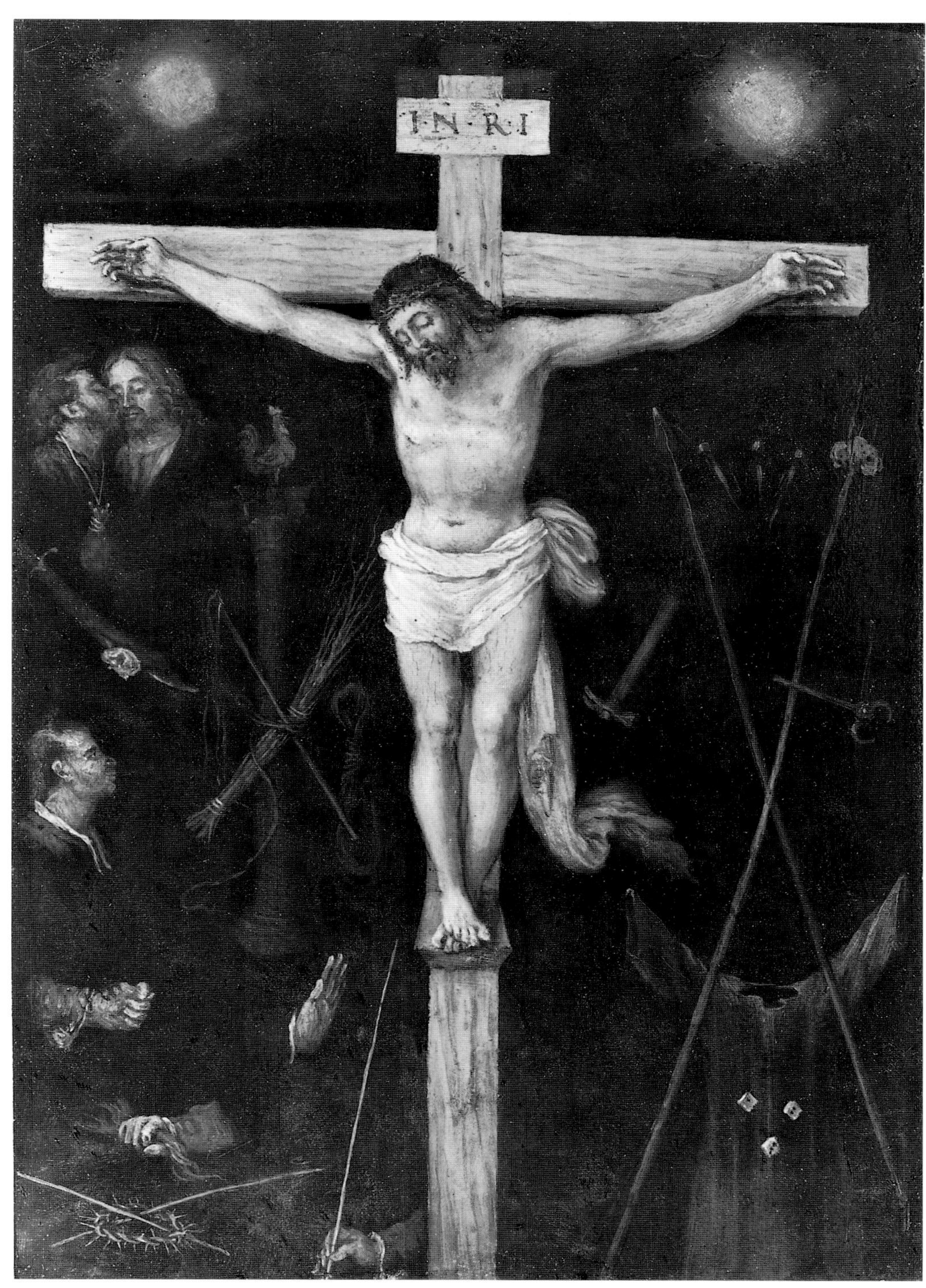

145 Lotto. *Mystic Crucifixion* (?*c.*1540). Panel, 18 × 14.3 cm. Florence, Berenson Collection. Reproduced with permission of the President and Fellows of Harvard College.

he noted in the *Libro* that the local nobleman Tommaso Costanzo had offered him only ten scudi for his portrait, which according to the painter was less than half its value; and then, to add further injury, the patron refused to accept the completed work because he claimed it was not a sufficiently good likeness.[45] By the autumn of 1545 Lotto had decided to revert to his earlier plan to spend his last years in Venice, and to be buried at Santi Giovanni e Paolo; and in the will he drafted a few months after his return, he reflected bitterly on his inability to earn an adequate living while in Treviso.

Despite his now vast experience as a painter of altarpieces, Lotto received only a handful of commissions of this type between 1542 and 1545, and even these were of modest dimensions and for comparatively unprestigious sites. The principal surviving example is a *Lamentation*, painted during the first half of 1545 for the altar of the Holy Sacrament in the Dominican nuns' church of San Paolo, Treviso (pl. 146).[46] Although it is true that he may have been content to offer his Dominican employers concessionary terms, the paltry fee of sixteen ducats – little more than one sixth of what he had received in 1506 for the not much larger *St Christina* altarpiece (pl. 24) – is symptomatic of his generally low remuneration during this phase. In keeping with its tragic subject, obviously chosen as appropriate to the dedication of the altar, the work is characterised by a mood of profound melancholy, expressed by the anguished facial expressions and the gloomy shadows, and further heightened by the instability and claustrophobic compactness of the figure composition. In its use of superimposed

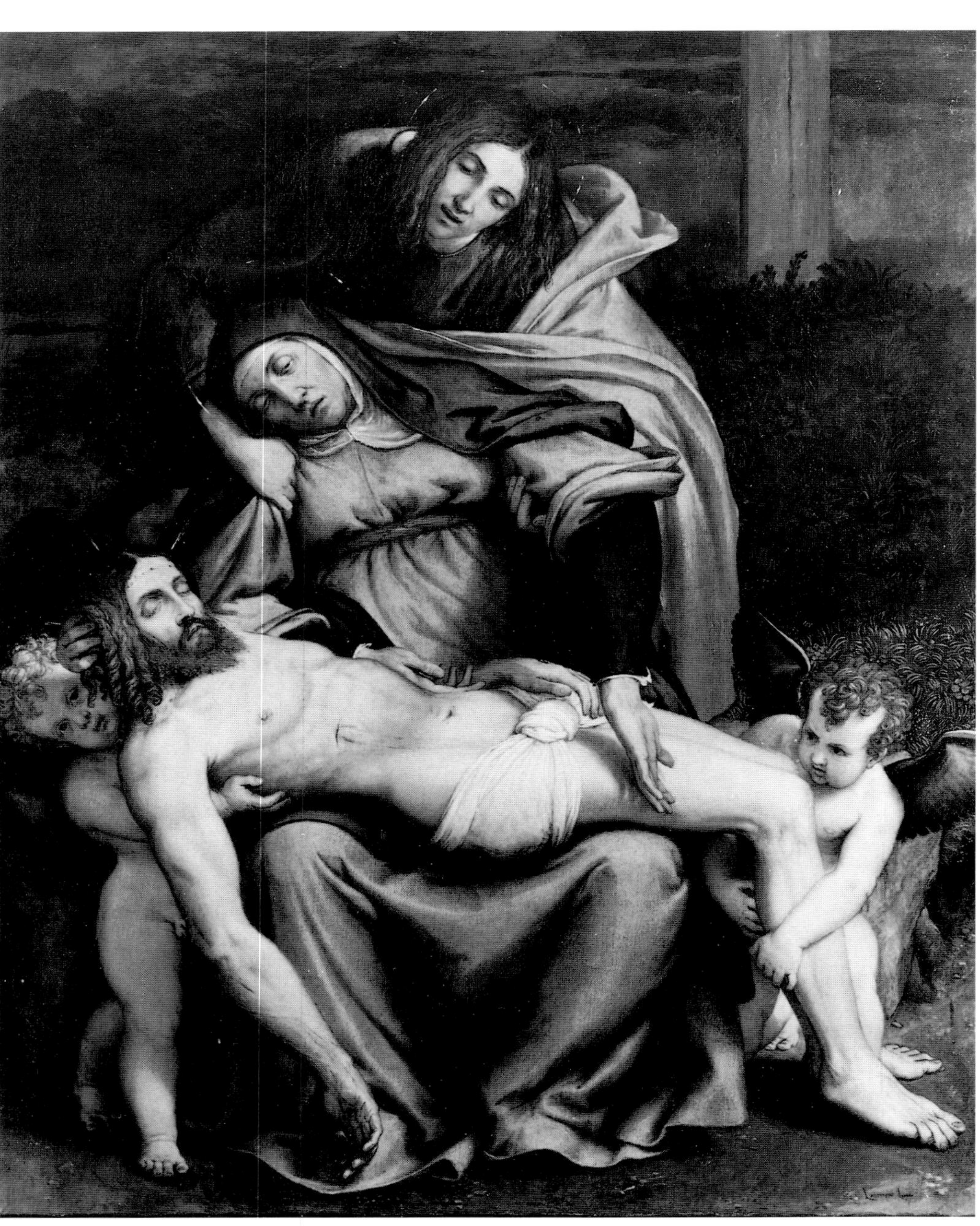

146 Lotto. *Lamentation* (1545). Canvas, 185 × 150 cm. Milan, Pinacoteca di Brera.

planes, and also in the artificially serpentine pattern created by the limbs and draperies, the work suggests that Lotto has meditated on Francesco Salviati's version of the subject, painted in Venice in 1540 (Milan, Brera); but even more than in the *Venus and Cupid* (p. 139), the graceful beauty of the Florentine *maniera* is deliberately sacrificed to an almost ugly expressiveness. As in the Monte San Giusto *Crucifixion* (pl. 127), and earlier in the *Christ taking Leave* (pl. 63) of the Bergamo period (pp. 124, 56), the deathly pale Virgin has fallen into a faint; and although this motif is entirely consistent with Lotto's own highly charged religious sensibility, the fact that he records the Virgin as 'tramortita' in his entry for the commission in the *Libro* implies that it had been specifically requested by the prioress of San Paolo. This is somewhat curious, since from the beginning of the century Dominican theologians had argued that the Virgin had foreknowledge of the coming Resurrection, and would, therefore, have endured her ordeal with stoical calm – in contrast to the Franciscan view, which held that following the Crucifixion, the Virgin suffered a spiritual death that paralleled that of her son.[47] But it may well be that for the nuns of San Paolo nice theological distinctions of this kind were of much less interest than the powerful emotional attraction of the image of the swoon.

The austere starkness of the *Lamentation*, which is unrelieved by any particular beauty of colour or detail, undeniably marks a step towards Lotto's decline as a painter of religious pictures for a public context. The portraits that he painted in Treviso, by contrast, and in particular the three now in the Brera gallery in Milan (pls 147–8, 150), remain on a very high plateau of quality indeed, and even show a willingness to experiment with new compositional formulae.[48] In many ways they approximate more closely to Titian's portraits of the 1520s (see pl. 4) than to Lotto's own earlier portraiture, in their use of a vertical format, planar poses, a dark neutral background, a limited palette and a severe restriction of accessories. This is particularly true of the *Man with a Glove* (pl. 150), perhaps identifiable with Lotto's portrait of one Liberale da Pinedel, painted in 1542–3,[49] in which the highly expressive face and hands are thrown into relief by the sombre but sumptuous black costume. But although the sitter shares with those of Titian a collected dignity of pose, he lacks their frank optimism and controlled vitality; characteristically for Lotto he appears more vulnerably human, with his abstracted gaze deeply suggestive of inner thoughts and feelings. A comparatively introspective melancholy pervades the features of *Febo da Brescia* (pl. 147), a portrait which, together with that of his less strongly characterised wife, *Laura da Pola* (pl. 148), may certainly be identified with a pair commissioned from Lotto in April 1543.[50] Although husband and wife are represented on separate fields, the painter has returned here to the genre of the double portrait, last practised two decades earlier in Bergamo; and, as in the *Marsilio* and Hermitage portraits (pls 80, 82), the couple is shown seated, with at least a hint of a domestic environment. But the stylistic and compositional contrast with the Bergamask portraits is striking; and, as with the *Man with a Glove*, a muted sobriety of colour and ornament is combined with a sophisticated elegance of deportment virtually unprecedented in Lotto's portraiture.

With portraits such as these – broadly yet confidently executed, and psychologically profound yet imparting a convincing sense of social poise – Lotto's skills ought to have been in high demand in any city in Italy. But his failure to convince wealthy patrons in Venice and Treviso of his genius, even when they did employ him, may have been in part due to a prickliness of personality, and to a deficiency of those social graces that were so important for the public success of Titian and Raphael. As has been seen (p. 89), Lotto's letters to the Consorzio della Misericordia are frequently fretful or defensive in tone; and his apparent need always to provide elaborate justifications of his own conduct may have made many employers quickly lose patience. Similarly, his accounts of his stays with Mario d'Armano (Appendix B) and Giovanni dal Saon

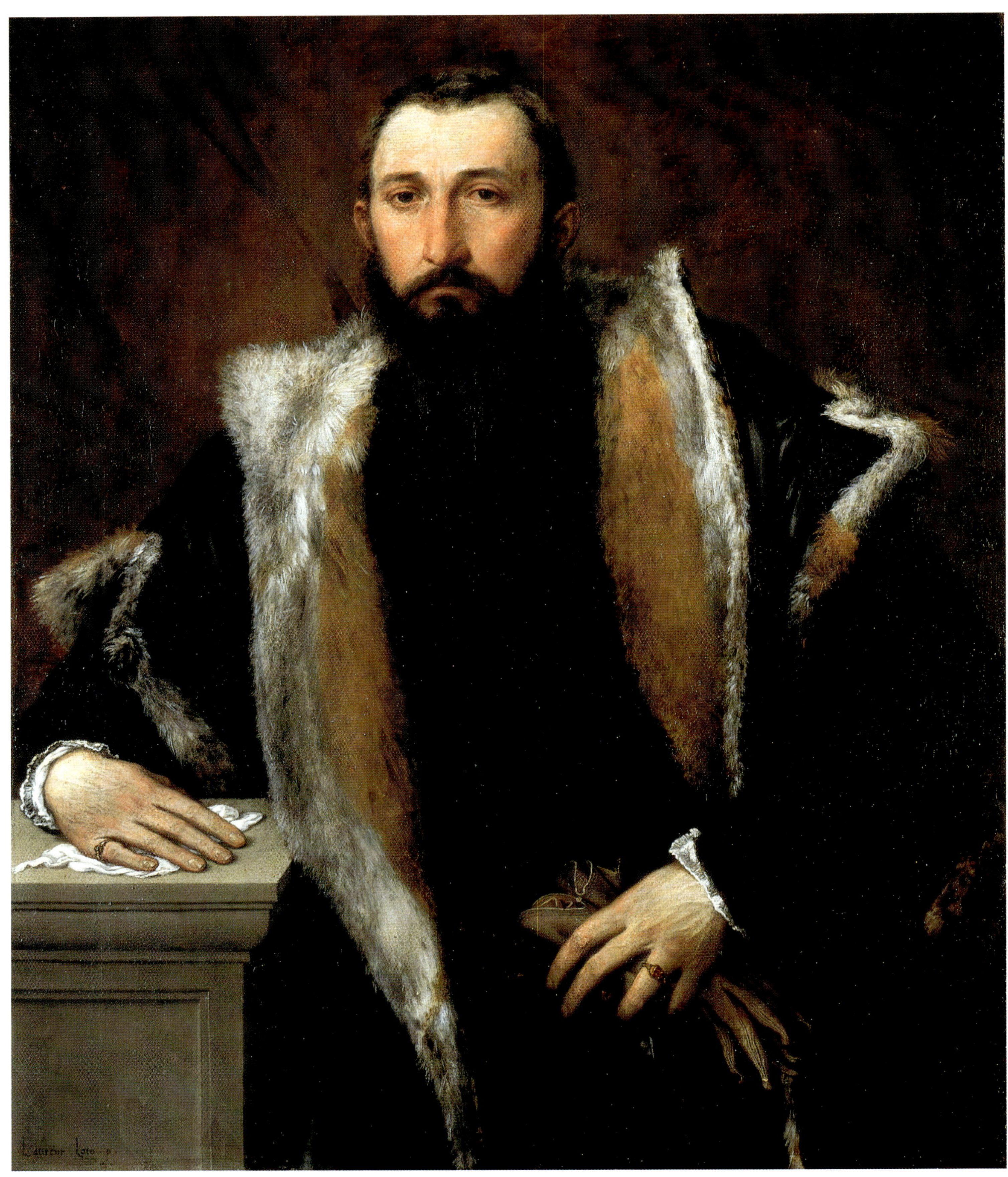

147 Lotto. *Febo da Brescia* (1543). Canvas, 91 × 76 cm. Milan, Pinacoteca di Brera.

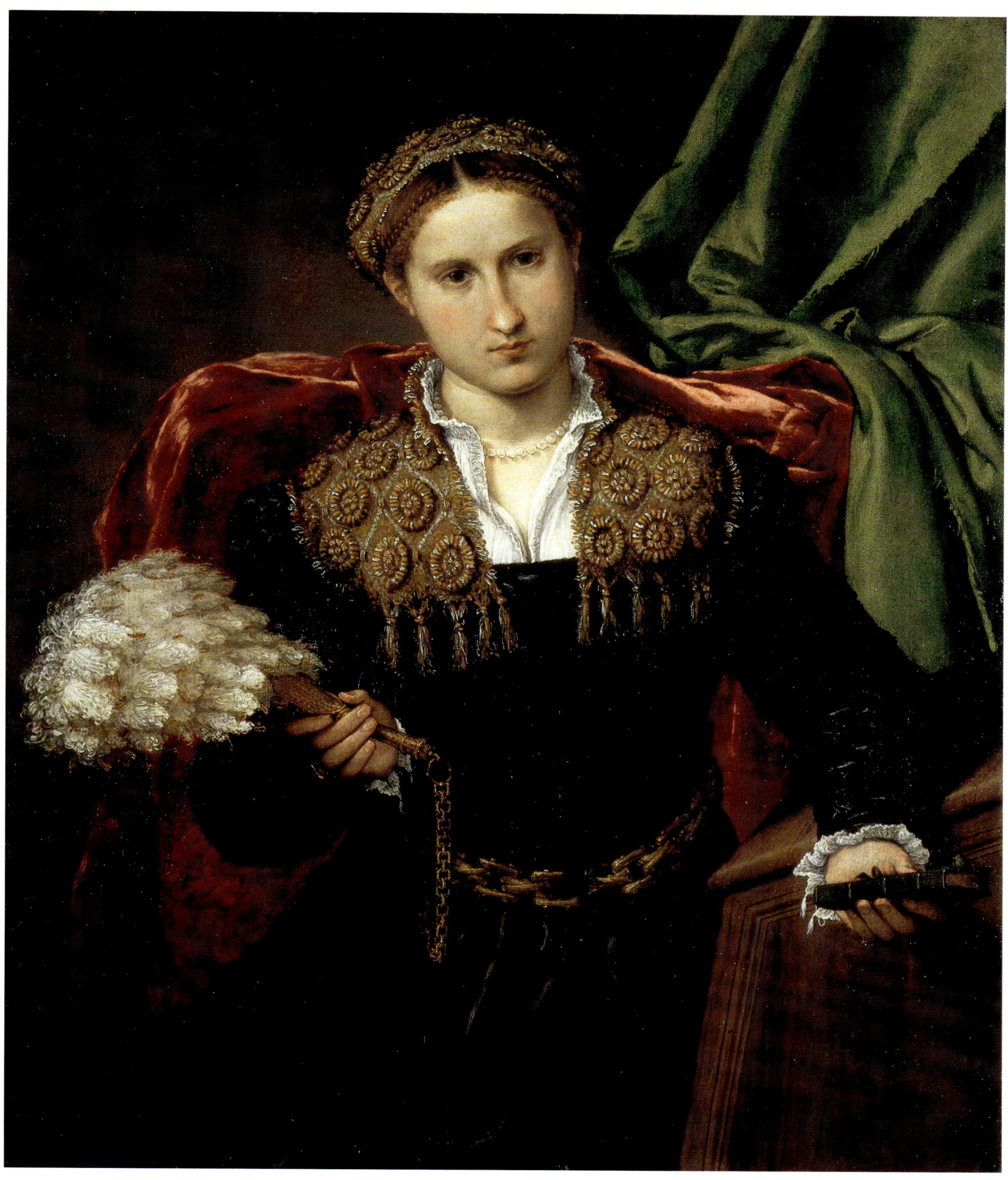

148 Lotto. *Laura da Pola* (1543). Canvas, 91 × 76cm. Milan, Pinacoteca di Brera.

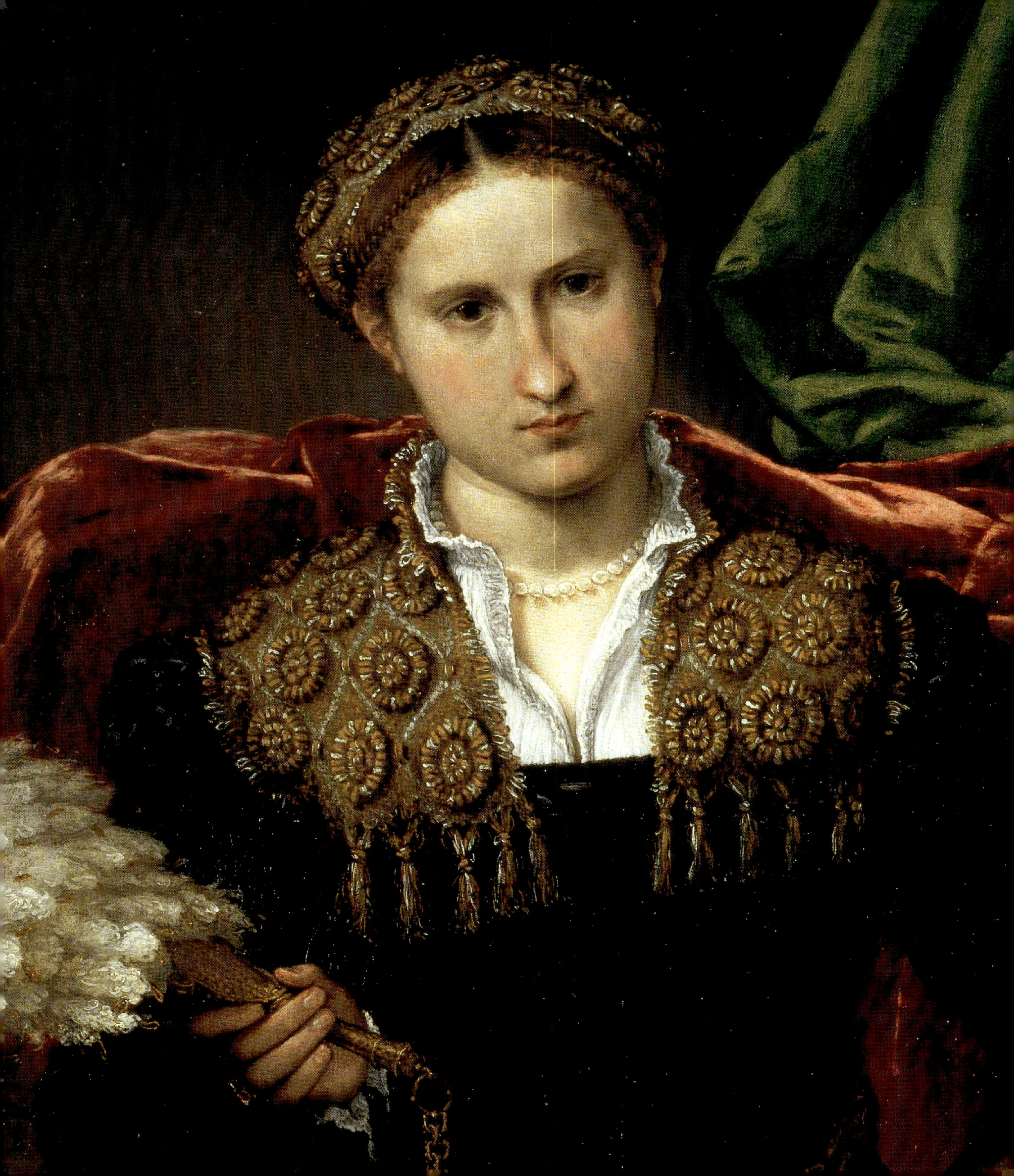

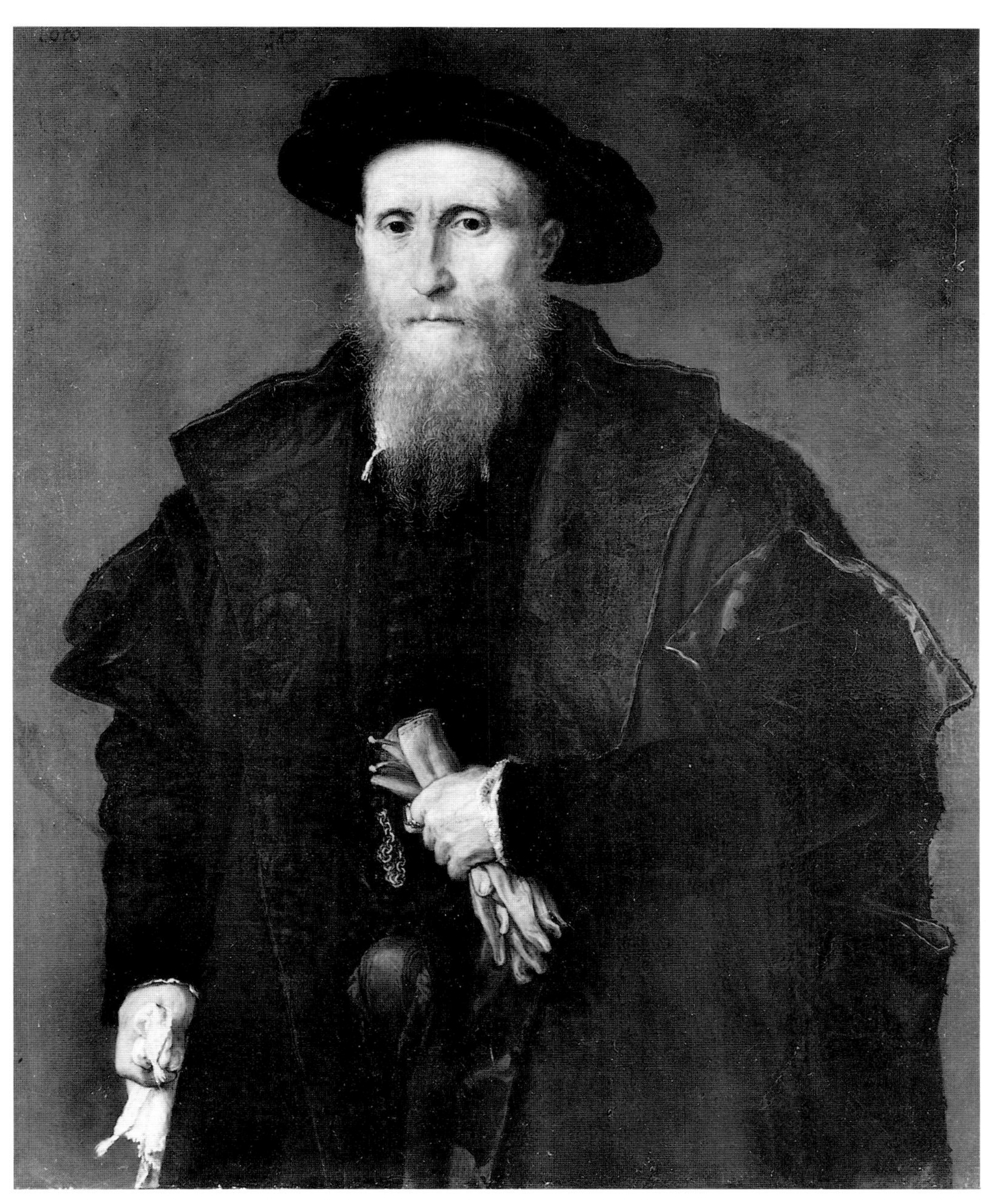

150 Lotto. *Man with a Glove* (*c.*1542–3). Canvas, 90 × 75 cm. Milan, Pinacoteca di Brera.

(Appendix C) reveal him to have been exceptionally thin-skinned, easily hurt by gossip (real or imagined), and pathologically fearful of appearing to exploit the generosity of others. There is a note of self-pity in the phrase near the beginning of his will that he was 'old, alone, without any stable domestic arrangements, and very anxious of mind'; and in fact, this was a not quite accurate description of his situation in the autumn of 1542, since his cousin had just given him a written assurance that he and his family loved him dearly, and would welcome him back into their house whenever he wanted. As a bachelor with no close relatives, Lotto clearly yearned for domestic stability and for the emotional security of a close family circle; and it is touching to note from the account-book how frequently he bought little presents for the children of his various hosts. At the same time, however, an evident restlessness of temperament and a sense of anxious dissatisfaction with his lot meant that the goal of domestic contentment was constantly to elude him.

149 (*facing page*) Detail of pl. 148.

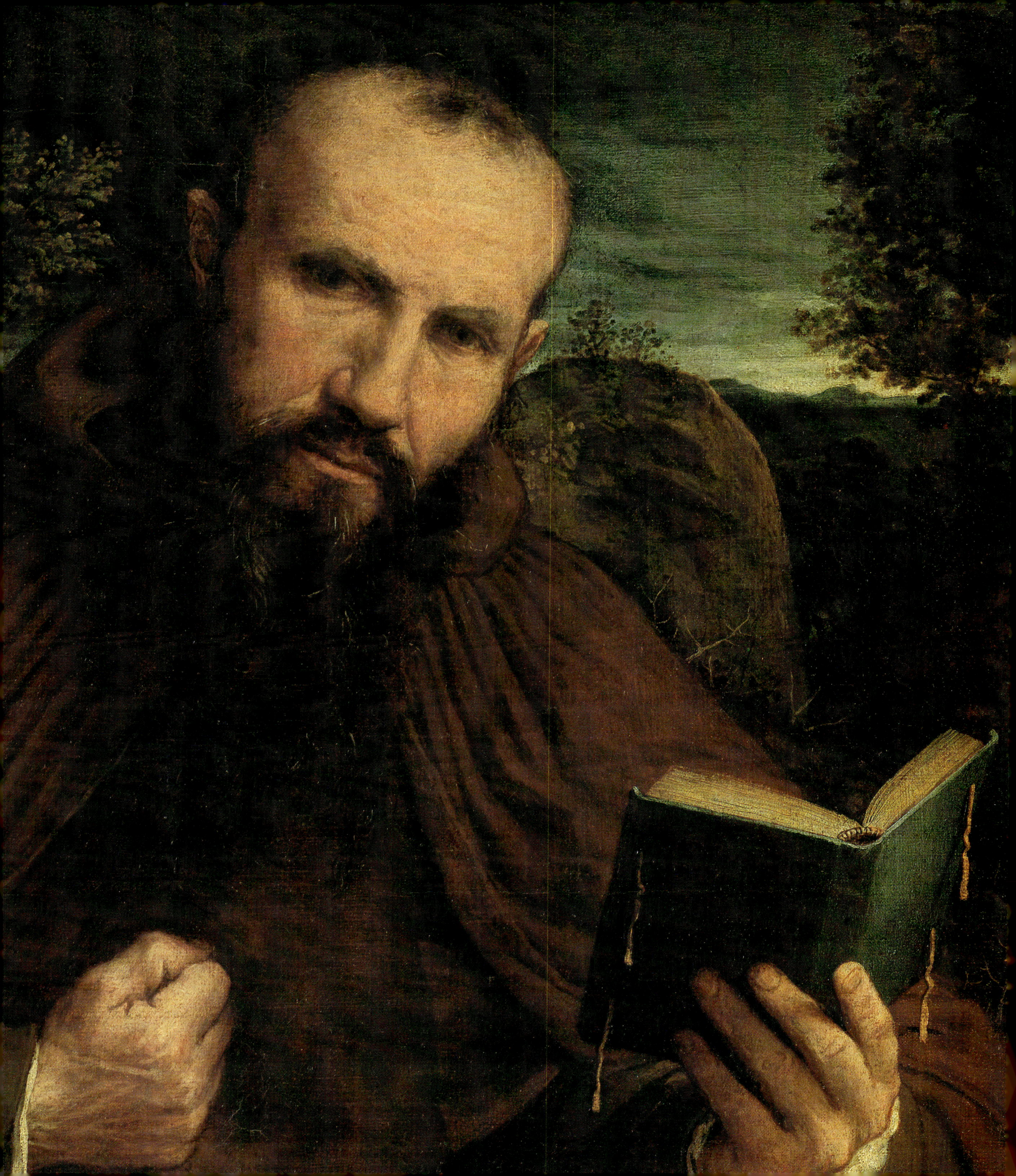

Chapter 6

THE LAST YEARS 1546–1556/7

The final decade of the ageing painter's life was one of constant movement. His two changes of residence during the earlier 1540s were followed by at least seven between 1546 and 1554. To some extent these were motivated, as in the earlier career, by sound professional considerations; but much more than before, his constant shifts of course appear to have been driven by his restless state of mind. During these last years he continued to receive important public commissions – indeed, his two late altarpieces for Ancona and Jesi were the largest he ever painted – but it is also clear that personal difficulties and humiliations increasingly weighed on his spirit. His travels finally ended in 1554 when he resolved to enter the religious community at the Santa Casa in Loreto as a lay brother; and there is an undeniable pathos, as well as a sense of exhaustion, in his entry in the *Libro* on 15 August: 'So as not to have to travel any more in my old age, I have resolved to end my days in this holy place, and to remain here as an oblate for the rest of my life.'[1]

On his return to Venice at the end of 1545 he took up residence not with Mario d'Armano, but with another family man, one Giovanni della Volta. The portrait painted in 1547 of his landlord, together with his wife and two children (London, National Gallery),[2] constitutes a very rare example of a Venetian family portrait, and it undoubtedly owes its origin to the intimacy of their relationship. In the will made by Lotto in March 1546, however (Appendix C, pp. 179–81), none of the three families with which he had recently been involved was to receive any legacy, and the chief beneficiary was to be rather the Hospital of the Derelitti (Destitute) at Santi Giovanni e Paolo, one of four major hospitals founded by the Venetian government in 1527, originally as a shelter for refugees from famine, but subsequently also used to house orphans and the sick.[3] As emerges from the will, Lotto himself was a governor of this hospital; and he appointed as chief executors his fellow-governors, Giovanni Maria Giunta – son of Luc'Antonio Giunta, publisher of the Brucioli Bible (p. 114) – and Vincenzo Frizier, cloth-merchant 'at the sign of the tree' ('l'Albero') at Rialto. The affairs of the hospital were evidently very close to Lotto's heart, and he clearly felt a personal sympathy with the pious and philanthropic ideals of an institution that in its early stages had been closely associated with the saintly figure of Girolamo Miani, a leading light of the Catholic Reform movement in Venice. As has been seen (p. 111), another institution with which Lotto was involved, charitable as well as professional in function, was the Venetian guild of painters; and it is revealing that in clause seven of his will, he provides the means for two young painters, to be chosen by the guild, to marry two young women of the hospital – thereby ensuring that all four began their adult life with the kind of domestic establishment that he never himself enjoyed.[4] In the will he also reaffirms his wish, already expressed at the time of the delivery of the *St Antoninus* altarpiece in 1542 (p. 142), to be buried in the nearby cemetery of Santi Giovanni e Paolo.

151 Detail of pl. 155.

Later in the same year Lotto was commissioned to paint another altarpiece for a

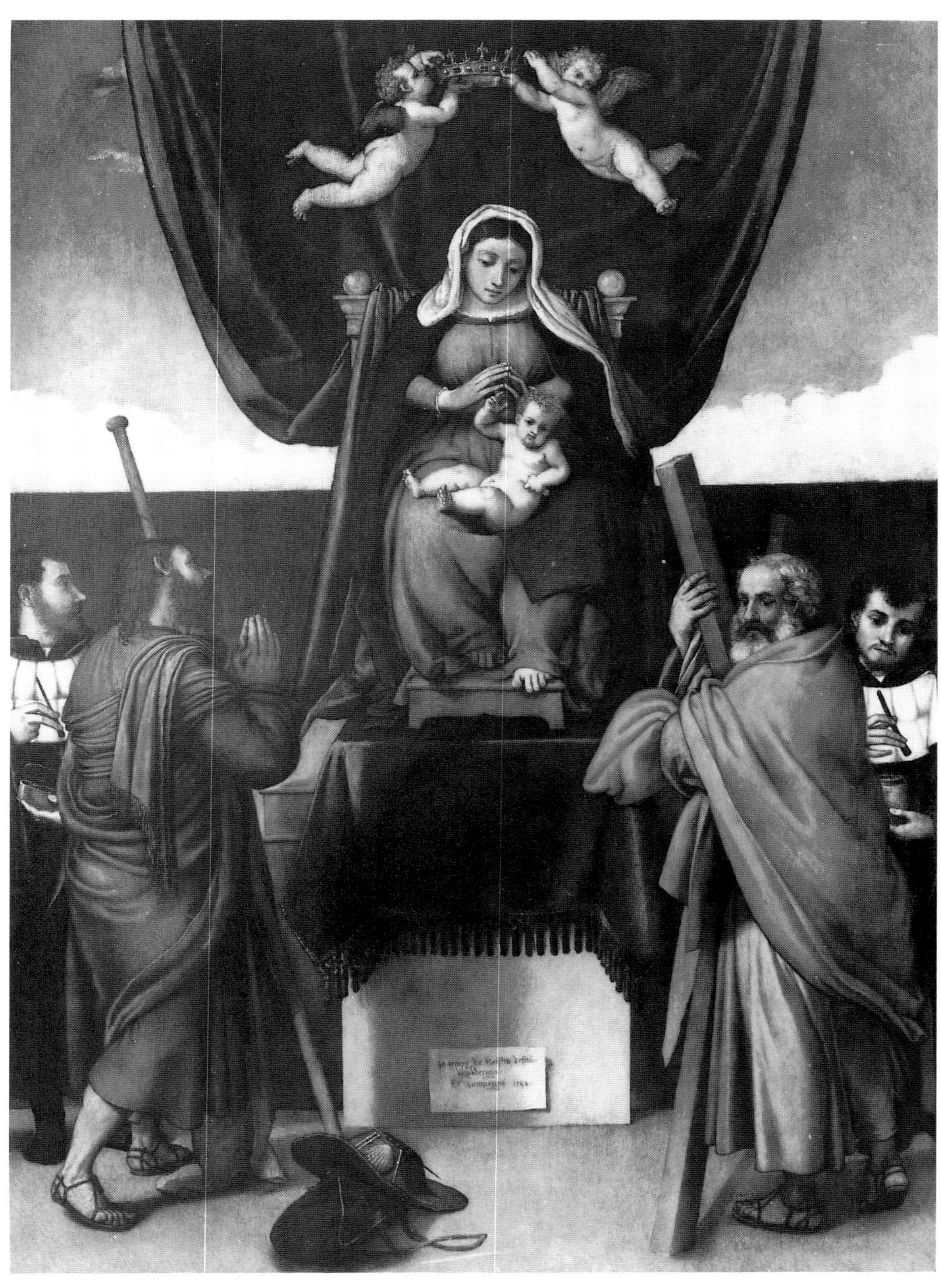

152 Lotto. *Virgin and Child with Saints* (1546). Canvas, 240 × 171 cm. Venice, San Giacomo dell'Orio.

Venetian church: a *Virgin and Child with Saints* for the altar of the Immaculate Conception in the parish church of San Giacomo dell'Orio (pl. 152). The titular of the church, James Major, stands in the place of honour at the Virgin's right hand, while the physicians Cosmas and Damian are included as former titulars of the altar.[5] Compositionally, this *sacra conversazione* represents a rather dull repetition of that painted in Ancona eight years previously (pl. 130); and even taking account of its poor state of preservation, it is evident that much of the vitality of the earlier work, conveyed by the rippling movement of the poses and draperies and by the dappled fall of light and shade, has also been lost. Part of the reason for this disappointing perfunctoriness may be that during the period of the work's execution in the second half of 1546, Lotto was ill, and had to be looked after for six weeks by his friend, the goldsmith Bartolomeo Carpan.[6] This circumstance also has some relevance for what is known of Lotto's attitude towards the rapidly unfolding religious crisis in Venice, and in Italy in general. The failure of the Colloquy of Regensburg in 1541 meant that all hope that the Protestants would return to the Catholic fold was finally destroyed, and after years of prevarication about ecclesiastical reform, the Council of Trent was convened in 1545. During the course of the 1540s the papal curia, particularly through its legate Giovanni della Casa, put increasing pressure on the Venetian government resolutely to suppress any manifestation of heresy; and although as ever, the Venetians dragged their feet, resenting any attempt by Rome to interfere in their affairs, they eventually accepted that religious conformity was in their own national interest, and in 1547 formally reconstituted the local branch of the Holy Office, or Inquisition.[7] In 1560 Carpan was denounced to this tribunal as a Lutheran of many years' standing;[8] and indeed, in September 1546 – in the same autumn, in other words, in which Lotto stayed in his house as an invalid – Carpan is known to have hosted a clandestine meeting there, in which fellow-guildsmen debated contentious religious issues, including the Calvinist doctrine of predestination, with the renegade Augustinian preacher Fra Agostino da Genova. Fra Agostino had recently been censured by his superiors for his unorthodox sermons in Venetian parish churches, including that of San Giacomo dell'Orio;[9] and Lotto's close recent association both with the church and with Carpan makes it unthinkable that he was not well acquainted with Fra Agostino's ideas – especially also given his known attentiveness to sermons (p. 89). This is not to conclude that he was an unthinking disciple of the friar; and against this association it may be pointed out that the patron of the San Giacomo altarpiece, a devotional confraternity dedicated to the Immaculate Conception, would have represented a bastion of Catholic orthodoxy. Consistent with this is the entirely conventional iconography, which implicitly upholds the Catholic doctrine, diametrically opposed to that of predestination, of salvation through the intercession of the saints, and in particular of the Virgin as Queen of Heaven and Mother of God. Similarly, if Lotto himself had actually believed in predestination rather than 'good works', he would not have left money in his will for the boys and girls of the hospital to pray to God for the salvation of his soul. But against the background of the increasing polarisation of the religious debate, and of increasing intolerance of nonconformism, the time was rapidly approaching when Evangelical sympathisers could no longer equivocate, and had to choose where their loyalties lay. It is only to be expected that the dilemma would have caused considerable anguish to a sensitive and spiritually restless personality such as Lotto.

Artistically more impressive than the San Giacomo altarpiece, and by contrast charged with an urgent religious intensity, is the *St Jerome* in the Prado (pl. 153). Several small-scale representations of the subject are recorded in Lotto's accounts during the 1540s. The Prado version has been plausibly identified with that begun for Lotto's fellow-governor of the Hospital at Santi Giovanni e Paolo, Vincenzo Frizier, on 24 July 1546.[10] Certainly, with its pictorial austerity and its emphasis on the saint's self-mortification and penance, the work is in perfect accord with the reforming ideals of the Hospital, and may be interpreted as a sort of Spiritual Exercise in visual form.[11] As in the *St Jerome* painted forty years earlier for Bishop Rossi (pl. 22), and in contrast to the sunnier and more luxuriant versions painted in Rome and Bergamo (pls 36, 59), the scene is set in a rocky wilderness at twilight. But the later version is more overtly dramatic, with its more pronounced contrasts of light and shade and especially, with its more boldly scaled figure, his arms outstretched in imitation of the Crucified Saviour whose image he contemplates.

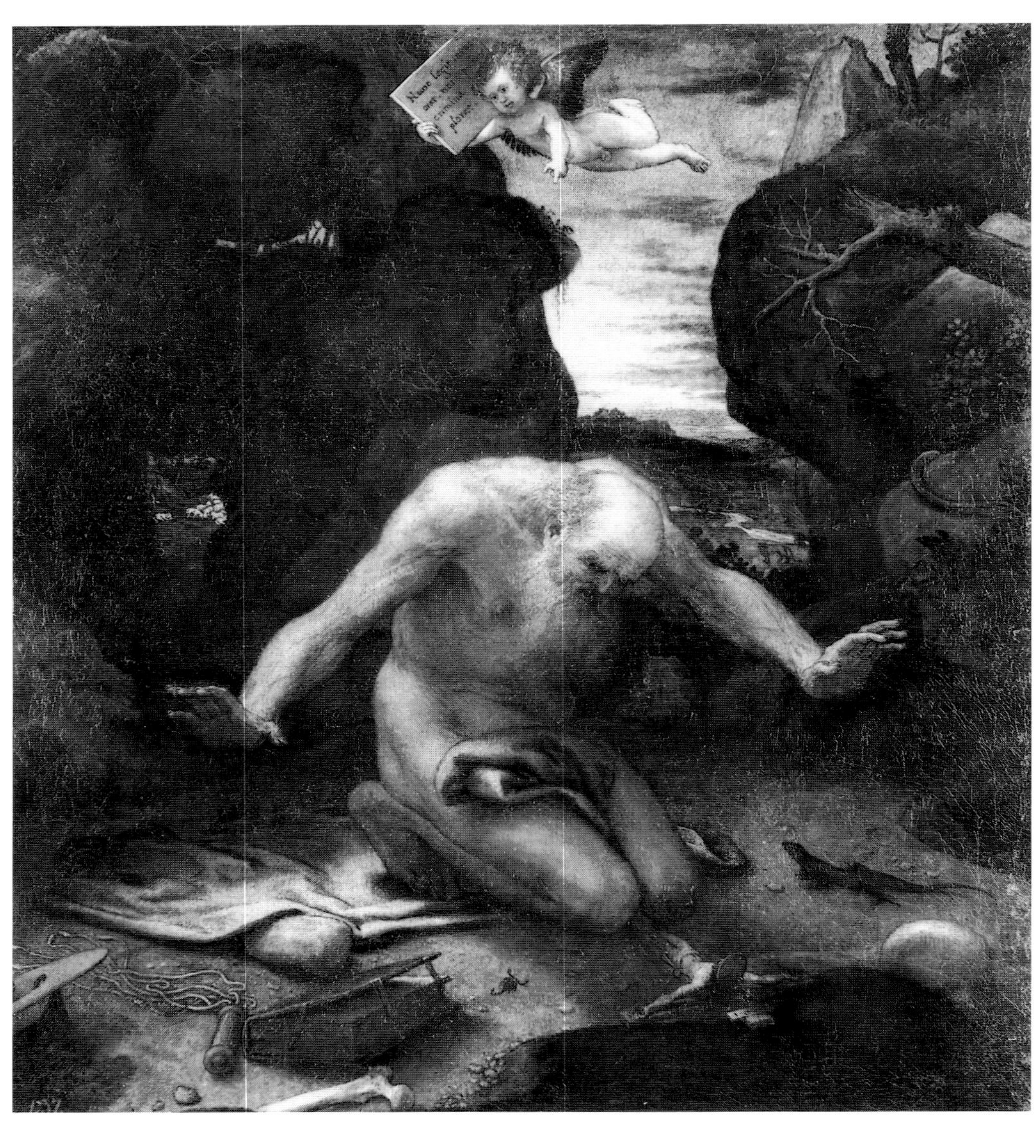

153 Lotto. *St Jerome* (1546). Canvas, 99 × 90 cm. Madrid, Museo del Prado.

When undertaking the *St Jerome* for his friend and *confrère* Vincenzo Frizier, Lotto also undertook to paint his portrait.[12] This portrait has never been identified, but it is worth wondering whether it might be identical with the haunting *Portrait of a Man* now in Palazzo Doria in Rome (pl. 154). The Doria picture is usually dated to a few years earlier than 1546, by stylistic analogy with the *Man with a Glove* and the *Febo da Brescia* (pls 150, 147). Yet although it is in a very worn condition, it appears always to have lacked the tonal subtlety of the Trevigian portraits, and to be more reductively planar in composition. It also lacks their social grace, and is characterised instead by a direct and personal character consistent with the supposition that Lotto knew the sitter well. Like the earlier Borghese *Portrait of a Man* (pl. 5; p. 137), the Doria man wears a sorrowful expression, and gestures as if in pain towards the area of his abdomen, in this case presumably his liver, which, like the spleen, was traditionally regarded as the source of melancholy. His gesture draws attention also to the pair of rings on his little finger, placed at the centre of the composition; and especially since he wears no other rings, the pair may indeed in this case allude to mourning for a dead wife. In this context the Latin inscription on the right (ANN AETATIS SVE XXXVII), although sometimes interpreted as referring to his own age, certainly refers to that of a late wife[13] –

especially since it is encircled by a wreath of ivy, the evergreen leaves of which symbolise eternity, or more precisely, eternal love. The significance of the fictive relief on the left, representing a winged putto standing on a pair of scales, is rather harder to elucidate.[14] But the putto, like Cupid, surely alludes in some way to love, in this case probably the chaste love associated with his counterpart, Anteros, rather than the sensual love associated with Cupid himself; while, according to an inscription decoding one of the hieroglyphics in the *Hypnerotomachia Poliphili*, scales signify 'RECTA AMICITIA'—true friendship—as well as justice (pl. 48).[15] The combined motif had, in fact, already been used by Lotto twice before, once in a Bergamo *intarsia* in 1524,[16] and again in the same year, on the ring of St Catherine in a representation of the *Mystic Marriage* for Zanin Cassotti (p. 53). This latter appearance in the context of divinely sanctioned marriage may serve to confirm an allusion in the portrait to the sitter's beloved late wife.

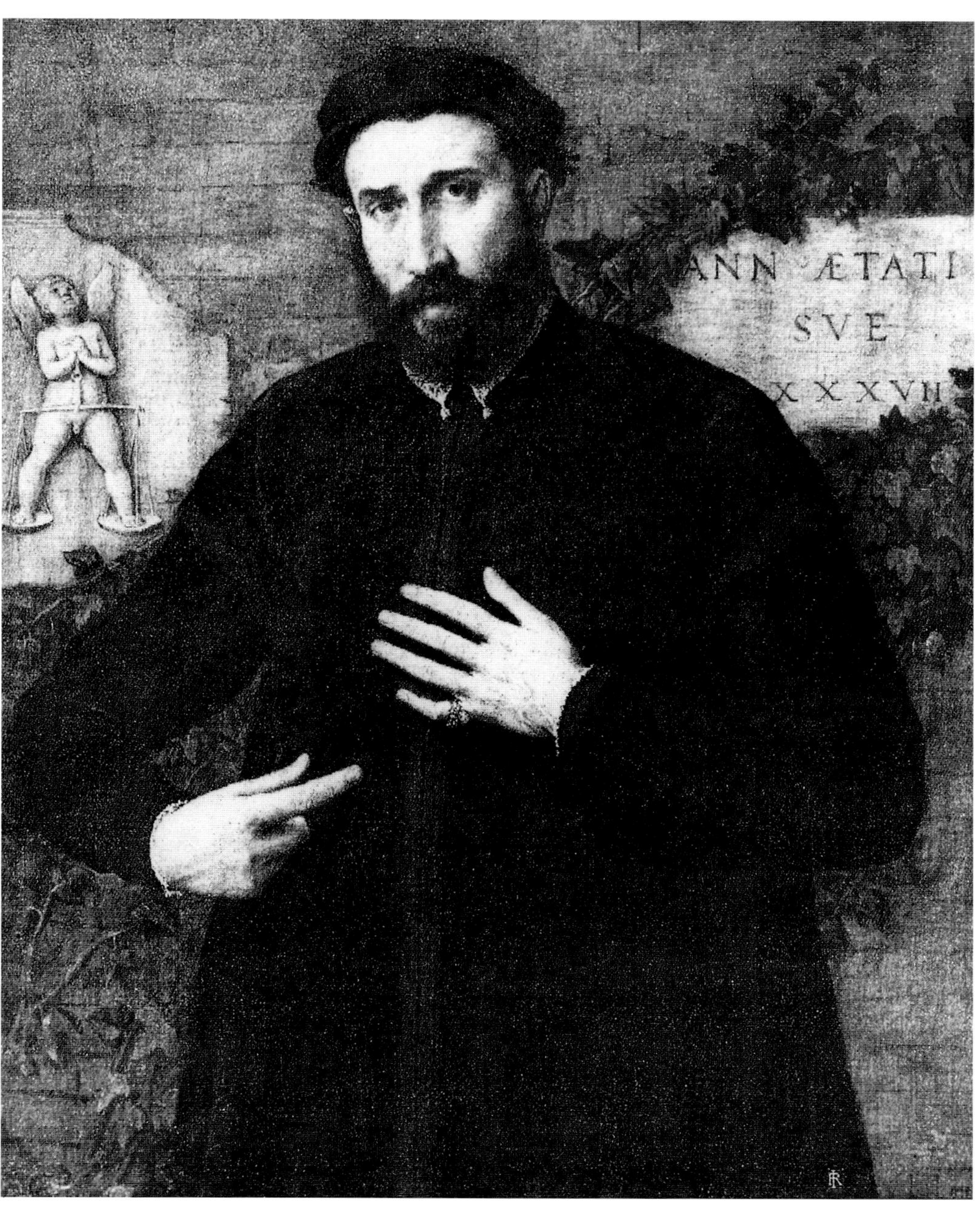

154 Lotto. *Portrait of a Man* (*c.* 1546). Canvas, 95 × 80 cm. Rome, Palazzo Doria.

Unfortunately, although it is known that Vincenzo Frizier was a married man with two daughters,[17] it is not clear whether or not his wife was still alive in the summer of 1546 when he commissioned his portrait, and the identity of this with the Doria portrait remains to be proved. But the dating of the work to the later rather than the earlier 1540s does appear to be confirmed by comparison with a portrait that can definitely be linked to a reference in the account-book: the *Fra Gregorio Belo* (pl. 155), begun by Lotto in December 1546, and completed before October the following year.[18] Belo was a member of the order of Hieronymite friars at San Sebastiano in Venice; and in homage to St Jerome, after whom the order was named, the sitter is shown against a setting of wild, twilit landscape and beating his breast in humble penitence. The visionary nature of the vignette showing the Crucifixion in the upper left corner sugests that it is taking place in Fra Gregorio's mind's eye, just as Jerome's attention is entirely absorbed by his contemplation of the crucifix in Lotto's panel for Vincenzo Frizier (pl. 153). Although the effect of movement is somewhat more dynamic than in the Doria portrait, the two works resemble one another in their austere colour-schemes, based on earth tones, and in their essentially planar compositions. There is independent evidence to suggest that in this case, too, Lotto knew the sitter well; and his obvious empathy with his state of mind is directly reflected in the compelling immediacy of the portrait, with its insistent, demonstrative use of gaze and gesture, and with no trace of the aristocratic reserve of the Treviso portraits.

In the same year as the *Belo* portrait, Lotto received a commission of a type completely different from anything he had undertaken so far in his Venetian career. On 20 July 1547 he undertook to paint a canvas representing 'the Madonna, Child, two little angels, and Sts James and Lawrence', incorporating portraits of two patrician magistrates, Jacopo Pisani and Lorenzo Giustinian, to hang above the panelling in their office in the Mint.[19] In other words, the now lost picture was of the official, votive type, traditional for the Doge's Palace and other government buildings. In some ways the commission, which was perhaps awarded on the recommendation of Jacopo Sansovino as architect of the Mint, marks a belated recognition of Lotto by the Venetian authorities. But on the other hand, he was not particularly well paid for it, and nor did he himself apparently regard it as a significant breakthrough. Contemporaneously, he began renewing his old contacts with the Marches, and in November he undertook a sizeable altarpiece for the small town of Mogliano, near Fermo.

The Mogliano *Virgin in Glory with Saints*, which remains *in situ* above the high altar of the church of Santa Maria di Piazza, is a decidedly uninspired piece of work, and it could hardly have impressed any Venetian who may have seen it in the painter's studio before it was shipped to its destination in the summer of 1548.[20] It was probably through deliberate oversight that Paolo Pino, in his *Dialogue on Painting* published in the same year, omitted Lotto from his list of principal painters then active in Venice—a list that included not just Savoldo, Paris Bordone, Bonifacio and Tintoretto, but also the third-rate Gian Pietro Silvio.[21] Certainly, the contrast between Lotto's tired altarpiece and the thirty-year-old Tintoretto's explosive *Miracle of the Slave* (Venice, Accademia), painted for the Scuola di San Marco in April, provides a vivid illustration of how far Lotto had been overtaken by the swift pace of artistic events. In the same month, the influential critic Pietro Aretino wrote an open letter to both painters: to Tintoretto acknowledging that his astonishing *Miracle* had won 'the voice of public praise';[22] and to Lotto as follows:

> O Lotto, good as goodness itself and virtuous as virtue: Titian in Augsburg, surrounded by the favours of the whole world, greets and embraces you by way of the letter he sent me two days ago. He says that the pleasure he receives from the approval by the Emperor of his works would be doubled if you would look at them

155 Lotto. *Fra Gregorio Belo* (1546–7). Canvas, 87.3 × 71.1 cm. New York, Metropolitan Museum of Art, Rogers Fund, 1965.

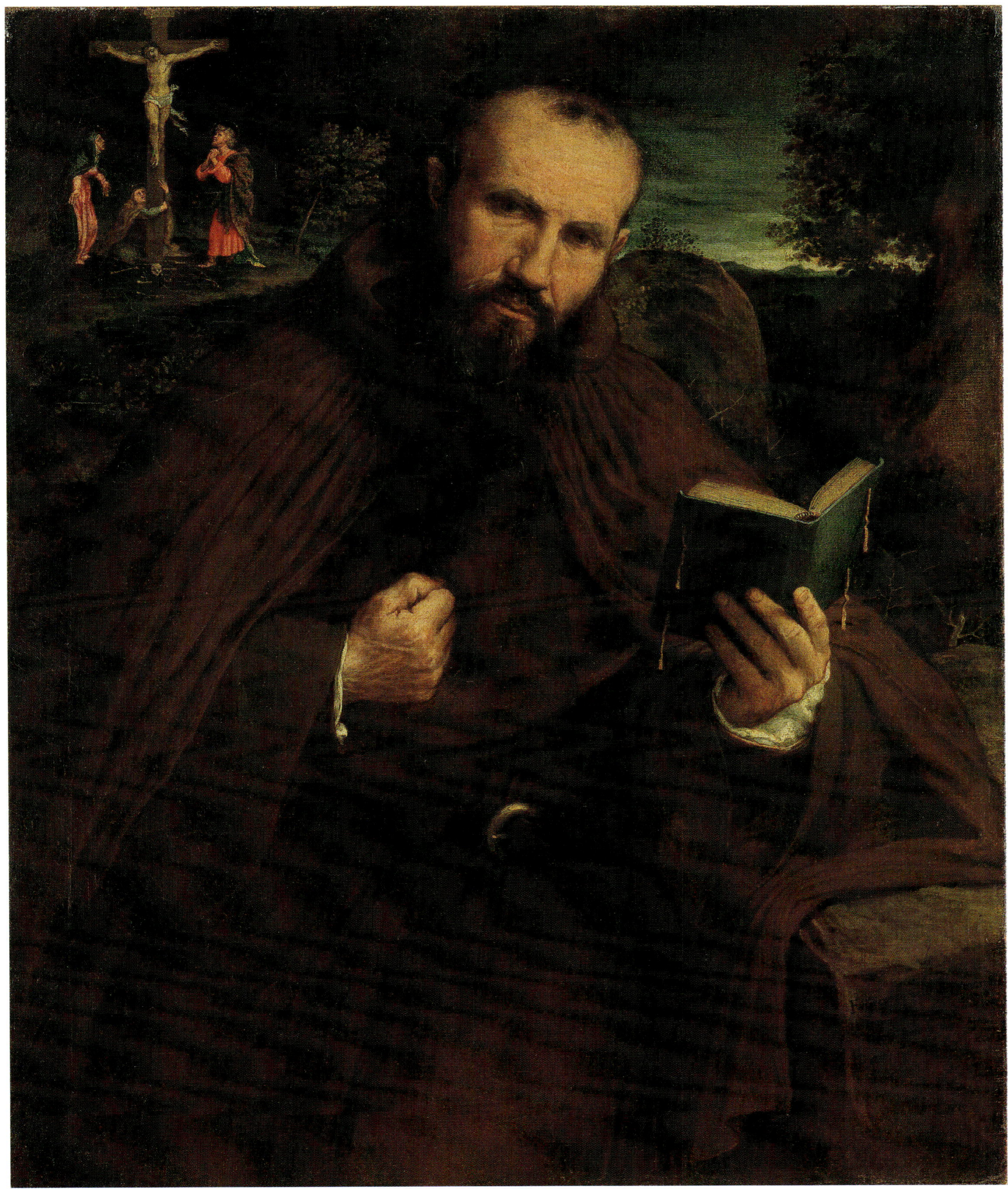

and give him your verdict. No serious painter could go wrong in doing this, because your advice is based on long experience of art and nature and because it is guided by a sincere benevolence, which judges the efforts of others neither more kindly nor more harshly than if they were your own. Hence it is possible to say that whoever places you in front of his pictures and portraits is showing them to himself, and is seeking his own advice. There is no envy in your breast; rather, you are glad to see artists achieve feats that you accept are beyond the range of your own brush. Yet this still performs miracles not easily attainable by those who are interested only in their own work. And even if you are outclassed in the profession of painting, you cannot begin to be equalled in your attention to religion. Therefore heaven will compensate you with a glory that surpasses earthly praise.

April 1548, in Venice.[23]

This letter is usually interpreted in purely negative terms, as one of crushing condescension. It is certainly true that it would be ingenuous to take all of Aretino's compliments at face value, and there is an undoubted irony in the comment that Lotto may take solace in religion since he is outclassed as a painter. Aretino is also likely to have taken a sadistic pleasure in implicitly contrasting the positions of Titian, at that moment receiving the plaudits of the imperial court at Augsburg, and of Lotto, struggling to earn his living in Venice. But it is not therefore necessary to conclude that every sentence of the letter is laced with heavy sarcasm. Aretino was a close friend of Titian and his staunchest propagandist, and he was bound to compare every artist unfavourably with him, including Michelangelo himself. But he was also highly perceptive as a critic, and a good judge of human character, and he was perfectly willing to give credit where it was due. It may well be, therefore, that Titian sincerely valued Lotto's opinion of his work, and that Aretino, with equal sincerity, admired Lotto's personal qualities, and the religious piety reflected in his works. Indeed, Aretino's summary judgement of Lotto–that although surpassed by Titian, he nevertheless achieved miracles of painting rivalled by few other painters of his age–corresponds with remarkable accuracy to the judgement of posterity. Lotto apparently remained on amicable terms with Aretino, since in the following January the two met one another, in the company of their mutual friend Jacopo Sansovino and two wealthy patrons, in the workshop of the sculptor Danese Cattaneo to admire his recently completed bust of Pietro Bembo.[24] All this is not, however, to exclude the likelihood that Lotto's sensitivities were stung by Aretino's double-edged praise; and the publication of the letter may well have influenced his decision by 1550 never to return to Venice.

Apparently the Mogliano altarpiece, for all its inadequacies, had been favourably received in the Marches, because a year after its installation there Lotto was commissioned to paint a monumental *Assumption of the Virgin* for the high altar of San Francesco alle Scale in Ancona (pl. 156).[25] As is recorded in detail in the *Libro* (Appendix D, p. 181), the contract was signed in Venice on 1 June 1549 between Lotto and the heirs of the Anconite nobleman, Lorenzo Todini, who had recently died leaving funds for the decoration of the chancel of the large Franciscan church–called 'alle Scale' because of its dramatic situation on steeply rising ground overlooking the port and the Adriatic. It was agreed that the canvas should be executed on the spot at San Francesco, presumably because of its colossal dimensions: larger, indeed, than any previous altarpiece by Lotto, including the Colleoni Martinengo altarpiece (pls 47, 52). He duly arrived in Ancona exactly a month later, and took up residence within the convent. The promised fee was the not ungenerous sum of four hundred scudi; but as was by now frequently the case for Lotto, he was short of ready cash, and had to finance his journey with the help of a loan from his friend the architect Giovanni dal

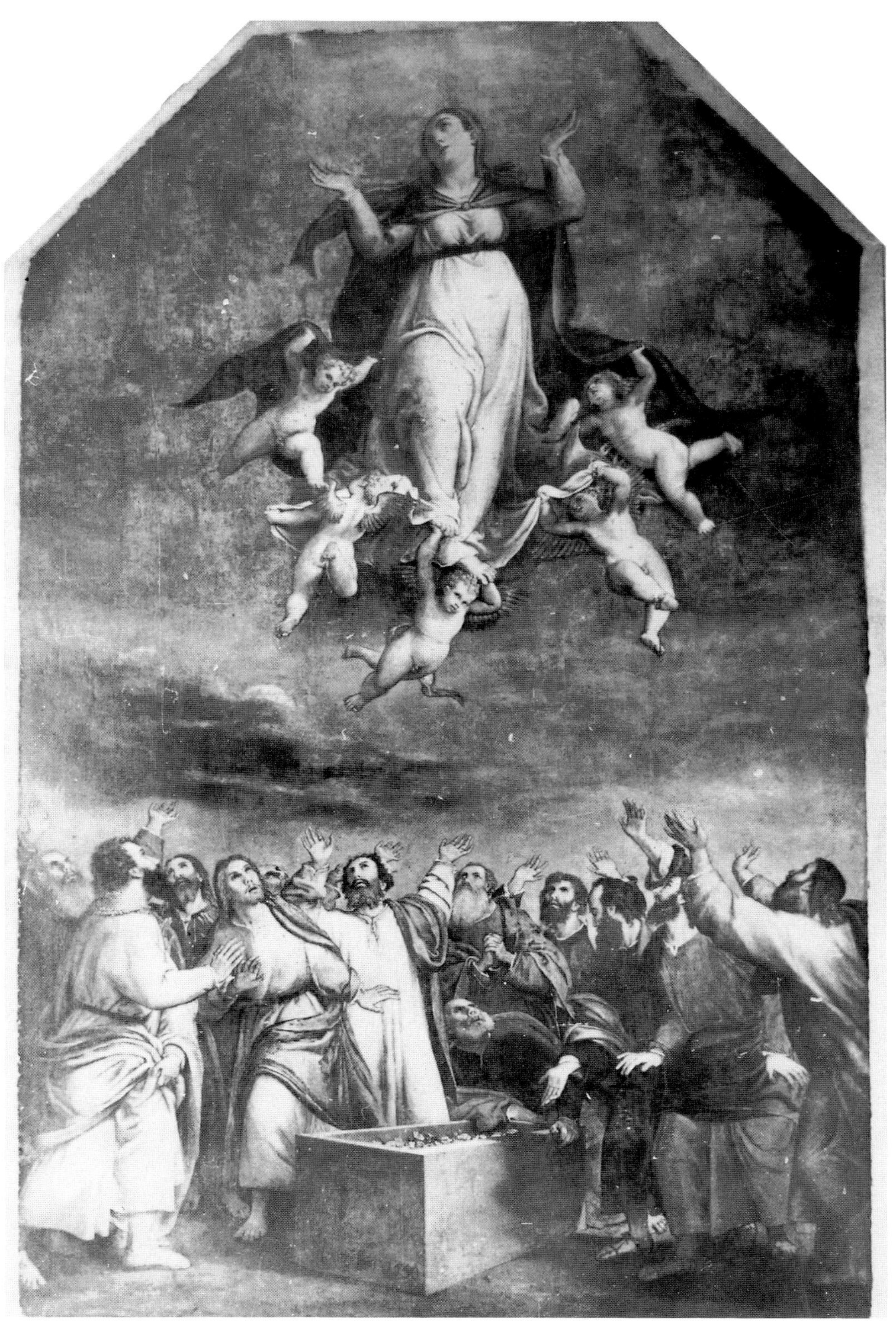

156 Lotto. *Assumption of the Virgin* (1549–50). Canvas, 670 × 403 cm. Ancona, San Francesco alle Scale.

Coro. Giovanni was himself a native of Ancona, and was perhaps involved in initiating the commission; he was certainly involved in its execution, since Lotto made him responsible for subcontracting the frame for the altarpiece from a woodcarver in Venice. Lotto took with him to Ancona, surely because of the size of the work, two studio hands; and although both young men abandoned him soon after their arrival, he was joined in April 1550 for several months by his former pupil Durante Nobili (p. 127).[26] After a succession of interim payements by the Todini heirs and their agents, Lotto received his final payment for the completed work in November 1550.

Even taking account of its now much damaged condition, the Ancona *Assumption* cannot unfortunately be regarded as any more successful as a work of art than the San Giacomo dell'Orio or Mogliano altarpieces. Its failure is due partly to the flaccid pictorial handling, much of it no doubt executed by Durante and the studio hands, but partly also to the weakness of Lotto's composition. To a much greater extent than in the Celana *Assumption* of 1527 (pl. 99), this follows the model of Titian's celebrated *Assunta* (pl. 94), inspired, perhaps, by the common Franciscan destination of the work, as well as by the comparably huge scale. Thus, as in Titian's panel, the customary landscape setting is eliminated; the apostles are arranged as a foreground screen, with their arms silhouetted against the sky; and the Virgin is presented frontally, supported by a semicircle of flying putti, and with her arms upraised in an orant gesture. Perhaps Lotto was wise when painting on this scale not to revert to the frenetic rhythms and touches of burlesque of the Celana *Assumption*. Even so, his placing of an interval between the two zones creates a fatal compositional disjunction, and his attempt at heroic grandeur in the figures and storm-clouds is embarassingly miscalculated. In this instance, at least, Aretino's verdict on Lotto in comparison with Titian may be regarded as charitable.

Yet, as in the previous decade, Lotto in his final years in the Marches remains much more true to himself on the intimate scale of portraiture and pictures for private devotion, and also of drawing. A still impressive example of a late portrait is the *Crossbowman* (pl. 157), identifiable as one Battista della Rocca Contrada, painted in Ancona in 1551–2.[27] In its colour-range, comprising chiefly blacks, browns and flesh-tones, it continues to resemble the Doria *Portrait of a Man* (pl. 154) and the *Gregorio Belo* (pl. 155), although to some extent Lotto has also reverted to his habits of the late 1520s, in the diagonal, active pose, and the use of a table for accessories. There is also a revived attention to telling detail, evident in the careful representation of the complicated mechanism of the crossbow, with its metal fittings and taut strings. Probably because he did not know him well, the sitter is presented without the overt emotion of the Doria portrait and the *Belo*; as always, however, the pose is strongly suggestive of character, and the face of an inner life of thought.

When Lotto left his native city for the last time in June 1549, he was still apparently intending to return once the *Assumption* was complete.[28] By November 1550, however, he must have decided to remain in the Marches, since eleven days before the final payment for the altarpiece, he moved from the convent of San Francesco into new lodgings in Ancona. He had presumably concluded that his work would be more in demand where he was; and in fact, the account-book records that during the course of the next two years he received several commissions of considerable prestige. In August 1551, for example, he painted the portrait of the vice-regent of Ancona, Giovanni Taurino da Montepulciano;[29] and this was followed in April 1552 by portraits of Vincenzo de Nobili, nephew to Pope Julius III, and of Nobili's son and majordomo.[30] Then in August 1552 he went to Jesi to sign the formal contract to paint another huge altarpiece, this time for the chapel of the wealthy Amici family in the Duomo.[31] This work is now lost, but from the documents it is possible to infer that it constituted, in some sort, a larger-scale version of the Mogliano altarpiece of 1547–8, with the Virgin and angels represented in glory in the upper part of the composition and six saints standing below. The massive wooden gilt frame, which, like that of the Colleoni Martinengo altarpiece (pl. 47), incorporated a painted pediment and predella, was again made the responsibility of Lotto's close friend and colleague, Giovanni dal Coro – who, however, died soon after the project was begun. As with the *Assumption*, it is clear that

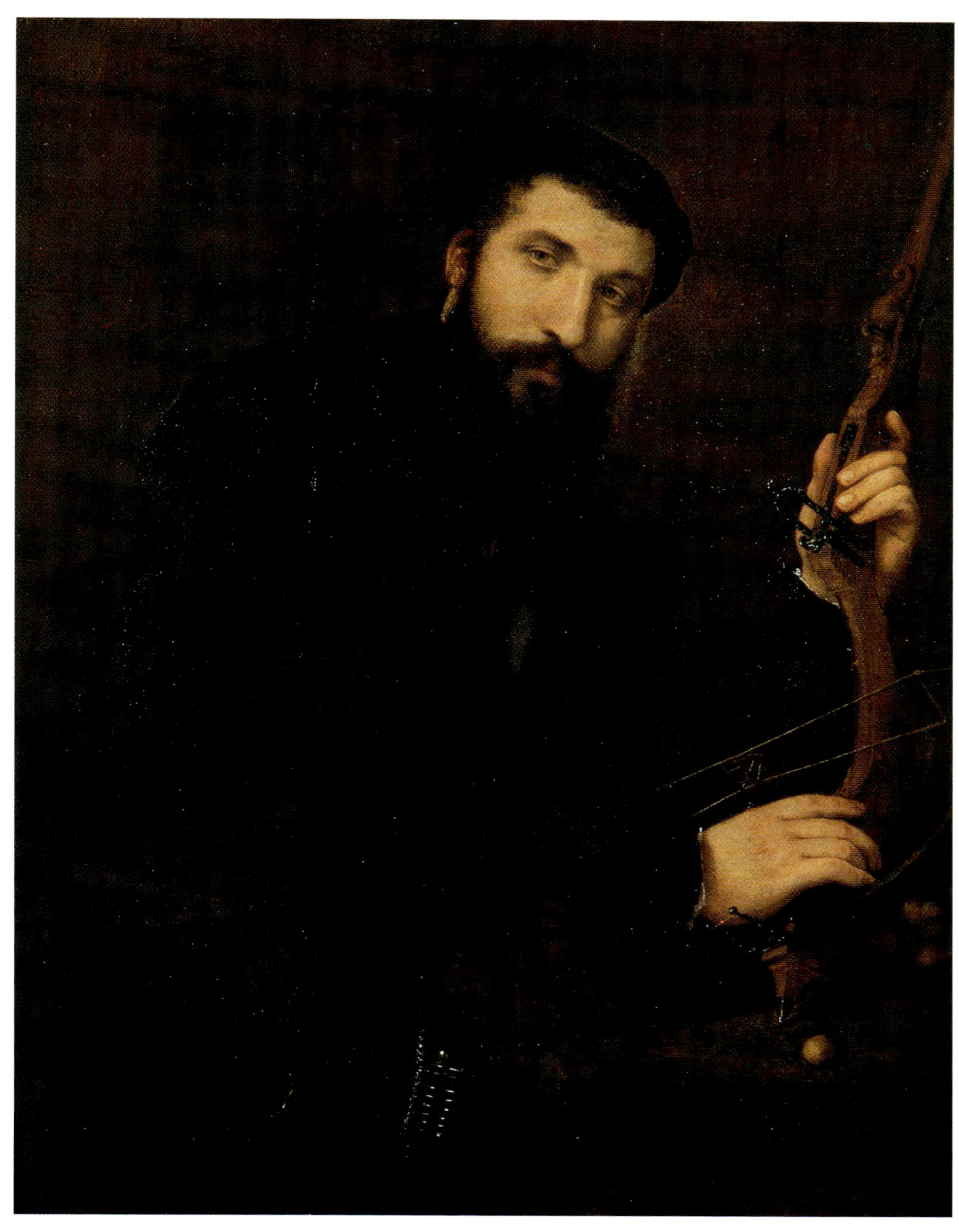

157 Lotto. *Crossbowman* (1551–2). Canvas, 94 × 72 cm. Rome, Musei Capitolini.

Lotto must have received considerable assistance in the execution, in this case from Antoniuccio da Jesi, an obscure figure by whom no works are now definitely recognisable.[32] The completed altarpiece was installed some time in late 1554 or early 1555, soon after Lotto's retreat to the Holy House.

But as well as bringing prestigious commissions such as these, Lotto's three years in Ancona between 1549 and 1552 brought their bitter disappointments. Before leaving Venice, Lotto gave Sansovino a consignment of six pictures, including the splendid Louvre *Holy Family* (pl. 137; p. 135), as well as some jewellery, which he asked him to sell; but Sansovino failed to find a buyer, and in May of the following year he returned them to Lotto in Ancona.[33] In August Lotto included the six pictures, together with ten more, and thirty of the coloured cartoons for the Bergamo *intarsie*, in a public

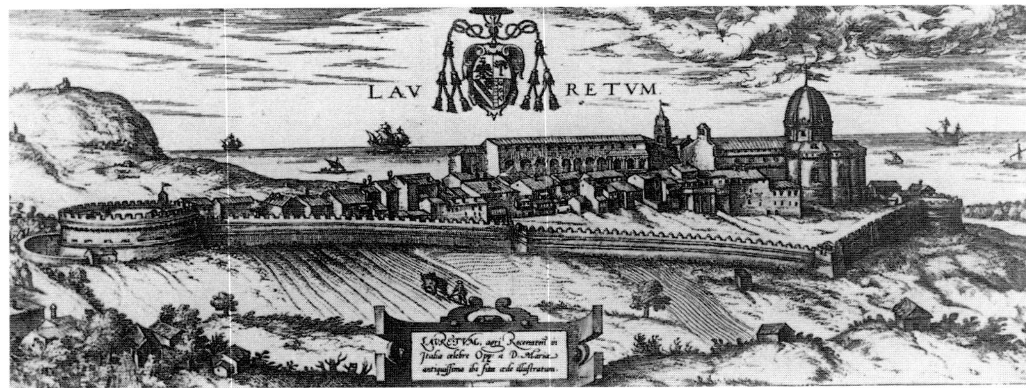

158 Engraved view of Loreto, with Basilica of the Santa Casa. From Ortelius, *Theatrum Orbis Terrarum* (1572).

auction held in the Loggia dei Mercanti.[34] Part of his purpose in holding the auction may have been, as has been suggested, to advertise his presence in the city.[35] But the reference to the cartoons in the 1546 will, as well as in many of the letters to the Consorzio della Misericordia (see Appendix A, p. 176), makes it clear that they were dear to him, and it seems unlikely that he would have put them up for auction unless he was in severe financial straits. Lotto hoped to raise four hundred scudi from the sale of forty-six pictures, but in the event, only seven were sold, for a total of little more than thirty-nine scudi. Even more humiliating was an episode that took place in March 1551, when Lotto made a gift of three devotional pictures to Francesco Bernabei who, as an agent of the Todini family, had been involved in making payments to the painter for the San Francesco *Assumption* (Appendix D, p. 182). Lotto carefully geared the subjects of the three pictures to Bernabei's personal interests, representing his name-saint, Francis, in two of them; and he also made it clear in an accompanying note that he expected no payment. But to his obvious chagrin, the pictures were immediately returned 'with an unpleasant letter',[36] and Lotto eventually gave them to someone else.

By August 1552, the septuagenarian painter had wearied of the competitive, mercantile environment of Ancona, and he retired to spend his remaining years within the Marian sanctuary of Loreto (pl. 158). He had already had contact with the governor of Loreto, the Protonotary Apostolic Gaspare de Dotti, who happened to be a Venetian, and for whom Lotto had painted a *St Francis receiving the Stigmata* in April, and some prophets and sibyls on the nave piers of the basilica in July.[37] Dotti now gave Lotto free board and lodging, a room to work in and an assistant to help him, in return for further occasional work.[38] Then, on the feast of the Nativity of the Virgin, 8 September 1554, Lotto took the partial religious vows of an oblate, and dedicated himself and all his possessions to the Santa Casa – thereby implicitly annulling the provisions of his will of 1546, and decisively renouncing any earlier leanings towards religious heterodoxy.[39] He received the official title of 'Painter to the Holy House' and his existing privileges, including that of receiving free workshop materials, were formally confirmed.[40] Now a member of a religious community, the elderly, devout and lonely painter at last found the family and the domestic stability that he had sought for so long. He had two more years to live: the last entry in the *Libro* dates from 1 September 1556, and a Loreto document of 9 July 1557 implies that he is deceased.[41]

Of the various works he is known to have painted in these last years few survive, and even of these, most were clearly executed with workshop assistance. An *Adoration of the Magi* (Loreto, Palazzo Apostolico), for example, identifiable with one of a series of pictures seen by Vasari above choirstalls in the apse of the basilica, is a mediocre work, attributable mainly or wholly to one of several pupils or assistants known to have worked with Lotto in this period.[42] Another of the series, however, which was apparently conceived by Lotto as a cycle devoted to the infancy of Christ, is a

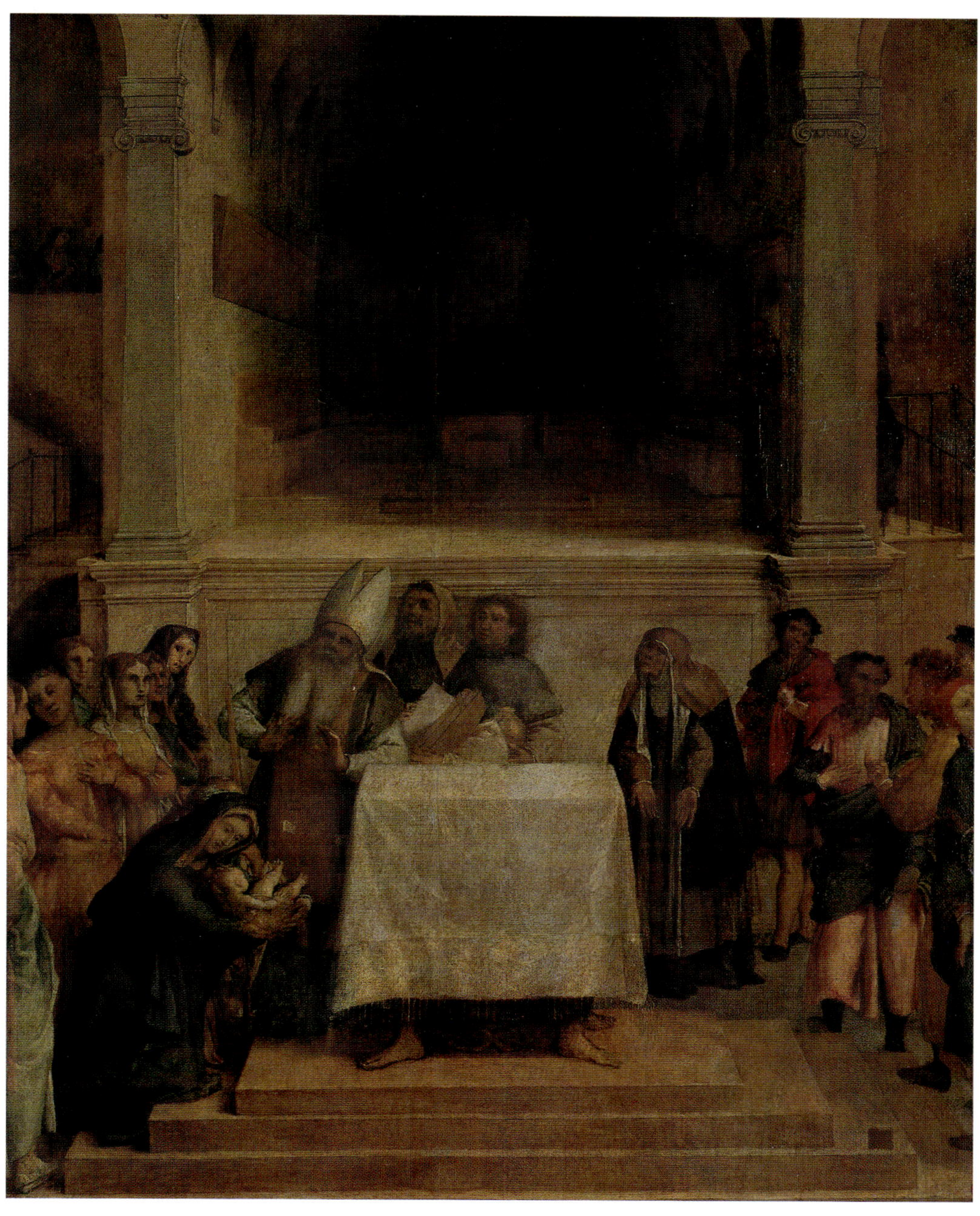

159 Lotto. *Presentation in the Temple* (*c.*1556). Canvas, 172 × 136.5 cm. Loreto, Palazzo Apostolico.

masterpiece that represents a moving testimony to his final thoughts as a painter (pl. 159).[43] In some ways the *Presentation in the Temple* marks a return to the spirit of the Trescore frescoes (pls 86–90), since it similarly shows a sketchy freedom of handling, using broad patches of colour, and the sacred narrative populated with a simple, unheroic humanity. In contrast to the traditional iconography of the subject, usually in the context of altarpieces, the Virgin and Simeon are not placed symmetrically and on a large-scale at the centre of the composition, but almost casually to one side, while the aged prophetess Anna peers intently across from the other. With disconcerting oddness, the central altar is supported on human feet. This informal, unidealised but highly expressive approach to narrative is also reminiscent of that of the Old Testament *intarsie* in Bergamo, the cartoons for which Lotto had failed to sell in Ancona; and in fact, the composition as a whole, with its strangely empty stage-space in the middleground, is loosely based on that of the *David and Goliath* (pl. 96). But the colours no longer have

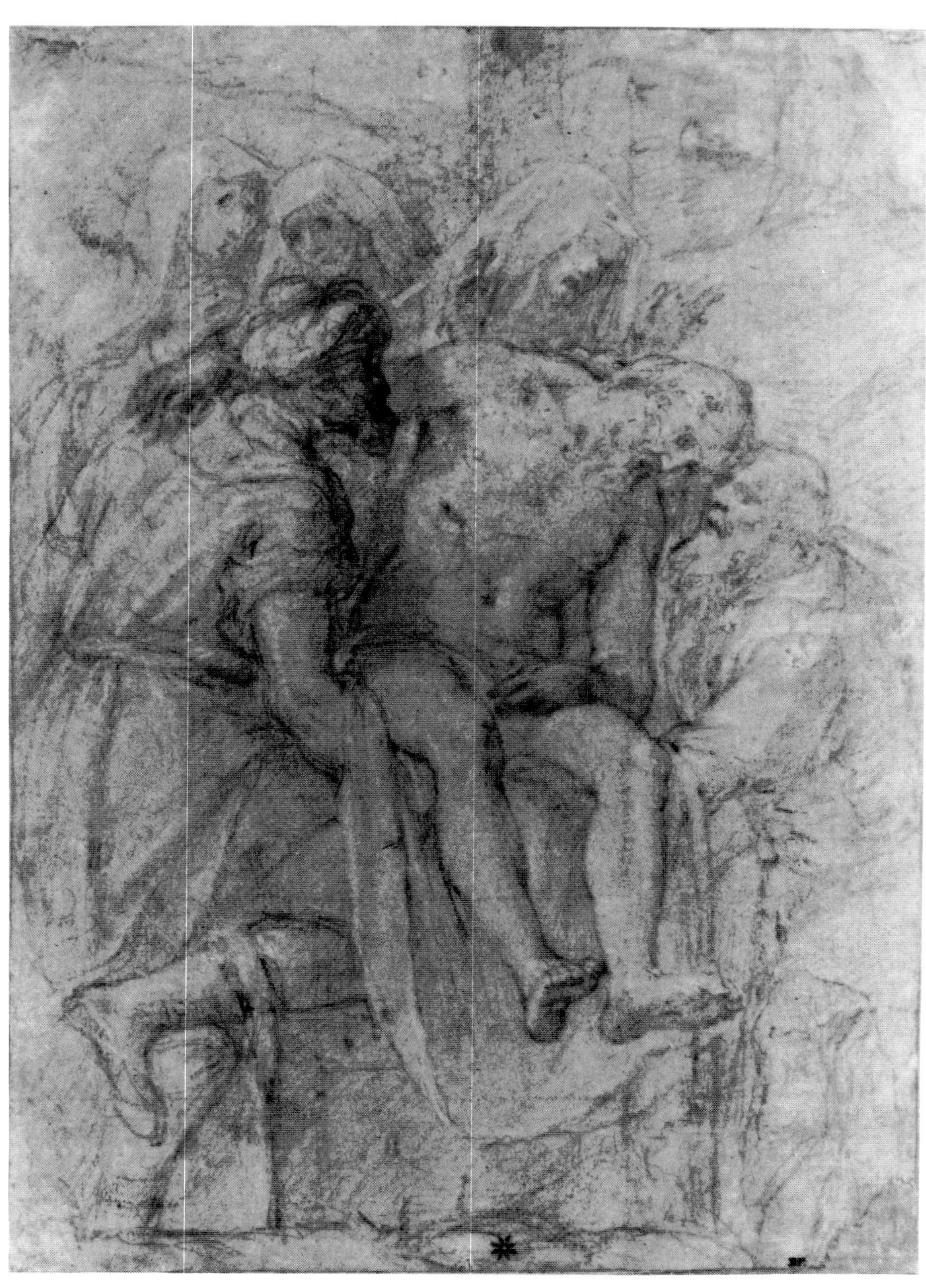

160 Lotto. *Entombment* (*c.*1556). Black chalk with white heightening. 34.3 × 24.5 cm. Paris, Musée du Louvre.

the decorative brightness of Lotto's Bergamo period, and they appear muted and dusky, and as if seen through a luminous mist; while the figures have become anatomically inarticulate, and appear as if fumbling to find their way. Very moving is the tenderness with which the kneeling Virgin holds up the Christ Child to the devout old man, to whom it had been 'revealed by the Holy Ghost that he should not see death until he had seen the Lord's Christ' (Luke 2: 26), and who now raises his eyes in thanks to heaven. It is as if Lotto is identifying himself with Simeon, and that this picture is his own Nunc Dimittis.

Probably contemporary with the *Presentation* is another meditation by Lotto on his approaching death, this time on the intimate scale of a drawing (pl. 160).[44] In the *Entombment* he has returned to the tragic theme of the apex of the San Domenico polyptych, executed in his incisive early style when in nearby Recanati half a century earlier (pl. 31). The drawing, however, is unconnected with any known painting, and its motivation is likely to have been entirely personal. Executed in soft black chalk with white highlighting on a grainy, originally blue paper, it shares the sketchy suggestiveness of the *Presentation*; and again, the almost formless heads seem to see more as if with an inner vision than with their outward eyes. Particularly intensely expressed is the emotion of another old man, perhaps identifiable as Joseph of Arimathea, who presses his forehead against that of Christ, and who turns his face upwards to recognise his Saviour.

* * *

Lotto's passing would hardly have been noticed by his colleagues in Venice, where by the mid-1550s the artistic scene was dominated by Tintoretto and Veronese, and even the ageing Titian had become more the honorary than the actual leader of Venetian painting. Neither Tintoretto nor Veronese, nor any other Venetian painter of their generation can be regarded as an artistic heir to Lotto; and nor can he be said to have made an abiding impact in any of the various other centres of his activity. During his ten-year stay in Bergamo he did help create, together with Previtali and Cariani, a phase of remarkable ferment, and a revolution in the taste of local patrons; but all this quickly dissipated after his departure, since his followers there had succeeded in absorbing only the most superficial aspects of his art. Similarly in the Marches, several of the painters periodically associated with Lotto continued to be active for several decades after his death; but all, including Durante Nobili, were mediocrities, and none, in any case, remained particularly faithful to their master's style. To some extent, Lotto's failure to exert any long-term influence on the course of Italian Cinquecento painting may be ascribed to the fact that, unlike most Venetian painters, he did not belong to a family of painters, and did not even make consistent use of assistants and pupils. But a more fundamental reason is that Lotto did not provide a formula that could have been profitably adopted or developed by followers. On the contrary, the character of his art was so personal that it was essentially inimitable.

But neither Lotto's lack of significant artistic progeny, not the undoubted disappointments of his later years, should be allowed to create the impression that he was ignored by his contemporaries, or that outwardly his career was a failure. Already in a document in Treviso of 1505 he is called 'pictor celeberimus', a very famous painter; and sixteen years later in Bergamo he was referred to in similar terms.[45] His patrons in his earlier career included a succession of high-ranking churchmen and noblemen, including Bishop Rossi, Pope Julius II, Alessandro Colleoni Martinengo, Domenico Tassi, Niccolò Bonghi, Zanin Cassotti and Battista Suardi, and also Bishop Negri of Traù (Trogir) in Dalmatia.[46] Some of these – most notably Colleoni Martinengo – rewarded him very highly indeed for his work (p. 45). In his later career, even in the less happy final years, socially prominent patrons continued to present themselves: Bishop Bonafede, the Protonotary Apostolic Pizoni, the Baglione family of Perugia, the Todini of Ancona, the Amici of Jesi. But an ability to attract patrons of the highest social rank is not the only criterion of professional success; and throughout his career, Lotto found loyal and enthusiastic customers among the middle- and lower-ranking clergy, and among the elected officials of lay confraternities. In his relations with the clergy, he obviously benefited in particular from his longstanding association with the Dominican order; and his expressed wish to be buried in a friar's habit followed a series of major commissions from the Dominican houses of Recanati, Bergamo and Cingoli, as well as of Venice. This special relationship did not, however, preclude fruitful contacts with the other orders, and Lotto also painted altarpieces for the churches of the Franciscans, the Carmelites and the Augustinian hermits. Lay confraternities represented a even more important category of patron: about one third of his extant altarpieces were painted for altars under their jurisdiction; and the *intarsia* designs for the Consorzio della Misericordia represented one of the most challenging commissions of his entire career. Furthermore, it would almost certainly be wrong to assume that Lotto turned to confraternities, some of which may have been rather modest in their social complexion, only because he lacked more prestigious patrons. On the contrary, he may well have felt a natural sympathy for the devotional aims of such institutions, and have been instinctively attracted by the type of commission they offered.

Sometimes a contrast is made between Lotto's relative success in Bergamo and the provincial towns of the Marches, and his apparent failure ever to secure a firm foothold in Venice.[47] It may be true that Lotto did not achieve a recognition in his native city commensurate with his extraordinary talents; and as has been mentioned (p. 96), apart from the lost votive canvas for the Mint (p. 156), he was never awarded any public commission by the Venetian government or the Scuole Grandi. Yet it is important not to exaggerate the degree to which his presence in the city was overlooked. Although Lotto lived in Venice for a total of only thirteen years, he gained during this time four commissions for altarpieces, two of them for conspicuous sites in major conventual churches (pls 95, 102). This is a respectable record that compares well, if not with that of Titian, at least with that of most of Lotto's other contemporaries, including Palma Vecchio, Pordenone, Savoldo, Bonifacio and Paris Bordone. But Lotto seems, in any case, to have been more highly regarded in Venice in the sphere of domestic painting, where his patrons included the patricians Marco Loredan, Lucrezia Valier (or more probably, her husband Benedetto Pesaro) and Marcantonio Giustinian,[48] as well as the wealthy and refined citizen Andrea Odoni. To judge from the descriptions of Venetian art collections by Marcantonio Michiel, the tastes of their owners were remarkably catholic; and there is no reason to suppose that they merely tolerated Lotto as a sort of second-rate, less expensive version of Titian. Rather, they may well have derived a particular pleasure from those features of style and iconography that set him apart from the mainstream of Venetian pictorial tradition.

Yet Lotto's art as a whole is impressive not only for its distinctiveness and originality, but for its sheer quality. It is perhaps, above all, his achievement as a portrait painter, which rivals that of Raphael, Titian and Holbein, that qualifies him to be regarded as one of the great artists of sixteenth-century Europe. But the same outstanding characteristics of his portraiture – compositional and iconographical inventiveness, brilliance of technique, daring and piquant colour combinations, expressive intensity, humane wit – are equally characteristic of his religious pictures; and with the addition of a spiritual urgency rooted in Lotto's own profound Christian commitment, these may likewise be counted among the greatest contributions to the religious art of an age of crisis. Lotto, in short, is a painter worthy of our highest admiration, as well as of our warmest affection.

NOTES

INTRODUCTION

1 See Biographical Outline, pp. xi–xiii.
2 F. Cappelletti in *Gatti nell'arte* (1987), p. 112.
3 The letters are preserved in the Biblioteca Civica, Bergamo. For published editions: Chiodi (1968); *Libro* (edn. 1969), pp. 261–96; Chiodi (1977) (which adds four more letters to the previous thirty-five); Cortesi Bosco (1987), vol. II.
4 *Libro* (edn. 1969), pp. 3–255; preserved in the archive of the Palazzo Apostolico, Loreto.
5 Muraro (1992).
6 Muraro (1984).
7 Chiappini di Sorio (1983).
8 Vasari (1550; edn. 1976), pp. 552–3.
9 Vasari (1568; edn. 1976), pp. 552–4.
10 For the attributions of the *Goldsmith* and the *Man with a Golden Paw* (pl. 104; from Archduke Leopold Wilhelm's collection) to Titian and Correggio respectively: Mariani Canova (1975), nos. 195, 177. The *Odoni* portrait (pl. 105) was attributed to Titian in the seventeenth century and to Correggio in the eighteenth: Shearman (1983), p. 144. For Van Dyck and the *Goldsmith* portrait: Vertova (1981).
11 The will was discovered by Bartolomeo Cecchetti in 1887, and the *Libro* by Pietro Gianuizzi in 1892/3.
12 Berenson (1895). In the 1956 edition the opening chapters on Lotto's antecedents and training were substantially revised, but the highly perceptive conclusion ('Resulting Impression') was retained almost unaltered.
13 The most important monograph of the immediate post-war period is Banti and Boschetto (1953); this appeared in the same year as the major, near-comprehensive Lotto exhibition in the Doge's Palace in Venice (Zampetti, 1953). The volume by Mariani Canova (1975) in the *Classici dell'Arte* series still provides the most serviceable catalogue of the whole oeuvre. More recently, the principal book-length works have been partial studies. Of particular monuments: Cortesi Bosco (1980); Cortesi Bosco (1987). Of particular periods: Mascherpa (1971); Gentili (1985). Of Lotto's altarpieces: Matthew (1988a). Volume of conference papers: Zampetti and Sgarbi (1981). Exhibition catalogues: Zampetti (1953); *Bergamo per Lorenzo Lotto* (1980); Dillon (1980); *Lorenzo Lotto a Loreto e Recanati* (1980); Dal Poggetto and Zampetti (1981).

I TREVISO

1 For recent surveys of the early Treviso period: Gentili (1985), pp. 15–137; Dal Pozzolo (1993). For a convenient summary of the documents: Gargan (1980), pp. 9–18. A document (Gargan, 1980, p. 9 no. 1) recording the existence of a certain 'maestro Lorenzo depentor' in Treviso is often assumed, following Liberali (1963), pp. 4–6, to refer to Lotto; but the absence of a surname makes the assumption impossible to verify.
2 This relatively late birthdate is also proposed, on internal grounds of style, by Rearick (1981), p. 24.
3 According to Dal Pozzolo (1993), p. 33, the inscription is sixteenth-century, but not autograph.
4 For painting in Treviso: Lucco (1988), pp. 208–11; Fossaluzza (1990); Manzato (1992).
5 For the literary culture of late fifteenth and early sixteenth-century Treviso: Gargan (1980); Martignago (1992); Pastore Stocchi (1992), with references. For Colonna (1433/4–1527), Augurelli (*c.*1456–1524) and Bologni (1454–1517), see the respective entries in *Dizionario biografico degli Italiani* XXVI (1982), pp. 299–303; IV (1962), pp. 578–81; XI (1969), pp. 327–31.
6 For Rossi: Liberali (1963), pp. 13ff; Galis (1977), pp. 190–2; Gentili (1985), passim.
7 An X-ray photograph is published in Berenson (1895; edn. 1956, pl. 5). This shows that the donor figure was obliterated before the Baptist was inserted, probably in the middle of the sixteenth century. But the donor was holding a cross, and so was certainly a cleric; and the picture is known to have come from the Rossi collection in Parma. Furthermore, an inventory of the bishop's possessions of 1511 records 'uno quadro dove è retrattato suso la figura de Monsignore rev.mo di Rossi'—a picture clearly distinct from Lotto's independent portrait of Rossi (pl. 10), recorded elsewhere in the inventory. See Liberali (1963), pp. 26–7; Liberali (1981), pp. 73–4.
8 For this episode and its probable relation to the commission: Biscaro (1898), pp. 146–7; idem (1901), p. 161. As Dal Pozzolo (1993), p. 45 n. 2, has pointed out, a potential problem in linking the picture to the event is created by the fact that the inscribed date reads '1503. adi 20 septembrio', whereas the assassination attempt took place nine days later. On the basis of this discrepancy one might wish to go on to challenge the reliability of the date provided by the inscription, which is not in Lotto's hand (above, n. 3). Yet the eclectic and immature style of the picture does seem to confirm that it is Lotto's earliest; and the balance of evidence still favours Biscaro's theory of its origin.
9 For a list of twenty-seven versions: Heinemann (1962), pp. 37–8 no. 135.
10 This proposal was first put forward by Berenson (1895), pp. 80ff. Although in the 1956 edition of his book he laid less emphasis on the formative influence of Alvise on Lotto, the original proposal remains essentially convincing. For a recent survey of critical opinion on Lotto's training: Dal Pozzolo (1993), pp. 44–5 n. 1 (with a conclusion in favour of Alvise).
11 The portrait is usually dated 1505, as its original cover was once inscribed with the date of 1 July 1505 on its reverse (see following note). But work on the portrait may well have begun at least a year earlier.
12 According to an inscription formerly on the reverse of the panel: Shapley (1979), p. 278.
13 For portrait covers in general and the *Alvise Contarini* in particular: Pope-Hennessy (1966), pp. 211–12; Dülberg (1990), pp. 124–6, 236–7; for Dürer's *Holzschuher*: Dülberg (1990), pp. 190–91.
14 For the early history of the Renaissance *impresa* and its use in portraiture: Lippincott (1990).
15 For varying interpretations: Tervarent (1958), cols. 211–12; Liberali (1963) (with reference to the particular circumstances of Rossi's life); Pope-Hennessy (1966), pp. 211–12; Galis (1977), pp. 192–203; Shapley (1979), p. 278; Gentili (1985), pp. 84–7; Pochat (1985); Cortesi Bosco (1987), pp. 346–8 (with reference to the theological mysticism of Jean

Gerson); Dülberg (1990), pp. 124–6, 236–7.

16 For the association with the book of Job and Gregory's *Moralia*: Gentili (1985), p. 87.

17 As pointed out by Galis (1977), p. 203. It is worth noting that the composition of Raphael's so-called *Dream of the Knight* (London, National Gallery), close to Lotto's *Allegory* in both date and theme, is likewise bisected by a tree.

18 Formerly Berlin, Kaiser-Friedrich-Museum, destroyed 1945. For the borrowing from Dürer's *Penitence of St John Chrysostom*: Lucco (1983), p. 465.

19 For the debt of early Lotto to Dürer: Pignatti (1973), pp. 261–5.

20 Berenson (1956), p. 4.

21 As suggested by Galis (1977), pp. 212–17, followed by Gentili (1985), p. 90. Other, less likely candidates include the early Vienna portrait (pl. 26), as suggested by Mascherpa (1980a), p. 15. Dal Pozzolo (1992), p. 119, argues that it served as the cover for a now lost portrait of the poet Giovanni Aurelio Augurelli.

22 For varying interpretations, many of which overlap: Tervarent (1958), cols. 390–91; Galis (1977), pp. 435–46; Shapley (1979), pp. 275–7; Arasse (1981), pp. 370–76; Gentili (1985), pp. 87–90; Pochat (1985); Dülberg (1990), pp. 144–5; Cortesi Bosco (1992); Dal Pozzolo (1992).

23 Some scholars have read the inscribed date as 1500 rather than 1506: see the survey of opinions by S. Béguin in *Le Siècle de Titien* (1993), pp. 274–5. But for a recent, convincing insistence that the date should be read as 1506: Dal Pozzolo (1993), pp. 337–8, who follows Liberali (1981), p. 83, and Gentili (1985), p. 129, in identifying the picture with a 's. Jeronimo' recorded in an inventory of Rossi's possessions.

24 Gentili (1985), p. 131.

25 The documents originally published by Biscaro (1898) and Liberali (1963) are summarised by Gargan (1980), pp. 14–15, and Matthew (1988a), pp. 398–401.

26 For a reconstruction of the original, now lost frame: Manzato (1981).

27 See Gentili (1985), p. 103, who also points out that the book held by St Jerome is decorated with an image of the dead Christ, and that the Child holds a goldfinch, a traditional symbol of the Passion.

28 For the Asolo *Assumption*: Dillon in Dillon (1980); Gentili (1985), pp. 118–28; Matthew (1988a), pp. 318–22; Humfrey (1993), p. 353.

29 Gentili (1985), p. 124.

30 Humfrey (1993), pp. 354–5. The suggested date of *c.*1510 for this picture may be too late by five to seven years.

31 As first proposed by Von Einem (1956), p. 163 n. 64; see Humfrey (1993), pp. 248–50. As well as interpreting Lotto's picture as an *Immaculate Conception*, Dal Pozzolo (1990), pp. 99ff, suggests that the figure of the Virgin constitutes a portrait of Caterina Cornaro, the exiled Queen of Cyprus, who held court in Asolo and who was compared by one of her court poets with the Virgin Mary. But while such an analogy was clearly possible in the rarified context of chivalric poetry, it would have been quite unacceptable in the public and devotional context of an altarpiece.

32 The portrait has traditionally been dated to *c.*1506–8 – in other words, to Lotto's first Marchigian period (see Mariani Canova, 1975, p. 90). An earlier dating to *c.*1504–5, already proposed by Seidenberg (1964), pp. 41–2, now seems to be more generally preferred: Zampetti (1983), no. 3; Gentili (1985), pp. 76–82. Perhaps, however, this should be advanced to *c.*1506, given the greater maturity of the work compared with the *Rossi* portrait.

33 Grabski (1981), pp. 384–5.

34 For the reference to the interpretation by Valeriano: Gentili (1985), pp. 79–2. Less convincing is the author's attempt to identify the sitter of the portrait as Broccardo Malchiostro, Rossi's close adherent and Parmese compatriot, who was also intended as a victim of the assassination plot of 1503. One of the arguments put forward in favour of this identification is the supposed resemblance between Lotto's sitter and a donor portrait in Francesco Bissolo's *St Justina* altarpiece of 1530 (Treviso, Duomo); this donor has been shown, however, to represent not Malchiostro, but another adherent of Rossi, Giovanni de' Novellis (Carboni, 1987). Dal Pozzolo (1990), p. 110 n. 45, accordingly suggests that Lotto's portrait represents the young de' Novellis; but the resemblance between the two portraits is in any case not very close.

35 Galis (1980), p. 367.

36 Critics are unanimous in dating this picture to Lotto's early career in Treviso.

37 Although usually identified as Jerome, the figure bears none of this saint's customary attributes, and the scroll indicates rather that he is an Old Testament prophet. Jeremiah was one of several prophets venerated as saints in Venice, with a parish church dedicated to him. Similarly unlikely is the traditional identification of the female saint as Clare, as the colour of her hood is not the Franciscan brown worn by her neighbour Francis, but violet.

38 Gentili (1985), pp. 112–14.

39 Although sometimes dated close to the Recanati polyptych of 1506–8 (pl. 31), the picture more probably precedes Lotto's move to the Marches, since it may be identified with a *Mystic Marriage* by Lotto recorded by Ridolfi (1648; edn. 1914), p. 144, in the Galdini collection in Treviso. See Kultzen and Eikemeier (1971), pp. 91–3, with references.

40 Although it is unusual for Joseph to hold a book, he does so in Vasari's *Holy Family with St Francis* (Los Angeles, County Museum of Art), as was pointed out to me by David Ekserdjian. As an object of devotion, the old man is in any case, unlikely to represent the hermit, who according to legend, showed Catherine a miraculous image of the Virgin and Child. For this reading: Kultzen and Eikemeier (1971), pp. 91–3.

41 But the attribution to Lotto, first proposed by Biscaro (1898), still has staunch supporters. For a survey of recent critical opinion: Fossaluzza (1990), pp. 566–8, n. 67.

42 Pignatti (1973), p. 261.

2 THE MARCHES AND ROME

1 For recent surveys of Lotto's career 1506–13: P. Zampetti in Dal Poggetto and Zampetti (1981), pp. 194–5; Oldfield (1984a); Gentili (1985), pp. 141–205. For the Roman phase, see also n. 13 below.

2 Humfrey (1993), pp. 129, 135.

3 For Recanati and Loreto in the fifteenth and sixteenth centuries: Moroni (1980); Grimaldi (1980).

4 For the documents relating to the Recanati polyptych: Grimaldi (1980), pp. 81–2; see also the summaries in *Libro* (edn. 1969), pp. 321–2; Matthew (1988a), p. 403.

5 For the polyptych: P. Zampetti in Dal Poggetto and Zampetti (1981), pp. 196–9; Gentili (1985), pp. 141–50; Matthew (1988a), pp. 402–5.

6 For the iconographic programme: Mariani Canova (1981), pp. 340–41 (with an emphasis on the Dominican aspect); Gentili (1985), pp. 141–50 (with a counter-emphasis on the civic aspect). The two popes were identified by Vasari (1568; edn. 1976), p. 553, simply as 'Gregory' and 'Urban'. Mariani Canova (1981), p. 341, proposed that they should be identified rather as Gregory IX (who canonised St Dominic) and Honorius III (who confirmed the Dominican rule), but suggested as alternatives Innocent V and Benedict XI (the first two Dominican popes to be beatified). Gentili (1985), pp. 143–6, reaffirmed Vasari's identifications by pointing out that the pope on the (spectator's) right, holding a panel with the images of Sts Peter and Paul, must be Urban V (who discovered relics of the saints in the Lateran), and by suggesting that his companion may be Gregory XII (a former bishop of Recanati and Macerata). But as the writer admits, this last suggestion must remain hypothetical, since Gregory XII was never canonised. The Dominican saints in the upper register are identifiable as Vincent Ferrer and Catherine of Siena, and their companions as Lucy (with the glass jar) and Sigismund (a rare saint, specifically identified by Vasari).

7 Vasari (1568; edn. 1976), p. 553. Of the three predella panels, the *Preaching of St Dominic* is generally identified with a picture now in the Kunsthistorisches Museum, Vienna (but doubt about the identity has recently been expressed by Dal Pozzolo, 1993, p. 43); the other two are lost.

8 A more relevant precedent than the San Zaccaria altarpiece is the earlier San Giobbe altarpiece of *c.*1480 (Venice, Accademia),

which includes a coffered barrel vault. The Frari triptych of 1488 (Venice, Frari) provides a precedent for Lotto's use of side panels that are physically separate but illusionistically linked to the central panel.

9 See especially also the altarpiece of the Milanesi (Venice, Frari), left unfinished by Alvise at his death in 1503/5, and subsequently completed by Marco Basaiti.

10 Crivelli's *Pietà* of 1493 (pl. 32) was painted for the church of San Francesco in Fabriano, not far from Recanati.

11 See, for example, the contrasting positions of Strieder (1982), p. 128, and Anzelewsky (1980), pp. 129, 132.

12 Cortesi Bosco (1990), p. 48, plausibly suggests that, in keeping with standard practice, the Recanati polyptych would have been required to be in place above its altar in time for the feast of St Dominic (4 August). In that case, Lotto may have reached Rome by the autumn. The identity of the bishop saint may also have some bearing on the question of where the Borghese picture was painted. Correctly pointing out that this figure cannot be Louis of Toulouse, as had traditionally been supposed, Gentili (1985), p. 156, has proposed instead that he is Flavian, a patron saint of Recanati, who although represented in a slightly different guise in Lotto's polyptych, was in fact sometimes venerated as a martyr. Implicit in this proposal is the assumption that the picture was painted while Lotto was still at Recanati. But as kindly pointed out to me by David Ekserdjian, the saint is certainly to be identified rather with the early Christian martyr Ignatius of Antioch, after whose death in the Colosseum, according to *The Golden Legend* (edn. 1969), p. 148, 'his heart was opened, and there the name of Jesus Christ was found written in letters of gold'. The saint's customary attribute is accordingly a heart, and in Lotto's panel it is duly inscribed with the IHS monogram. The fact that the cult of Ignatius centred above all on Rome, where several churches claimed to possess his relics, lends further weight to the supposition that Lotto painted the picture when already in Rome towards the end of 1508.

13 For the Roman visit: Zocca (1953); Longhi (1980); Volpe (1981); Zampetti (1987); Cortesi Bosco (1990).

14 Longhi (1980), p. 116; Oldfield (1984a), pp. 22–3. An alternative suggestion proposed by Liberali (1963), p. 18, that Lotto was summoned by Julius II on the recommendation of Bernardo de' Rossi, seems less likely, especially since Rossi did not take up residence there until 1511.

15 According to the payments published by Zocca (1953), pp. 341–2, nn. 11, 14, Lotto was working in the room next to the papal library ('propre librarium superiorem')—in other words, either the Stanza dell'Incendio or the Stanza d'Eliodoro. Since the fresco decoration of a room customarily began with its ceiling, and since Perugino was already occupied on the ceiling of the Stanza dell'Incendio, it may well be that Lotto's task was to paint the fields between the eight original ribs on the ceiling of the Stanza d'Eliodoro. Consistent with this supposition are both the length of Lotto's documented activity in the Stanza (six months) and his total payment (150 ducats). Further, it is known that the ceiling decoration by Raphael, executed *c.*1514 after he had completed the wall frescoes, was painted to replace an existing scheme.

16 Volpe (1981), pp. 133–4; Contardi and Gentili (1983); Gentili (1985), pp. 170ff.

17 Volpe (1981), p. 134, suggests the influence of Raphael's exactly contemporary *Madonna Alba* (Washington, National Gallery of Art), but the relationship is rather generic.

18 Oldfield (1984a), pp. 23–4; M. Lucco in *Pinacoteca di Brera* (1990), p. 163; Lucco (1994), pp. 348–9.

19 For the *Transfiguration*: P. Zampetti in Dal Poggetto and Zampetti (1981), pp. 204–6; Gentili (1985), pp. 184–9; Matthew (1988a), pp. 406–9; Cortesi Bosco (1990), pp. 54–9.

20 For the documents: Oldfield (1984a), pp. 36–7.

21 For the *Entombment*: I. Chiappini di Sorio in Dal Poggetto and Zampetti (1981), pp. 201–2; Gentili (1985), pp. 189–95; Matthew (1988a), pp. 356–8; Cortesi Bosco (1990), pp. 59–62.

22 For the documents and the confraternity: Matthew (1988b).

23 Denied by Volpe (1981), p. 134, and Gentili (1985), p. 192; upheld most recently by Cortesi Bosco (1990), p. 59.

24 Galis (1977), pp. 9–10; Gentili (1985), p. 193.

25 Oldfield (1984a), p. 24.

26 Cortesi Bosco (1990), p. 59.

27 Oldfield (1984a), p. 24. Cortesi Bosco (1991), p. 56, has pointed to a general compositional resemblance between Lotto's altarpiece and Perugino's *Transfiguration* fresco in the Collegio del Cambio, Perugia.

28 Matt. 17:5; Mark 9:7; Luke 9:35.

29 Cortesi Bosco (1990), p. 54. For the threat of schism posed by the anti-papal Council of Pisa, see also Jedin (edn. 1957), pp. 106ff.

30 Vasari (1568; edn. 1976), p. 553.

31 Oldfield (1984a), pp. 35–6. This conclusion was accepted by Matthew (1988a), p. 407, and Humfrey (1990b), p. 107.

32 M. Lucco in *Pinacoteca di Brera* (1990), pp. 161–3.

33 Ibid.

34 For the *St Vincent Ferrer*: P. Zampetti in Dal Poggetto and Zampetti (1981), pp. 207–8; Gentili (1985), pp. 197–200; and Cortesi Bosco (1990), pp. 51–4, to whom the following interpretation is indebted. Zampetti and Gentili both date the fresco slightly later than 1512/13, and believe that Lotto must have returned briefly from Bergamo in 1514/15 to execute it.

35 'Timete Deum et date illi honorem, quia venit hora iudicii eius' (Rev. 14:7).

36 For Fra Bartolomeo's *St Vincent Ferrer* (now Museo di San Marco) and *Christ* (now Arezzo, Casa Vasari): Fischer (1990), p. 199; for Lotto's response: Oldfield (1984a), p. 26.

37 Steinberg (1977), p. 108.

38 According to Lanzi (1795–6; edn. 1834), III, p. 72, the *St Nicholas* altarpiece of 1527–9 (pl. 103), which similarly shows a saint enthroned in clouds above a panoramic landscape, 'represented a reworking of the idea' of the *St Vincent Ferrer* fresco.

39 Lucco (1987a), p. 150. The picture is given a slightly later dating to *c.*1516–17 in Pallucchini and Rossi (1983), p. 120.

40 For the possibilty that Palmezzano based his composition on Bellini: Joannides (1992), p. 164. As pointed out by Gentili (1985), p. 201, the African character of Judith's maidservant has a precedent in the grisailles of Mantegna and in an engraving by Mocetto; but these show the figures in full-length.

41 Ricciardi (1993), p. 315, quotes an Aldobrandini family inventory of 1626 ('un quadro con una Iudith con la testa di Holoferne di mano di Lorenzo Lotto') and another of 1682 ('un quadro di una Giuditta con la testa di Oloferne di mano di Lorenzo Lotti in tavola alto palmi uno et un quarto con cornice di ebano'). Furthermore, as Mauro Lucco has pointed out to me, Lotto's picture was clearly known to Carlo Saraceni, whose workshop produced close variants of it in the first decade of the seventeenth century. For two of these variants, now in Dresden and Verona, see Ottani Cavina (1968), pp. 135–6.

42 Chiodi (1980), p. 13.

43 Cortesi Bosco (1990), p. 48, plausibly argues that Lotto did not definitively transfer to Bergamo until late in 1514; less plausible, however, is her suggestion that he maintained his base in Rome during these years.

3 BERGAMO

1 For surveys of Lotto in Bergamo: Mascherpa (1971); P. Zampetti and F. Cortesi Bosco in *I Pittori Bergamaschi* (1980), pp. 1–87; Oldfield (1984c). For Bergamask painting of the earlier sixteenth century and its political and cultural background: Nova (1988).

2 For a transcription of the 'contract' (actually an abbreviated notary's record): *Libro* (edn. 1969), p. 259; R. Tardito in *La Pala Martinengo* (1978), p. 54.

3 For documentary evidence of Previtali's return to Bergamo in 1512–13: P. Zampetti in *I Pittori Bergamaschi* (1980), p. 89. Cariani returned from Venice to live in Bergamo in mid-1517, but his movements in 1512–13 are not precisely recorded. See E. De Pascale in Pallucchini and Rossi (1983), p. 93.

4 For the Colleoni Martinengo altarpiece: Cortesi Bosco (1977); *La Pala Martinengo* (1978); *I Pittori Bergamaschi* (1980), pp. 45–6; Bertelli (1981); Cortesi Bosco (1983); Oldfield (1984a), pp. 26–30; Matthew (1988a). The saints represented (from left to right) are: Alexander, Barbara, James (or Roch?), Dominic,

Mark; Catherine of Alexandria, Stephen, Augustine (or Ambrose?), John the Baptist and Sebastian. For the church of Santi Stefano e Domenico: Mascherpa (1978).

5 For Colleoni Martinengo, his patronage and bequests: Oldfield (1984a), pp. 37–8.

6 Mascherpa (1971), pp. 15–16; Chiodi (1980), p. 15. Oldfield (1984a), p. 33 n. 33, points to several documents recording the presence of Bergamask merchants, including members of the Cassotti family, in Recanati in 1511–12; Matthew (1988a), p. 229, adds to this information by also referring to the business activities of the Marchetti (related by marriage to the Cassotti) in the Marches.

7 Cortesi Bosco (1983).

8 For a purely visual interpretation of the dual rebus: Galis (1980), p. 374, with reference to Matt. 11:30 ('iugum enim meum suave est') and Romans 6:18 ('servi facti estis justitiae'). For the political dimension, with reference to the Myth of Venice: Cortesi Bosco (1983).

9 For Lotto and Correggio: Gould (1981). The author concludes that the two painters exerted a mutual influence on one another, but the problem of how they knew one another's work remains unresolved.

10 Berenson (1956), p. 39.

11 Arasse (1981), p. 366.

12 Bertelli (1981), p. 189.

13 Cortesi Bosco (1977).

14 For the photomontage, which uses Isabello's frame in San Pietro Martire at Alzano Maggiore, originally made for Palma Vecchio's *Death of St Peter Martyr*, now in San Martino at Alzano: Mascherpa (1978), pp. 46–9.

15 For the reconstruction: Mascherpa (1978), pp. 46–7. The author includes the *Angel* now in Budapest (Szépmüvészeti Múzeum) and the three predella panels now in the Accademia Carrara, Bergamo; but he convincingly argues against the inclusion of a number of other small-scale panels that have sometimes been associated with the altarpiece.

16 For the Santo Spirito altarpiece: *I Pittori Bergamaschi* (1980), pp. 47–8; Cortesi Bosco (1981a), pp. 313–15; Matthew (1988a), pp. 338–44. The adult saints represented (from left to right) are: Catherine of Alexandria, Augustine, Sebastian and Anthony Abbot.

17 For the identity of the patron: Cortesi Bosco (1981a), p. 321; for further comments on the contacts between the Marchetti and the Marches: Matthew (1988a), pp. 229–30.

18 Pallucchini and Rossi (1983), pp. 130–31; Humfrey (1990b), pp. 114–19.

19 For Palma's altarpiece: Rylands (1992), pp. 44–6; Humfrey (1993), p. 356.

20 For the San Bernardino altarpiece: *I Pittori Bergamaschi* (1980), p. 46; Matthew (1988a), pp. 335–7; Massi (1993). The saints represented (from left to right) are: Joseph, Bernardino, John the Baptist and Anthony Abbot.

21 For the Ponteranica polyptych: Mascherpa (1971), pp. 71–3; P. Zampetti in *I Pittori Bergamaschi* (1980), pp. 48–9; Cortesi Bosco (1984a), pp. 67–77; Matthew (1988a), pp. 387–92. The date 152[. . .]. is inscribed at the feet of the Baptist, but the last digit is completely abraded.

22 Cortesi Bosco (1984a), pp. 64–77.

23 As argued by Mascherpa (1971), pp. 71–3, who relevantly compares the *Resurrected Christ*, the standing saints and the angel respectively with the *Christ the Vine*, the saints in roundels, and the angel bringing white vestments to St Barbara in the Trescore frescoes of 1523–4 (pl. 86). But the convoluted draperies are also close to those of the Celana *Assumption* of 1527 (pl. 99), while the phosphorescence of the angel's robe resembles that in the Jesi *Annunciation* (Pinacoteca Civica), probably likewise of 1526–7 (p. 92).

24 Mascherpa (1971), pp. 71–3. For more information on the vicissitudes of the frame: Cortesi Bosco (1982).

25 For family chapels at Santi Stefano e Domenico: Mascherpa (1978), p. 40; at Santo Spirito: Cortesi Bosco (1981a), pp. 313, 321.

26 Transcribed in Chiodi (1968), pp. 8–10; *Libro* (1969), pp. 259–60.

27 For the correct identification of Marsilio: Cortesi Bosco (1980), p. 55 n. 15. The other certainly identifiable picture belonging to Cassotti is the *Mystic Marriage of St Catherine*, dated 1524 and now in the Palazzo Barberini, Rome.

28 Frimmel (1888), p. 68.

29 The picture was painted in part payment for Lotto's rent. See Chiodi (1968), pp. 12–13.

30 Cortesi Bosco (1981a), p. 313; Oldfield (1984a), pp. 31, 46.

31 Although Berenson (1956), p. 37, preferred to identify the Tassi *St Jerome* with the one dated 1515, now in Allentown, Pennsylvania, he convincingly dated the Bucharest version likewise to Lotto's Bergamask period (*c.*1520). Mariani Canova (1974) suggested that the latter might be identifiable rather with one of the three St Jeromes painted in Treviso between 1544 and 1546. This late dating was accepted by M. Giammaroli and P. Di Mambro in Contardo and Gentili (1983), pp. 115–16, and by Aikema (1984), p. 344; recent opinion, however, has reverted to the traditional, or even to an earlier dating: Aikema (1993), pp. 304–5 n. 8; Dal Pozzolo (1993), p. 44. For a survey of further opinions: T. Enescu in *Capolavori europei dalla Romania* (1991), p. 39.

32 See sale catalogue of Old Master Drawings, Sotheby's, London, 14 January 1992, lot 34. My thanks to Mauro Lucco for bringing this drawing to my attention.

33 Ridolfi (1648; edn. 1914, p. 144); Tassi (1793), I, p. 125. For recent discussions of the two pictures and an evaluation of the sources: Colalucci (1991); Massi (1991).

34 For further examples: Massi (1991), pp. 109–12.

35 Cortesi Bosco (1976a), pp. 11–16; Colalucci (1991).

36 Ciaranfi (1936), p. 326 (with the mistaken conclusion, accepted by a number of other critics, that the picture was identical with the Tassi *Nativity*); Torriti (1981), pp. 220–22.

37 This picture was kindly brought to my attention in this connection by Mauro Lucco.

38 Arasse (1981), pp. 367–70.

39 For this picture: Colalucci (1990). As the author points out, the wooden object in the right foreground is not a mousetrap, as was asssumed by Shapley (1979), pp. 280–81.

40 Colalucci (1990), p. 82; idem (1991), p. 56 n. 4.

41 For the woodcut, datable to 1515: Rosand and Muraro (1986), pp. 88–9. For Lotto's painting and its interpretation: Gentili (1981), pp. 417–18; Brock (1990).

42 Gentili (1981), p. 417, transcribes the cartouches as follows: 'Vidimus eam cum iuvene commisceri / Ni nobis assenties testimonio nostro peribis' (We saw her consort with a young man. If you do not submit to us you will perish from our testimony); and 'Satius duco mori quam peccare. Heu me' (I would rather die than sin. Alas!).

43 Brock (1990), pp. 57–63. Cortesi Bosco (1995), p. 14 n. 24, tentatively identifies the patron as the distinguished Bergamask judge Benedetto Ghislandi, with whom Lotto is known to have had close relations in 1518.

44 Mascherpa (1980b).

45 '. . . ire velle ad alia loca sive civitates vel terras . . . per Italiam sive extra Italiam ac partes gallicas sive Germanie.' Quoted by Mascherpa (1980b), p. 17.

46 For the identity of the patron: Cortesi Bosco (1981b); in his will he bequeathed the picture to the nunnery of Santa Grata in Bergamo. The work is usually dated *c.*1522, but the resemblance of the figure of St Sebastian to that of the Baptist at the extreme right of the Colleoni Martinengo altarpiece (pl. 47) of 1513–16 suggests a slightly earlier date.

47 A close replica of the picture (London, National Gallery) carries the date 1521; technical investigations have shown that although undeniably weaker in quality, it too underwent modifications during the process of execution, suggesting that Lotto worked on both pictures simultaneously. For the correct identification of the friar saint (previously called Anthony of Padua) as the Augustinian Hermit Nicholas of Tolentino: Ekserdjian (1991); as a hermit and a fellow-Father of the Church with Augustine himself, Jerome was also a favourite saint of the order (see p. 127). For a detailed reading of the furniture and accessories represented in the Boston picture as allusions to Christ's passion, death and resurrection: Goffen (1978).

48 Useful biographical information on the patron Niccolò Bonghi (born 1462) is provided by Di Tanna (1990a). But the author's suggestion that the figure of St Catherine represents a portrait of Bonghi's wife Dorotea is not entirely convincing.

49 Ridolfi (1648, edn. 1914), p. 144.

50 The hat and costume of Niccolò have been

drastically altered by now removed overpaint on two different occasions in the picture's history: see Gould (1975), pp. 133–4; and especially Cortesi Bosco (1981a), who also provides detailed biographical information on the sitters.

51 'Medicorum Esculapio / Joanni Ausgustino Ber / gomatj.' The inscription on the letter on the table is addressed to Niccolò: 'Dno Nicolao de la tur / re nobili bergom . . .' Gould (1975), pp. 133–4.

52 For example, by Berenson (1956), pp. 31–2; Seidenberg (1964), pp. 52–3; Gould (1966); Cortesi Bosco (1981a).

53 I am grateful to Jill Dunkerton for this information.

54 The detail of the fly may have been inspired by a similar detail (now lost) in Dürer's *Feast of the Rosegarlands*, for which see Bialostocki (1986), p. 20.

55 Caversazzi (1913). For further biographical information on Lucina Brembate: Gentili (1981), pp. 418–19; idem (1989), pp. 174–7.

56 Ovid, *Metamorphoses*, IX.306–23; this source was suggested by Claudie Balavoine, at a conference of the Society for Renaissance Studies at the University of Glasgow, 5 November 1994. See also Friedmann (1969), pp. 2–4. Gentili (1981), pp. 418–19, while also emphasising the references to childbirth, interprets the weasel-head rather as a symbol of evil and misfortune, to be warded off by the amulet.

57 For the rise of the conjugal portrait and its social background: Hughes (1986).

58 For the following, see especially Hall (1976), whose interpretation is largely followed by Hughes (1986), pp. 20–21. The relationship with German bridal portraiture was already noted by Pope-Hennessy (1966), p. 227. For the symbolism of the yoke and the laurel, see also Tervarent (1958), cols. 225, 232–3.

59 For German double portraits of the later fifteenth and earlier sixteenth centuries: Buchner (1953), cats. 197–207. Buchner's cat. 198, in which an angel hovers above the heads of the bridal couple, is related to Lotto's portrait by Pope-Hennessy (1966), p. 227. See also Wilk (1978), pp. 61–2, who refers to two further examples of particular relevance for Lotto: an engraving after the Housebook Master (with the monogram *bg*), in which a half-length couple exchange wedding gifts; and a now unidentifiable Flemish double portrait recorded by Michiel (Frimmel, 1888, pp. 102–3) in the house of Cardinal Grimani in Venice in 1521.

60 For this identification: Amaglio (1992), followed by Cortesi Bosco (1993).

61 Giovanni Maria, his wife and children are recorded living in the house of his father Zanin Cassotti by Michiel (Frimmel, 1888, p. 68).

62 Galis (1977), p. 238. The author points out that the priest follows the gospel quotation with the words 'It should never be lawful to put asunder those whom thou by matrimony hadst made one' ('numquam licere disjungi'). Lotto's inscription thus constitutes an abbreviated conflation of the two sentences.

63 For squirrel symbolism in general: Tervarent (1958), col. 153. For recent interpretations of Lotto's squirrel: Hughes (1986), p. 20; Di Tanna (1990b); Cortesi Bosco (1993).

64 Pope-Hennessy (1966), p. 233. For the drawing, see also Pouncey (1965), p. 12; Rearick (1981), p. 29.

65 Chiodi (1980).

66 The fresco is recorded by Michiel (Frimmel, 1888, p. 64). For the identification of the drawing: Cohen (1975). For an earlier, sketchier version of the same composition: Rearick (1981), pp. 26–7.

67 For a recent discussion: Barbieri (1991).

68 For the following, see the detailed and authoritative account by Cortesi Bosco (1980).

69 Criticising this anti-heretical interpretation by Cortesi Bosco (1981a), Calì (1981), pp. 245–51, unconvincingly proposes that the Christ-Vine image reflects a certain sympathy for the Protestant position felt by reformers within the Catholic Church. See the further comments by Cortesi Bosco (1984b) and by Gentili (1985), pp. 209ff.

70 Katz (1978).

71 Before the correct identification of the protagonist of Lotto's frescoes as St Brigid of Ireland by Cortesi Bosco (1980), they were thought to represent scenes from the life of St Clare of Assisi.

72 For the history of the commission: Cortesi Bosco (1987), I, pp. 9ff.

73 For the documents: Annibaldi (1980), pp. 151–2. Some subsequent writers have inferred from an acknowledgement of payment by Lotto dated 22 April 1525 that he was back in Jesi on that date; but it is clear from the context that he received the payment through Giovanni Marchetti. For Giovanni and his brother Balsarino: Cortesi Bosco (1981a), p. 321; idem (1984a), p. 57.

4 VENICE

1 The idea that the *St Antoninus* altarpiece was commissioned as early as 1525/6 was first proposed by Oldfield (1984b), but was rejected by Cortesi Bosco (1987), I, p. 158, and Aikema (1989). Further supporting arguments in favour of Oldfield's idea have been advanced by Matthew (1988a), pp. 60–61, 425–6.

2 *Libro* (edn. 1969), p. 233; cf Matthew (1988a), p. 425. Also relevant in this connection is the observation by Galis (1977), p. 37, that Lotto's references to the altarpiece in his account-book in 1540 concern only his expenses, and exceptionally, do not summarise the terms of the contract. This implies that he had already recorded this information in a now lost account-book dating from the period before 1538.

3 See P.L. De Vecchi in *I Pittori Bergamaschi* (1980), p. 352. The iconography of Marconi's altarpiece has recently been illuminatingly discussed by Gardner (1995); there is inadequate foundation, however, for the author's supposition that the two altarpieces were originally placed against the choir-screen, and were only later moved to their present positions.

4 Chiodi (1968), p. 101; Libro (edn. 1969), pp. 265–7; Cortesi Bosco (1987), II, pp. 9–10.

5 Romano (1976), p. 87. But cf pp. 14, 142, 153.

6 *Libro* (edn. 1969), pp. 272, 286 respectively.

7 *Libro* (edn. 1969), pp. 286, 291 respectively.

8 For interpretations of the covers, each with a different emphasis: Van den Berg-Noë (1974); Galis (1977), pp. 89–189; idem (1980); Cortesi Bosco (1987), I, pp. 125–38. The last is certainly mistaken in her denial of the connection, amply demonstrated by Galis, between Lotto's covers and Renaissance hieroglyphic culture.

9 'Quali picture de ditte tavolete siano di quella corespondenza in significato a li altri quadri sopra quali se ponerano respectivamente.' Chiodi (1968), p. 28. Cf Galis (1980), p. 363 n. 3; Lippincott (1990), p. 72.

10 *Libro* (edn. 1969), p. 286 ('Circha li disegni de li coperti, sapiate che son cose che non essendo scritte, bisogna che la imaginatione le porti a luce').

11 For interpretations of the *David mourning Absolom* cover: Galis (1977), pp. 136–8; idem (1980), pp. 373–4; Cortesi Bosco (1987), I, pp. 428–30.

12 An opinion shared by Galis (1977) and Cortesi Bosco (1987), despite their otherwise very different views on the interpretation of Lotto's covers.

13 Libro (edn. 1969), p. 276.

14 For this work, painted for a side altar in San Floriano, Jesi: I. Chiappini di Sorio in Dal Poggetto and Zampetti (1981), pp. 308–9; Matthew (1988a); Lampacrescia (1989). The central *St John the Evangelist*, recorded in a sketchy drawing after Lotto (Pouncey, 1965, p. 23) has disappeared. The flanking *Annunciation* is usually and plausibly dated on stylistic grounds to *c.*1526–7.

15 Matthew (1988a), pp. 345–7.

16 For the Celana *Assumption*: Mascherpa (1971), pp. 88–90; Matthew (1988a), pp. 348–50. For a proposed preparatory drawing: Rearick (1983).

17 Cortesi Bosco (1987), I, p. 144.

18 Pilo (1981), p. 159. Pordenone did not settle in Venice until the beginning of 1528, and throughout 1526–7 he was active in the Friuli (see Furlan, 1988, pp. 29–30); it is perfectly possible, however, that he made brief visits to Venice during this period.

19 I. Chiappini di Sorio in Dal Poggetto and Zampetti (1981), pp. 304–7; Matthew (1988a), pp. 359–61; Mozzoni (1993).

20 F. Pappagallo in Mozzoni (1993), p. 42.

21 Matthew (1988a), pp. 418–22; A. Augusti in *Le Siècle de Titien* (1993), pp. 495–6.

22 Ridolfi (1648; edn. 1914), p. 145; Zanetti (1771), p. 208.

23 'Tempore de Ih. Baptista Donati guardian et Georgii de Mundis vicarii et sotior(um)

MDXXVII'. For the confraternity: Gramigna and Perissa (1981), p. 70.

24 Galis (1977), p. 230. Lotto used a similar composition for his Trinity of *c.*1517, now in Sant' Alessandro della Croce, Bergamo.

25 See especially the description by Michiel (Frimmel, 1888, pp. 100–4) of the Grimani collection.

26 Dolce (1557): see Barocchi (1960), p. 184; Roskill (1968), pp. 154–5.

27 Vasari (1568; edn. 1976), p. 552; Ridolfi (1648; edn. 1914), p. 145.

28 Ridolfi (1648; edn. 1914), p. 145 ('Il signore Jacopo Pighetti gentiluomo bergamasco per la cognitione delle belle lettere ornamento della sua patria possiede un pietoso Redentore con la Croce in ispalla'). See Chastel (1982); S. Béguin in *Le Siècle de Titien* (1992), pp. 493–4. The latter was hesitant about identifying the Louvre picture with that of Pighetti, apparently because she inferred that Ridolfi saw the picture in Bergamo; but for Pighetti's residence in Venice, see Savini Branca (1964), p. 260.

29 For which see Brown (1987), p. 238. For this, the Giorgione and the relation of both compositions to a prototype by Leonardo: *Leonardo and Venice* (1992), pp. 344–56.

30 The iconography of the woodcut, datable to the beginning of the sixteenth century, was already compared to that of Solario's painting by Brown (1987), p. 238.

31 Ridolfi (1648; edn. 1914), p. 145. For the Reynst brothers and the Falck engraving: Logan (1979), pp. 134–5; Béguin (1981), pp. 101–2.

32 Vasari (1568; edn. 1976), p. 552; for the identification of this with the Reynst picture: Béguin (1981), pp. 101–2. Tommaso da Empoli is mentioned in Lotto's account-book in 1541, when Lotto painted his wife's portrait (*Libro*; edn. 1969, p. 132); it is not clear how or when he acquired the *Night Nativity*, which must originally have been commissioned by the patrician Marco Loredan.

33 For Lotto and Savoldo: Longhi (1928; edn. 1968), pp. 115–19; Martin (1995), p. 67.

34 Vasari (1568; edn. 1984), p. 430.

35 Critics are generally agreed that the picture dates from *c.*1528 (or slightly later): Berenson (1956), pp. 70–71; Zampetti (1983), no. 33. The saint at the right has always been called James, but as pointed out by Cortesi Bosco (1987), I, p. 466, he does not hold a pilgrim's staff but a spear, and may accordingly be identified as Thomas.

36 Boschini (1660; edn. 1966), p. 334.

37 For a formal analysis of Lotto's Venetian portraits: Seidenberg (1964), pp. 55–66. For a discussion of several of them against the background of Lotto's social and intellectual world: Puppi (1981).

38 Most critics agree in dating the portrait to *c.*1526; a close stylistic and compositional analogy is provided by the *Portrait of a Dominican* (Treviso, Museo Civico), which is inscribed with that date.

39 Gentili (1989), pp. 168–9. The author proposes a date of *c.*1524–5.

40 The portrait is traditionally dated to *c.*1527–30: Berenson (1956), p. 100; Caroli (1980), p. 182; Zampetti (1983), no. 35.

41 Ridolfi (1648; edn. 1914), p. 140: 'Fece il Palma ancora molti ritratti di Dame con ornamenti e vesti all'antica e frà gli altri uno della Zattina di gratioso aspetto con bionda capigliatura, che tien in mano una Zampina dorata, alludendo al suo cognome.' This passage was relevantly related to Lotto's portrait by Rylands (1992), pp. 92–3, 108 n. 21, 325, who also raised the possibility that Ridolfi was mistaken in his attribution to Palma, and that the female portrait may also have been by Lotto. The very exactness, however, of the repetition of the attribute makes it seem unlikely that the two portraits were painted as pendants of a man and his wife (or beloved).

42 See Morano di Custoza (1979), no. 3424.

43 For this much-discussed portrait, see in particular Larsson (1968); Shearman (1983), pp. 144–8; Coli (1989). For a useful compilation of biographical information and documents on the sitter: Battilotti and Franco (1978), pp. 79–82.

44 See, for instance, the *Portrait of a Man* (Cleveland Museum of Art), perhaps also of 1527; the *Bishop Tommaso Negri* of 1527 (Split, Santa Maria delle Grazie alle Paludi); and the *Man as St Wenceslas* (lost; copy in Lovere, Galleria dell'Accademia Tadini).

45 This relationship is discussed in detail by Martin (1995), pp. 21–3, 28–30.

46 Frimmel (1888), pp. 82–6.

47 Conveniently republished in Battilotti and Franco (1978), pp. 79–82.

48 Larsson (1968), p. 25.

49 Burckhardt (1898), p. 265; Pope-Hennessy (1966), pp. 228–31; Shearman (1982), p. 147.

50 Coli (1989). Consistent with the author's interpretation is the choice of the statuette of *Hercules mingens*—that is, of Hercules urinating in the direction of a crouching goddess, perhaps identifiable as Venus. The author also identifies the headless female torso next to the head of Hadrian as a Venus; for other critics, however, this is a Diana or a nereid.

51 The portrait is customarily dated to *c.*1524–8: Berenson (1956), p. 470; Seidenberg (1964), p. 61; Zampetti (1983), no. 32.

52 Galis (1977), pp. 233–4. The author claims to discern other objects in the picture, most notably a lute in the left background, and a dead bird on the right, and she duly incorporates them into her interpretation. But the paint surface is very worn in these areas, and neither of the two shadowy forms is properly legible.

53 Gentili (1981), pp. 420–21. Although likewise discerning a lute and a dead bird in the background, the author correctly points out that the reptile is not the self-transforming chameleon, as was assumed by Galis (*loc. cit.*), but the cold-blooded lizard. See also Tervarent (1958), cols. 234–5.

54 According to the eminent French physician André du Laurens (Andreas Laurentius), whose *Discours de la conservation de la veue, des maladies melancoliques etc* (Paris, 1597) constituted a synthesis of Renaissance notions of melancholy, sufferers were advised to seek relief by scattering their rooms with the petals of roses, violets and waterlilies. See Starobinski (1960), pp. 42–4. My thanks to Mauro Lucco for drawing my attention to this passage.

55 Jaffé (1971).

56 'NEC VLLA IMPVDICA LV / CRETIAE EXEMPLO VIVET' ('Nor shall any unchaste woman live through the example of Lucretia'). Livy, *Ab Urbe Condita*, I, 58.

57 Vertova (1981). For the date: Berenson (1956), p. 470; Mariani Canova (1975), p. 112.

58 But he may well have, especially since by 1532 he certainly did know a mutual friend in Treviso, his future landlord Giovanni dal Saon (*Libro*, p. 297).

59 Grabski (1981), pp. 385–7.

60 For the relevance of the *paragone* debate to Lotto's portrait: Puppi (1981), pp. 397–8; Vertova (1981). The latter's conclusion that the portrait was painted rather as a practical model for a sculptor carving or modelling a portrait bust of the sitter is not entirely convincing.

61 For the dating of the drawing and for possible connections with Venice: Pedretti (1975), pp. 10–11; for Lotto's knowledge of it, or of a related drawing: Marani (1987), p. 43; idem in *Leonardo and Venice* (1992), p. 35.

62 Vasari (1568; edn. 1976), p. 552. It remains possible, however, that Vasari's comment represents no more than a rhetorical device for linking the biographies of the two painters.

63 Document in Ludwig (1901), p. 69.

64 For Lotto's association with Sansovino and Serlio: Puppi (1981); Tafuri (1985; edn. 1989), pp. 58–64.

65 Letters of 5 and 12 August, 16 September, 7 October 1527: *Libro* (edn. 1969), pp. 275–7, 282–3.

66 Document in Ludwig (1903), p. 42.

67 Frimmel (1888), p. 84; Battilotti and Franco (1978), p. 79.

68 First proposed by Romano (1976); accepted by Cortesi Bosco (1976b) (but denying any religious heterodoxy on Lotto's part); Calì (1981), pp. 257–8; Fontana (1981), pp. 287–8; Aikema (1984), p. 349 n. 8; Nova (1988), p. 110. Scepticism has been expressed by Zampetti (1980), p. 24; Chiappini di Sorio (1981), pp. 332–3; Gentili (1985), pp. 210–12.

69 For Brucioli and his Bible: R.N. Lear in *Dizionario biografico degli Italiani*, XIV (1972), pp. 480–85. For a recent evaluation of the term 'Evangelism': Gleason (1993), pp. 191ff. As the author explains, it refers to a loosely organised, undogmatic movement that aspired towards the moral reform of the individual Christian through God's word in the Bible, and stressed faith in divine mercy through Christ's death on the cross.

70 Tafuri (1985; edn. 1989), pp. 64–70.

71 Cortesi Bosco (1980), p. 59 n. 42.

72 Martin (1993), pp. 51ff, with references.

73 This topic has been the subject of much critical debate during the last fifteen to twenty years, with scholars often taking sharply polarised views. For a sample of opinion: Calì (1981); Fontana (1981); P. Zampetti in Dal Poggetto and Zampetti (1981), pp. 439–40; Cortesi Bosco (1984b); Gentili (1985), pp. 209–26; Tafuri (1985; edn. 1989), pp. 58–64. The pioneering sketch by Berenson (1896; edn. 1956), pp. 145–6, although inevitably outdated, still offers a remarkably balanced view.

74 For the *St Lucy* altarpiece: P. Dal Poggetto in Dal Poggetto and Zampetti (1981), pp. 317–21; Cortesi Bosco (1984a); Matthew (1988a), pp. 364–6. For the documents: Annibaldi (1980).

75 *The Golden Legend* (edn. 1969), pp. 34–7.

76 The presence of a small, wheel-shaped symbol, placed at the top of the green curtain in the central panel of the predella, and again in the centre of the main panel near its lower edge, has been convincingly interpreted by Cortesi Bosco (1984a), pp. 63–4, as a device for punctuating the flow of the narrative, indicating to the spectator that the scene represented in the main panel belongs chronologically to the point marked by the green curtain. The choice of a wheel is obviously appropriate to denote the passage of time.

77 A panel representing *St Lucy at the Stake* (Jesi, Museo Diocesano; currently exhibited in the Pinacoteca Civica), of identical dimensions to the three predella panels and vaguely Lottesque in style, was published by P. Dal Poggetto in Dal Poggetto and Zampetti (1981), p. 317, with the suggestion that it represents an early copy after a fourth, now lost predella panel by Lotto. Cortesi Bosco (1984a) rejected this suggestion, rightly arguing that the total width of the four panels is excessive in relation to the width of the main panel, and pointing out that it would have been unusual and unsatisfactory for there to have been an even number of predella panels, with a caesura coinciding with the central axis. In addition to these arguments, it may be pointed out that the episode of St Lucy at the stake represents yet another unsuccessful attempt to have her martyred, and iconographically it is not a necessary complement to the other scenes. Cortesi Bosco proposed that the fourth panel is a copy after an option that Lotto decided to reject; more probably, however, it was a late eighteenth- or early nineteenth-century addition *ex novo*, made at a time when the predella had become detached from the main panel.

78 See Humfrey (1993), pp. 76–8.

79 The document is listed among the papers of the Venetian notary Daniele Giordan, but is missing from its place in his files. The same is true of a will made by Lotto two years earlier with the same notary. See Ludwig (1905), pp. 131, 135.

80 Rylands (1992), pp. 137–40.

5 THE MARCHES, VENICE AND TREVISO

1 For a survey of Lotto's career in the Marches in the 1530s: P. Zampetti in Dal Poggetto and Zampetti (1981), pp. 302–3. For a biographical survey of the period covered by the account-book: P. Zampetti in *Libro* (edn. 1969), pp. XXIX–XLVIII.

2 For the *Crucifixion*: I. Chiappini di Sorio in Dal Poggetto and Zampetti (1981), pp. 314–16; Dal Poggetto (1984); Angelucci (1990); Matthew (1994). When the picture was cleaned in 1981 the last two digits of an inscribed date of 1531 were shown not to be authentic.

3 For Bonafede and his patronage: Angelucci (1990); Matthew (1993a).

4 Massi (1990).

5 Vasari (1568; edn. 1976), p. 554. For this work, usually dated to *c.*1535, see R. Varese in Dal Poggetto and Zampetti (1981), p. 326; Matthew (1988a), pp. 290–97, 369–73. A preparatory drawing for the *St Christopher* is published by Lucco (1994), with a dating to *c.*1533–4; the author dates the painting to slightly later, *c.*1536–7.

6 Matthew (1988a), p. 290. For the traditionally close association of the images of Christopher, Sebastian and Roch with that of the Virgin of Loreto: Grimaldi (1987); idem (1993), pp. 211ff, 240, 340.

7 Lotto had already used these motifs in this sense in the Bergamo *intarsie*; see Matthew (1988a), pp. 295–6. Muraro (1981), p. 311 n. 35, interprets them as a more personal expression of devotion by the painter.

8 Matthew (1988a), pp. 291–2, 308–9 n. 47.

9 Berenson (1956); Caroli (1975), p. 186; P. Zampetti in Dal Poggetto and Zampetti (1981), pp. 310–12.

10 Compare, for example, the *Visitation* (Jesi, Pinacoteca Civica) (with its similar display of still-life objects on a shelf) and the *Virgin and Child with Angels* (formerly Osimo, Palazzo Comunale), both of *c.*1534–6; and the *Holy Family with St Jerome* (Florence, Uffizi), dated 1534. In type, the head of the Virgin is very close indeed to that in the Fermo altarpiece of 1535 (pl. 129).

11 Quoted by Matthew (1988a), p. 410.

12 For the recently rediscovered Fermo altarpiece: Zampetti (1981); P. Zampetti in Dal Poggetto and Zampetti (1981), pp. 229–31; Matthew (1988a), pp. 412–13. Like that of the Ancona altarpiece (see following note), the top was probably originally arched.

13 Zampetti (1981). See also P. Zampetti in Dal Poggetto and Zampetti (1981), pp. 332–4, and R. P. Benedetti Panici, ibid, pp. 364–5.

14 For the Ancona altarpiece and its contract: Micaletti (1991); Polverari (1992). The canvas has been cut at the sides, and especially at the top, which was originally arched.

15 Identified by Michele Polverari; discovery announced in *Corriere Adriatico*, 19 July 1994.

16 For the Cingoli altarpiece, its patron and iconography: Aikema (1981). See also P. Dal Poggetto in Dal Poggetto and Zampetti (1981), pp. 338–41; Matthew (1988a), pp. 351–2.

17 Matthew (1988a), pp. 107–8.

18 Most recently and fully by K. Christiansen in *The Age of Caravaggio* (1985), pp. 63–5. But a more relevant comparison might be with two other works of a similar type, both certainly painted in the Marches: the *Holy Family with St Jerome* of 1534 (Florence, Uffizi), and the related *Holy Family* of 153(?)5 (London, Courtauld Institute Galleries). The somewhat coarse quality of the latter suggests that it may have been executed in collaboration with Lotto's assistant Durante Nobili (p. 127).

19 Catena's design, which recurs in another version in Dresden, derives in turn from a drawing by Giulio Romano, executed in Raphael's studio (Chatsworth, Devonshire Collection). See Robertson (1954), pp. 56–8. Christiansen (see previous note) convincingly argues that since both Giulio's drawing and Catena's Dresden picture show the figures in full length, Lotto's composition must have been based on the ex-Mexborough version, in which the Virgin similarly appears in three-quarter length.

20 See most recently F. Caroli in *Giovanni Girolamo Savoldo* (1990), pp. 287–8. The author does not, however, quote the convincing suggestion by Béguin (1981), p. 102, that the picture dates rather from the mid-1530s.

21 Originally in the local church of the Franciscan Observants, it was stolen from the Palazzo Comunale in 1911 and was never recovered. See P. Zampetti in Dal Poggetto and Zampetti (1981), p. 328.

22 Panazza (1958), p. 135.

23 Possible candidates for a pair of Baglione brothers of a suitable age in the mid-1530s are the two sons of Grifonetto Baglione: Braccio II (1495–1559), who with papal support won some influence in Perugia in the years 1533–4, temporarily winning ascendancy over a rival branch of the family; and his younger brother, Sforza Baglione. For a family tree: Astur (1964), pp. 462–3; for the power struggles of the 1520s and 1530s: Black (1970), especially p. 263.

24 Ricci (1918); Astur (1964), p. 61.

25 S. Béguin in *Le Siècle de Titien* (1993), pp. 496–7.

26 The iconography of both episodes is discussed in detail, with reference to literary texts, by Lavin (1955).

27 Pouncey (1965), pp. 14–15.

28 This work, previously considered lost, has recently been identified by Lucco (1994) with a portrait now in a private collection.

29 Ricciardi (1989). The identification was accepted by S. Béguin in *Le Siècle de Titien* (1993), pp. 497–8, but somewhat inconsistently in view of her convincing dating of the portrait on stylistic grounds to *c.*1535.

30 For the sitter's gesture: Gentili (1981), pp. 422–3. The author, followed by Ricciardi (1989), further maintains that the presence of a

pair of rings on the sitter's little finger proves that he is a widower; but pairs of rings frequently appear on the same finger in Italian Renaissance portraits without necessarily signifying a state of widowhood.

31 For the confraternities in Florence and Venice, and the social policy of the Venetian government: Pullan (1971), pp. 232, 267, 373. For Lotto's altarpiece against this background: Mariani Canova (1981); Mazza (1981); Aikema (1989); Aikema and Meijers (1989), pp. 85–8.

32 Humfrey (1993), pp. 76–8.

33 In June and July 1541 Lotto made drawings of *poveri*: *Libro* (edn. 1969), p. 236.

34 For a dating to the mid to late 1520s, and for a detailed and convincing discussion of the picture's iconography: Christiansen (1986). See also S. Béguin in *Le Siècle de Titien* (1993), pp. 494–5. Zampetti (1957) has identified Mario d'Armano's *Venus* rather with a picture in a private collection in Bergamo; but this is a vertical composition, whereas Lotto's abbreviated reference in his account-book (*Libro*, edn. 1969, p. 238 n. 2) to Mario's *Susannah*, painted as a pendant to the *Venus*, shows that their format was horizontal.

35 The most likely candidate for the prints is the pair of woodcuts by Hans Brosamer (Hollstein, 596–7), first published in Nuremberg in 1530, and widely circulated during the subsequent decade.

36 See above, chap. 4 n. 73.

37 Fontana (1981); Martin (1993), p. 132.

38 For the *Beneficio*: Martin (1993), pp. 84–7, with reference to some of the vast critical literature.

39 The picture is inscribed on the reverse, apparently in the hand of Lotto's friend the architect Giovanni dal Coro: 'Questo quadro è fatto di mano di Messer Lorenzo Lotto, omo molto divoto, et per sua divotione il fece la septimana santa et fu finito il Venerdì Santo all'ora della Passione di N.S. Gesù Cristo. Io Zanetto del Co. ho scritto acciò si sappia e sia tenuta in quella venerazione che merita essa figura' ('This picture was painted by Mr Lorenzo Lotto, a very devout man, for his own devotion during Holy Week, and was finished on Good Friday at the hour of the Passion of Our Lord Jesus Christ. I, Giovanni dal Coro, wrote this so that it would be known, and so that this image would be held in the veneration that it deserves'). The picture is difficult to date: Berenson (1956), pp. 88–9, related it to the Monte San Giusto *Crucifixion* and the *St Lucy* predella of the early 1530s, but it may well date from a decade later.

40 *Libro* (edn. 1969), pp. 84–6.

41 For a biographical survey of the second Trevigian period: Chiappini di Sorio (1981).

42 Document in Libro (edn. 1969), p. 297.

43 *Libro* (edn. 1969), pp. 84–5.

44 *Libro* (edn. 1969), pp. 54–5, 241, 248, 251.

45 *Libro* (edn. 1969), pp. 174, 229.

46 Documents in *Libro* (edn. 1969), pp. 154–5. For the *Lamentation*: M. Lucco in *Pinacoteca di Brera* (1990), pp. 168–70; Matthew (1993b).

47 For this controversy and its reflection in religious imagery: Hamburgh (1981), with references.

48 For these three portraits: Seidenberg (1964), pp. 72–4; M. Lucco in *Pinacoteca di Brera* (1990), pp. 163–8.

49 *Libro* (edn. 1969), pp. 120–21, 247. In favour of the identification is the fact that this is one of Lotto's larger Trevigian portraits, and that Pinedel paid him the comparatively high fee of twenty ducats. Furthermore, as pointed out by Ricciardi (1993), p. 320, Pinedel's son and heir married the daughter and heiress of Febo da Brescia and Laura da Pola; and this family connection may well account for the very similar dimensions and common provenance of the three portraits. Although Lotto's sitter is sometimes described as a old man, his hair and beard are red, with no traces of grey; and his age also, therefore, seems consistent with that of Pinedel, who, as shown by Ricciardi, was aged forty-seven or eight in 1542–3.

50 *Libro* (edn. 1969), pp. 56–7.

6 THE LAST YEARS

1 *Libro* (edn. 1969), p. 151.

2 *Libro* (edn. 1969), p. 98.

3 For the Hospital of the Derelitti (Ospedaletto): Pullan (1971), pp. 247–8, 262; Aikema and Meijers (1989), pp. 149ff. For Lotto's association with the Hospital: Manzelli (1981); Aikema (1984).

4 Rosand (1971).

5 For the altar and the patron: Matthew (1988a), pp. 432–6.

6 As recorded in the account-book, the contract for the altarpiece was signed on 27 August 1546, and the completed work was to be delivered in time for the feast of the Immaculate Conception on 8 December. On 24 November Lotto made a payment to Carpan's maidservant, who had looked after him during the month and a half of his illness. *Libro* (edn. 1969), pp. 36–7 and pp. 20–21 respectively.

7 Santosuosso (1973); Martin (1993), pp. 89, 132.

8 Fontana (1981), pp. 281–3.

9 For Carpan and Fra Agostino: Martin (1993), pp. 89, 132.

10 *Libro* (edn. 1969), p. 182. For the identification: M. Giammarioli and P. Di Membro in Contardi and Gentili (1983), pp. 107–16; Aikema (1984); Aikema (1993).

11 For the religious background to the iconography: Aikema (1994). The author's suggestion, however (p. 344), that the picture was meant to serve as an altarpiece for the Hospital chapel is inconclusive; and so is his insistence that the phrase in the account-book signifies that it was an official rather than a private commission. 'Ducati 8 tra doi fratelli' indicates more simply that, as was his frequent custom, Lotto was charging his dear friend and *confrère* much less than the standard rate for his *St Jerome*, and probably for his portrait as well.

12 *Libro* (edn. 1969), p. 182.

13 Gentili (1981), pp. 421–3; Ricciardi (1993).

14 See the various detailed interpretations by Gentili (1981), pp. 421–3; Grabski (1981), pp. 387–90; Cristaldi (1984).

15 As pointed out by Claudie Balavoine, conference for Society for Renaissance Studies, University of Glasgow, 5 November 1994.

16 Cortesi Bosco (1987), pp. 340–7, with detailed iconographic interpretation.

17 F. Signori in Muraro (1992), p. 347.

18 *Libro* (edn. 1969), pp. 74–5. For the portrait and the sitter: Zeri and Gardner (1973), pp. 40–41; M. Giammaroli in Contardi and Gentili (1983), pp. 119–24.

19 *Libro* (edn. 1969), pp. 32–3. This Lorenzo Giustinian, a Procurator of San Marco, was identical with the co-donor of Veronese's altarpiece for San Francesco della Vigna in 1550–1: Humfrey (1990a).

20 *Libro* (edn. 1969), pp. 26–7, 41, 104–5. For the Mogliano altarpiece and its commission: I. Chiappini di Sorio in Dal Poggetto and Zampetti (1981), pp. 446–7; Matthew (1988a), pp. 379–82. For a biographical survey of the phase 1548–51: Chiappini di Sorio (1984).

21 Barocchi (1960), p. 126.

22 *Lettere* (1957), II, pp. 204–5.

23 *Lettere* (1957), II, pp. 218–19; *Libro* (edn. 1969), pp. 305–6.

24 *Lettere* (1957), II, pp. 274–5 (letter to Monsignor de' Martini, 5 January 1549).

25 For the work and the commission: P. Zampetti in Dal Poggetto and Zampetti (1981), pp. 450–52; Matthew (1988a), pp. 315–17.

26 *Libro* (edn. 1969), pp. 119, 110, 43 respectively. The studio hands were named Paolo Rossino and Giuseppe Belli; the latter was the son of one of the craftsmen with whom Lotto had worked on the choirstalls in Bergamo.

27 *Libro* (1969), p. 28.

28 *Libro* (1969), p. 98 ('jo vado for de Venetia per qualche tempo').

29 *Libro* (1969), pp. 186–7. This portrait has been tentatively identified with the *Portrait of a Gentleman* (Milan, Brera) by M. Lucco in *Pinacoteca di Brera* (1990), p. 172.

30 *Libro* (1969), pp. 186–7.

31 Documents in *Libro* (1969), pp. 307–9. For the commission: Matthew (1988a), pp. 447–51.

32 *Libro* (1969), pp. 18–19. See also P. Zampetti in Dal Poggetto and Zampetti (1981), pp. 375–6, 464.

33 *Libro* (1969), pp. 98, 114–15.

34 *Libro* (1969), p. 128.

35 Chiappini di Sorio (1984), p. 99.

36 *Libro* (1969), pp. 62–3.

37 *Libro* (1969), pp. 76, 146.

38 *Libro* (1969), p. 147.

39 At this very time the Santa Casa was beginning to represent another source of contention between orthodox Catholics and the Protestant reformers. In 1554, for example, the apostate bishop Pietro Paolo Vergerio published a

blistering attack on the cult of the Virgin of Loreto, claiming it to be based on superstition and fostered by papal greed. Grimaldi (1993), pp. 17–18.

40 Document in *Libro* (1969), pp. 310–12, and in *Lorenzo Lotto a Loreto e Recanati* (1980), pp. 95–6.

41 *Libro* (1969), pp. 219, 316; *Lorenzo Lotto a Loreto e Recanati*, p. 98.

42 Vasari (1568; edn. 1976), p. 554. For the attribution: R. Varese in Dal Poggetto and Zampetti (1981), p. 457.

43 For this picture: R. Varese in Dal Poggetto and Zampetti (1981), pp. 460–61.

44 Pouncey (1965), p. 17; F. Viatte in *Le Siècle de Titien* (1993), pp. 478–9.

45 See respectively Gargan (1980), p. 13; Cortesi Bosco (1987), p. 17 ('pictorem famosissimum').

46 See above, chap. 4 n. 44.

47 This is the viewpoint frequently expressed by the leading expert on Lotto in the second half of this century, Pietro Zampetti. See, for example, *Libro* (1969), pp. XXVI–II.

48 This Giustinian, whose portrait Lotto painted in Venice in 1541 (*Libro*, 1969, pp. 132–3), was the nephew of Lorenzo Giustinian, one of the two officials portrayed in Lotto's lost votive picture for the Mint of 1547 (p. 156). For their family relationship: Humfrey (1990a), p. 301.

APPENDICES OF DOCUMENTS

Appendix A
Letter from Lotto to Girolamo San Pellegrino, 1526

This is the sixth of the series of thirty-nine extant letters written by Lotto to the Consorzio della Misericordia in Bergamo in connection with his designs for the *intarsia* decoration of the choir of Santa Maria Maggiore (see pp. 2, 82–3, 89–92). Most of the letters (now in the Biblioteca Civica, Bergamo) are addressed to the governors of the confraternity, but several, including the present one, are addressed instead to the Consorzio's legal representative, the notary Girolamo San Pellegrino. The translation is based on a transcription in Cortesi Bosco (1987), II, pp. 9–10.

To Girolamo San Pellegrino

From Venice, 18 July 1526

Honoured Messer Girolamo,
In a separate letter I am writing to the governors–as briefly as possible, so as not to be tedious–to reassure them that although I am far away, I am being no less attentive to them than I was to their predecessors. Indeed, I am doing more than was requested of me; and if my progress so far has been slow, it is because I have been preoccupied with many unpleasant worries–which however, thanks be to God, are now honourably resolved. You know how much I deserve the generous support of the city of Bergamo in my transfer to Venice. I lived so long among you that people there were astonished at my leaving, and thought that I must have had some special reason. Indeed, my words and feelings already bear witness to my loyalty; and my actions now and in the future will give further confirmation of this to you, and especially to the Misericordia. People have heard about the altarpiece that is being planned for the choir, because many honourable men here have seen the designs that I was able to bring with me, since they were no longer needed by you. The costliness and magnificence of both projects was further confirmed to them by the reports I have been giving of the excellence and grandeur of the church and of the city, so that those who have never been there are now eager to see it. I hope, therefore, that you will all be grateful to me, and particularly so your *intarsiatore* Giovanni Francesco. Please greet him for me, and send him my best wishes, and remind him that I have written to him several times without receiving any reply. Despite this, I still bear him affection, and admire his qualities from afar, because I am a Christian by temperament and conviction, and defy anyone to deny it. He knows well that for his honour and advancement I have acted like a brother on his behalf, and that as a result I have suffered injury from Fra Damiano, an ignoramus lacking in true Christianity. Thanks to him I have had to move to a much more expensive lodging than I had previously, and from this it should be clear to everybody what a malevolent character he is. But by mentioning this, I do not wish to reproach Master Giovanni Francesco, nor ask him for any compensation beyond that of his continuing friendship.

I beg you that my drawings be looked after as carefully as possible during the work; and afterwards please put them in you own safekeeping, so that they do not get manhandled. I would also be grateful if once they have been transferred, you could send them back to me. I have been planning and wanting to visit Bergamo on account of my many interests and needs there; and in this case I would have transferred the designs to panel myself provided that we had come to an agreement about the large ones. But as for this year, such a visit cannot be arranged without great damage to my reputation here. You will understand that so soon after my arrival it is important for me to act prudently, and to treat people here with the greatest consideration.

Send me the subjects for the remaining panels, because I have only three left, one of which I am using for a large scene representing the Crossing of the Red Sea, to place opposite that of the Flood. The other two I am using for the pilasters, because the tall fields there are suitable for showing scenes of rising into the sky: Elijah ascending into heaven; and the Tower of Babel. Please devise two more of this type, and send me the measurements for all the panels.

I did not want to insist further with the governors about what I did when I provided the large design for the Flood, since I was unhappy about the excessive work that was demanded of me. The same will be true of the fields for the pilasters, and in fact I made a mistake when I evaluated the terms of the contract. I begged the governors to judge the case wisely, considering that the Misericordia intends to do well by everybody, and not by just one individual; and if there had been any regrettable misunderstanding with any of its employees, it was its duty towards the holy place to rewrite the contract, and to acknowledge that this would be a good thing to do, and that there is no merit in sparing the money of God. They answered me that I would be satisfied; but since then I have heard nothing more from them on the subject. I would have written something, but I decided not to, because it might have looked as if I wanted to break the first agreement. It would have appeared so especially to his excellency Lodovico Rota, with whom I had an earlier disagreement regarding the standard; and he would immediately have said, 'There goes that importunate Lotto again!'–so I feared that I might only make matters worse. You know the whole story, and understand much better than anyone else what is involved in our kind of work; and I would like, therefore, to leave the matter in your hands. You may, if you think fit, explain that I have written respectfully to you under separate cover, to ensure that my efforts are not in vain, and that in future the governors are not grudging in what they commission – as they usually are when dealing with practitioners of our craft, most of whom prefer to reduce the quantity of work rather than expand it – and will accordingly, God willing, give me adequate compensation. I know that you will do this from you good nature, especially since everyone there, including the craftsmen, well know how much time I have wasted on having to make changes, and on having to ask advice about things that were their concern, and which really did not have anything to do with me. I have not been shown the same courtesy as has been shown to other employees, most of whom have done much less than I; and you must finally have realised how much time has been wasted on persons who are disloyal. You have many years' experience of my loyalty, and even now I am at you disposal; and yet I have not received any reward beyond what is demanded by simple obligation. I therefore pray you to handle this matter as you yourself think fit, showing the governors this letter if necessary. At the same time, you should know that I have also spoken on the subject with his excellency Nicolò Besuccio, who I think will put in a good word for me, enabling you to speak more freely in support of my case.

You may tell Master Giovanni Francesco that when doing the large panel he should be careful that the main figures in the David pulling the sling on Goliath are not too close to one another, and that it may be helpful to move David closer to the suit of armour, or even further away, and put the armour where he now is. In this way everything will work better, because the tops of the steps will be made visible, and so will appear more beautiful. If he cannot manage this, the design could be redrawn by Master Andrea, or else by Master Jacopino, or else by Boselli, or best of all by our own Francesco, if he is there.[1] In the same way, in the Absolom hanging by his head from the oak-tree, his chin is too far from his chest, so that it does not really look as if he is hanging; and Giovanni Francesco could improve it by arranging for the chin to be closer to the neck and chest, and for the forehead to be out of the perpendicular, again to make it look more realistic. Nothing else occurs to me. God protect the whole city from evil, and make my dear friends happy. Farewell.

Your servant and brother,
Lorenzo Lotto

Mr Girolamo: the large design was glued on to a wooden panel, but for ease of transport I unglued it. I beg you to have Master Giovanni Francesco glue an additional paper border two inches wide around it as soon as possible, and then to glue it on to a panel like the other one with Noah. This is because it is large, and would be damaged if handled too much.

1 Lotto is referring respectively to the Bergamask painters Andrea Previtali (*c.*1470/80–1528), Jacopo Scipioni (*c.*1470–1532), Antonio Boselli (*c.*1470/80–*c.*1532) and Francesco Bonetti (*c.*1470/80–*c.*1556).

Appendix B

Lotto's List of Expenses in the House of Mario d'Armano, 1540–1542

Lotto lived with the family of his younger cousin Mario d'Armano in Venice for two years from July 1540 to October 1542 (see pp. 139–42). The following record of his contribution towards household expenses was approved by Mario at the time of Lotto's departure, and was subsequently incorporated into the painter's acount-book (now in the Archive of the Palazzo Apostolico, Loreto). Among the names mentioned are those of Mario's son Alvise and his daughters Armana, Moranda, Lucrezia and Lauretta. Mario's wife is referred to simply as 'madonna' ('my lady'). The sums on the right are given in lire and soldi, with 20 soldi to the lira; the Venetian ducat was worth 6 lire and 4 soldi, and the scudo slightly more. The translation is based on a transcription in *Libro* (1969), pp. 211–16.

Various expenses incurred in the house of Mario d'Armano my nephew, namely to offset the cost of my food there, even though he never made any request for reimbursement.

First, on 3 July 1540, a barrel of olive oil, which I ordered from the Marches, containing 2 measures, at wholesale value of 10 lire the measure — L20 s0

A barrel of vinegar also from the Marches, containing 3 measures — L3 s12

Two oz of saffron, also from the Marches — L2 s8

For latches for the stable door, for chains, and for having them welded in place — L0 s19

On [. . .] July, given to Armana, to help her buy a fleece, 1 golden scudo and five soldi — L7 s1

29 July, for a pair of orange satin shoes for Lauretta — L0 s12

2 August, for 4 lbs of soap which I had sent to Captain Barbato — L0 s12

26 August, sent to my lady by the hand of Gasparo, to pay for a porter to bring wine to master Alvise — L0 s18

Same day, for a pair of hams which I had from Sinnibaldo of Jesi, weighing 12 lbs at 9 soldi per lb, and a pecorino cheese weighing 7 lb at 6 soldi per lb, totalling — L7 s17

6 September, a cheese from Ragusa weighing 12 lbs at 5 soldi per lb — L3 s0

10 September, for a trestle dining table of walnut, which Mario ordered from me, with its metal attachments — L11 s10

And for the green cloth cover and Bergamask tapestry, 10 quarters high by 4 braccia, at 36 soldi the braccio — L7 s4

Earlier in September, for the frame of the picture of Venus which I gave him,[1] i.e. for woodwork in nut, gilding and cover in black Lyons cloth with the lettering he requested — L32 s0

About the end of September, 1 braccio of yellow cloth for making stockings for the little girl Lauretta — L2 s10

17 October, two little pictures with portraits of Martin Luther and his wife,[2] which Mario gave to Tristan with gilt frames, a bargain at 6 ducats — L37 s4

1 Probably the picture now in New York (pl. 123); see above, p. 139.
2 See above, pp. 140–42.

28 October, to Gasparo, who asked me for a *mocenigo* to buy a pair of shoes L1 s4

3 November, for my lady to buy canvas for Lucrezia, 2 ducats given to Armana L12 s8

10 December, given to Lucrezia in the convent of San Bernardo, a twelve-soldi coin L0 s12

to buy her a bound copy of the Lives of the Holy Fathers L3 s2

for a psalter with an Italian commentary, bound in paper L2 s5

a book in quarto, Gerson's Disdain of the World[3] L0 s4

For things taken by Ottavio, namely a pair of hams weighing 14 lbs, at 9 soldi per lb L5 s16

a 12 lb cheese, at 9 soldi per lb L3 s12

3 oz of saffron, at 24 soldi per oz L3 s12

a jar of rosewater L2 s0

28 December, for having made a pair of shoes for Lauretta at the time of Armana's confinement L0 s10

Seven lbs of soap, which I gave to Nena to do the laundry, at 3 soldi per lb L1 s1

For Alvise's journey to Padua, 2 *mocenighi* L2 s8

30 December, to Lucrezia at San Bernardo L0 s12

For Moranda's boat journey back from San Bernardo L0 s8

3 January 1541, for bookplates,[4] sent by courier to Alvise in Padua L0 s9

Given to Armana by Gasparo L0 s3

30 January. Given to my lady for soap L0 s12

A present for Moranda of a cameo mounted in a simple gold frame, showing a Crucifix with the Virgin, St John and two little angels, valued by honest experts at 25 ducats L155 s0

Total = 53 ducats L4 s17

8 February, to my lady, by the hand of Gasparo L0 s4

To Gasparo, to buy 2 lbs sausages, with good quality oil and salad L0 s13

17 February, given to the Turkish woman to buy white salt L0 s2

for the portrat of Alvise with its frame, 8 ducats L49 s12

for the portraits of Armana and Moranda, 18 ducats L112 s12

for their frames L6 s12

for refining silver to make four goblets, similar to the two small ones already in the house L2 s4

for gold to gild all six L1 s18

for work on the cups L3 s12

the same four goblets weighing a total of 8 oz, containing two carats, at 5 lire 5 soldi per oz L42 s0

27 February, to my lady, for her amusement at carnival L0 s6

to my lady, by the hand of Catarina L0 s4

8 March, for a pair of shoes for Lauretta L0 s10

Earlier, at the time of Armana's confinement, for another veil which she bought L7 s0

23 April, for a pair of shoes for Lauretta L0 s10

[. . .] May, for the picture of Susannah, which Mario commissioned to accompany the Venus, 25 ducats[5] L155 s0

for the frame, matching that of the Venus L32 s5

Earlier, when Ottavio came to the house, he brought a barrel with some oil, a ham and some cheeses, to a total value of about 1 ½ ducats L9 s0

The picture of the Venus, without its frame, given to Mario, worth 30 ducats, but given to him without charge L186 s0

The picture of the swooning Madonna, which I promised to donate to the hospital if Armana should give birth in time to protect her from malicious gossip; worth 40 ducats, but again given without charge L248 s0

[. . .] October, given to the Turkish woman to make me a fur coat L3 s0

For the picture of the Madonna with one figure on either side, for Master Alvise's tutor, 8 ducats L49 s12

[. . .] December, for a little ring inset with a diamond and a ruby for Lauretta, 3 golden scudi L20 s8

To change the little picture of Mario's uncle into a St Sebastian, 2 ducats L12 s8

January 1542, for a picture of the Madonna with three little angels, which Mario wanted to have ready for when Lucrezia took the veil 12 ducats L74 s8

For a pregnant sow, given when Enza, daughter of Armana was born, total cost L18 s6

[. . .] February, for a piece of blue cloth for the Turkish woman, 1 braccia and a half quarter L1 s16

A cotton veil for the Turkish woman, 6 quarters L0 s14

For the base of the double bed . . . ,[6] for dismantling it and for making various adjustments and repairs to it L5 s0

10 March, to my lady, by the hand of Daniel L0 s2

For arranging the bed in the little bedroom and refitting its screws, and for arranging other beds and for other things L10 s10

Earlier, when I moved into the house, I spent for the frame for the glass for the high window in the bedroom above the staircase, and for the cloth and for covering with earth and for rails and little curtains for the two big windows in the street *c.*9 soldi L9 s0

16 April, to Mario, a good-sized picture for a bedroom, showing the Madonna and Child, Joseph and the child Baptist, with the Three Magi, but no frame. Mario gave this picture as a present to Domenico Pasqualigo de Candia, a Venetian gentleman, and . . . [?][7] by way of Giovanni dal Canevo. Its true value is 20 ducats. L124 s0

Total = L1177 s11

[. . .] July 1542, for the frame and the cover of the little Madonna picture for Lucrezia. The woodwork cost 3 lire 5 soldi, the gilding with its cover, i.e. the metal frame with its cloth L14 s8

For Lucrezia, the wooden crucifix, poychromed and with a gilded frame L34 s0

Total = L48 s8

Note that on the said day and year, at the beginning of a new year, in order not to be dependent on Mario, I wanted to come to an arrangement with him. So I gave him a written statement promising to give him 3 ducats a month for living in his house at his expense. There was

3 The mystical treatise *De contemptu mundi* (otherwise known as the *Imitation of Christ*) by Thomas à Kempis was attributed in Lotto's day to Jean Gerson.

4 The meaning of the phrase 'tavole da libri' is not clear.

5 See above, p. 140, and chap. 5 n. 34.

6 The meaning is obscured here by damage to the original document.

7 See previous note.

no need for expenses incurred during the previous two years to enter into the discussion, since I had already kept careful account, and given abundant recompense. Then, wishing to move house to go and live a more quiet life in Treviso, because of the many disturbances in the house, I asked him permission to leave, for the sake of preserving our mutual affection as blood relatives.

1 September 1542. The said Mario decided to present me with a document in his own hand confirming that he had received full satisfaction from me in respect of my stay in his house. This was because I had paid him back handsomely, and would owe him nothing more in the future. He wrote as follows:

Copy of the document written by Mario d'Armano my nephew
In the name of Jesus and Mary, 1 September 1542, in Venice. I, Mario d'Armano, have no other relatives on my mother's side than the honoured Lorenzo Lotto, cousin of my late mother, both the legitimate offspring of two sisters and two brothers, and nor has he any relatives closer than I; and I was very glad, therefore, when he chose to come to live in my house. I regarded him more as a father than as an uncle, and my family loved and revered him in the same way, as we always will. No malicious, envious or hostile person should have any doubt that I could have asked him for any payment at any time, and nor did he himself have any such doubt; but because of the pleasure we take in one another's company and the affection he have for one another, it would have been unreasonable for one relative to have asked another for payment. Besides, he did reimburse me in many different ways, as an affectionate uncle and dear father would. Nevertheless, I, the aforesaid Mario d'Armano, am happy to make it known though this autograph document that the aforesaid uncle has made me generous and abundant compensation for his stay in my home up to the present day. I absolve him from any debt and confirm that I shall never ask him for anything, and I declare that I have already received full satisfaction, not only for the period up to now, but for any future period in which we are together. Indeed, I can say with true sincerity that I would be very happy if Divine Providence, to the confusion of his and my enemies, were to permit us to live together again for a long time in the grace of God.

I, the aforesaid Mario d'Armano wrote this in
my own hand and signed it below.

This is the copy of the document written by Mario d'Armano which I inserted here, and which I made from the original in my own possession, as a precaution against the loss of the original.

Item, after my departure from him I returned to Venice at the beginning of December 1542, and brought him a present of veal, sausages and other little things amounting to 8 lire 10 soldi
L8 s10

24 January, I sent sausages, tripe and leeks — L2 s2

Total = L11 s2

Appendix C
Lotto's Will, 1546

Made soon after his return to Venice from Treviso at the end of 1545 (see pp. 2, 151), this is Lotto's only extant will (now in the Archivio di Stato, Venice). He is known, however, to have made at least three earlier ones, in 1531, 1533 (see p. 118) and 1542; and the present one was in turn revoked when he became an oblate at the Santa Casa, Loreto, in 1554 (see p. 162). The translation is based on a transcription in *Libro* (1969), pp. 301–5.

In the name of almighty God, of the holy Trinity and of the whole court of heaven. On this day, 25 March 1546 in Venice, in the Volta della Corona at San Matteo di Rialto.

I, Lorenzo Lotto, Venetian painter, sound of mind and body, aged about sixty-six, am mindful that our Lord God, for the salvation of our souls, assumed human flesh through the Holy Spirit, and was born as Jesus Christ, son of God, of the Virgin Mary; and that he came to teach us the way to know him, and to save us through the grace of the universal Father, creator of heaven and earth. Since death is inevitable, and since we have no certain knowledge of when, where or how it will come, I wish to make provision for my departure from this life. With this document, therefore, I make my last will and testament, partly so that I am satisfied that my few worldly goods will be distributed according to my intentions, and partly so that these are made clear to my heirs.

With this my last will I annul and cancel every previous document and testament, and in particular the one I made in Treviso in 1542 in the house of my friend Giovanni dal Saon. At that time, my friends and well-wishers there saw that I was old, alone, without any stable domestic arrangements, and very anxious of mind; and our mutual dear friend Antonio Carpan, goldsmith in Treviso, moved by this circumstance and acting as an intermediary, made arrangements with the aforesaid friend and myself that I should go and live in his house. In this way, I would be very well settled, with every basic material need taken care of, bringing me peace of mind; and we also expected that my host's sons would benefit from learning the art and science of painting from me. Certainly he derives much pleasure from pictures; and he, together with his whole family, were happy to have me in his house, honoured and respected, without wanting me to pay a single penny towards my costs, until the end of my days. So I let myself be taken into this loving Christian family – with the intention, however, of retaining some independence from their generosity and charity. They were all so kind that I was happy to assure my host that if I died, he would not suffer unwelcome interference for any reason from any of my relatives; and accordingly I wanted to make it absolutely clear that after my death no relative of mine would have any claim on any part of my property. I therefore made him my sole heir; and when the document had been read to the said friend and to Antonio Carpan, the said intermediary, it was sealed in their presence, and witnessed by the notary Giovanni Francesco Federici in the hospital of Treviso. The document was then deposited with him as a record of my testament.

Several days later the said host wrote me a note formalising our arrangement. It was a great pleasure for him and his family to have me in their house as their guest, as already agreed, without any payment or request for payment from me, now or in the future. He gave it to me saying: Friend, keep this with you. I took it with the intention of doing him some favour in return, because he was always reluctant to accept any payment. A few days later, after our arrangement had become public knowledge, respectable people began to make unkind remarks behind my back, saying that I was a sponger, with my snout in other people's trough. So I complained to our friend, the aforementioned intermediary Antonio Carpan, that I was being talked about in this way, and mocked by my rivals. To protect myself, I tried to come to a new agreement, whereby even if my host would not accept a complete payment for his gracious hospitality, I could at least make an annual contribution; but he always refused, saying that he had already made a note of all this in his account-book, and he could not alter existing entries because he did not want to falsify his records. In the end, my only options were either to leave him, or for him to accept my sincere offer, which our confessor praised and highly approved. I therefore made out a document in the form I thought best, and gave it to my host, so that he himself could enter its terms into his account-book. Together with this document, I gave him back his own previous note; and he took both of them, and kept them for several days. Then he gave me back my document without further comment. I did not ask whether he had written down its terms, nor did I ask to see the book, because I trusted him; and assuming that he must have accepted my terms, I did not want to be disappointed in my expectations of him. As a result of all this, I became calmer, and began making occasional monetary contributions, without asking for a receipt. Every so often I also spent money on my own needs, and on occasional little presents for the women and children. I kept careful account of all this, and matters continued in this way for three years. However, for various reasons I then decided to leave Treviso, above all because I was not earning enough from my art to cover my expenses. So I had a discussion with my host, and asked permission to leave his house and Treviso. He could not oppose my free will, but since I did not have the cash to fulfil my desire to reimburse him as explained above, I wrote an autograph statement declaring that I owed him sixty ducats, at 6 lire 4 soldi to the ducat, without expressly saying that it related to expenses incurred during my stay. Since I was doubtful whether he would accept this, I gave this document to his eldest son, so that he would pass it on to him. My host acknowledged receipt, but said that among friends there was no need for me to have done such a thing. But I replied that I really had to do this, and that in fact I owed him more. In addition, therefore, I left two completed pictures with him, one with the portrait of Tommaso Costanzo in armour, and the other with Girolamo Mocenigo of the bishop's palace, for each of which about 25 scudi were still owed to me.[1] My host was then to collect and keep this money, and likewise another 15 scudi owing for some of my pictures given by Bartolomeo Carpan, jeweller in the Ruga,[2] to his pupil Lauro Orso, when he went to set up shop as a jeweller in Messina in Sicily. He took the pictures with him to sell there, and acquired in exchange a quantity of black satin to the value of the said 15 scudi, which here will be worth 20 scudi. This money was to be sent to my host, even though it is not mentioned in the statement referring to the sixty ducats, but was simply mentioned orally to him and to Bartolomeo Carpan, whose task it was to pass on to him the money from Sicily. Of this succession of events–how I first moved into my friend's house; how he intended that I should pay nothing; how I subsequently resolved to pay, for the aforementioned reasons; and how we conducted our business relations together–of all this, our mutual friends are informed and aware: that is, first of all the said Antonio Carpan and his two brothers Vittore and Bartolomeo Carpan, goldsmiths and jewellers; also Antonio dal Sarasin; also the reverend prior of the Maddalena, our confessor; also the priest Fra Bernardo da Vicenza; and finally, Giovanni dal Coro, architect and contractor of Ancona, resident in Venice.[3]

Since, therefore, I have returned to my native Venice, I am making a new will, declaring for the present and future my last wishes in this document, which now supersedes every previous one, as already explained. To the praise and glory of my Lord, creator and redeemer, to whom out of his goodness and divine clemency I beg for merciful pardon for my offences both against his divine majesty and against my neighbours, and for all my other sins.

First, I appoint as my executors my fathers and brothers in Christ, the governors of the Hospital of Santi Giovanni e Paolo. I ask Giovanni Maria Giunta and Vincenzo l'Albero[4] to assume this office for the love of Jesus Christ, or else any other governor who may be preferred. Therefore I commend my soul and spirit to the Lord God, and consign my corrupt body to the earth.

Second, as soon as I am dead, I wish the friars of Santi Giovanni e Paolo to have me buried in their cemetery, according to their rite, and dressed in their habit. They already agreed to do this when I gave them their altarpiece of St Antoninus, at no charge to myself or my heirs. The friars were consulted about this at a meeting of their chapter, and their consent was noted in their record book for 12 May 1542, fol. 95. This was during the priorate of the reverend Sisto de' Medici, and a copy was given to me for may own records.

Third, once my body, dressed as described, has been taken from my house, it shall be accompanied to the church of Santi Giovanni e Paolo for burial, as previously described, by the following: four priests of my parish carrying a cross, together with four candlesticks of modest expense, in honour of the cross and not of my body; four friars of Santi Giovanni e Paolo with four of their novices; and five pairs of poor boys from the aforesaid Hospital; but without representatives of any of the confraternities to which I belong.

Fourth, if I have any servants or apprentices in my employment, they shall be paid their dues, as will be found recorded in my account-book, together with the names of my business associates and the records of the little that I owe them. The payments shall be made from the proceeds of the sale of my pictures, since the necessary cash will not be found otherwise.

Fifth, my executors shall set aside any items of furniture and household goods of quality, so that they can be used. Any remaining pieces of no importance shall be given for the use of the poor in the aforementioned hospital.

1 Both these portraits are now lost, but they are extensively documented in the account-book: *Libro* (1969), pp. 174–5, 218, 229; and 90–91, 230, 302 respectively. For the Costanzo portrait, see also, p. 143.

2 For Lotto's friend Carpan: see above, pp. 110, 142, 153.

3 For Lotto's friend Giovanni dal Coro: see above, pp. 158–60.

4 For Lotto's friend Vincenzo Frizier: see above, pp. 151, 153–4, 156.

Sixth, all my artist's materials shall be kept together: drawings; plaster and wax models; unfinished pictures; and the Old Testament drawings used for the *intarsie* for the choir at Bergamo, numbering thirty in all, that is twenty-six small and four large. Also paints, brushes and various other items of equipment used in the practice of art, and these too shall be kept.

Seventh, an investigation shall be made through the Scuola de' Depentori to find two young painters living in Venice, either local or foreign, who are respectable, at the beginning of their careers, and keen to make use of my aforesaid materials. Similarly, two young women of the aforesaid Hospital shall be found, who are of a quiet disposition, healthy in mind and body, and capable of running a household; and these girls shall be given as wives to the aforesaid young men, together with dowries consisting of the reserved items, namely the furniture, household goods and artist's materials, divided equally in half. These items shall be given in addition to the normal dowry granted by the said Hospital. The proceeds from any sales shall be divided into three parts: two parts shall be given to each of the said young men as a dowry, and the third part shall be used to benefit the poor of the Hospital, for instance by providing linen or something similar. Of the aforementioned items comprising the dowries, an honest estimate shall be made of their value; and in keeping with normal practice, a declaration shall be made of the combined total of this sum and of the sum given by the Hospital.

Eighth, the ultramarine pigments with the prices written on them shall be sold; and similarly, the ground lapis lazuli shall be refined to make blue, and sold at the best possible price. All finished pictures shall also be sold. Likewise twelve cameos of naturally multicoloured stones, with the twelve astrological signs carved on them; these are separate and unmounted, and are modern, not antique. Also four other cameos with heads, which are similarly coloured, modern and unmounted. Also a white antique cameo, with a worn antique putto, mounted in gold to serve as a hat medallion. Also a gold ring inset with a beautiful antique cornelian, with a crane taking off and a yoke at its feet, and in its beak the sign of Mercury; this signifies the active and contemplative life, and the possibility of rising above earthly matters through spiritual meditation.

Ninth, I do not wish these items to be sold by auction; instead, the sale shall be carried out as well and quickly as possible, so that they are not acquired cheaply by strangers. Rather than sell them at a low price, it would be better if they went to friends: to the governors of the said Hospital, for instance; or else to other close friends, such as Bartolomeo Carpan and his brothers; or Giovanni dal Saon, my host; or Giovanni dal Coro, architect of Ancona; or Giovanni Maria, gilder.[5] All this shall be done in the way in which my executors shall deem the most appropriate, so that any proceeds can become part of the dowry.

Tenth, if in this will I make no mention of any blood-relatives, it is because those few that I have are already well-off, and have no need of my few possessions, and so will excuse me. Besides this, I pray my dear fellow-governors to put aside a small sum to pay the boys and girls of the Hospital to pray to God that in his grace and infinite goodness he will have mercy on my soul, so that I may attain eternal life, amen.

Since my executors have other onerous responsibilities, they may request Master Giovanni Maria, gilder at Ponte San Lio, for the love of Christ and for the sake of our good friendship, to take charge of my less important affairs. These include the division of my artistic effects, and for this purpose he should find a painter well qualified to provide the aforesaid evaluation. If he would like something for his trouble, he shall be satisfied as a dear friend.

From the sale of the aforesaid effects, ten ducats shall be given to Donna Lucia of Cadore, launderess at San Moisè, in Corte da Ca' Barozzi, or else to her son Giovanni Maria, at present aged about ten. This is because she has constantly shown me every Christian kindness. And with this I take my leave.

I, Lorenzo Lotto, aforesaid painter, have written the above will with my own hand and sealed it.

5 For Giovanni Maria, who had acted as Lotto's trusted agent in Venice during his absence in Treviso: *Libro* (1969), p. 365, with references.

Appendix D
Lotto's Receipts and Expenses for the Ancona Assumption, *1549–1550*

These extracts from Lotto's account-book (now in the archive of the Palazzo Apostolico, Loreto) refer to the commission and execution of the *Assumption of the Virgin* for the high altar of San Francesco alle Scale in Ancona (pl. 134; pp. 158–60). On the left-hand pages of the book (*verso*), Lotto recorded the mutual obligations incurred by himself and his patron, as well as his expenses; on the right-hand pages (*recto*), he recorded his receipts of payment. The translation is based on a transcription in *Libro* (1969), pp. 196–201.

fol. 137 verso

1 June 1549. Paid back to Giovanni dal Coro, architect of Ancona,[1] 20 ducats *ongari*, as recorded opposite, i.e. 16 in gold and 4 in currency at 7 lire 10 soldi to the ducat. Present Dario Franceschini of Cingoli, when I paid back the money and took back my receipt from Giovanni and destroyed it.

On 1 July 1549 I arrived in Ancona with my painter's materials and other luggage to make a start on the aforesaid work, and took up lodgings in San Francesco alle Scale. The picture is to be executed in an enclosed place in the church, reserved for my exclusive use. For this reason I plan to dissolve the guarantee made by Giovanni dal Coro recorded opposite, that I come to Ancona to undertake the commission, because I was obliged by the sum of 100 scudi which I had received in Venice as an advance. If I had not met this obligation, Giovanni himself would have been obliged to pay me back the said 100 scudi; but since I did come, and made an excellent start, the aforesaid obligation is no longer valid.

In Ancona, [. . .] July 1549, paid to Giovanni dal Coro, who received from me 20 golden scudi, to go and pay an advance for the frame-carving of the aforesaid altarpiece in Venice sc. 20

[. . .] August 1549, sent to Giovanni dal Coro in Venice, through Venturin della Vecchia,[2] 50 golden scudi, to spend on the frame-carving for the work for the Todini sc. 50

1 For Lotto's friend Giovanni dal Coro: see above, pp. 158–60.

2 The brothers Tommaso and Venturin della Vecchia were merchants of Ancona, with business premises in Venice: *Libro* (1969), p. 409, with references.

fol. 138 recto

29 May 1549. Received from Giovanni dal Coro, architect of Ancona, a loan enabling me to travel to Ancona, 20 golden ducats *ongari* at 7 lire 10 soldi to the ducat. This sum shall be returned to him whenever he wants, in Venetian or Marchigian currency, depending on where he is; and when this happens my receipt, witnessed by Dario Franceschini of Cingoli, shall be returned to me.

Record that on 1 July 1549 Giovanni dal Coro, architect of Ancona, gave me a guarantee in respect of the work I had to go and paint in Ancona for San Francesco alle Scale, commissioned by the heirs of Lorenzo Todini for 400 scudi, inclusive of expenses. I gave to the aforesaid Giovanni dal Coro a formal document absolving him from any responsibility that such a guarantee might incur, thereby pledging my present and future goods, on behalf of myself and my heirs, allowing him to dispose of them in any place, in the presence of good witnesses. I also received a cash advance of 100 scudi at 20 grossi per scudo, on behalf of Giovanni Francesco Todini and the other heirs sc. 100

27 April 1550. Received from Giovanni dal Coro receipts for the 70 scudi, recorded opposite, because of the money he spent in Venice on the framing of the work that I am doing for the Todini, the which money I consider well spent, i.e. 70 golden scudi sc. 70

fol. 138 verso

1 June 1549, in Venice. Agreement made with Giovanni Francesco Todini and his co-heirs of the late Lorenzo Todini, noblemen of Ancona, in accordance with letters from the executors of the said legacy. Present the representative of the said heirs, Antonio Saracini of Ancona. This agreement has been drawn up, as can be seen from the document, by a third person fulfilling the wishes of both parties. According to this agreement, I have to provide an altarpiece, to be executed in Ancona at my own cost, for a fee of 400 scudi, at 20 grossi to the scudo. This sum shall be paid to me on request, according to the needs of the painting and its frame. The original document, signed by the witnesses, is in the hands of the commissioners; I had a copy made for me in the hand of Ciriaco Todini, nephew of Giovanni Francesco.

fol. 139 recto

1 June 1549 in Venice. Received from Giovanni Francesco Todini, nobleman of Ancona, in the name of himself and his co-heirs, 100 scudi for the said work, paid by Antonio Saracini, in the workshop of Venturin and Tommaso della Vecchia. The sum is paid in Marchigian currency, at 20 grossi per scudo sc. 100

16 September in Ancona. Received from Giovanni Francesco Todini, on account for the said work, in San Francesco alle Scale, as confirmed in my own hand on the back of the agreement, 10 golden scudi in *paoli*, amounting to 11 $^1/_2$ scudi at the rate of 20 grossi per scudo sc. 11 $^1/_2$

3 October 1549. Received from the said Giovanni Francesco Todini, sent to Venice by way of the Della Vecchia brothers, 50 golden scudi for Giovanni dal Coro towards the costs of the frame, i.e. 57 $^1/_2$ scudi mozi.

29 October 1549. Paid by him towards my expenses here, 20 golden scudi, i.e. 23 scudi in currency. And 1 April 1550: paid by him 10 scudi in currency at 20 grossi per scudo sc. *mozi* 10

For the aforesaid work. Received a quantity of Florentine lake valued at 3 scudi *mozi* and 36 *bolognini* at 20 grossi sc. 3 bl. 36

For the aforesaid. Received 4 golden scudi from Antonio Saracini, in currency at 20 grossi sc. 4 bl. 48

26 April 1550. Received from the same 60 scudi in currency at 20 grossi sc. 60 bl. 0

6 July. Received on account from Giovanni Francesco Todini and the said heirs, 10 scudi in currency at 20 grossi, at my house, in the presence of Niccolò Giustinian sc. 10 bl. 0

31 July. Received on account from Giovanni Francesco Todini, paid by Francesco Bernabei, 20 scudi in *paoli* at 20 grossi to the scudo, and receipt given sc. 20 bl. 0

19 August. Receipt on account from Giovanni Francesco and Alessandro Todini, paid on their behalf by Francesco Bernabei, 25 scudi at 20 grossi to the scudo, and receipt given sc. 25 bl. 0

2 October. Received on account from Giovanni Francesco and Alessandro Todini, paid on their behalf by Francesco Bernabei, 25 scudi at 20 grossi to the scudo sc. 25 bl. 0

24 November 1550. Received from the said Messers Todini the final and remaining payment of 50 scudi in currency at 20 grossi to the scudo. Receipt formally drawn up by Girolamo Giustinian, notary sc. 50

BIBLIOGRAPHY

Aikema, B., 'La pala di Cingoli', in Zampetti and Sgarbi (1981), pp. 443–56

Aikema, B., 'Lorenzo Lotto and the *Ospitale de San Zuanne Polo*', in Rosand (1984), pp. 343–50

Aikema, B., 'Lorenzo Lotto: La pala di Sant'Antonino e l'osservanza domenicana a Venezia', *Mitteilungen des Kunsthistorischen Instituts in Florenz*, XXXIII (1989), pp. 127–40

Aikema, B., 'Lorenzo Lotto: Ancora San Girolamo', in Varese (1993), pp. 303–05

Aikema, B., and Meijers, D., *Nel regno dei poveri: Arte e storia dei grandi ospedali veneziani in età moderna, 1474–1797*, Venice, 1989

Amaglio, M.S., 'I ritratti di Antonio Agliardi e Apollonia Cassotti in un dipinto di Lorenzo Lotto', in *Rivista di Bergamo*, XLIII (1992), pp. 17–18

Angelucci, G., *Niccolò Bonafede: Dal palazzo al mausoleo, dalla piazza al quadro*, Macerata, 1990

Annibaldi, G. jun., 'Documenti d'archivio sull'allogazione a Lorenzo Lotto della pala d'altare della Santa Lucia di Jesi', *Notizie da Palazzo Albani*, IX (1980), pp. 143–52

Anzelewsky, F., *Dürer: His art and life*, New York, 1980

Arasse, D., 'Lorenzo Lotto dans ses bizarreries: Le peintre et l'iconographie', in Zampetti and Sgarbi (1981), pp. 365–82

Aretino: see *Lettere*

Astur, B., *I Baglioni*, Florence, 1964

Banti, A., and Boschetto, A., *Lorenzo Lotto*, Florence, 1953

Barbieri, C., 'La Nascita della Vergine di Lorenzo Lotto in San Michele al Pozzo Bianco', *Venezia Cinquecento*, I, no. 1 (1991), pp. 63–99

Barocchi, P., *Trattati d'arte del Cinquecento*, I, Bari, 1960

Battilotti, D., and Franco, M.T., 'Regesti di committenti e dei primi collezionisti di Giorgione', *Antichità Viva*, XVII, nos. 4–5 (1978), pp. 58–86

Béguin, S., 'A propos des peintures de Lorenzo Lotto au Louvre', in Zampetti and Sgarbi (1981), pp. 99–105

Berenson, B., *Lorenzo Lotto: An essay in constructive art criticism*, London, 1895. 4th, rev. edn., London, 1956

Bergamo per Lorenzo Lotto, Bergamo, 1980

Bertelli, C., 'Ricordi di viaggio nella pala Martinengo', in Zampetti and Sgarbi (1981), pp. 187–93

Bialostocki, J., *Dürer and his critics*, Baden Baden, 1986

Biscaro, G., 'Lorenzo Lotto a Treviso nella prima decade del secolo XVI', *L'Arte*, I (1898), pp. 138–53

Biscaro, G., 'Ancora di alcune opere giovanili di Lorenzo Lotto', *L'Arte* IV (1901), pp. 152–61

Black, C., 'The Baglioni as tyrants of Perugia, 1488–1540', *English Historical Review*, LXXXV (1970), pp. 245–81

Boschini, M., *La Carta del Navegar Pittoresco* (1660), ed. A. Pallucchini, Venice and Rome, 1966

Briganti, G. (ed.), *La pittura in Italia: Il Cinquecento*, 2 vols., Milan, 1987

Brock, M., 'La *Suzanne* de Lorenzo Lotto ou comment faire l'*histoire*', in *Arts et Langage*, vol. III of *Symboles de la Renaissance*, Paris, 1990, pp. 37–64

Brown, D.A., *Andrea Solario*, Milan, 1987

Brunetta, E. (ed.), *L'Età Moderna*, vol. III of *Storia di Treviso*, Venice, 1992

Buchner, E. *Das deutsche Bildnis der Spätgotik und der frühen Dürerzeit*, Berlin, 1953

Burckhardt, J., *Beiträge zur Kunstgeschichte von Italien*, Basel, 1898

Calì, M., 'La "religione" di Lorenzo Lotto', in Zampetti and Sgarbi (1981), pp. 243–77

Capolavori europei della Romania: Sessanta dipinti dal Museo Nazionale d'Arte di Bucarest, Venice, 1991

Carboni, P., 'La pala di Francesco Bissolo nel Duomo di Treviso', *Arte Veneta*, XLI (1987), pp. 128–30

Caroli, F., *Lorenzo Lotto*, Florence, 1980

Caversazzi, C., 'Una dama bergamasca di quattrocent'anni fa riconosciuta in un ritratto del Lotto', *Bolletino della Civica Biblioteca di Bergamo*, VII (1913), pp. 23–5

Chastel, A., 'Le "Portement de Croix" de Lorenzo Lotto', *La Revue du Louvre et des Musées de France*, XXXI (1982), pp. 266–72

Chiappini di Sorio, I., 'Il soggiorno trevigiano del Lotto dal 1540 al 1542: Speranze ed inquietudini', in Zampetti and Sgarbi (1981), pp. 243–77

Chiappini di Sorio, I., 'Carattere, comportamenti, religiosità di Lorenzo Lotto: Appunti e tentativo di un'analisi dei suoi scritti', *Ateneo Veneto*, CLXX, no. 2 (1983), pp. 207–24

Chiappini di Sorio, I., 'Lorenzo Lotto da Venezia ad Ancona, attraverso le annotazioni del Libro di Spese, 1548–1551', *Notizie da Palazzo Albani*, XIII (1984), pp. 95–100

Chiodi, L., *Lettere inedite di Lorenzo Lotto* (1962), 2nd edn., Bergamo, 1968

Chiodi L., 'Quattro lettere inedite di Lorenzo Lotto', *Bergomum*, LXXI (1977), pp. 17–36

Chiodi, L., 'Le abitazioni del Lotto a Bergamo', in *Bergamo per Lorenzo Lotto* (1980), pp. 13–16

Christiansen, K., 'Lorenzo Lotto and the tradition of epithalamic painting', *Apollo*, CXXIV (1986), pp. 166–73

Ciaranfi, A.M., 'La *Natività* di Lorenzo Lotto nella Reale Pinacoteca di Siena', *Bolletino d'Arte*, XXIX (1936), pp. 319–29

Cohen, C., 'The modello for a lost work by Lorenzo Lotto', *Master Drawings*, XII (1975), pp. 131–5

Colalucci, F., '*Muscipula diaboli*? Una psuedo-trappola per topi nell'*Adorazione* di Lorenzo Lotto a Washington', *Artibus et Historiae*, XI, no. 21 (1990), pp. 71–88

Colalucci, F., 'Lorenzo Lotto, don Pietro da Lucca, Elisabetta Rota e il tema del Congedo di Cristo dalla madre', *Venezia Cinquecento*, I, no. 1 (1991), pp. 27–61

Coletti, L., *Lotto*, Bergamo, 1953

Coli, B., 'Lorenzo Lotto e il ritratto cittadino: Andrea Odoni', in Gentili (1989), pp. 155–81

Contardi, B., and Gentili, A. (eds.), *Il S. Girolamo di Lorenzo Lotto a Castel S. Angelo* (catalogue of exhibition at Museo Nazionale di Castel Sant'Angelo, Rome), Rome, 1983

Cortesi Bosco, F., 'La letteratura religiosa devozionale e l'iconografia di alcuni dipinti di Lorenzo Lotto', *Bergomum*, LXX (1976), pp. 3–25 [1976a]

Cortesi Bosco, F., 'A proposito del frontespizio di Lorenzo Lotto per la Bibbia di Antonio Brucioli', *Bergomum*, LXX (1976), pp. 27–42 [1976b]

Cortesi Bosco, F., 'La metamorfosi della caverna: La pala di Lorenzo Lotto per la chiesa dei Santo Stefano e Domenico a Bergamo', *Bergomum*, LXXI (1977), pp. 3–16

Cortesi Bosco, F., *Gli affreschi dell'Oratorio Suardi: Lorenzo Lotto nella crisi della Riforma*, Bergamo, 1980

Cortesi Bosco, F., 'Il ritratto di Niccolò della Torre disegnato da Lorenzo Lotto', in Zampetti and Sgarbi (1981), pp. 313–24 [1981a]

Cortesi Bosco, F., 'Un amico bergamasco di Lorenzo Lotto', *Archivio storico bergamasco*, I (1981), pp. 63–73 [1981b]

Cortesi Bosco, F., 'Lotto e Cariani: Due disegni e un dipinto perduto', *Rivista di Bergamo*, no. 4 (1982), pp. 5–12

Cortesi Bosco, F., 'Riflessi del mito di Venezia nella pala Martinengo di Lorenzo Lotto', *Archivio storico bergamasco*, III (1983), pp. 213–49

Cortesi Bosco, F., 'Lorenzo Lotto dal polittico di Ponteranica alla commissione della Santa Lucia in Jesi', *Notizie da Palazzo Albani*, XII (1984), pp. 56–80 [1984a]

Cortesi Bosco, F., 'Il problema della posizione religiosa di Lorenzo Lotto', *Notizie da Palazzo Albani*, XIII (1984), pp. 81–9 [1984b]

Cortesi Bosco, F., *Il Coro intarsiato di Lotto e Capoferri per Santa Maria Maggiore in Bergamo*, 2 vols., Milan, 1987

Cortesi Bosco, F., 'Per Lotto a Roma e Raffaello'. *Notizie da Palazzo Albani*, XIX (1990), pp. 45–74

Cortesi Bosco, F., '*Divina vigilia*: Il sonno vigilante dell'Anima nel dipinto di Lorenzo Lotto K291 della National Gallery di Washington', *Notizie da Palazzo Albani*, XXI (1992), pp. 25–49

Cortesi Bosco, F., 'I coniugi di Lotto all'Eremitage e la loro "impresa"', in Varese (1993), pp. 336–49

Cortesi Bosco, F., 'Sulle tracce della committenza di Lotto a Bergamo: Un epistolario ed un codice di alchemia', *Bergomum*, LXXXIX (1995), pp. 1–44

Cristaldi, R. V., 'Homo ille melancolicus: Il "trentasettene" di Lorenzo Lotto', *Synaxis*, II (1984), pp. 201–38

Dal Poggetto, P., 'Restauri di opere del Lotto in occasione della mostra di Ancona', *Notizie da Palazzo Albani*, XIII (1984), pp. 138–43

Dal Poggetto, P., and Zampetti, P. (eds.), *Lorenzo Lotto nelle Marche. Il suo tempo, il suo influsso* (catalogue of exhibition, Ancona 1981), Florence, 1981

Dal Pozzolo, E. M., 'Lorenzo Lotto 1506: La pala di Asolo', *Artibus et Historiae*, XI, no. 21 (1990), pp. 89–110

Dal Pozzolo, E. M., '*Laura tra Polia e Berenice* di Lorenzo Lotto', *Artibus et Historiae*, XIII, no. 25 (1992), pp. 103–27

Dal Pozzolo, E. M., 'Osservazioni sul catalogo di Lorenzo Lotto, 1503–1516', *Arte Veneta*, XLV (1993), pp. 33–49

Di Tanna, M., 'Lorenzo Lotto, 1523: *Nozze mistiche di S. Caterina*', *Osservatorio delle Arti*, no. 4 (1990), pp. 58–67 [1990a]

Di Tanna, M., 'Dal bestiaro lottesco: Lo *sciurus vulgaris*', *Osservatorio delle Arti*, no. 5 (1990), pp. 44–50 [1990b]

Dillon, G. (ed.), *Lorenzo Lotto a Treviso: Ricerche e restauri*, Treviso, 1980

Dizionario biografico degli italiani, Rome, 1962–

Dolce: see Barocchi (1960), pp. 141–206; Roskill (1968)

Dülberg, A., *Privatporträts. Geschichte und Ikonographie einer Gattung im 15. und 16. Jahrhundert*, Berlin, 1990

Ekserdjian, D., 'A note on Lorenzo Lotto's *Virgin and Child with Saints Jerome and Nicholas of Tolentino*', *Journal of the Museum of Fine Arts, Boston*, III (1991), pp. 87–91

Fischer, C., *Fra Bartolommeo: Master Draughtsman of the High Renaissance*, The Hague, 1990

Fontana, R., '"Solo, senza fidel governo et molto inquieto de la mente"', in Zampetti and Sgarbi (1981), pp. 279–97

Fossaluzza, G., 'Treviso', in *La Pittura nel Veneto: Il Quattrocento*, ed. M. Lucco, Milan, 1990, pp. 541–71

Friedmann, H., 'Footnotes to the painted page: The iconography of an altarpiece by Botticini', *Metropolitan Museum of Art Bulletin*, XXVIII (1969), pp. 1–17

Frimmel, T., *Der Anonimo Morelliano: Marcanton Michiels Notizie d'opere del disegno*, Vienna, 1888

Furlan, C., *Il Pordenone*, Milan, 1988

Galis, D., 'Lorenzo Lotto: A study of his career and character, with particular emphasis on his emblematic and hieroglyphic works', PhD diss., Bryn Mawr College, 1977

Galis, D., 'Concealed wisdom: Renaissance hieroglyphic and Lorenzo Lotto's Bergamo *intarsie*', *Art Bulletin*, LXII (1980), pp. 363–75

Gardner, J., 'Frühchristliche Einflüsse im venezianischen Cinquecento. Ein Dominikaneraltar von Rocco Marconi in SS. Giovanni e Paolo', in H. R. Meier, C. Jäggi and P. Büttner (eds.), *Für irdischen Ruhm and himmlischen Lohn*, Berlin (1995), pp. 280–86

Gargan, L., 'Lorenzo Lotto e gli ambienti umanistici trevigiani fra quattro e cinquecento', in Dillon (1980), pp. 1–31

Gatti nell'arte (catalogue of exhibition at Palazzo Barberini, Rome), Rome, 1987

Gentili, A., '*Virtus* e *Voluptas* nell'opera di Lorenzo Lotto', in Zampetti and Sgarbi (1981), pp. 415–24

Gentili, A. (with M. Lattanzi and F. Polignano), *I Giardini di Contemplazione: Lorenzo Lotto 1503/1512*, Rome, 1985

Gentili, A., 'Lorenzo Lotto e il ritratto cittadino: Leonino e Lucina Brembate', in Gentili (1989), pp. 155–81

Gentili, A. (ed.), *Il Ritratto e la Memoria. Materiali I*, Rome, 1989

Giovanni Girolamo Savoldo (catalogue of exhibition at Monastero di Santa Giulia, Brescia, and Schirn Kunsthalle, Frankfurt, 1990), Milan, 1990

Gleason, E., *Gasparo Contarini: Venice, Rome and Reform*, Berkeley and Los Angeles, 1993

Goffen, R., '*A Madonna* by Lorenzo Lotto', *Bulletin of the Museum of Fine Arts, Boston*, (1978), pp. 34–41

Gould, C., 'Lorenzo Lotto and the double portrait. Transformations of the Della Torre picture', *Saggi e Memorie di Storia dell'Arte*, V (1966), pp. 45–51

Gould, C., *National Gallery Catalogues: The sixteenth-century Italian schools*, London, 1975

Gould, C., 'Lotto and Correggio', in Zampetti and Sgarbi (1981), pp. 169–71

Grabski, J., 'Sul rapporto fra ritratto e simbolo nella ritrattistica del Lotto', in Zampetti and Sgarbi (1981), pp. 383–92
Gramigna, S., and Perissa, A., *Scuole di Arti, Mestieri e Devozione a Venezia*, Venice, 1981
Grimaldi, F., 'La Santa Casa nel Cinquecento', in *Lorenzo Lotto a Loreto e Recanati* (1980), pp. 32–44
Grimaldi, F., *Santa Maria Porta del Paradiso liberatrice della pestilenza*, Loreto, 1987
Grimaldi, F., *La Historia della Chiesa di Santa Maria de Loreto*, Loreto, 1993
Hall, M. van, 'Messer Marsilio and his bride', *Connoisseur*, CXCII, no. 774 (1976), pp. 292–7
Hamburgh, H., 'The problem of "Lo Spasimo" of the Virgin in Cinquecento paintings of the "Descent from the Cross"', *Sixteenth Century Journal*, XII (1981), pp. 45–75
Heinemann, F., *Giovanni Bellini e i Belliniani*, Venice, 1962
Hughes, D. O., 'Representing the family: Portraits and purposes in early modern Italy', in *Art and History: Images and their meaning*, ed. R. I. Rotberg and T. K. Rabb, Cambridge, 1986, pp. 7–38
Humfrey, P., 'La Pala Giustinian a San Francesco della Vigna: contesto e committenza', in *Nuovi Studi su Paolo Veronese*, ed. M. Gemin, Venice, 1990, pp. 299–308 [1990a]
Humfrey, P., *La Pittura Veneta del Rinascimento a Brera*, Florence, 1990 [1990b]
Humfrey, P., *The Altarpiece in Renaissance Venice*, New Haven and London, 1993
I Pittori Bergamaschi dal XIII al XIX Secolo. Il Cinquecento I, Bergamo, 1980
Jaffé, M., 'Pesaro family portraits: Pordenone, Lotto and Titian', *Burlington Magazine*, CXIII (1971), pp. 696–702
Jedin, H., *A History of the Council of Trent*, I (English trans. from original German edn., 1949), London, 1957
Joannides, P., 'Titian's *Judith* and its context: The iconography of decapitation', *Apollo*, CXXXV (1992), pp. 163–70
Katz, M. B., 'The Suardi chapel. A document of Lotto's work with Raphael', *Arte Lombarda*, L (1978), pp. 82–6
Kultzen, R., and Eikemeier, P., *Venezianische Gemälde des 15. und 16. Jahrhunderts*, vol. IX of *Bayerische Gemäldesammlungen, Alte Pinakothek, München*, Munich, 1971
Lampacrescia, L., 'Un altra opera del Lotto nella chiesa di San Floriano a Jesi', *Paragone*, no. 473 (1989), pp. 99–104
Lanzi, L., *Storia pittorica della Italia* (1795–6), 4 vols., Florence, 1834
La Pala Martinengo di Lorenzo Lotto: Studi e ricerche in occasione del restauro, Bergamo, 1978
Larsson, L. O., 'Lorenzo Lottos Bildnis des Andrea Odoni in Hampton Court: Eine typolologische und ikonographische Studie', *Konsthistorisk Tidskrift*, XXXVII (1968), pp. 21–33
Lavin, M. A., 'Giovannino Battista: A study in Renaissance religious symbolism', *Art Bulletin*, XXXVII (1955), pp. 85–101
Le Siècle de Titien: L'âge d'or de la peinture à Venise (catalogue of exhibition at Grand Palais, Paris, 1993), Paris, 1993
Leonardo and Venice (catalogue of exhibition at Palazzo Grassi, Venice, 1992), Milan, 1992
Lettere sull'arte di Pietro Aretino, ed. E. Camesasca, 4 vols., Milan, 1957
Liberali, G., 'Lotto, Pordenone e Tiziano a Treviso', *Atti e Memorie dell'Istituto Veneto di Scienze, Lettere ed Arti*, XXXIII, no. 3 (1963)
Liberali, G., 'Gli inventari delle suppellettili del vescovo Bernardo de' Rossi, nell'episcopio di Treviso (1506–1524)', in Zampetti and Sgarbi (1981), pp. 73–92
Libro di Spese Diverse (1538–1556), ed. P. Zampetti, Florence, 1969
Lippincott, K., 'The genesis and significance of the fifteenth-century Italian *impresa*', in *Chivalry and the Renaissance*, ed. S. Anglo, Woodbridge, 1990, pp. 49–76
Logan, A.-M., *The Cabinet of the Brothers Gerard and Jan Reynst*, Amsterdam, 1979
Longhi, R., 'Quesiti caravaggeschi, II: I precedenti' (1928), repr. in *Edizione delle opere complete di Roberto Longhi*, IV, Florence, 1968
Lorenzo Lotto: see also *Libro*
Lorenzo Lotto a Loreto e Recanati, Loreto, 1980
Lucco, M., 'Venezia fra quattrocento e cinquecento', in *Dal medioevo al quattrocento*, vol. V of *Storia dell'arte italiana*, Turin, 1983, pp. 447–77
Lucco, M., 'La pittura a Venezia nel primo Cinquecento', in Briganti (1987), pp. 149–70 [1987a]
Lucco, M., 'La pittura nelle provincie di Treviso e di Belluno nel Cinquecento', in Briganti (1987), pp. 208–18 [1987b]
Lucco, M., 'Tre schede per Lorenzo Lotto', in *Hommage à Michel Laclotte: Etudes sur la peinture du Moyen Age et de la Renaissance*, Milan, 1994, pp. 346–56
Ludwig, G., 'Bonifazio di Pitati da Verona, eine archivalische Untersuchung', *Jahrbuch der königlich preussischen Kunstsammlungen*, XXII (1901), pp. 61–78
Ludwig, G., 'Archivalische Beiträge zur Geschichte der venezianischen Malerei', *Jahrbuch der königlich preussischen Kunstsammlungen*, XXIV (1903), suppl.; XXVI (1905), suppl.
Manzato, E., 'Lorenzo Lotto a Santa Cristina: Un artista nel contado', in Zampetti and Sgarbi (1981), pp. 115–25
Manzato, E., 'La pittura a Treviso durante il dominio veneto', in Brunetta (1992), pp. 221–96
Manzelli, M., 'Lorenzo Lotto governatore dell'Ospedale di S. Maria dei Derelitti in Venezia', *Arte Veneta*, XXXV (1981), pp. 202–3
Marani, P. C., *Leonardo e i Leonardeschi a Brera*, Florence, 1987
Mariani Canova, G., *L'opera completa del Lotto*, Classici dell'Arte Rizzoli, Milan, 1975
Mariani Canova, G., 'Lorenzo Lotto e la spiritualità domenicana', in Zampetti and Sgarbi (1981), pp. 337–45
Martignago, F., 'Il volgare a Treviso fra Umanesimo e Rinascimento', in Brunetta (1992), pp. 159–93
Martin, A. J., *Savoldos sogenanntes 'Bildnis des Gaston de Foix': Zum Problem des Paragone in der Kunst und Kunsttheorie der italienischen Renaissance*, Sigmaringen, 1995
Martin, J., *Venice's hidden enemies. Italian heretics in a Renaissance city*, Berkeley, 1993
Mascherpa, G., *Lorenzo Lotto a Bergamo*, Milan, 1971
Mascherpa, G., 'L'ancona perduta', in *La Pala Martinengo* (1978), pp. 40–53
Mascherpa, G., *Invito a Lorenzo Lotto*, Milan, 1980 [1980a]
Mascherpa, G., 'Il Lotto e il nord', in *Bergamo per Lorenzo Lotto* (1980), pp. 17–23 [1980b]
Massi, N., 'The self-portrait of Lorenzo Lotto in the *Crucifixion* of Monte San Giusto', *Source*, IX, no. 4 (1990), pp. 1–4
Massi, N., 'Lorenzo Lotto's *Nativity* and *Christ taking leave of his mother*: pendant devotional paintings', *Artibus et Historiae*, XII, no. 23 (1991), pp. 103–19
Massi, N., 'Lorenzo Lotto: The San Bernardino altarpiece', *Arte Cristiana*, LXXXI (1993), pp. 115–30
Matthew, L. C., 'Lorenzo Lotto and the patronage and production of Venetian altarpieces in the early sixteenth century', PhD diss., Princeton University, 1988 [1988a]

Matthew, L.C., 'New evidence for Lotto's career in Jesi', *Burlington Magazine*, cxxx (1988), pp. 693–7 [1988b]
Matthew, L.C., '*Patria*, papal service and patronage: Nicolò Bonafede at Monte San Giusto', *Renaissance Studies*, VII (1993), pp. 184–206 [1993a]
Matthew, L.C., 'Lotto's "Pietà" altarpiece of 1545', *Burlington Magazine*, CXXXV (1993), pp. 31–3 [1993b]
Matthew, L.C., 'Method and meaning in an altarpiece by Lotto', *Renaissance Studies*, VIII (1994), pp. 162–74
Mazza, A., 'La pala dell'*Elemosina di Sant'Antonino* nel dibattito cinquecentesco sul pauperismo', in Zampetti and Sgarbi (1981), pp. 347–64
Micaletti, R., 'Il contratto per la pala di Lorenzo Lotto in Sant'Agostino ad Ancona', *Venezia Cinquecento*, I, no. 1 (1991), pp. 133–6
Michiel: see Frimmel
Morano di Custoza, E., *Libri d'arme di Venezia*, Verona, 1979
Moroni, M., 'L'organizzazione territoriale di Recanati nella prima metà del Cinquecento', in *Lorenzo Lotto a Loreto e Recanati* (1980), pp. 9–17
Mozzoni, L. (ed.), *Lorenzo Lotto, 'La Madonna delle Rose': Restauro ed ipotesi critiche*, Jesi, 1993
Muraro, M., 'Asterischi lotteschi', in Zampetti and Sgarbi (1981), pp. 299–312
Muraro, M., 'I conti in tasca di Lorenzo Lotto', *Notizie da Palazzo Albani*, XIII (1984), pp. 144–64
Muraro, M., *Il Libro Secondo di Francesco e Jacopo dal Ponte*, Bassano del Grappa, 1992
Muraro: see also Rosand
Nova, A., 'La pittura nei territori di Bergamo e Brescia nel Cinquecento', in Briganti (1988), pp. 105–23
Oldfield, D., 'Lorenzo Lotto 1508–1513', *Notizie da Palazzo Albani*, XIII (1984), pp. 22–38 [1984a]
Oldfield, D., 'Lorenzo Lotto's arrival in Venice', *Arte Veneta*, XXXVIII (1984), pp. 141–5 [1984b]
Oldfield, D., 'Lorenzo Lotto 1509–1525', PhD thesis, University of East Anglia, 1984 [1984c]
Ottani Cavina, A., *Carlo Saraceni*, Milan, 1968
Pallucchini, R., and Rossi, F., *Giovanni Cariani*, Milan, 1983
Panazza, G., *I Civici Musei e la Pinacoteca di Brescia*, Brescia, 1958
Pastore Stocchi, M., 'La cultura umanistica', in Brunetta (1992), pp. 137–57
Pedretti, C., *Disegni di Leonardo da Vinci e della sua scuola alla Biblioteca Reale di Torino*, Florence, 1975
Pignatti, T., 'The relationship between German and Venetian painting in the late Quattrocento and early Cinquecento', in J. Hale (ed.), *Renaissance Venice*, London, 1973, pp. 244–73
Pilo, G.M., 'Lotto, Sebastiano del Piombo, Pordenone: Significato di tre esperienze romane', in Zampetti and Sgarbi (1981), pp. 147–62
Pinacoteca di Brera: Scuola Veneta, Milan, 1990
Pochat, G., 'Two allegories by Lorenzo Lotto and Petrarchism in Venice around 1500', *Word and Image*, I (1985), pp. 3–15
Polverari, M. (ed.), *Lorenzo Lotto: La Pala dell'Alabarda*, Ancona, 1992
Pope-Hennessy, J., *The portrait in the Renaissance*, Princeton, 1966
Pouncey, P., *Lotto Disegnatore*, Vicenza, 1965
Pullan, B., *Rich and poor in Renaissance Venice: The social institutions of a Catholic state*, Oxford, 1971
Puppi, L., 'Riflessioni su temi e problemi della ritrattistica del Lotto', in Zampetti and Sgarbi (1981), pp. 393–8
Rearick, W.R., 'Lorenzo Lotto: The drawings, 1500–1525', in Zampetti and Sgarbi (1981), pp. 23–36
Rearick, W.R., 'A drawing by Lorenzo Lotto', *Notizie da Palazzo Albani*, XII (1983), pp. 92–7
Ricci, E., 'La leggenda di S. Mustiola e il furto del Sant'Anello', *Bolletino di Storia patria per l'Umbria*, XXIV (1918), pp. 133–55
Ricciardi, M.L., 'Lorenzo Lotto: il Gentiluomo della Galleria Borghese', *Artibus et Historiae*, X, no. 19 (1989), pp. 85–106
Ricciardi, M.L., 'Le piccole verità, ovvero cronaca di una identificazione mancata', in Varese (1993), pp. 315–24
Ridolfi, C., *Le Maraviglie dell'Arte* (1648), ed. D. von Hadeln, I, Berlin, 1914
Robertson, G., *Vincenzo Catena*, Edinburgh, 1954
Romano, G., 'La Bibbia di Lotto', *Paragone*, XXVII, nos. 317–19 (1976), pp. 82–91
Rosand, D., review of *Libro* (ed. 1969), in *Art Bulletin*, LIII (1971), pp. 407–9
Rosand, D. (ed.), *Interpretazioni Veneziane: Studi di Storia dell'Arte in Onore di Michelangelo Muraro*, Venice, 1984
Rosand, D., and Muraro, M., *Titian and the Venetian woodcut*, Washington, 1986
Roskill, M., *Dolce's 'Aretino' and Venetian art theory of the Cinquecento*, New York, 1968
Rylands, P., *Palma Vecchio*, Cambridge, 1992
Santosuosso, A., 'Religious orthodoxy, dissent and suppression in Venice in the 1540s', *Church History*, XLII (1973), pp. 476–85
Savini Branca, S., *Il collezionismo veneziano del '600*, Padua, 1964
Seidenberg, M., *Die Bildnisse des Lorenzo Lotto*, Lörrach, 1964
Shapley, F.R., *Catalogue of the Italian Paintings*, Washington, 1979
Shearman, J., *The Early Italian Pictures in the Collection of Her Majesty the Queen*, Cambridge, 1983
Spiazzi, A.M., 'La pala di Santa Cristina', in Dillon (1980), pp. 101–23
Starobinski, J., *Histoire du traitement de la mélancolie des origines à 1900*, Basle, 1960
Steinberg, R., *Fra Girolamo Savonarola, Florentine art and Renaissance historiography*, Athens, Ohio, 1977
Strieder, P., *Dürer. Paintings, prints, drawings* (trans. from the German), London, 1982
Tafuri, M., *Venezia e il Rinascimento*, Turin, 1985. Eng. trans. as *Venice and the Renaissance*, Cambridge, Mass, 1989
Tassi, F.M., *Vite de' pittori, scultori ed architetti bergamaschi*, Bergamo, 1793
Tervarent, G. de, *Attributs et symboles dans l'art profane, 1450–1600*, Geneva, 1958
The Age of Caravaggio (catalogue of exhibition held at Metropolitan Museum of Art, New York, and Museo Nazionale di Capodimonte, Naples), New York, 1985
The Golden Legend, trans. G. Ryan and H. Ripperger, 2nd edn., New York, 1969
Torriti, P., *La Pinacoteca Nazionale di Siena: i dipinti dal XV al XVIII secolo*, Genoa, 1981
Van den Berg-Noë, H.A., 'Lorenzo Lotto e la decorazione del coro ligneo di S. Maria Maggiore in Bergamo', *Mededelingen van het Nederlands Instituut te Rome*, XXXVI (1974), pp. 145–64
Varese, R. (ed.), *Studi per Pietro Zampetti*, Ancona, 1993
Vasari, G., *Le Vite de' più eccellenti pittori, scultori ed architettori* (1st edn., 1550; 2nd edn., 1568), ed. R. Bettinari and P. Barocchi, Florence, IV/1, 1976; V, 1984
Vertova, L., 'Lorenzo Lotto: Collaborazione o rivalità fra pittura e scultura?', in Zampetti and Sgarbi (1981), pp. 401–14
Volpe, C., 'Lotto a Roma e Raffaello', in Zampetti and Sgarbi (1981), pp. 127–45

Von Einem, H., 'Die "Menschwerdung Christi" des Isenheimer Altares', in *Kunstgeschichtliche Studien für Hans Kauffmann*, ed. W. Braunfels, Berlin, 1956, pp. 152–70

Wilk, S., *The sculpture of Tullio Lombardo. Studies in sources and meaning*, New York and London, 1978

Zampetti, P., *Mostra di Lorenzo Lotto* (exhibition catalogue), Venice, Doge's Palace, 1953

Zampetti, P., 'Un caopolavoro del Lotto ritrovato', *Arte Veneta*, XI (1957), pp. 75–81

Zampetti, P., 'Una vita errabonda', *Notizie da Palazzo Albani*, IX (1980), pp. 13–27

Zampetti, P., 'Anno 1535: Lorenzo Lotto e Durante Nobili', in Zampetti and Sgarbi (1981), pp. 237–42

Zampetti, P., *Lotto*, Bologna, 1983

Zampetti, P., 'Esiste una congiuntura Lotto-Raffaello?', in *Studi su Raffaello*, ed. M. Sambucco Hamoud and M.L. Strocchi, Urbino, 1987, pp. 125–31

Zampetti, P., and Sgarbi, V. (eds.), *Lorenzo Lotto: Atti del Convegno Internazionale di Studi per il V Centenario della Nascita (Asolo, 1980)*, Venice, 1981

Zampetti: see also Dal Poggetto

Zampetti: see also *Libro*

Zanetti, A.M., *Della Pittura Veneziana*, Venice, 1771

Zeri, F., and Gardner, E., *Italian Paintings: Venetian School*, Catalogue of the Collection of the Metropolitan Museum of Art, New York, 1973

Zocca, E., 'La decorazione della Stanza d'Eliodoro e l'opera di Lorenzo Lotto a Roma', *Rivista dell'Istituto Nazionale d'Archeologia e Storia dell'Arte* n.s. III (1953), pp. 329–43

INDEX

PHOTOGRAPH CREDITS

Amsterdam, Rijksmuseum 82
Ancona, Pinacoteca Civica 130
Antella (Florence), Scala 66, 70
Bergamo, Da Re 47, 54, 55, 57, 58, 74, 86, 87, 88, 89, 90, 91, 92, 96, 97, 98, 99
Berlin, Staatliche Museen zu Berlin–Preussischer Kulturbesitz (Photo: Jörg P. Anders) 63
Boston, Courtesy Museum of Fine Arts, ©1996/ All Rights Reserved 72
Brescia, Civici Musei d'Arte e Storia 108, 135
Bucharest, Muzeul National al României 59
Cambridge, Fitzwilliam Museum 143
Edinburgh, National Galleries of Scotland 27
Florence, Berenson Collection 145
Jesi, Pinacoteca Civica 101, 123
Leipzig, Museum der Bildenden Künste 83
London, National Gallery 12, 13, 62, 75, 118
London, Prudence Cuming 45
Malibu, California, Collection of the J. Paul Getty Museum 133
Macerata, Luigi Ricci 126, 127
Madrid, Museo del Prado 80, 153
Madrid, Copyright © Fundacion Colección Thyssen-Bornemisza 34
Milan, Sporetti 112
Milan, Soprintendenza per i Beni Artistici e Storici 53, 146, 150
Modena, Soprintendenza per i Beni Artistici e Storici 10
Munich, Bayerische Staatsgemäldesammlungen (Photo: Artothek) 28
New York, The Metropolitan Museum of Art 142, 155
New York, Pierpont Morgan Library 8
Ottawa, National Gallery of Canada 71
Paris, Réunion des Musées Nationaux 4, 49, 106, 116, 137, 138, 160
Peissenberg, Artothek 28
Rome, Antonio Idini 157
Rome, Banca Nazionale del Lavoro 44
Rome, Istituto Centrale per il Catalogo e la Documentazione 36
Rome, Soprintendenza per i Beni Artistici e Storici 5, 35, 104
Urbino, Soprintendenza per i Beni Artistici e Storici delle Marche 2, 31, 43, 131, 156, 159
Venice, Mark Smith 103
Venice, Osvaldo Böhm 95, 102, 117, 138, 152
Venice, Soprintendenza per i Beni Artistici e Storici 9, 23, 94
Verona, Soprintendenza per i Beni Artistici e Storici del Veneto 3
Vienna, Kunsthistorisches Museum 26, 109, 110, 114, 119
Washington, DC, The National Gallery of Art 16, 17, 21, 67, 76, 105
Windsor, Royal Collection Enterprises 115